America

At a time when the expanded projection of US political, military, economic and cultural power draws intensified global concern, understanding how that country understands itself seems more important than ever.

America First, a collection of new critical essays, tackles this old problem in a new way, by examining some of the hundreds of US films that announce themselves as titularly 'American'. From early travelogues to contemporary comedies, national nomination has been an abiding characteristic of American motion pictures, heading the work of Porter, Guy-Blaché, DeMille, Capra, Sternberg, Vidor, Minnelli and Mankiewicz. More recently, George Lucas, Paul Schrader, John Landis and Edward James Olmos have made their own contributions to Hollywood's Americana.

What does this national branding signify? Which versions of Americanism are valorized, and which marginalized or excluded? Out of which social and historical contexts do they emerge, and for and by whom are they constructed?

Edited by Mandy Merck, the collection contains detailed analyses of such films as *The Vanishing American, American Madness, An American in Paris, American Graffiti, American Gigolo* and *American Pie.*

Contributors: Pam Cook, Ana María Dopico, Peter William Evans, William R. Handley, Rembert Hüser, Barry Langford, Esther Leslie, H. N. Lukes, Mandy Merck, Diane Negra, Paul Smith, Eric Smoodin, Kristen Whissel and Sharon Willis.

Mandy Merck is Professor of Media Arts at Royal Holloway, University of London. She is the author of *Perversions: Deviant Readings* (1993), *In Your Face: Nine Sexual Studies* (2000) and *Hollywood's American Tragedies* (forthcoming 2007). She is editor of *After Diana* (1998) and co-editor of *Coming out of Feminism?* (1998) and *The Art of Tracey Emin* (2002).

America First

Naming the nation
in US film

Edited by
Mandy Merck

 Routledge
Taylor & Francis Group

LONDON AND NEW YORK

First published 2007
by Routledge
2 Park Square, Milton Park, Abingdon,
Oxon OX14 4RN

Simultaneously published in the USA and Canada
by Routledge
270 Madison Ave, New York, NY 10016

*Routledge is an imprint of the Taylor & Francis Group,
an informa business*

Editorial selection and material © 2007
Mandy Merck
Chapters © 2007 the Contributors

Typeset in Perpetua/Bell Gothic by
Florence Production Ltd, Stoodleigh, Devon
Printed and bound in Great Britain by
Antony Rowe Ltd, Chippenham, Wiltshire

British Library Cataloguing in Publication Data
A catalogue record for this book is available
from the British Library

Library of Congress Cataloging in Publication Data
   America first: naming the nation in US film
   [edited by Mandy Merck].
      p.cm
   1. United States—In motion pictures.
   2. National characteristics, American, in motion
   pictures.   3. Motion pictures—United States.
   I. Merck, Mandy.
   PN1995.9.U64M47 2007
   791.43′658—dc22   2006030352

ISBN10: 0–415–33791–7 (hbk)
ISBN10: 0–415–33792–5 (pbk)
ISBN13: 978–0–415–37495–8 (hbk)
ISBN13: 978–0–415–37496–5 (pbk)

Contents

Contents

Illustrations

Photographic copy source: British Film Institute

Notes on contributors

Pam Cook is Emeritus Professor of European Film and Media at the University of Southampton. She is co-editor of *The Cinema Book* (1999), and her most recent publication is *Screening the Past: Memory and Nostalgia in Cinema* (2005). She is currently working on a monograph about Baz Luhrmann.

Ana María Dopico is an Associate Professor in the Department of Comparative Literature and the Department of Spanish and Portuguese at New York University. She is the author of *Houses Divided: Genealogical Imaginaries and Political Visions in the Americas* (forthcoming). She is the editor of *Jose Martí: Revolution, Politics and Letters*, a two volume selection of Martí's prose works for the Library of Latin America (forthcoming in 2007 and 2008). She is presently at work on *Cubanologies: Altered States of the Nation*.

Peter William Evans teaches film at Queen Mary, University of London. He has written widely on Hollywood, British and Spanish cinema. His publications include the co-authored books *Blue Skies and Silver Linings* (1985), *Affairs to Remember* (1989) and *Biblical Epics* (1993). He is the author of *The Films of Luis Buñuel* (1995), *Women on the Verge of a Nervous Breakdown* (1996) and *Carol Reed* (2005).

William R. Handley is Associate Professor of English at the University of Southern California. He is the author of *Marriage, Violence, and the Nation in the America Literary West* (2002) and co-editor of *True West: Authenticity and the American West* (2004). He is currently co-editing a collection of essays on the film *Brokeback Mountain*. In 2005, he served as President of the Western Literature Association.

Rembert Hüser is Assistant Professor of German at the University of Minnesota. He is co-editor of *Das Buch Zum Vorspann: The Title Is a Shot* (2005), an anthology on film title sequences, and author of *Hitchcock: The First Three Minutes* (2007).

Barry Langford is Senior Lecturer in Film Studies at Royal Holloway, University of London. Recent publications include *Film Genre: Hollywood and Beyond* (2006) and essays on a wide variety of subjects in film, media studies and critical theory, including Chris Marker's politics, revisionist Westerns, narrative temporalities in *The Lord of the Rings*, images of disaster in the urban theory of Michel de Certeau, modernity and trauma in Walter Benjamin and Siegfried Kracauer and the political unconscious of TV sitcoms.

Esther Leslie is Professor of Political Aesthetics in the School of English and Humanities at Birkbeck, University of London. She is the author of *Synthetic Worlds: Nature, Art and the Chemical Industry* (2005), *Hollywood Flatlands: Animation, Critical Theory and the Avant Garde* (2002) and *Walter Benjamin: Overpowering Conformism* (2000).

H. N. Lukes is the gender politics post-doctoral fellow / assistant professor at New York University's John W. Draper programme. Her work has appeared in *The Oxford Literary Review*, *GLQ* and *Homosexuality and Psychoanalysis* (2001). She is currently working on a project addressing the roles of adaptation and allegory in transatlantic queer film and literature.

Mandy Merck is Professor of Media Arts at Royal Holloway, University of London. She is the author of *Perversions: Deviant Readings* (1993), *In Your Face: Nine Sexual Studies* (2000), editor of *After Diana* (1998) and co-editor of *Coming out of Feminism?* (1998) and *The Art of Tracey Emin* (2002). Her next book is *Hollywood's American Tragedies: Dreiser, Eisenstein, Sternberg, Stevens* (2007).

Diane Negra is Reader in the School of Film and Television Studies at the University of East Anglia. She is the author of *Off-White Hollywood: American Culture and Ethnic Female Stardom* (2001), co-editor of *A Feminist Reader in Early Cinema* (2002), editor of *The Irish in Us: Irishness, Performativity and Popular Culture* (2006) and co-editor of *Interrogating Postfeminism: Gender and the Politics of Popular Culture* (2006). Her current project is entitled *Perils and Pleasures: Postfeminism and Contemporary Popular Culture*.

Paul Smith teaches in the doctoral programme in Cultural Studies at George Mason University. His books include *Discerning the Subject* (1988), *Clint Eastwood: A Cultural Production* (1993), *Millennial Dreams* (1997) and *Primitive America* (forthcoming).

Eric Smoodin is Professor of American Studies and Director of Film Studies at the University of California, Davis. He is the author, most recently, of *Regarding Frank Capra: Audience, Celebrity, and American Film Studies, 1930–60* (2004).

Kristen Whissel is Assistant Professor of Film Studies at the University of California, Berkeley. Her articles on the early American cinema and modernity have appeared in *Camera Obscura*, *Screen*, *The Historical Journal for Film, Radio and Television* and *A Feminist Reader in Early Cinema* (2002). She is the author of *Picturing American Modernity: Traffic, Technology and the Silent Cinema* (forthcoming). She is currently working on a book on digital special effects and contemporary film.

Sharon Willis is Professor of French and Visual and Cultural Studies at the University of Rochester. A co-editor of *Camera Obscura*, she is the author of *Marguerite Duras: Writing on the Body* (1987), *High Contrast: Race and Gender in Contemporary Hollywood Film* (1997) and co-editor of *Male Trouble* (1993). She is currently completing a book on popular cinema's representation of the civil rights movement, provisionally titled *Islands in the Sun*.

Acknowledgements

I am grateful to the department of Media Arts, Royal Holloway, University of London, for providing the leave to complete this project, and to the Program in Film at the Department of Rhetoric, University of California at Berkeley, for the Visiting Scholar invitation with which it began. Thanks also to my colleague Barry Langford for his contribution to this collection and his advice at various stages of its preparation and to Jennifer Doyle for her intellectual support and warm hospitality during my visits to the USA. Finally, I would like to register my gratitude for invitations to speak at three stimulating conferences which started this project off in 2003: 'New Sex: Changing Conditions of Gender, Sexuality and Intimacy', George Mason University, Fairfax, Virginia; 'The Flesh Made Text', School of English, Aristotle University of Thessaloniki, Greece; and 'US Icons and Iconicity', European Association for American Studies, University of Graz, Austria.

Introduction

Naming the nation
in US film

Mandy Merck

Across the range of American cultural, film and media studies, one constant assumption is that films made in the United States of America have been and continue to be significantly imbricated with changing notions of American national identity. And at a time when the expanded projection of US political, military, economic and cultural power draws intensified global concern, to understand the ways in which that country understands itself seems, more than ever, an essential project. Yet concretizing the relationship between so multifarious, amorphous and – in regard to merely one country within an identically named hemisphere – grandiose a national signifier as 'American' on the one hand, and, on the other, film-making institutions such as 'Hollywood', whose own history and practices are themselves often inadequately understood, has proved predictably troublesome.

This collection of new critical essays tackles this old problem in a new way, approaching cinematic refractions of American identity through a series of close analyses of some of the hundreds of US films that have underscored their role in interpreting and constituting 'America' by announcing themselves as titularly 'American'. Madness, beauty, graffiti, tragedy, romance, splendour and, of course, (apple) pie – all of these and many more have, at different historical moments and through the agency of film-makers with widely various artistic, cultural and political agendas, found themselves rendered definitively 'American'.

The contributors to this volume propose that, through detailed consideration of the ways that individual US films have thus reiterated their 'Americanness' – in the context of a global film market quickly dominated by American cinema an apparently redundant gesture – other aspects of the evolving American imaginary can be interrogated and clarified. What does this national branding signify?

1

Why does it continue to be such a widespread practice in US film? What models of being – or doing – 'American' are conjured by such films? Out of what social and historical contexts do they emerge, and for and by whom are they constructed? Which versions of Americanism are valorized, and which marginalized or excluded? How is 'Americanness' differently constituted in the early twentieth and twenty-first centuries, in Classic and New Hollywood? Is the declaration of national identity an assertion of strength or anxiously defensive? Is it reliably ironic (as in literary precursors from Dreiser to Mailer), naïvely celebratory or shrewdly populist? How might national entitlement evoke patriotic enthusiasm, cultural prestige, instant nostalgia, epic grandeur or political disenchantment? Is the issue one of representing a presumptively pre-existing nation/national identity or that of constituting it anew?

I

Remarking on the national pride displayed by early nineteenth-century Americans, Alexis de Tocqueville famously concluded that it was a product of the political participation and social mobility afforded by democracies. Unlike their European contemporaries, even those from whose countries they had recently emigrated, Americans seemed intensely convinced of the dependence of their own success on that of the nation and anxiously concerned to preserve and defend it. Laudable as Tocqueville found this identification of private and public interests, he complained that American chauvinism exhibited the disadvantages of any other, including an aversion to criticism and an insatiable appetite for praise: 'One cannot imagine a more disagreeable and talkative patriotism. It fatigues even those who honor it' (Tocqueville 2000: 585).

Something of this national vanity may be discerned in what is described as American exceptionalism – the idea that its system of government (rather than, for example, its geographical location, natural resources or economic prosperity) has protected it from the violent revolutions and authoritarian rule which have characterized the historical development of other modern states.[1] More broadly, this belief persists in what Anatol Lieven describes as the country's civic nationalism, the widespread conviction that America is, 'in the words of former Secretary of State Madeleine Albright, the "indispensable nation" – whether chosen by God, by "Destiny", by "History" or simply marked out for greatness and leadership by the supposed possession of the greatest, most successful, oldest and most developed form of democracy' (Lieven 2005: 32). But as a recent president of the International American Studies Association reminds us, such claims to national uniqueness are not unique to the USA and, arguably, have been sustained by its academic Americanists as much as its politicians (Kadir 2003: 19). Without reinforcing this national mythology, or its monolithic representation of American culture, this collection is one attempt to take cognizance of the 'extraordinary degree' to which US public discourse, in the words of William R. Brock, 'seems to be marked . . . by appeals to the special character and destiny of the American people' (Brock 1974: 59).

One way to do so would be to consider Brock's view that, despite the general approbation with which the word 'American' is used in the USA, a 'wealth of overtones' (Brock 1974: 59) is discernible in its assertion of national values. (As he notes, its obverse, 'un-American', can connote not only foreignness, but also danger, immorality, subversion and delusion.) Brock's observation offers the possibility that, despite its claim for exceptional status, such national naming may offer varied meanings of just what that exception entails. Thus a recent *New York Times* discussion of two very different US periodicals concludes that the titles of *American Magazine* (a do-it-yourself bimonthly distributed by Wal-Mart) and *America* magazine (a hip-hop style rag backed by pop producer Damon Dash) say 'something about the mutability of the word "America" and the bifurcated republic it represents' (Carr 2004: B1), here differentiated by culture, ethnicity, location and generation. Whether these examples illustrate the distinction that Paul Willemen (2006: 34) draws between specifically nationalist discourses and those, as apparently in this case, preoccupied with national identity, that preoccupation remains a conspicuous feature of US culture. At the very least, the resort to such similar titles by two contemporary US magazines underlines the continuing popularity of the national signifier to name the country's cultural commodities.

More than 16,000 products and services are identified with the word 'America' in the US Patent and Trade Office's records, making it, in the words of Washington, DC lawyer Edward W. Gray, 'what trademark attorneys would call a "weak mark" . . . A term like "America" conveys all sorts of meanings' (Carr 2004: B4). Given the widespread resort to this national signifier to designate intellectual goods, one connotation would seem to be that of a proprietary identification or brand – *Brand America: The Mother of All Brands*, as a recent study of the country's commercial ethos would have it (Anholt and Hildreth 2004). Claiming a historical congruence between the aspirational individualism of the nation's founders and the global dominance of its leading corporations, Simon Anholt and Jeremy Hildreth identify US brands such as Microsoft, Nike and Time-Warner with the traditional insignia of the Stars and Stripes and the Statue of Liberty. But if 'America' is a brand composed of other brands – commercial and national – how fixed or coherent is its meaning?

In a discussion of political ideology (1989: 96), Slavoj Žižek maintains that iconic US brands such as Marlboro do not derive their national significance from their products' fabricated association with generically 'American' character-istics (Western landscapes, stetsons and denim, the lined faces of herdsmen and smokers). Rather, the US becomes 'Marlboro country' via its identification with the product. This reversal is argued to be even more apparent in regard to that quintessentially American brand Coca-Cola, whose Americanness is so ineffable that it can only be expressed as 'the real thing'. If we consider Žižek's observation in regard to American brands and titles that literally name the nation, can they be said to represent effectively national properties or merely to nationalize them by that naming? Does the term 'American' represent so contingent an identity that its founding moment – as Kadir would have it – fittingly occurred as a geographer's pun on the name of the Italian navigator Amerigo Vespucci to designate not North but South America in 1507? Or, as Ernesto Laclau (2005: 106–7) argues in reply to Žižek, do the particular commodities that solicit this national identification attest to a systematic – if not necessarily logical – homogeneity in the symbolic framework of US society?

II

Although the conspicuously American practice of national nomination did not originate with the US cinema, it was employed from the outset in titling its products.[2] Regrettably neglected, such titling is important because of its contribution to what Stephen Heath has described as a film's '"narrative" image, which is a film's presence, how it can be talked about, what it can be sold and bought on, itself represented as – in the production stills displayed outside a cinema, for example' (Heath 1981: 121). Far more prominent than such stills is the title (or titles in today's multiplexes) displayed on a cinema's marquee or in a film's advertising. Heading the bill, the title is usually the first or most prominent signifier in this 'static portrait' of a film's 'negotiable meaning' (Heath 1981: 133–4). The fact that it may have been selected from a score of equally or more apt possibilities out of commercial or political calculation, or that it may contradict other aspects of the film's meaning, does not negate its effectivity in constructing this narrative image.

Thus *America First* seeks to examine the repeated use of the terms 'America', 'American' and to a lesser extent 'United States' (more commonly 'US') in the titles of films from the earliest era of their production. The American Film Institute's authoritative Catalog of US films made between 1893 and 1970 includes 191 with 'American' in their title and sixty-three with the word 'America'. (The British Film Institute's *Film Index International*, less comprehensive than the AFI Catalog but including documentaries and major television movies up to the year 2004, includes 324 US-made entries whose titles include these designations.)[3] The first examples of these are, perhaps unsurprisingly, travelogues or 'views'.

One of the earliest of these subjects was the spectacular American Falls at Niagara, New York. Between 1896 and 1906, this scenery was filmed repeatedly by the Edison Manufacturing Company, American Mutoscope and Lubin, with titles such as *American Falls from Canadian Side* (Lubin, 1903) indicating the various perspectives of their filming. An Edison catalog note proclaiming an 1896 view of the falls from the Incline Railroad as the most popular due to the facilities offered by that company indicates the already burgeoning connections between the nation's tourism and its nascent cinema, a connection formalized by commercial alliances between a number of railroads and production companies. The early cinema's contribution to the iconic status of this scenery as an image of the nation (natural, vast, mighty, white) is disturbingly suggested by the poet Vachel Lindsay's description of the Klan riding to rescue the Cameron family in *The Birth of a Nation* (D. W. Griffith, 1915) 'as powerfully as Niagara pours over the cliff' (Lindsay 1970: 75).

With the onset of the Spanish–American War in 1898, the US military became a popular film subject in 'actualities' which continued the practice of national designation. The sensationalist press coverage of the conflict, with its stories of Spanish atrocities and the mysterious explosion that destroyed the American battleship *Maine* in Havana Harbour, generated 'war fever' and a market for films representing it. One month after Congress passed a resolution demanding Spanish withdrawal from Cuba, Edison issued a special supplement to its film catalog, *War Extra*. Throughout the conflict, Edison, Lubin and American Mutoscope repeatedly filmed troops on parade and battleships sailing into harbour as well as reconstructions of US forces firing on Filipino trenches or advancing in Cuba. Such films were titled according to the official name of their subject (e.g., *U.S. Battleship 'Oregon'*, American Mutoscope, 1898), or the manoeuvre portrayed (*American Cavalry Charging with Drawn Swords*, Lubin, 1898), nationally nominating a rapidly enlarging genre of what were even then described as 'war pictures'. The patriotic fervour of the period was amplified by a subject offered by several companies to conclude an evening's roster of entertainments: *The American Flag*. As Selig Polyscope proclaimed in 1898, '"Old Glory" fluttering on the breeze never fails to rouse an audience to the highest pitch of enthusiasm' (Savada 1995: 24).

Edison's catalogue entry for an actuality titled *U.S. Battleship Indiana* exemplifies some of the characteristics nationalized by these films. Filmed from a moving yacht as it is refuelled at anchor, the battleship is described as 'the most powerful fighting machine in the world to-day'. The scale of its threat is emphasized by repeated references to its 'great length', its decks 'covered with marines and sailors', the 'large gang of negroes . . . hustling' coal from an 'immense barge' alongside, and its 'powerful 13-inch, 8-inch and 6-inch guns bristl[ing] from their turrets' (Edison 1898: 9). Size, numbers and coordination are stressed in this spectacle of the country's preparations for war with its imperial rival. At the end of a decade of national conflict over financial corruption, immigration and labour unrest, and only thirty-three years after a devastating civil war provoked by the issue of slavery, the reunited ship of state is portrayed as a spectacle of lethal weaponry, mechanical efficiency, racial hierarchy and masculine energy.

The war actuality's 'synthesis of militarized masculinity, powerful technology, and patriotism' (Whissel 2002: 147) offered abundant opportunities for romantic narratives, and their elaboration into fictional narratives occurred soon after. By 1903, American Mutoscope and Biograph had jointly produced a compilation of three fictional scenes to be combined with two war views. Filmed by the innovative cinematographer G. W. 'Billy' Bitzer, *The American Soldier in Love and War* portrays a young American officer who leaves his lover to fight in the Philippines, where he is wounded, nursed back to life by a Filipino woman and eventually reunited with his sweetheart and her father. From these beginnings, a self-consciously national nomination frequently characterized films by the US cinema's early pioneers.

Among the most notable of these was Edwin S. Porter's technical triumph, *Life of an American Fireman* (1903). As Charles Musser's painstaking analysis of this film makes clear, the fire-rescue film was already an established US and UK subgenre by the filming of this production in autumn 1902. Moreover, these films were predicated on an international tradition representing heroic firemen in lantern shows (the English *Bob the Fireman*), fairground spectacles (*Fighting the Flames*, first produced for the Paris Exposition of 1901), painting (Millais's *The Rescue*, 1855) and printed illustrations (the US publishers Currier and Ives' 1855 *Life of a Fireman*).

Not mentioned by Musser is another Currier and Ives series, also created by the lithographer Louis Maurer, under the title *American Fireman* (1858). These illustrations complement the crowded urban scenes of the 1855 series with vertical images of a single statuesque figure in a series of poses later recalled in the fire-rescue film: *Rushing to the Conflict* (pointing to the fire, trumpet in hand), *Prompt to the Rescue* (of an unconscious woman in a nightgown), *Facing the Enemy* (directing the hose at the fire), and *Always Ready* (pulling the wagon from the firehouse). So popular was the *American Fireman* series that Currier and Ives commissioned additional scenes after Maurer left the firm and reissued these and the earlier series in the 1880s.[4]

Although the heroic fireman was not a uniquely American figure, his national reclamation by Currier and Ives marked two major transformations in mid-nineteenth century US urban life: the mass immigration which made the firehouse an idealized site of cross-cultural male camaraderie (Maurer was himself a German immigrant) and the professionalization of the fire companies that transformed the volunteer fireman into an object of national nostalgia. Half a century later, Edison prefaced its scenic description of 'the strongest motion picture attraction ever attempted in this length of film' with the declaration: 'The record work of the modern American fire department is known throughout the universe, and the fame of the American fireman is echoed around the entire world. He is known to be the most expert, as well as the bravest, of all fire fighters' (Edison Films, 1903, quoted in Musser 1991: 215).

Reflecting on the nationalization of this figure, Musser notes the late nineteenth-century urban fire fighter's unifying role in US society as both a proletarian hero and the protector of bourgeois property, as well as Porter's supercession of localism in filming four different cities' fire departments. In these respects, *Life of an American Fireman* anticipates the national designation of a subsequent Porter film, *Life of an American Policeman* (1905). Like its predecessor, which begins with the fireman dreaming of (inferentially) his own wife and baby, Porter's policeman is first seen with his family. The bonds of kinship are then combined with those of community, as various policemen aid a lost child, avert a would-be suicide, control a runaway horse and die while attempting to capture a dangerous robber. (The claim to authenticity is underscored by the use of actual locations and participants to restage real events.) And here, again, the identification of such civic functionaries with both the family and the nation, not unusual in Porter's films, is formalized by its title.

The title *Life of an American Policeman* also, of course, refers back to its prestigious predecessor, whose marshalling of four fire departments, 300 firemen and 'countless pieces of apparatus' (Musser 1991: 217), together with its innovative temporal construction and shot variations, justified Edison's superlatives. 'We show the world', the company announced, 'the every movement of the brave firemen and their perfectly trained horses' (Musser 1991: 215), a claim that allied the supremacy of the American fireman with that of the American film-maker. In the case of this film, that association was literally true: James White, producer of several fire-rescue films for Edison, took the title role in *Life of an American Fireman*. His next would be as the company's European sales manager.

Soldier, fireman, policeman: the gender of these exemplary Americans establishes a pattern which persists throughout the history of US cinema. In films that announce their titular 'Americanness', the American subject is almost invariably male, even on the rare occasions in which such films are directed by women. Such a rarity is *Making an American Citizen* (1912), one of the few surviving films directed by the French-American Alice Guy-Blaché for her own company Solax. This one-reel (15-minute) melodrama is an early example of films that dramatized immigrant experience, anticipating Chaplin's better-known 1917 *The Immigrant*. Both directors had themselves recently arrived in the USA, Guy-Blaché in 1907 and Chaplin in 1910, and both films feature couples who come to the USA from Europe. But from there the two films differ markedly. Where Chaplin's pits the little tramp and the young woman (Edna Purviance) he meets aboard ship together against the poverty, hunger and derision that await them in New York, Guy-Blaché's film contrasts a cruel immigrant husband with his downtrodden wife and the American men who intervene on her behalf.

Making an American Citizen opens in the (presumably Russian) countryside, with Ivan Orloff (Lee Beggs) riding in a cart while whipping his wife (Blanche Cornwall) as she leads the horse that draws it. The next scene takes place in view of the Statue of Liberty, as Ivan abuses his exhausted wife in Manhattan's Battery Park until an American man forces him to carry the couple's luggage. In subsequent scenes, the indolent immigrant continues to assault his wife while various American men protest. Eventually he is taken to court, where he again threatens his wife, is sentenced to hard labour and ultimately reformed. At the film's end, Ivan is finally employed, and he joins his wife in prayer over dinner.

Such a narrative, as well as its unusual female direction, lends itself to a feminist interpretation, but it also anticipates the assumed masculinity of the American citizen, however egalitarian he is 'made' (here, literally forced) to become. Liberty may be female, and, as such, an ironically gendered reproach to Ivan's misogynist cruelty, but, as Marina Warner observes, she cannot function as a character. Unlike Uncle Sam, from 1812 the personification of the initials US stamped on military supplies, 'Liberty, like many abstract concepts expressed in the feminine, is in deadly earnest and one-dimensional . . . Liberty is not representing her own freedom' (Warner 1985: 12.) And, similarly, Ivan's wife, however freed from his despotism by her arrival in the US, is neither the subject of Guy-Blaché's film nor of American citizenship.

Ivan Orloff's transformation from a lazy tyrant into a dutiful and god-fearing husband can be read as an allegory of the early US cinema's own Americanization. As Richard Abel has pointed out, the nickelodeon's appeal to immigrants, women and children provoked considerable anxiety in the years just prior to Guy-Blaché's film. Many theatres had Jewish proprietors or managers and exhibited foreign-produced films (notably, as Abel points out, from the French Pathé company). Their 'sensational' stories and stylized imaging afforded pleasures which did not require literacy. Meanwhile, the racist reaction to the wave of Italian and Jewish immigration in the first decade of the century produced demands for a wholesome character-building cinema on the model of Horatio Alger's dime novels, celebrating the social ascent of their hard-working 'native born' heroes. Together with the frontier manliness nostalgically promoted by politicians such as Teddy Roosevelt, these factors combined to nationalize the virile adventure story as 'the quintessential American subject' (Abel 1999: 126).

But if this masculinization of the US cinema was the tendency in this period, it was not without exceptions. Abel notes the dashing heroines in the 1910 films *A Western Maid*, *Female Bandit* and *The Cowboy Girls*, who ride fearsome horses, rescue children and capture rustlers. Five years after *Making an American Citizen*, *The Little American* (DeMille, 1917) refigured the titular citizen to address the controversy over the USA's entry into the First World War. Here the eponymous American is significantly female, a gendering requisite to the film's representation of her country as the innocent victim of German imperial ambition, espionage and attacks on its shipping. With the characteristically waiflike Mary Pickford in the title role, the prevailing national fantasy of American youth and ingenuousness is deployed to make her the outraged witness of Hunnish brutality. As Kristen Whissel demonstrates in this collection (pp. 23–43), the shocked tones in which the US Government announced its discovery of German intrigues is given an equivalently sensational treatment in this melodrama's dramatization of a virginal nation's violated neutrality.

Cecil B. DeMille's direction of *The Little American* is additional evidence of the continuing contribution of the country's foremost film-makers to its nationally nominated filmography. As this collection shows, DeMille and Porter were just two of the distinguished directors whose work flew the national colours. Joining them eventually were Capra, Sternberg, Vidor, Minnelli and Mankiewicz, with Orson Welles a further addition had *Citizen Kane* been released under its first-draft title, *American*. Reconstructing that film's production history, Pauline Kael points out that *William Randolph Hearst, American* was the title of the authorized biography of Welles's model for Kane, desperate to display his patriotism after his newspapers' attacks on the subsequently assassinated President McKinley.

> What [the film's original] title was meant to signify was indicated by Kane in the 'News on the March' segment when he said, 'I am, have been, and will be only one thing – an American.' That was pure flag-waving Pop before we had a name for it: 'American' as it was used by the American Legion and the Daughters of the American Revolution.
>
> (Kael 1971: 55)

(Kane's declaration may also be taken to reference Hearst's support for isolationism prior to the country's entry into the Second World War, when the publisher was a leading supporter of the 'America First'[5] movement.)

In 1922, representatives of the Daughters of the American Revolution wrote to Will Hays, the former Indiana politician who had become head of the Motion Picture Producers and Distributors of America, suggesting a film about the American War of Independence. Hays approached D. W. Griffith, who in turn engaged the popular writer Robert W. Chalmers, author of a short story about a British captain who leads the Iroquois against settlers in New York's Mohawk Valley. The ensuing film became a 95-minute epic recreating, with the help of the US army, key historical events such as Paul Revere's ride, Washington's army wintering at Valley Forge and the Battle of Bunker Hill, in some of their original locations.

America (1924) chronicles the conflict between revolutionaries and loyalists, ultimately drawn together by the atrocities of the renegade captain (a bravura performance by Lionel Barrymore) and his Indian cohorts. At its centre is a romance between the Massachusetts Minute Man Nathan Holder (Neil Hamilton) and Nancy Montague (Carol Dempster), the beautiful daughter of a Virginia Tory who insists on her marriage to Barrymore's captain. The name 'Montague' is not the only reference to *Romeo and Juliet*: Griffith includes a comic version of the balcony scene in which Nathan is left dangling from Nancy's window sill, and her brother later challenges him to a duel. But the two lovers are finally united after the villainous officer orders an Indian attack against the settlers at Fort Sacrifice and then menaces Nancy at a spectacular orgy of drunken Indians and their dissolute leaders. Throughout the film (readily adapted for British audiences, under the name *Love and Sacrifice*, via intertitles proclaiming the common values of the revolutionary colonists and their country of origin), white rebels and Tories are contrasted with savage Indians and the Montagues' silent slaves.

To be sure, *America* is not Griffith's sole representation of its indigenous peoples, who are effectively counterposed to its titular nation. Both his 1909 adaptation of James Fenimore Cooper's *The Last of the Mohicans* and his 1910 adaptation of Helen Hunt Jackson's novel of interracial marriage *Ramona* (in which Pickford portrays the half-Scottish half-Indian heroine) represent Indians in a more elegiac mode, as doomed survivors of dispossession and bigotry. A year after *America*, and the granting of US citizenship to Native Americans, Hollywood returned to this theme in a film of Zane Grey's 1922 *Ladies Home Journal* serial *The Vanishing American*. But as William Handley details in this volume (pp. 44–64), Grey's criticism of the white destruction of Native American culture was largely eliminated in the film to emphasize the evolutionary inevitability of its downfall and assimilation. Not only is the film's Indian hero (who dies of influenza in Grey's original) killed by another Indian, he effectively agrees to his own annihilation as the price of an emphatically religious redemption of his people, vanishing with them into Christian 'America'.

In 1931, the attempt of another Hollywood *auteur*, Josef von Sternberg, to engage with an explicitly tragic America became the subject of litigation and a box-office failure. With its emphases on economic injustice, sexual hypocrisy and futile religiosity, Theodore Dreiser's *An American Tragedy* was a daunting project for Hollywood, and the author was warned that Hays would never permit its adaptation. Nevertheless, Sergei Eisenstein was initially commissioned to attempt one during his brief sojourn at Paramount, producing the remarkable treatment which survives in Ivor Montagu's memoir of their time at the studio (Montagu 1978). Sharpening the novel into 'a monstrous challenge to American society' (Eisenstein 1949: 96), as production chief B. P. Schulberg complained, Eisenstein's approach was duly rejected, leaving Paramount with an ageing best-seller on their books. Employed to make a quick and inexpensive adaptation, Sternberg eliminated what he later described as the novel's 'sociological elements' (Sternberg 1966: 46), stressing instead the more spectacular aspects of its courtroom drama. Although Dreiser's suit to prevent the film's release failed, so also did *An American Tragedy*, a title the novelist had chosen because 'it could not happen in any other country in the world' (Lingeman 1990: 235). Twenty years later, at the height of the congressional Un-American Activities investigations, George Stevens was only able to undertake a remake by romanticizing the story's class dynamics and renaming it *A Place in the Sun* (1951).

III

In 1997, the American Film Institute issued *Within Our Gates*, a reference work cataloguing nearly 2,500 US feature films focusing on issues of immigration, xenophobia, interracial marriage and the struggle of disparate ethnic communities for social acceptance within American society. Prefacing this work, the Chief Executive Officer of its sponsor, Bank of America Corporation, retells the story of the bank's founder, A. P. Giannini (Gevinson 1997: xii). Giannini was the son of an Italian immigrant who, in 1904, opened a multilingual bank in the international North Beach neighbourhood of San Francisco. Catering to the Mediterranean, Chinese and Russian immigrants in the area, as well as to women after their achievement of suffrage in 1921, Giannini's Bank of Italy also became an early lender to the motion-picture business. Starting with a $500 loan to a local nickelodeon proprietor for a new film, the bank went on to finance the CBC Film Sales Company, which, in 1920, produced a celebrity newsreel series called *Screen Snapshots*. Among the directors of the series was the young Frank Capra.

A. P. Giannini's bank would later be renamed the Bank of America, and his brother A. H. 'Doc' Giannini would become a key backer and board member of Columbia Pictures – and the apparent model for the banker hero of Capra's 1932 depiction of Depression-era financial panic, *American Madness*. Despite (or, quite possibly, because of) its extraordinary timeliness and powerful execution, Capra's film, originally titled *Faith*, was not a success. Reflecting on the international origins and interests of both its model hero and its domestic audience, Eric Smoodin raises in this volume (pp. 65–82) the possibility that the film was, in effect, *too* American – too national in its disconcerting dramatization of the country's economic crisis.

As *Within Our Gates* testifies, the theme of immigration was a staple of both American dramatic films and documentaries. Writing in this collection, Rembert Hüser (pp. 83–104) charts a convergence of these modes in King Vidor's 1944 epic of immigration and industry, *An American Romance*. Vidor's celebration of the steel industry's contribution to the war effort centres on a Czech immigrant determined to work in the Minnesota iron fields. In a literalization of the figure of the melting pot, Steven Dangos will refine ore into steel while reshaping himself as paterfamilias, industrial magnate, American. Although publicized as a conventional love story, the hero's romance is clearly with the nation's alchemical powers of transformation, metallurgical and human. But, as Hüser points out, the film's own alchemy was less potent, failing to integrate its lengthy documentary sequences of steel and plane production into its archetypal story of immigrant success.

If, as Pam Cook reiterates in this collection (pp. 105–22), national identity must be understood as a dynamic relationship between the home nation and its 'others', the Second World War's transformation of this relationship was bound to have a significant impact on the meaning of 'American'. Elevated to a global super-power, the post-war USA sought to reinforce its standing through foreign investment and trade agreements as well as military strength. As the Cold War escalated, the Marshall Plan was one such strategy to further western Europe's reconstruction and to consolidate its commercial ties with the USA. Appropriating the title of George Gershwin's composition, *An American in Paris* (Vincente Minnelli, 1951) is an uneasy musical fantasy on the theme of cultural influence, in which the increasing fact of Europe's Americanization is displaced onto ex-GI Gene Kelly's attempt to embrace all things Parisian, including Leslie Caron. In the spirit of the Marshall Plan, the film promotes cultural exchange between the nations, reversing their traditional characterizations to make the American an artist and the Frenchwoman a shop assistant. But, as Cook observes, theirs is both Hollywood's Paris and art cinema's, a painted set shadowed by delusion, on which the two lovers cannot dance away their differences.

As the Cold War intensified, the dangerous illusions of the American abroad became the subject of Graham Greene's dystopian portrait, *The Quiet American*. Anticipating the country's disastrous intervention in Vietnam, and negatively reviewed on its US publication, Greene's novel posed another challenge to Hollywood adaptation, and writer-director Joseph Mankiewicz predictably eliminated its hero's CIA connections in his 1958 version, which starred the Korean War and Western hero Audie Murphy. Half a century later, Australian director Philip Noyce returned to the novel as a potential explanation of the USA's (and its ally Australia's) political motivations in East Asia. But although the Cold War had long since become history, and the Vietnam War an acknowledged debacle, his film's release was threatened by a new conflict, manifested in the attacks of 11 September 2001 (9/11). Reading these adaptations together, through their triangulation with the European writer Greene and his literary avatar the English journalist Fowler, Peter William Evans explores in this collection (pp. 123–35) two rather different attempts to characterize a specifically American colonialism.

The Cold War conflicts over the Berlin Wall and the Cuban Missile Crisis in 1961–2, as well as the early years of the Vietnam War, loom in the background of *The Americanization of Emily* (Arthur Hiller, 1964). But the film's action is set in 1944, with its black-and-white cinematography more redolent of Zanuck's elaborate reconstruction of the Normandy invasion in *The Longest Day* (1962). Writing in this collection (pp. 136–56), Sharon Willis identifies such reconstructions as the subject of this dark comedy, in which the death of a US naval officer on Omaha Beach is staged to enhance the prestige of the service. Condemned for its defiantly un-American challenge to the glorification of war, *The Americanization of*

Emily's sustained dialogue, disjointed structure and ironic ambiguity is certainly un-Hollywood, owing more to the 'Golden Age' of live drama on US television. Unusually too for such films of national nomination, it offers a titular female figure in the war widow played by Julie Andrews, then undergoing her own Americanization as the object of Hollywood Anglophilia. As Willis concludes, the film's definition of Americanization is public relations, embodied in its suavely cynical fixer Charlie Madison (James Garner), fittingly offered as a sacrifice not to war but to the avenue of promotion after which his character is named.

Despite Emily's ultimately triumphant Americanization, her US counterparts remained oppressed or off centre, if not voiceless, in the nationally nominated films of the 1960s. The Hollywood version of Norman Mailer's *An American Dream* (Robert Gist, 1966) opens with a powerful performance by Eleanor Parker as the bitchy wife of a television talk-show host played by Stuart Whitman. But when the fight between them climaxes in her fatal fall from a window, the ensuing story is that of anti-hero Whitman, who is betrayed by old flame Janet Leigh in his attempt to make his wife's death look like suicide.

Not surprisingly, in a decade of profound sexual transformation, the unhappy marriage repeatedly figures in the US cinema as a nationally identified malaise. Signalling its sophistication in its titular echo of Vittorio De Sica's 1964 *Marriage Italian Style* (*Matrimonio all'Italiana*), and co-written by future sitcom giant Norman Lear, *Divorce American Style* (Bud Yorkin, 1967) chronicles the bitter end of the seventeen-year marriage of a wealthy Californian couple played by Dick Van Dyke and Debbie Reynolds. Including a silent scene in which the warring couple arrive simultaneously at their bank to close down their accounts and a sequence in which Jason Robards attempts to escape alimony by fixing up Van Dyke with his ex, the film nevertheless concludes as a belated comedy of remarriage when the principals discover that divorce is even worse. In the following year's *The Secret Life of an American Wife* (George Axelrod, 1968), another Californian comedy of marital unhappiness, Anne Jackson is the discontented spouse of Hollywood agent Walter Matthau. In a desperate attempt to assert her erotic appeal, she poses as a call girl and ultimately regains her husband's attention by attracting that of his arrogantly sexy client, played by Patrick O'Neal.

Made in the aftermath of the 1960s fracturing of the post-war social consensus, *American Graffiti* (George Lucas, 1973) is the trail-blazer for the 'nostalgia' film and a representative example of the 1970s preoccupation with defining – and recovering – 'Americanness'. It inaugurates the cycle of films that discover a lost American Eden in a very resonant cultural moment: 1962–3, prior to Dallas, the March on Washington, the Gulf of Tonkin and the arrival of the Beatles, a last sun-drenched instant of American innocence. Other significant films in this cycle include *Big Wednesday* (1976), *The Wanderers* (1978) and – less satirically than one might assume – *Animal House* (1978). In this collection, Barry Langford (pp. 157–76) explores these films' conjuring of a racially and culturally homogenous youth culture focused emphatically on personal issues (sex, career, young adulthood) rather than the public and political concerns that would come to dominate the decade. As with its peers, *American Graffiti*'s assumed subject position is emphatically white, straight and male. In so far as this subjectivity is presented through a frame of retrospective melancholy (most famously through the film's much-imitated closing character biographies), the film is heavily invested in the white male pathos which characterized much 1970s US cinema.

The questionable innocence of another white male American is the theme of a neo-noir thriller of the Reagan era, albeit one seen through a filter of Armani pastels. Glamorously employed in the sex work more typically undertaken by women, blacks and gays, the protagonist of *An American Gigolo* (Paul Schrader, 1980) is a postmodern Horatio Alger hero with designer boots. As H. N. Lukes points out in these pages (pp. 177–98), Schrader's glossy adaptation of Robert Bresson's *Pickpocket* (1959) combines the era's rejection of the more relaxed style of the 1970s with its conservative cleansing of identity politics under the rubrics of law, order and a return to traditional American values. But the film's redemption of its hustler hero is an unconvincing narrative of love triumphing over commodity fetishism – doomed in the face of its own indulgence in those pleasures and because the very idea of an American gigolo is invidious to national understandings of male sexual power.

One year after *An American Gigolo*'s release, a cult movie beloved for its dark humour, tongue-in-cheek dialogue and (then) state-of-the-art horror effects staged a coming-of-age experience which might be understood as a refusal of a solipsistic national identity. *An American Werewolf in London* (John Landis, 1981) represents the transformation of its student protagonists as an encounter with a world outside national/natural borders. In a period that saw close ties between Reaganism and Thatcherism, Britain figures in this film as a point of engagement with and possible bulwark against the horrors of remembered European violence. Diane Negra examines the film's unusual engagement with British culture, including a closing message of congratulation to the newly married Prince and Princess of Wales, in this collection (pp. 199–213). Despite representing Europe as a traumatic proving ground for young American males, it offers a valuable case study in the manner in which popular culture both feeds and challenges the Anglo-American 'special relationship'.

If the Reagan 1980s did not usher in the 'morning in America' promised in the President's highly successful 1984 campaign for re-election, the decade did signal a new dawn in the national entitlement of US feature films. The generic range across which this designation was applied is indicated by its varying use in *American Pop* (Ralph Bakshi, 1981), *American Flyers* (John Badham, 1985) and *American Rampage* (David de Coteau, 1989). Bakshi's animated feature returned to the theme of immigration to chronicle the rich musical contribution, from ragtime to punk, made by four generations of a Russian-American family. *Saturday Night Fever* director Badham collaborated with Steve Tesich, the writer of *Breaking Away* (Peter Yates, 1979) to follow two brothers' efforts to train for a bicycle race in the postcard beauty of the Rockies. And exploitation-film director De Coteau screened the story of a woman cop pursuing a cocaine kingpin down the mean streets of Los Angeles. In each case, the choice of the adjective 'American' appears as circumstantial as it is thematic. De Coteau clearly needed to distinguish his film from William Friedkin's 1988 thriller *Rampage*, in which a district attorney hunts for a serial killer who drinks his victims' blood. *American Flyer* suggests the nationalized family values and sporting prowess represented by its star, Kevin Costner, but it also makes nostalgic reference to the classic bike company of the 1950s. *American Pop* stresses its immigrant family's contribution to their adopted culture while echoing its successful pop-history predecessor, *American Hot Wax* (Floyd Mutrux, 1978), a biopic about the anti-racist white disc jockey Alan Freed.

IV

The impetus to nominate the national concerns of the American cinema continued into the 1990s, with two such films declaring emphatically political themes. *American Me* (co-written by Floyd Mutrux and directed by Edward James Olmos, 1992) dramatizes its narrating gang lord's power over the internal economies of prison life and his disastrous attempt, on parole, to take control of the drug trade in East Los Angeles. The autographical voice-over creates a counterpoint to the film's panoptic gaze, proclaiming his own self-fashioning in the face of its assertion of the silencing powers of the State. The significance of this Latino breakthrough film has been widely attributed to the authenticity of its documentary style, the celebrated commitment of its activist director and star, and the notoriety of its violence. But as Ana María Dopico argues in this volume (pp. 214–43), *American Me*'s most notable feature is the way it deploys the power of the cinema to create both objectification and identification. Thus its hero and its spectators are implicated in what Foucault described as the 'carceral continuum' between penitentiary and society, in which the State's powers of observation and imprisonment are effectively internalized.

In 1995, 168 Americans died in Oklahoma City at the hands of a right-wing extremist, Timothy McVeigh. *American History X* (Tony Kaye, 1998), the story of a white man's involvement with the radical right, appeared three years later. On the face of it, *American History X* is an attempt to counter the crossing out of such episodes in the nation's history. The heart of its story – and the ostensible meaning of its title – is the special course given by a black high-school teacher (Avery Brooks) to 'save' a teenager (Edward Furlong) from the influence of his brother (Edward Norton), an imprisoned neo-Nazi, by making the teenager re-remember the brother's story of violence and imprisonment. But the brother's story is unfinished: in prison he has seen the error of his ways and has renounced his neo-Nazi past, but on his return to the community, his renunciation will lead to the teenager's murder. Exploring in these pages the film's contentious representation of the histories it purports to relate, Paul Smith (pp. 244–58) concludes that *American History X* resolves social contradictions into a figure of personal redemption, a move generic to American cinema that contributes powerfully to its evacuation of history and memory.

The failure of historical memory is also the demonstrable effect, if not the intention, of the hit teen comedy *American Pie* (Paul Weitz, 1999). Frequently described as a political improvement on the crude voyeurism of the 1981 *Porky's*, *American Pie*'s graphic representation of adolescent sexual initiation is combined with a contemporary storyline in which female characters study postmodern feminist thought and control their relationships with their inexperienced male peers. The supposed sensitivity with which the film treats its teenage girls has provoked extensive comment but not its strange choice of title, given the absence of Don McLean's hit from its soundtrack. As I inquire in this volume (pp. 259–76), what's American about *American Pie*? Certainly its 'gross-out' humour, which this comedy did much to revive. When the central character asks a more experienced friend to describe reaching 'third base', he's told that it's like 'warm apple pie'. Cut to his mother's newly baked dessert on the kitchen table in the film's signature scene. But in a scenario in which the girls are clearly more mature than the boys and the boys fantasize about having sex with their friends' mothers, the pie in question inevitably recalls the patriotic simile 'as American as Mom's apple pie'. Here the oedipality remarked by one critic begins to make sense, as well as the film's repressed connections with *Porky's* 1950s America of segregation and anti-Semitism.

In another film of the 1990s, *Made in America* (Richard Benjamin, 1993), the nation's apparent progress beyond the racist realities of the pre-civil-rights era is also cast into doubt. The late Michael Rogin's discussion of this film's failure to engage with the tabooed miscegenation that is its ostensible subject is an exemplary study of the vagaries of American entitlement (in all its senses) in Hollywood. As he points out, despite its apparently liberal ridicule of national anxieties about interracial sex, *Made in America*'s surprise ending unites its black mother (Whoopi Goldberg) and the white man (Ted Danson) believed to be her sperm donor, 'without violating racial descent . . . The movie's title is a quadruple entendre, alluding not only to sex, babies, and melting-pot patriotism but also to the product for sale, *Made in America* itself, racialized entertainment as commodity' (Rogin 1996: 9).

The proliferation of explicit Americana across the cinema of the 1990s includes, in an era distinguished by films heroicizing the nation's chief executive, *The American President* (Rob Reiner, 1995). In an overt plea for personal privacy in the Oval Office, this Clinton-era romance between a widowed President (Michael Douglas) and a high-powered lobbyist (Annette Bening) proposes them as an ordinary couple, albeit one who weekend at Camp David. If the American theme requires the lobbyist to be the girl next door, as demonstrated by her initial awkwardness and indiscretion, she quickly summons fluent French when she attends a state dinner on her first date. The film's Clintonian combination of American informality with an equally American display of power is even more evident in her suitor, who briefly interrupts his folksy wooing to order an air strike on Middle Eastern militants.

Consolidating the decade's penchant for national nomination, the much-lauded *American Beauty*[6] (Sam Mendes, 1999) took Bening from her Doris Day persona in the previous film to the brittle neurosis of Mary Tyler Moore in *Ordinary People* (Robert Redford, 1980). The consequent exculpation of her unhappy spouse (Kevin Spacey) from his midlife yearnings for a toned body and a teenage girl was widely ignored, as were the film's demonization and derision of its homosexual characters. Instead, plaudits were aimed at its satire of suburban conformity and the stylized reflexivity employed by its British theatre director. The five Academy Awards it received celebrated the *American Beauty* of a putative Hollywood art cinema, rather than its long-nationalized theme of marital breakdown.

Released in the millennial year of 2000, *American Psycho* (Mary Harron) takes its title, but not its feminist perspective, from its literary source, Bret Easton Ellis's 1991 satire of the Wall Street world of mergers and acquisitions. Co-written by Harron and Guinevere Turner, the film intensifies the novel's milieu of designer labels and desirable restaurants with its display of the expensive art in Patrick Bateman's (Christian Bale) apartment, including Richard Prince's Marlboro cowboy and a woman powdering her face in one of Cindy Sherman's *Untitled Film Stills*.[7] In a story already quoting Hitchcock, these blatantly citational works offer clues to Bateman's psychopathology. The toning mask he applies in his elaborate morning ablutions functions like the skull of Norman's mother, figuring the villain's merged and acquired subjectivity. Surrounded by highly mediated references to the simulacral America of Hollywood and Marlboro country, Bateman's mirrored masculinity maintains the traditional gendering of its representative citizen, but his patriarchal power is now exposed as wholly performative. (In a well-judged sequel, Bale's masked Bateman mutated into 2005's *Batman*.)

The attacks of 11 September 2001 and the subsequent failures of American intervention in the Middle East have prompted many reconsiderations of the nation and its history of self-assertion. Considering pre-9/11 polls in which US respondents' declarations of national pride and superiority greatly exceeded those from Britain and France, Anatol Lieven observes that such figures are more comparable with surveys in Mexico and the Philippines, where 'this pride has usually been seen as reflecting a certain actual national insecurity and even an inferiority complex' (2005: 20). Writing in the 'collective paroxysm' that followed the attacks, Djelal Kadir maintains that 'Assertiveness generally masks uncertainty, and America's discourse, most obviously at critical times such as the historical present, emerges simultaneously as blustery assertion and as uncertain question' (2003: 11).

Assertion and uncertainty are the contrary characteristics of the protagonist of *American Splendor* (Shari Springer Berman and Robert Pulcini, 2003), the outspoken but troubled Cleveland clerk and comic *auteur* George Pekar. His America is the nerd culture which came to attention first in his comics and then in this cinematic portrait of the artist. Hollywood's appropriation of the American comic has traditionally exploited the feats of its superheroes in the action movie, but Pekar's work is part of a different current in US comics and their film adaptations, representing everyday frustration and failure. Tracing this tradition back through the work of Chris Ware, Art Spiegelman and R. Crumb to Winsor ('Little Nemo') McCay, Esther Leslie considers the relation between its values and the ambivalences of this biopic (pp. 277–95). Part drama, part documentary, part drawing, *American Splendor* raises questions about identity and authenticity in Pekar's search for recognition. Yet in the wake of 9/11, it can ultimately be read to join America's superheroes in defying trauma by reaffirming the national norms of family, fame and fortune.

Nowhere is this drive to normalization more clearly evident than in the 2005 road movie *Transamerica* (Duncan Tucker). Here the abiding national thematics of personal mobility and transformation are embodied in the character of a preoperative transsexual (*Desperate Housewives'* Felicity Huffman) 'transitioning' from male to female, from solitude to family, from Los Angeles to the heartland and back again. The heroine's reconciliatory journey across a rainbow America encompasses her Latina therapist, her (ambivalently) gay hustler son, a black mammy figure from his childhood, a romantic Native American, a Jewish father, a menopausal mother and a sister in recovery from drug addiction. Making good the film's sole demographic exclusion, Dolly Parton's accompanying theme draws a clear parallel between sexual and evangelical conversion: 'And when I'm born again, you're going to see a change in me.' If the allusion recalls a substantial section of US society ill disposed to such alterations of one's God-given corporeality, the suggestion – driven home by Nashville's drag-queen soprano – is that even these oppositions can be reconciled in a nation dedicated to the pursuit of self-development.

Ethnic reconciliation is also the project of *American Dreamz*, a 2006 comedy of US politics produced, written and directed by *American Pie's* Paul Weitz. The film's premise is the television success of *American Idol*, an actual US talent show indicatively retitled from its UK prototype, *Pop Idol*. Amping up the antagonisms that make reality television war by other means, its diabolical English presenter (Hugh Grant) ensures that an Arab, a Jew and a blonde Midwestern cheerleader engaged to a veteran just returned from Iraq will appear in the competition's finals. When a politically penitent president (Dennis Quaid) attempts to recover his popularity by appearing as a judge on the show, the stage is set for a suicide bombing live on television. In a film whose central joke is the universal appeal of US media (avidly consumed by the mujahidin who arrange the bombing), the ostensible critique of imperialist warfare gives way to a softer satire of celebrity culture, this era's definition of the American dream to die for. Reversing the 's' at the end of its title to ironize an already ironic indictment of the country's aspirational ethos, as well as its idolatry of fame, *American Dreamz* succeeds in asserting little more than the national narcissism it sets out to lampoon.

If not the empty signifier described by Slavoj Žižek, Hollywood's 'America' has been represented as a plucky waif in wartime (*The Little American*, 1917) and a desperate housewife with a dick (*Transamerica*, 2005). More commonly masculinized, the nationally designated protagonist has been nostalgically rewritten (*American Graffiti*, 1973), punitively disciplined (*American Gigolo*, 1980) and belatedly normalized (*American Splendor*, 2003). The American history of racism has been religiously redeemed (*The Vanishing American*, 1925) and crucially misremembered (*American History X*, 1998), but it has also been reasserted – albeit from behind bars (*American Me*, 1992). Meanwhile, the white immigrant has been offered citizenship on condition of 'his' reformation into a national subject (*Making an American Citizen*, 1912; *An American Romance*, 1944). 'Americanization' has figured as an avowedly political mission in Europe (*An American in Paris*, 1951; *The Americanization of Emily*, 1965) and a stealthier one in Asia (*The Quiet American*, 1957 and 2002). But teen horror (*An American Werewolf in London*, 1981) has offered a surprising measure of engagement with the nationally 'other'. The American economic order has been represented as tragically unjust (*An American Tragedy*, 1931), periodically insane (*American Madness*, 1932) and increasingly feminized (*American Pie*, 1999). The national signifier has featured in the titles of travelogues, war pictures, adventure stories, romances, immigration sagas, Westerns, courtroom dramas, musicals, romances, melodramas, horror films, gross-out comedies, biopics, animations, prison pictures, documentaries and road movies. Judging from such recent titles as *Team America: World Police* (2004), *An American Haunting* (2005) and *American Gun* (2006), it shows no sign of abeyance.

As this collection demonstrates, the American cinema has developed across a century and more of economic, political and cultural crises, which it has variously repressed, addressed and imaginatively surmounted in its successive iterations of the nation's name. If the consequent identification of its films with that nation seems extraordinarily close, this may be because both are so invested in 'Americanitis', as the Russian film-maker Lev Kuleshov dubbed the 1920s enthusiasm for the US cinema's movement, heroics and – especially – modernity (Levaco 1974: 127). Although far from true in a country whose political institutions are now among the oldest, and least changed, in the world, the USA retains its abiding self-image as 'a perpetual project in-the-making' (Kadir 2003: 11). Should this collection reveal anything, it is the way such 'Americanness' is offered as a fantasy of renewal in each motion picture bearing its name.

Acknowledgement

My thanks to Barry Langford and Susan Nash for their very helpful contributions to this introduction.

Notes

1   In his significantly titled memoir of marital crisis, market speculation and film spectatorship, *American Sucker* (2004: 255), film critic David Denby cites the Victorian writer Walter Bagehot in attributing the nation's immunity from political upheaval to the 'stupidity' of its preoccupation with consumption.
2   The designation 'the Great American Novel', first used by John William DeForest to describe *Uncle Tom's Cabin* in an 1868 article in *The Nation*, itself became the title of two notable American novels, by William Carlos Williams and Philip Roth, who also wrote *An American Pastoral*. See Sanford Pinsker, *The Comedy That 'Hoits': An Essay on the Fiction of Philip Roth*.
3   My thanks to Caroline Sisneros of the American Film Institute's Louis B. Mayer Library for these statistics.
4   For illustrations of these images, see Sara Duke, '"Always Ready:" The American Fireman as Historic and Cultural Icon', *The Library of Congress Information Bulletin*, September 2002, www.loc.gov/loc/Icib/0209/firemen.html.
5   The American Film Institute Catalog records no feature with the title *America First*, although it notes that it was the original title of the 1918 film *Lafayette, We Come!* (directed by Leonce Perret for Perret Productions), in which an American pianist studying in France falls in love with a mysterious woman who is eventually revealed to a French spy impersonating a German agent.
6   The title reprises that of a 1927 First National picture starring Billie Dove as an impoverished beauty who has to choose between a wealthy young man and the chemist who woos her.
7   I am indebted to Chris Townsend for this observation.

References

Abel, Richard (1999) *Red Rooster Scare: Making Cinema American, 1900–1910*, Berkeley, Calif.: University of California Press.

Anholt, Simon with Hildreth, Jeremy (2004) *Brand America: The Mother of All Brands*, London: Cyan Books.

Brock, William R. (1974) 'Americanism', pp. 59–84 in Dennis Welland (ed.), *United States: A Companion to American Studies*, London: Methuen.

Carr, David (2004) 'This Land Is Whose Land? 2 Magazines, 2 Answers?' *New York Times*, 12 April.

Denby, David (2004) *American Sucker*, New York: Penguin.

Edison Manufacturing Company (1898) *'War Extra' Catalogue*, 20 May.

Eisenstein, Sergei (1949) 'A Course in Treatment', pp. 84–107 in Jay Leyda (ed.), *Film Form*, San Diego, Calif.: Harvest.

Gevinson, Alan (ed.) (1997) *American Film Institute Catalog: Within Our Gates – Ethnicity in American Feature Films, 1911–1960*, Berkeley, Calif.: University of California Press.

Heath, Stephen (1981) *Questions of Cinema*, London: Macmillan.

Kadir, Djelal (2003) 'Introduction: America and Its Studies', *PMLA* 118 (1): pp. 9–24.

Kael, Pauline (1971) *The Citizen Kane Book*, London: Methuen.

Laclau, Ernesto (2005) *On Populist Reason*, London: Verso.

Levaco, Ron (ed.) (1974) *Kuleshov on Film: The Writings of Lev Kuleshov*, Berkeley, Calif.: University of California Press.

Lieven, Anatol (2005) *America Right or Wrong: An Anatomy of American Nationalism*, London: Harper Perennial.

Lindsay, Vachel (1970) *The Art of the Moving Picture*, New York: Liveright.

Lingeman, Richard (1990) *Theodore Dreiser: An American Journey 1908–1945*, New York: G. P. Putnam's Sons.

Montagu, Ivor (1978) *With Eisenstein in Hollywood*, New York: International Publishers.

Musser, Charles (1991) *Before the Nickelodeon: Edwin S. Porter and the Edison Manufacturing Company*, Berkeley, Calif.: University of California Press.

Pinsker, Sanford (1975) *The Comedy that 'Hoits': An Essay on the Fiction of Philip Roth*, Columbia, Miss.: University of Missouri Press.

Rogin, Michael (1996) *Blackface, White Noise*. Berkeley, Calif.: University of California Press.

Savada, Elias (ed.) (1995) *The American Film Institute Catalog of Motion Pictures Produced in the United States: Film Beginnings, 1893–1910 – Film Entries*: Metuchen, NJ: Scarecrow Press.

Sternberg, Josef von (1966) *Fun in a Chinese Laundry*, London: Secker & Warburg.

Tocqueville, Alexis de (2000) *Democracy in America*, trans. and ed. by Harvey C. Mansfield and Delba Winthrop, Chicago, Ill.: University of Chicago Press.

Warner, Marina (1985) *Monuments and Maidens: The Allegory of the Female Form*, London: Weidenfeld & Nicolson.

Whissel, Kristen (2002) 'The Gender of Empire', in Jennifer M. Bean and Diane Negra (eds), *A Feminist Reader in Early Cinema*, Durham, NC: Duke University Press, pp. 141–65.

Willemen, Paul (2006) 'The National Revisited', in Valentina Vitali and Paul Willemen (eds), *Theorising National Cinema*, London: British Film Institute, pp. 29–43.

Žižek, Slavoj (1989) *The Sublime Object of Ideology*, London: Verso.

Chapter 1

The Little American (1917)

Kristen Whissel

The US cinema's silent era witnessed the production of a number of films that focus upon war, immigration, or both and, as such, are centrally concerned with the formation of a sense of national identity. Often, they do so by staging violent encounters with a 'foreign' entity. As their titles suggest, films such as *The American Soldier in Love and War* (Billy Bitzer, 1903), *Making an American Citizen* (Alice Guy-Blaché, 1912), *American Aristocracy* (Lloyd Ingraham 1916), and *The Little American* (Cecil B. DeMille, 1917) self-consciously strive to use emergent and newly institutionalized visual and narrative forms to articulate and assert the moral, political and cultural specificity of what it meant, in the early twentieth century, to be American. Such films dramatize conflicts with newly colonized subjects, recently arrived immigrants and only apparently 'American' traitors in order to mobilize and soothe anxieties aroused by the assertion of the USA's recently consolidated military and political power. This should be no surprise, for the American cinema's silent era (1895–1927) coincided not only with one of the greatest periods of immigration to the USA from Europe and Asia but also with the nation's involvement in three wars – the Spanish–American War (1898) and Philippine–American War (1899–1902) and the First World War (1917–18). At the same time that these phenomena transformed prevailing conceptions of national identity, the American cinema, too, struggled to define its own 'Americanness'. As Richard Abel has shown, during the first decade of the twentieth century, the American film industry mobilized a moral panic around foreign films in order to define a nationally specific cultural identity for its product and to secure the US market for domestically produced films (Abel 1999).

Hence, it is no surprise that the films mentioned above should participate in ongoing constructions of national identity for its audiences. Somewhat more surprising (and perhaps pertinent to current debates about twenty-first century discourses on US military aggression and 'dangerous' or disloyal immigrants) is the way in which these early twentieth-century films strongly associate American military ventures with romantic love, American power with powerlessness and, in some instances, the demand to 'convert' foreign entities to 'Americanism'. In *The American Soldier in Love and War*, a young man is sent to the Philippines to fight in the USA's bloody suppression of the national independence movement. Yet from the start, the assertion of imperial power is associated with family love, romantic sentiment and powerlessness: the soldier leaves behind a father and a doting sweetheart, falls valiantly during battle and is rescued by a 'native' Filipino woman who protects him from an insurgent (caricatured as a 'savage') who threatens to club the fallen soldier. She nurses him back to health until his sweetheart arrives to take him back to the USA. Here, as Amy Kaplan notes, war and love are inseparable, and American military power is converted into a need for protection from savage violence (Kaplan 2002: 154–6). In *Making an American Citizen*, a recent Russian immigrant to the USA is taught four lessons in 'Americanism' that convert him from a merciless wife-beater who treats his spouse like a beast of burden. In scene after scene, passers-by and neighbours intervene as he pummels his wife when she collapses with exhaustion while carrying heavy loads or hoeing their garden, fails to remove his boots swiftly enough or spills a bit of dinner. After being tried and sentenced to six months' 'penal servitude' and hard labour for abusing his wife, Ivan is 'completely Americanized' and emerges from prison as a caring and doting husband who observes conventionally gendered divisions of labour, blows kisses to his wife and possesses good table manners. 'Americanization' thereby becomes associated with the pacification of violence and the use of (physical, social and juridical) power to protect and defend rather than exploit the powerless.

In *American Aristocracy*, Douglas Fairbanks plays Cassius Lee, a blue-blooded but penniless entomologist who falls in love with the already engaged daughter of a wealthy 'hat-pin king'. Without money or the proper social ties, he is unable to break into her social circle of the *nouveau riche* industrial class except as an imposter: Cassius agrees to act as a stunt double for his beloved's fiancé, who is trying to impress his increasingly disenchanted bride to be. In the process, Cassius discovers that his rival has converted his factory to a gunpowder plant and is shipping supplies to Mexico (and presumably into the clutches of Germany) – a plot which has gone undiscovered thanks to the smart set's distraction (the men are entirely absorbed in their business ventures) and callous indifference to the war overseas. In the end, Cassius rescues both his sweetheart and the nation from traitors and spies armed only with exuberant physical agility, a sense of national duty and feelings of romantic love. In this film's national imaginary, the extraordinarily powerful American 'aristocracy' – the industrial class – is most vulnerable to the corruptions of war-profiteering and infiltration by alien enemies and requires rescue, and conversion to a new sense of patriotism, by the heroic actions of an ordinary and, by comparison, powerless American.

Made shortly after the USA declared war on Germany and officially entered the First World War, Cecil B. DeMille's *The Little American* unites these films' concerns with a benevolent and even highly moralized image of American military power and with the thorough 'Americanization' of the immigrant or 'hyphenated' American. In the final reel of this film, the heroine, Angela Moore (Mary Pickford), faces a court martial of German military officers who try her as a spy for France. The scene is remarkable for its formal composition: illuminated Lasky-style by a pale pool of light, the heroine stands in the middle of the darkened frame surrounded by soldiers and officers and freely admits to revealing to the French military the position of German artillery guns placed around the occupied chateau she recently inherited from a great-aunt. As her fiancé, Karl von Austreim (Jack Holt) – a German-American serving in the 'Prussian' army – looks on, the officers rebuke Angela and revoke her immunity as a citizen of a neutral country. Finally,

Figure 1 The Little American.

in a moment the entire film has been working towards, the camera cuts to a close-up of the Little American as she declares with righteous indignation, 'I was neutral, until I saw your soldiers destroying innocent women and shooting old men! Then I became a human being!'

By first linking neutrality to a failure to see ('I was neutral until I saw . . .') and by opposing neutrality to humanity, this climactic sequence puts on trial not the fictional actions of a single American who intervenes heroically on behalf of suffering France, but the entire policy of American neutrality that preceded the USA's entry into the war on 6 April 1917. It is not surprising that *The Little American* would interrogate and pronounce judgement upon American neutrality, for the film went into production on 13 April 1917, just a few days after President Wilson asked Congress to declare war on Germany, and was released on 2 July 1917. In the process of narrating the nation's shift from neutral, non-combatant status to belligerency, *The Little American* participated in the broader official and unofficial project of reconfiguring national identity for the new wartime context by articulating, in the clearest melodramatic terms, the moral and ethical imperatives behind the USA's transformed status.

The imperative for Angela's conversion from neutral to combatant is significant: she is moved to *act* and speak against Germany by the clear perception of scenes of suffering and persecution. By making action contingent upon perception, *The Little American* ties American neutrality to a previous failure to see the true nature of the war as a struggle between extremes of villainy and virtue. Moreover, neutrality itself increasingly figures in the film as a form of repression and powerlessness imposed upon the individual (and the nation). Neutrality becomes a condition of anguished spectatorship that forces the individual to perceive spectacles of extreme suffering yet prohibits anything other than verbal protest against the indifferent villain, much as the spectator at the moving-picture show shouts ineffectively in response to the injustices played out upon the screen.

The early reception of *The Little American* suggests that a highly moralized dramatization of their country's conversion from neutrality was precisely what American audiences craved in the tumultuous summer of 1917. Indeed, *The Little American* reveals much about the role – imagined and real – played by the moving pictures in mobilizing national sentiment and activity for the new war effort as the USA prepared (reluctantly) to enter into the most deadly conflagration in the history of the civilized world. The film was given almost unanimously positive reviews in trade periodicals and newspapers in major cities. It was held over for a second capacity week after opening at the Castle Theatre in downtown Chicago and drew record crowds at Clune's Auditorium in Los Angeles and at the Strand Theatre in New York (*Motography*, 25 August 1917, p. 385). 'Never has a production played at the Strand Theater aroused such enthusiasm as was displayed during the showing of this picture', reported Strand manager Harold Edel (*Motography*, 21 July 1917,

p. 118). In turn, *The Little American*'s huge success with audiences created opportunities for the Wilson administration to combine its advocacy of the Allied cause with promotional activities for the film. For example, after appearing in San Francisco for the opening of *The Little American*, Mary Pickford agreed to be the guest of honour at a Liberty Bonds drive attended by 10,000 people and was reported to be 'largely instrumental' in raising $11 million for the Liberty Loan Committee of San Francisco (*Motography*, 14 July 1917, p. 105). And Cavalry Lieutenant Jas. Douglas wrote to Jeanie MacPherson, co-author of the screenplay for *The Little American*,

> We have placed a recruiting officer outside of the theatre where *The Little American* is being shown, and grab many young men as they come out after seeing this wonderful play. I don't know how soon we are going to the front, but if we ever reach the firing line, I wish that just before going into battle, we could show *The Little American* to our boys, for I know they would be in the right frame of mind to charge all the way up to Wilhelm's castle in Berlin.
>
> (*Motography*, 11 August 1917, p. 299)

As part of a training programme 'to inspire patriotism and acquaint the public with the needs of the war', *The Little American* was also shown at the National Committee of Patriotic and Defense Societies' Speakers' Training Camp in Chautauqua, New York (*Motography*, 21 July 1917, p. 145). In short, *The Little American* seemed to confirm the claims of film-industry executives and shore up the hopes of the Wilson Administration that moving pictures could act as a mobilizing force in building much-needed consensus around – and galvanizing American activity for – the nascent war effort.

However, *The Little American*'s troubled history with censors in Chicago also foregrounds the degree to which the war and its cinematic representation could be equally divisive and generate anxiety, suspicion and embittered feelings amongst fellow Americans. The film was for a short while banned from screens in Chicago by the city's censorship board on the ground that it was offensive to German-Americans. As Leslie Midkiff DeBauche has shown, the banning of the film sparked a heated debate in the editorial pages of Chicago's newspapers and trade periodicals and ultimately prompted allegations of treason in some (DeBauche 1997: 63–9). Indeed, after stating that 'Patriotic pictures are not merely the choice of the day; they are a necessity. The more objectionable they are to Germany and Germans, the better for the prosecution of America's cause', an editorial in *Motography* went on to argue,

> For any man, censor or plain citizen, to defend his confiscation of American property on the grounds of friendship for Germans looks to us like plain treason. We would strongly advise that the producer whose picture is held up on such

grounds as these communicate at once with the United States Secret Service Department. And for the sake of American liberty, the pursuit of justice should not stop with the inevitable vindication of the film, but should be continued until these 'German friends' and their friends are put wherever it is that the government is putting its internal enemies.

(Motography 14 July 1917, p. 68)

Artcraft Pictures sued, and a jury decided on 15 July that the picture should be shown in Chicago (DeBauche 1997: 65). But controversy over the film did not end there. In August, *Motography* reported that,

> *The Little American* . . . seems destined to stir up trouble wherever it goes. Mayor Van Lear of Minneapolis was very doubtful as to whether he ought to allow the film to be shown in the twin city, because like Chicago's censor chief Major Funkhouser, he thought it was very wrong to do anything to offend our German citizens. Are all the executive positions held by pro-German officials?
>
> *(Motography* 11 August 1917, p. 316)

To understand *The Little American*'s capacity simultaneously to mobilize Americans for the war effort and to provoke accusations of treason against American citizens, we must consider how the film directly addressed two issues at the forefront of American culture in the early months of the war: the USA's conversion from its neutral status to belligerency and the loyalty of one of the nation's largest and previously most esteemed immigrant groups. *The Little American* deployed a number of conversion scenarios in order to play out and soothe anxieties around both of these problems in a way that reimposed a sense of moral and ethical certainty upon a world which seemed entirely given over to horrifying uncertainty and instability. The film renders its protagonists (and by extension its audience) powerless in the face of scenes of extreme suffering in order to provide compelling motivation for their conversions from neutrality and 'Prussianism' to support for the Allied cause.

Mobilizing Melodrama in Official War Discourse

Tropes of astonished spectatorship and restored visual clarity ('I was neutral until I saw . . .') and the revelation of a moral occult through unmistakable signs of virtue and villainy were not only operative in wartime melodramas such as *The Little American*, but were also mobilized in official wartime discourse published by the Government. War pamphlets published and broadly distributed to civilians by the Government's newly formed Committee on Public Information (CPI) also imagined the USA as an astonished spectator converted from neutrality by the revelation of previously concealed scenes of villainy and suffering. The mobilization of the melodramatic imagination in these pamphlets and the consistent use of tropes of revelation suggest that just as the excesses of the war seemed to provide new legitimacy for the frequently disparaged genre of the melodrama, so, too, did the melodrama help to legitimate the USA's conversion from neutrality and to make sense of the nation's new identity as a combatant in the world war.

The successful mobilization of the codes of melodrama during the war in official and unofficial wartime discourse undoubtedly had much to do with what seems to be the shared sense that the world war had made real the previously fictional worlds of the sensation melodrama. The same outrageous coincidences that governed the fate of characters on stage and screen now seemed to govern the fate of entire populations. Moreover, tales of intercepted telegrams, stolen briefcases carrying shocking secrets, astonishing double-crosses and deadly encounters with nefarious technologies defined the new factual existence of the wartime world. Stock figures (evil villains and persecuted innocence) and 'situations' (sudden reversals of fortune, a prevalence of chance in governing fate, a hyper-violent clash between competing interests) seemed to have leapt from the melodramatic page, stage and screen to reconfigure current events into the genre's characteristic nightmare scenarios. It is not surprising then, that an article published in *Moving Picture World* suggested that the war had given the film industry a new opportunity to participate in the life of the nation precisely because what was once the realm of the most sensational fiction had become regular occurrences in everyday life:

> The war has driven from our vocabulary, so far as strange events are concerned, the meaning and the very word 'improbable.' Things imagined before now daily happen; desperate chances rarely believed in have now become a regular occurrence. The wildest adventure, almost inconceivable, the craziest melodrama, has now become prosy. Exciting romance of our youthful fancies is now the bitterest truth of realism. We cannot realize that we are living in a marvelous period of human activity, participating in a clash of purposes, of commercial interests, of lofty thoughts, of noble sentiments inspiring democracy against desperate schemes to save autocracy.
>
> (*Moving Picture World*, 7 July 1917, p. 60)

The very premise that the 'craziest melodrama' had become commonplace and that the shocks and excesses of the reality of war far exceeded any fiction made it possible to impose the melodrama's familiar and familiarizing moral schema onto a conflict that, as Paul Fussell has shown, otherwise defied logic and frustrated attempts to reconcile the present with the past (Fussell 2000: 5–9, 57). Whereas previously the USA was understood by its citizenry as a distant and dispassionate spectator of the admitted horrors of the war, intervening only to make appeals to the belligerents on behalf of the principles of humanity and peace, wartime discourse refigured the country as a reluctant and self-sacrificing participant in a most shocking sensation melodrama played out on a world stage. Conversion from the former position to the latter was a matter of finally seeing a complete picture of the war that revealed the true moral identities and ethical stakes of the players. For example, the CPI pamphlet 'Why We Are Fighting Germany' defines America's decision to enter into the war as the only possible choice given the astonishing picture of barbarity that had finally revealed itself to the nation's eyes. Here, Germany is a figure of anachronistic villainy, a feudal lord armed with modernity's most infernal machines.

> We are fighting Germany because in this war feudalism is making its last stand against on-coming democracy. *We see it now*. This is a war against an old spirit, an ancient outworn spirit. It is a war against feudalism – the right of the castle on the hill to rule the village below . . . Feudalism plus science, thirteenth century plus twentieth . . . With poison gas that makes living a hell, with submarines that sneak through the seas to slyly murder noncombatants, with dirigibles that bombard men and women while they sleep, with a perfected system of terrorization that the modern world first heard of when German troops entered China, German feudalism is making war upon mankind.
>
> (Lane 1917: 6, emphasis added)

In a striking fashion, this pamphlet synthesizes scenarios from the earliest melo-dramas of post-revolutionary France (the *ancien régime* trampling the rights of the people) (Brooks 1985: 1–30) with the key tropes of contemporary sensation melodramas. Ben Singer defines the latter as an early twentieth-century instantiation of the genre which placed emphasis on 'action, violence, thrills, awesome sights and spectacles of physical peril' (Singer 2001: 48) and frequently deployed terrifying new technologies to do so. Characterizing Germany in these terms provided a familiar moral coda for reclassifying the combatants and gave pathos to the Allied side. Moreover, the invocation of spectacles of defenceless men and women bombed from above or unsuspecting passengers sunk to the bottom of the ocean encouraged America to imagine itself as a hero(ine) rushing to defend the powerless against the powerful, the virtuous against the villainous.

Other pamphlets similarly picture the nation as a collective audience propelled into action by seeing previously hidden spectacles of German villainy and civilian suffering. The first such pamphlet reprinted a heavily annotated version of the President's 'War Message' to Congress, in which Wilson deployed tropes of hidden German intrigue and obscured machinations suddenly revealed to a disbelieving nation. Indeed, Wilson made Prussian autocracy synonymous with powers of concealment which, in turn, helped define German autocracy in opposition to American democracy.

> Self-governed nations do not fill their neighbor states with spies or set the course of intrigue to bring about some critical posture of affairs which will give them

an opportunity to strike and make conquest. Such designs can be successfully worked out only under cover and where no one has the right to ask questions. Cunningly contrived plans of deception or aggression, carried, it may be from generation to generation, can be worked out and kept from the light only within the privacy of courts or behind the carefully guarded confidences of a narrow and privileged class.

(Wilson 1917: 18)

Such hidden German machinations took place, Wilson explained, not only on European soil in the decades preceding the war, but also on American soil in the early years of the conflict:

Indeed *it is now evident* that its spies were here even before the war began and it is unhappily not a matter of conjecture, but a fact proven in our courts of justice, that the intrigues which have more than once come perilously near to disturbing the peace and dislocating the industries of the country, have been carried on at the instigation, with the support, and even under the personal directions of the Imperial Government accredited to the United States.

(Wilson 1917: 20, emphasis added)

Citing the revelation of the infamous Zimmerman Telegram (in which Germany promised to help Mexico regain its 'lost' territories of Arizona, Texas and New Mexico should it help invade the USA) as another notorious example of Germany's previously occluded secret plans 'to stir up enemies against us at our very doors', Wilson declared,

We are glad now that we see the facts with no veil of false pretense about them, to fight thus for the ultimate peace of the world and for the liberation of its peoples, the German peoples included; for the rights of nations, great and small, and the privilege of men everywhere to choose their way of life and of obedience.

(Wilson 1917: 22, emphasis added)

Like *The Little American*, Wilson frames the nation's shift from neutrality to belligerency in terms of a revelation of the moral stakes of the war. His 'War Message' declares on behalf of the nation, 'We were neutral until we saw . . .'.

This focus on the sudden perception of revealing signs able to uncover the 'truth' about the war can be linked to two trends operative in American and European culture during the conflict. The USA could claim failed perception to explain its neutral past by invoking the broad sense that, from the first outbreak of hostilities, the war had so profoundly overturned civilization that ordinary perception and traditional forms of representation were no longer adequate to the task of making the catastrophe intelligible. Such an understanding, Stephen Kern argues, can be linked to the First World War's radical transformation of the experience of time and space, thanks in part to the deployment of novel military strategies and technologies which created entirely new scopic regimes. While the aeroplane bomber gave rise to a newly abstract, totalizing aerial perspective and the periscope allowed military personnel on submarines to see their victims without being seen, trench warfare imposed an extended blindness upon soldiers and new forms of camouflage (inspired by Cubism) denatured objects and concealed them from vision. Hence, when she recalled the war, Gertrude Stein wrote,

> Really the composition of this war, 1914–1918, was not the composition of all previous wars, the composition was not a composition in which there was one man in the center surrounded by a lot of other men but a composition that had neither beginning nor an end, a composition of which one corner was as important as another corner, in fact the composition of cubism.
>
> (Stein 1959: 11)

If Cubism provided Stein and others with the means to describe the breakdown of traditional perspective and 'older', pre-war forms of perception during the war, then melodramatic spectacles of suffering and villainy seem to have provided American culture with a compensatory perceptual counterpart that restored to the wartime world visual clarity and, with it, moral certainty. Like those moments on the stage and screen when villainy and virtue suddenly reveal themselves with astounding force, the melodramatic moments of astonishment cited by authors of CPI pamphlets are what Peter Brooks describes as moments 'of ethical evidence and recognition' (Brooks 1985: 26). The resumption of unrestricted submarine warfare (and the revelation that its cessation was a matter of convenience, not human rights, for the German military), the discovery of spies on American soil and the interception of the Zimmerman Telegram are all instances that, as Brooks argues of the melodrama, ' "prove" the existence of a moral universe which, though put into question, masked by villainy and perversion of judgement, does exist and can be made to assert its presence and its categorical force among men' (Brooks 1985: 20). CPI pamphlets share with *The Little American* a tendency to narrate the war as the real world's descent into the condition of the no-longer fictional scenarios of the sensation melodrama and to think of the USA as a spectator who gradually perceives with increasing astonishment and anguish the true moral stakes of the drama and the imperative to shift from spectator to participant.

The Conversion of the Pre-War World

The Little American represents the historical moment which immediately preceded the outbreak of war as an idyllic and innocent time, but one displaying signs of the coming conflagration. While these signs are initially invisible to the Little American, they would have been utterly legible to the contemporary spectator ready to reinterpret American neutrality and German villainy in the 'light' of more recent events. By infusing the film's opening scenes with signs of war, the film aids in the construction of a war narrative which links neutrality with misplaced faith and desire.

The film opens on 4 July 1914 – Angela Moore's birthday – and introduces its heroine in close-up against an American flag which blows in the wind as Pickford salutes the camera. This introduction and the coincidence of Independence Day and Angela's birthday strongly links her origins and identity to the nation's, allowing her character to function more broadly as, in the words of one astute reviewer, 'a symbol of America's attitude toward Germany since the commencement of the war' (*Exhibitor's Trade Review*, 14 July 1917, p. 416). To mark both occasions, flags decorate every corner and surface of the Moores' parlour. In turn, each of the suitors who visit Angela bestow gifts that further tie her origins to the nation's: Jules de Destin (Raymond Hatton) – a representative from the French embassy – brings a bouquet of red, white and blue roses, while Karl von Austreim brings a box of candies arranged to resemble the Stars and Stripes and a small silk American flag. Both appeal to Angela's romantic feelings through her own feelings of nationalism: moreover, the display of patriotic sentiment binds desire, consumerism and Pickford's own star image to what Theodore Roosevelt and others described during the war as '100% Americanism'. Indeed, as Leslie Midkiff DeBauche has shown, Pickford's already-established star persona as 'America's Sweetheart' undoubtedly provided a context within which audiences might receive her explicitly nationalized wartime role as the patriotic 'little American' (DeBauche 1997: 45). One might easily argue that, given the wartime context of its exhibition, the film helped strengthen America's love for its sweetheart by establishing Angela's love of nation as the foundation for all other forms of sentiment and desire.

This textual association of Angela with super-patriotism aids in the film's construction of the pre-war world as one in which relationships and rivalries already have a strong nationalist overtone. In a rather striking three-shot taken against an American flag suspended from the parlour ceiling, Karl and Jules greet each other with barely concealed irritation and vie for the attention of an uncomfortable Angela, foreshadowing the upcoming struggle between the Allies and Central Powers for American aid. Here the melodramatic love triangle maps onto the personalized plane of romance the ensuing division of the world into three categories: the Allies, the Central Powers and neutral nations. But when Angela chooses Karl, the romantic triangle is reduced to a couple very early in the film, allowing the narrative to drive towards a simple opposition between Allied versus Central forces: initially aligned with opposing points in the political triangle, by the end, all three will join the Allies to fight against Germany.

In turn, Angela's desire for Karl helps play out anxieties around the loyalty of German-Americans during the war, for the film is as concerned with the conversion from 'Prussianism' of the German-American who falls under the influence of the Fatherland as it is with the conversion of the American neutral to the position of 'human being'. Shortly after the outbreak of hostilities, German-Americans experienced a radical change in their status as immigrants in the USA. The loyalty of many was called into question, and German culture was gradually forced out of public life: German studies were banned from many schools, restrictions were placed on German-language newspapers and German music disappeared from concert halls. Once the USA entered the war, German-Americans were forced to prove their loyalty through the purchase of Liberty Bonds and even public flag-kissing (Kazal 2004: 184–5). The fact that the only German-American character in the film has been educated in Germany would have resonated strongly with audiences at a time when many aspects of German 'Kultur' – music, philosophy, art – had been linked in the national imagination to pan-German plots for world domination.

The Little American represents the crisis of German-American wartime identity due to the suspicion that the loyalties of the 'hyphenated American' were highly transient, fluctuating between apparent identification with and affection for the democratic USA and a more deep-seated and compelling allegiance to autocratic Germany. Hence Karl is a figure of national/ethnic mobility: having complete allegiance to neither, he spends his time divided between Germany and the USA, his father's homeland and his mother's. However, his proposal to Angela holds forth the possibility of an arrest in his movement between identities and locations: early on in the film, he promises, 'I am not going back to Germany, Angela, because I've fallen in love with a Little American.' Karl's pledge of love and residency coincides with and is countered by the sudden and unexpected arrival of a sinister-looking stranger who pulls Karl away from Angela and orders him to return to Germany. After instructing Karl to hold up his business card to a light to reveal a watermark of the German double eagle, he commands, 'You will leave in the morning on the *Imperator* for Hamburg, where you will join your regiment. In the meantime, *absolute* silence!'

The secret agent's abrupt arrival and departure and his cloaked identity and intentions pose a more extreme form of Karl's own fluctuating movement between seeming and being, between one national identity and another. The concealed watermark emblematizes the belief that the American component of the German-American's identity was only superficial, with loyalty to Germany deep in the soul. In turn, Karl's swift departure gives expression to fears that the 'pull' of the Fatherland might mobilize ethnic sympathies across the Atlantic, thereby undermining national unity on the domestic front. With a sudden reversal typical of the sensation melodrama, Karl returns to Angela and bluntly announces without explanation that he will depart for Germany immediately and cannot ask for an answer to his proposal. Given that the war had reconfigured German and American identities into incommensurable antitheses, it is not surprising that the narrative works ultimately to fix Karl's identity and his mobility. By the end of the film, he will renounce the Kaiser and then be confined to an Allied prisoner-of-war camp.

Partial and Periscopic Vision

Setting its opening in the month prior to the outbreak of war allows *The Little American* to re-enact scenarios of partial vision and obscured views: like the rest of the nation, Angela fails to see the signs of the coming conflict and of the secret manoeuvres of German agents on American soil. Such a scene would have resonated strongly at a time when audiences had recently read sensational stories about secret agents cultivating the allegiance of German-Americans on American soil and hatching plots to blow up munitions factories. Angela simultaneously fails to see the Agent's secret activities (a point-of-view shot from Karl and the Agent's perspective shows her innocently staring off into the distance as the orders to mobilize are given) and, like the rest of the nation, misrecognizes the worthiness of the suitors who vie for her affection.

In keeping with the notion of blindness to Germany's secret machinations, *The Little American* places its heroine on the final voyage of the fictional ocean liner, the *Veritania*, to restage the horror of the sinking of the *Lusitania* by a German submarine on 7 May 1915. Through a sustained use of cross-cutting between the *Veritania* and the submarine that sinks it, DeMille foregrounds what Kern calls the war's great 'drama of simultaneity' which united disparate and distant events into a single catastrophe of civilization (Kern 1983: 294–5). As Angela boards the *Veritania*, a shot which shows her presenting her passport to an official and kissing her family goodbye is followed by a shot of a German commander issuing the order, 'All ships suspected of carrying munitions to the enemy are to be sunk.' Cross-cutting inflects melodramatic coincidence with a more profound sense that since its outbreak all actions and gestures have become inseparable from war. Hence, editing gives Angela's kiss goodbye an added measure of finality. Ensuing shots of her sitting and reading on the deck of the *Veritania* are followed by the title, 'Efficient Prussianism' and a shot of the top of a submarine slicing through the surface of the water. The rapid fulfilment of orders and accelerated pace of military action contrasts with the slow temporality and leisurely pace of life on board the ocean liner, while the submarine's swift and barely visible movements conveys the rapid approach of an unforeseen destiny. Moreover, by comparing civilian with military activities, DeMille reveals the capacity of 'Efficient Prussianism' to convert all that seems familiar, happy, mundane and secure into its opposite. In the ensuing scenes, a glamorous shipboard ball is transformed into a horrifying spectacle of mass death, and a beautiful chateau first becomes a hospital for the wounded and then a German military headquarters, where young women are violated and young boys and old men are executed.

The elaboration of simultaneity, blindness and speed through editing dramatizes the scopic regime created by new military technologies which took control over the skies and seas, giving the German military apparent omniscience and invisibility. Cross-cutting reveals the awful truth about the submarine's approach and confirms that the passengers on board the *Veritania* exist in a terrifying state of blindness. DeMille cuts from a shot of a sailor peering through the periscope to a masked shot of (a miniature of) the *Veritania*. A cut back to the inside of the submarine reveals the Captain looking through the periscope, but rather than show another point-of-view shot of the ship, the scene cuts to Angela dressing for the evening, suggesting that the Captain is well aware that civilians are on board. Further cross-cutting emphasizes the radical difference and disjunction between the spaces of civilian and military life. Shots of the choreographed movements of couples dancing in the ship's ballroom alternate with shots of the sailors' coordinated movements as they load torpedoes into the submarine's guns. A waiter hands out packets of streamers and confetti to the party-goers (in what is, in effect, the civilian world's harmless equivalent of the distribution of arms), and the revelers throw confetti at one another in an ironically joyful mimesis of battle; in later shots, the streamers that cascade from the ceiling above resemble the chains used by the German sailors to hoist their torpedoes into gun chambers.

To underscore the relative blindness of the American passengers to German hostility, DeMille has Angela utter the highly ironic remark, 'Today ocean travel has no thrills – we might as well be dancing at Sherry's'. If the rapid movement of the submarine confirms the war front's extreme mobility, the irony of Angela's statement confirms neutrality's failure to shield the civilian from annihilation. Moments later, we see a shot of the torpedo speeding through the water towards the ship followed by a close-up of Angela's joyful face, her hair covered in streamers and confetti. The alternation between submarine/torpedo and ballroom is finally disrupted by a shot of the Captain of the *Veritania* on lookout frantically scanning the surface of the water with a searchlight. The camera cuts between the ballroom, the lookout and the inside of the submarine as the German Captain, peering through the periscope, watches the torpedo hit its mark and raises his arm in triumph. Finally, the camera cuts to the exterior of the submarine as the *Veritania*'s searchlight discovers it too late. This re-enactment of the sinking of the *Lusitania* gave audiences the opportunity to watch the drama unfold from a position of historical hindsight on the USA's blind faith in the safety of merchant ships and Germany's respect for neutrality. And while the omniscience with which editing endows the spectator provides the knowledge that accompanies unobstructed vision, it ultimately serves to intensify the powerlessness of the anguished spectator who watches the horrifying drama from a (historical, geographic or politically imposed) distance but is unable to intervene.

Once the torpedo hits, the unified scene of joyful dancing is transformed into one of individuated mass suffering as the ship lists and the floor begins to fall away beneath the dancers' feet. The film cuts to the outside of the sinking ship as the submarine's searchlight illuminates the stream of mostly female bodies plunging from the decks into the dark waters below. The abrupt shift of action from a horizontal to a vertical plane and the contrast between the brightly lit interior of the ballroom and the darkened night illuminated only by slowly roving searchlights effectively pictures the war's power to overturn past happiness into a benighted world of suffering. DeMille's use of the submarine's searchlight is important in this respect: rather than illuminate the sinking ship and its drowning passengers in order to facilitate their rescue, it makes the spectacle of suffering visible to the German crew of the submarine. In increasingly eerie shots, the searchlight picks out passengers as they plunge from the deck to the dark ocean below and as they struggle to stay above the surface of the water: in one shot, a young child struggles towards the camera with a panicked expression; in another, more surreal image, a woman in a tiara splashes helplessly as a chair floats effortlessly on the surface of the water nearby.

Reaction shots of the submarine's captain and crew reveal that they are impervious to the shocking spectacle of death made visible. Ultimately, the searchlight illuminates the inhumanity of the German military on a moral spectrum of spectatorship that opposes its indifference to the intended response of moving picture audiences (the sinking seems calculated to outrage). *The Little American* thereby places neutrality's constrained spectatorship between the polarized extremes of the spectator moved by pathos into dynamic action and the German sailors who observe with extreme detachment the suffering of the *Veritania*'s passengers as they struggle to survive. The presentation of the spectacular sinking sequence highlights the radical difference between the two extremes and foregrounds the intolerability of neutrality as a response to the war.

Scenes of Suffering

It is significant that, upon her arrival in France, Angela's appearance has been radically transformed. Dressed in a borrowed soldier's overcoat and hat and shuffling about in shoes many sizes too large, Pickford's character now more closely resembles the childish ragamuffin protagonists – such as the one she played in *Rags* (James Kirkwood, 1915) – on which her star persona was largely based. Dirty and tripping over her own feet, Angela approaches the chateau and gazes about in childlike wonder. Dwarfed by the structure's imposing size, she wanders through the massive reception hall and stumbles into the parlour where the servants have gathered. Despite the presence of a portrait of Angela which sits nearby, the servants fail to recognize her. Indeed, she has the appearance of a war refugee, not the well-bred daughter of a US senator. This temporary de-maturation of Angela is strategic: this representative of America arrives on the war front not as the figure for powerful and invested intervention but as the embodiment of powerless innocence – a disinterested ingénue whose reaction to the scenes of suffering she sees will be based upon a child's unadulterated sense of right and wrong. In this way, the ragamuffin often played by Pickford momentarily appears in this scene as the 'Little American' in order to loan the USA her innocence, vulnerability and unworldly sense of injustice, as well as her impetuous inability to resist the German military's violent abuse of authority and power.

Angela soon matures into her former self when she learns that her aunt has passed away, that she is now the 'Lady of Chateau Vangy', and that the town has fallen to the Germans. A long shot of the town shows the German military occupying its ruins; in the right side of the frame, a group of soldiers stand around a civilian who kneels upon the ground before them. A medium shot closes in on the group and reveals Karl beating a civilian on the head as he forces the man to shine his boots. In a tableau that momentarily arrests the forward movement of the narrative, three other soldiers stand around and watch with amusement as Karl humiliates the civilian. Moments later, this shot is echoed by one that records an entirely different response to the suffering of the defeated. After Vangy falls, Angela is urged by her staff and a French soldier to flee before the chateau is overrun. However, as she rushes to leave, she agrees to allow it to be used as a makeshift hospital for wounded French soldiers. The sight of the soldiers being brought into the chateau one after another, as if on a conveyor belt, arrests her departure. As Angela gazes upon the wounded with pity, a stretcher pauses in front of her; the wounded soldier salutes Angela and she salutes him in return. In a striking composition, she is joined on the staircase by three maids who are transfixed by the sight of another injured soldier as he is carried into the chateau. Moved by the soldier's dire condition, the women agree to stay behind and nurse the men with Angela, despite the danger to their own lives.

Once again, the film inserts textual spectators between its own audience and the scenes of suffering it uses to melodramatize the war. Previously united by an exchange of romantic looks, the former sweethearts are now opposed to one another by their antithetical responses to the horrors of war: utterly transformed by Prussianism, Karl inflicts suffering and delights in the exercise of power and its effect on the powerless; in contrast, Angela is moved to pity by the sight of the fallen and desires to mitigate suffering even at her own peril. When another soldier approaches Karl and exclaims, 'We've been billeted to Chateau Vangy where one may find old wine and young girls', it is clear that Angela and Karl are fated to meet again. Once they do so, the film exposes both to scenes of suffering in order to convert each to a new position: whereas Karl will be converted from ruthlessness to pity, Angela will be moved from mere pity to action. Before these conversions take place, both must experience extreme powerlessness in the face of intolerable scenes of persecution.

Angela's mobilization to the war front and the invasion of Chateau Vangy by German forces facilitates the wartime compulsion to imagine the horror of an invasion of America by Germany. When drunken German soldiers smash their way into the chateau, Angela stands on the staircase holding a small silk flag and exclaims, 'You are breaking into the home of an American citizen – I must ask you to leave!' The soldiers laugh and chase her through darkened hallways and break down the locked door of a room where the other women hide. Karl is amongst them, and, under the cover of darkness, he traps Angela, and the two struggle in the dark, neither aware of the other's identity. In the midst of the attack, Karl's hand accidentally hits an electric light switch, illuminating the room. In a moment of anguished recognition, he falls to his knees in shame and begs Angela's forgiveness. The exchange that ensues establishes a structure of appeal and powerlessness that reduces both Karl and Angela to helpless spectators of the horrors of war. When Angela demands, 'If there is a spark of manhood left in you – go and save those women!' Karl can only reply, 'You don't understand. I can't give orders to a superior officer.' When Angela appeals to Karl's superiors on behalf of the women, she is told, 'My men must have recreation', and is forced to remove and dry an officer's boots while Karl looks on helplessly. Later, when he follows Angela upstairs, Karl sees one of the violated maids stumble into Angela's room and clutches his hands in agony at the sight of destroyed innocence. Angela, in turn, reacts with pity as the maid collapses at her feet. As their anguished responses suggest, Karl and Angela will remain at a dramatic impasse as spectators set apart from the suffering they observe yet against which are powerless to intervene. While Angela's appearance 'cures' Karl of his baser instincts and forces him to watch the atrocities from a critical distance, he in turn protects her from the other soldiers, thereby allowing her to maintain the neutral's position of an observer set apart from the hostilities.

This impasse sets up a (historically familiar) triangulated structure in which a representative of the USA fruitlessly appeals to an indifferent Germany on behalf of innocent civilians and non-combatants who fall victim to the war's all-pervasive violence. The only narrative solution seems to be for Angela to leave; however, this would leave unchanged the triangulation of forces which seems to ensure the triumph of villainy over virtue. After Karl obtains a passport to allow her to cross back into French territory and return to the USA, an old woman approaches them, falls to her knees and beseeches, 'Mademoiselle – you are an American – don't let them shoot my people!' This is followed by a cut to old men and boys being lined up before a firing squad for 'insolence' to German soldiers and an officer giving the 'ready' command, then back to Angela as she turns in horror to Karl, who shakes his head in shame. The film cuts back and forth between Angela and the squad as the latter aims and then fires. Angela shields the eyes of the old woman, who collapses in grief and falls out of the frame. A sudden cut to Angela's former suitor Jules at his post on the French front explains her decision to tear up her passport and remain behind enemy lines: horrified by this spectacle, she will now act on behalf of France.

That this execution should motivate Angela into taking action is not surprising, for the staging of the firing squad plays out with violent force the oppositions of armed and unarmed, military and civilian, powerful and powerless, life and death and, thereby, reveals in stark and rather polarized terms the moral stakes of the war. The cross-cutting between the 'ready, aim, fire' sequence of commands and the series of appeals from the old woman to Angela and from Angela to Karl intensifies the sense of Angela's – and the spectator's – powerlessness. Melodrama provokes emotion and even tears, as Franco Moretti argues, through structures of powerlessness and through the presupposition of two 'mutually opposed facts: that it is clear how the present state of things should be changed and that this change is impossible' (Moretti 1983: 162) – impossible, in this case, so long as Angela and America remain neutral. Hence, the sight of the group execution becomes a catalyst for individual and historical change, allowing Angela's conversion from spectator to participant to function as an allegory for the USA's conversion from powerless neutrality to dynamic intervention.

Coup de téléphone

DeMille dramatizes this sudden shift from horrified and powerless spectatorship to outraged activity through an act of self-sacrificing heroism. Angela sneaks away to a room in which is hidden a spy telephone connected to Jules's post on the war front. She calls him with information on the positions of the German artillery around the chateau, resulting in direct hits on the German guns. Not knowing that the strike has initiated a search for a spy, Angela reports to Jules the result of the attack, no longer acting as constrained spectator of the war's atrocities but as the eyes of Allies, directing French fire from a distance ('You are shooting too high for the gun by the garage!' she tells Jules). The telephone materializes her new connection to the Allies and allows Angela to articulate in clear terms her dedication to her new cause: when Jules warns her of the danger she is in, she responds, 'Don't worry about me! You have no choice when it's one woman – or the battle line of France!' To signal the reduction of the Allied–neutral–Central triangle to a new binary, DeMille cuts from Angela giving orders over the phone to the German Commander issuing orders to Karl to search the house for a spy and wires, effectively placing the lovers on opposite sides of the conflict. Karl locates the hidden telephone wire and follows it into the room, discovering Angela on the phone. When he tries to sneak her out of the room, he finds that they are trapped by soldiers at the door and window. Realizing that Karl will be executed, too, if he is implicated in her actions, Angela orders him to 'Make them think you've captured me – it's the only way!' She pulls her hair down and draws his pistol to give credibility to the violent struggle she stages to save him from the firing squad. The plan works, and Karl is commended for capturing a spy as Angela is taken away as a prisoner.

This performance positions Karl once again as agent actively involved in Angela's persecution (he testifies at the court martial that he found her using the telephone) and then as a spectator constrained against intervening on her behalf. After Angela testifies that she had used the telephone and Karl acts as a witness against her, he retreats into the back of the frame. In a tight three-shot, two officers stand on either side of Angela as one claims, 'You may lighten your sentence – if you will telephone the French false positions of our guns.' When she refuses, one grabs her by her hair and shakes her while yelling in her ear. A close-up reveals Karl's horror as the officers abuse Angela. Unable to endure the sight, he is finally moved to cry out on Angela's behalf. Ensuring his own death, Karl pushes his way past the other soldiers and throws down his sword. He gathers Angela in a protective embrace and exclaims, 'I'm done with you and your Emperor! I'd rather die free than live in the grip of your damnable "system."' The soldiers close in upon them and the Commanding Officer sentences both to death, 'the woman as a spy and the man for treason!'. The impassioned speeches delivered by Angela and Karl effectively condemn German brutality and American neutrality, allowing for a clear articulation of the terms of their respective conversions.

In this respect, the neutral and the hyphenated American are 'saved' by the firing squad they face. The repetition of its dramatically polarized scenario confirms that with the renunciation of neutrality, the world has been reduced from a triangle to a binary opposition between the forces of good and evil. Hence, just before the order to 'fire' is given, a French shell explodes in the space which separates the condemned from the firing squad, giving Karl and Angela the opportunity to escape with their lives. The moral victory of this new alliance of Americans (little and hyphenated) with the Allies expresses itself as military victory, as the French push the Germans back out of Vangy.

Hyphenated Conclusions

In the tumultuous summer of 1917, *The Little American* provided audiences with a fictional narration of the recent historical past which provided a morally charged motivation for the abandonment of neutrality, asking audiences to think of themselves as formerly constrained spectators of the horrors of war finally provoked into dynamic action by the unbearable perception of scenes of German tyranny and civilian suffering. In doing so, the film provided an occasion for newly belligerent Americans to think of themselves as self-sacrificing hero(ines) rushing to the aid of suffering France. There is some evidence that the film had the effect of mobilizing sentiment for the new war effort. While the reviewer for *Motography* noted that the 'vivid reality' with which scenes depicting 'the intimate, heart-rending sides of the war' might 'mar the entertainment seriously for sensitive people', he went on to note that nevertheless,

> these scenes tend to arouse a feeling of hatred or retaliation, or, perhaps, in the majority of cases, a sympathetic desire amounting to patriotism that this country, upholding its traditions of liberty and justice, shall deal a telling blow to the end that the things that sustain peace shall thrive and stand and those that are inimical to it shall be exterminated.

(Motography, 28 July 1917, p. 208)

While melodramatic scenes of suffering facilitate and even compel the Little American's total, impassioned conversion from neutrality, they do less to mitigate anxieties around the imaginary features of 'hyphenated Americanism'. Though Jules helps Angela secure a passport for Karl, the film ends before he is actually freed from a prisoner-of-war camp for German soldiers. The final shot of the couple shows a fashionably dressed Angela kissing a heavily bandaged Karl through the wire prison fence which separates them. This ending is deeply ambivalent, for it leaves the German-American simultaneously imprisoned and free, officially at liberty to (de)mobilize back to the USA yet still confined as an enemy. The film ends abruptly before resolving Karl's ambiguous status as enemy-ally and free-prisoner precisely because it remains anxious about his status as a German-American. Indeed, its narrative turns several times upon Karl's shifting loyalty from the USA and the Little American to Germany and back again. If anything, the film confirms the suspicion of the German-American's fluctuating loyalties, his tendency to embrace with apparent dedication what had become in wartime mutually exclusive identity categories and national sympathies. Hence, it is no surprise that the film ends by suggesting that Karl is free, a friend and an American yet simultaneously prefers to delay his liberation to an unseen narrative future, suspending his movement back to the USA. That the film should posit confinement with future liberation as a fitting conclusion for this character is not surprising, for during the summer of 1917 anxiety around the loyalty of German-Americans intensified; by autumn, Wilson required all German aliens to register with the Government and forbade them to move without permission. By the end of 1918, more than 6,000 such aliens were held in federal internment camps (Luebke 1974: 255–6). Hence, just as *The Little American* deployed sensational scenes of suffering to mobilize its heroine (and, by extension, its audience) into dynamic, self-sacrificing action, so too did it mobilize the loyalties of the German-American between mutually exclusive poles and, with them, broader anxieties about the newly fallen status of the USA's most established immigrant group. In this way, *The Little American* demonstrates how the war and cinematic representations of it participated in a broader discursive struggle over the meanings of 'American' as the USA prepared to enter the war.

References

Abel, R. (1999) *The Red Rooster Scare: Making Cinema American 1900–1910*, Berkeley, Calif.: University of California Press.

Brooks, P. (1985) *The Melodramatic Imagination: Balzac, Henry James, Melodrama and the Mode of Excess*, New York: Columbia University Press.

DeBauche, L. M. (1997) *Reel Patriotism: The Movies and World War I*, Madison, Wisc.: University of Wisconsin Press.

Fussell, P. (2000) *The Great War and Modern Memory*, 2nd edn, Oxford: Oxford University Press.

Kaplan, A (2002) *The Anarchy of Empire in the Making of U.S. Culture*, Cambridge, Mass.: Harvard University Press.

Kazal, R. (2004) *Becoming Old Stock: The Paradox of German-American Identity*, Princeton, NJ: Princeton University Press.

Kern, S. (1983) *The Culture of Time and Space, 1880–1918*, Cambridge, Mass.: Harvard University Press.

Lane, F. K. (1917) 'Why We Are Fighting Germany', *War Information Series*, Washington, DC: Committee on Public Information.

Luebke, F. (1974) *Bonds of Loyalty: German-Americans and World War I*, DeKalb, Ill.: Northern Illinois University Press.

Moretti, F. (1983) *Signs Taken for Wonders*, London: Verso.

Singer, B. (2001) *Melodrama and Modernity: Early Sensational Cinema and Its Contexts*, New York: Columbia University Press.

Stein, G. (1959) *Picasso*, New York: Scribner's.

Wilson, W. (1917) 'The War Message and the Facts Behind It: Annotated Text of President Wilson's Message, April 2, 1917', *War Information Series*, Washington, DC: Committee on Public Information.

Chapter 2

The Vanishing
American (1925)

William R. Handley

'[T]he only people who can rightfully be called Americans. . . . the Alpha of the alphabet of American history', *The Overland Monthly*, on 'American Aborigines' at the 1898 Trans-Mississippi Exhibition in Omaha, Nebraska

(Dippie 1982: 207)

Cultural rhetoric about the 'vanishing' of the 'first American' was almost as old as the USA in the early twentieth century when, at the peak of its use, 'vanishing' was as wishfully proleptic as 'first American' was wishfully anachronistic. Less paradoxically than it may seem, this interest in Indians' vanishing occurred at a time when the Indian population had been increasing – and when Indians were among the first and most frequent fascinations of early cinema. During the silent-film era, 'vanishing' Americans appeared in 300–800 pictures, as characters, extras, actors, and themes – probably more than any non-white group. In some silent films, Native Americans directed all-Indian casts. Between 1910 and 1913 alone, at least two films, on average, appeared each week with Indian themes, characters, or actors.[1] The cinematic genre of the Western had yet to become known as a singular noun: in the trade press, the designation for these films was 'Indian and Western subjects'. Indeed, half of all films in these categories produced between 1907 and 1910 had Indian-themed stories or an Indian central character or hero. A few studios, such as Biograph, specialized in making Indian pictures (Abel 1999: 164).

These facts may seem surprising, especially since Indian subjects had been significantly waning from popular print media. In 1904, *The Bookman* claimed 'the Indian as a factor had dropped out' of the dime novel in the past two decades (Abel

1999: 167). The waning of Indians in print media began around 1890, the year of the massacre at Wounded Knee, a year that also marked a sense that US wars with Indians had ended and that frontier territory no longer existed. In 1893, Frederick Jackson Turner argued that the 300-year 'frontier' phase of US history – which he called 'settlement' and later historians called 'conquest' – explained American development and character. In his thesis (republished in his 1920 essay collection at the height of his influence), Indians appeared only as 'Indian wars' and early 'stages of civilization'.

Indigenous peoples did not appear much in American historiography as historical agents for at least another generation. But from the end of the nineteenth century they appeared in exhibitions, travelling shows, photographic studies and films, which extended their figural reach in the American national imaginary. Film was the newest medium for Indian and Western subjects at a time when film also became a central medium of American modernity. In visualizing what was thought to make Americans different from other national groups, Indian films were a new and significant medium of Americanization. As a movement, Americanization marked a conflict about who could rightfully be called Americans, a reaction to the First World War and to a fear of the tens of millions of polyglot immigrants who had arrived in the previous three decades. It was just before the war, according to Brian Dippie in his important study of two centuries of white attitudes and policy towards native peoples, that 'popular interest in the Vanishing American reached a peak' (1982: 211). The Immigration Act of 1924, which severely restricted the flow of immigrants from southern and eastern Europe, codified nativist campaigns in favour of assimilation and against immigration.

Indians' imagined relation to Americanness was starkly different from that of new immigrants, which is not to say that the American–Native relation was, or ever had been, a simply positive case of identification between white Americans and the mirror-image of their native other. Similar to the diametrically opposed Euro-Christian figurations of indigenous peoples from the time of first contact (seen as innocents of the new paradise or sons of the Devil), Indians were either first or last in the symbolic ladder of true Americanness. Not even African-Americans were as elastic in relation to national symbolic culture. Hence, it is not surprising that the same year (1924) of the Immigration Act's draconian quotas against immigrants, Native Americans received citizenship through the Indian Citizenship Act. Divergent as they might seem politically, both legislative acts were, during a decade of nativism, eugenics and jingoism, belated and symbolically freighted attempts to shore up an American national culture. Native Americans symbolically fulfilled 'nativist' American needs. After over a century of proclamations that native cultures were doomed to extinction, Indians were perceived in the 1920s to have a culture – and one more alive and spiritual than was to be found in the increasingly mechanized world Americans inhabited. Americans could shore up their culture not only by keeping immigrants out but by assuming and absorbing, in an authenticating act of cultural theft, a culture of 'first Americans'. (That the Daughters of the American Revolution – organized in the 1890s – and Indians could share the category is precisely to the point: the contradictions of history and its uses would not be resolved by rhetoric.)

Heating up in the 1920s, Americanization was a crisis in American culture which was itself a 'crisis *of* culture', as Walter Benn Michaels puts it, citing Calvin Coolidge in 1923: 'We do not need more government, we need more culture.' Indians provided a source and model for American culture as 'the exemplary instance of a society that could be understood as having a culture' – and, moreover, an 'authentic' one, in contrast to the mechanized and materialist society of modernity. Yet it was those very modern forces, which were seen to destroy Indians' older cultural values, that rendered Indians at the same time as 'the exemplary instance of what it means no longer to have a culture', which, Michaels argues, they could not have become had they not been perceived as vanishing (Michaels 1995: 35, 36).

Those who most defended Indians – those who 'valued' what their culture represented – were, for that reason, the most vociferous about their vanishing. Rodman Wanamaker, whose father was a wealthy Philadelphia businessman and with whom he shared sentimental regrets about the Indian, sent out three 'expeditions' into western territories to commemorate and record, as Brian W. Dippie writes, 'what he fondly called the vanishing race'. Between 1908 and 1913, the expeditions brought back 11,000 pictures and 50 miles of film. Dippie describes Wanamaker's gathering of the 'Last Great Indian Council' as 'conducting the last rites for the first Americans' (1982: 212). The book that resulted in 1913, Joseph K. Dixon's *The Vanishing Race*, 'pounded home the title theme with an awesome persistence rarely matched in the annals of Vanishing American rhetoric' in lines like these: 'He would not yield. He died. He would not receive his salvation by surrender; rather would he choose oblivion, unknown darkness – the melting fires of extermination' (Dippie 1982: 213). James Wilson parenthetically notes about the cultural uses of this descriptor throughout the nineteenth century, '*vanishing* is a kind of innate quality, as in *vanishing cream*, something you do rather than something that is done to you' (Wilson 1998: xxii). Zane Grey's *The Vanishing American* shares in this relentless, purplish plunge towards the dying light it also postures to fight against. The novel's last sentence begins with two words which almost sound like relief: 'At last only one Indian was left on the darkening horizon – the solitary Shoie – bent in his saddle, a melancholy figure, unreal and strange against that dying sunset – moving on, diminishing, fading, vanishing – vanishing' (Grey 1925: 308). Six gerunds, five near-synonyms and a final double repetition of the adjective from the title page may seem a matter of poor writing, but the overdetermination also signals that once is never enough when it comes to watching Indians vanishing.

Western films and novels helped to forestall Americans' sense of cultural crisis by allowing them to visualize an imaginary, 'native' past on the stage of an ancient and unchanging landscape far removed from the turbulent, disorienting present – especially the Navajo and Hopi lands of the Southwest which were 'discovered' by artists and writers such as D. H. Lawrence, Mabel Dodge Luhan, Willa Cather and Zane Grey in the first decades of the century.[2] The climate of reform in which *The Vanishing American* appeared was animated by opposition to the appropriation of Navajo and Pueblo lands for corporate access to mineral and petroleum resources. Secretary of the Interior Albert B. Fall advocated developers' rights to access Indian lands, and in 1922, US Senator Holm O. Bursum of New Mexico followed suit by introducing a bill affirming squatters' rights, which required Indians to show proof of title to their land to block resource exploration. The question of these rights to Indian lands and the deteriorating state of reservations under federal administration drew large interest from the popular press; numerous articles appeared between 1922 and 1924 in major publications denouncing federal policies. Angela Aleiss cites titles which are accusations by themselves: 'Deplorable State of Our Indians', 'Sad Case of the American Indians', 'Let My People Go', 'He Carries the White Man's Burden', and 'Tragedy of the American Indian' (1991: 468). In 1922, an all-Pueblo council issued 'An Appeal to the United States' at the urging of the reformer John Collier, warning that the Bursum Bill 'will complete our destruction' (Collier 1923: 21). Mary Austin, Zane Grey, D. H. Lawrence and other writers lent their names and support to the cause (Dippie 1982: 277). In part as a result of this effort, Navajo and Pueblo Indians became 'the cynosures of reformist concern' in the 1920s (Dippie 1982: 295) and the representatives of Indian cultural survival and vitality (in particular contrast to Plains Indians). Navajo and Pueblo lands, in turn, became the iconic meeting ground for competing meanings of American 'nativeness'.

It was these Navajo and Pueblo lands which inspired the 1925 Famous Players-Lasky production (distributed by Paramount) of *The Vanishing American* (dir. George Seitz) and which were also used for its locations – long before John Ford and automobile advertisers arrived on the scene. If profitable proliferation of subsequent images of Monument Valley is any indication, American audiences grafted a sense of belonging on to these landscapes which spoke of an ancient past, which inevitably included the people whom Americans had sought to subjugate and culturally absorb but whose image increasingly absorbed Americans: the 'first Americans' who authentically preceded them, as opposed to the new immigrants from the Old World who were following in numbers far greater than the entire indigenous population. If, by precedent and place, Indians were as American as any American, then (the logic of identification went), Americans were as Indian as any Indian. Ventriloquizing white Americans' narcissistic imagination of the other as a mirror-image of its native desires, Marian, Grey's love interest for the Indian hero Nophaie, says to him in the novel, 'I think loving you and living out here has made me – a little more American than I was . . . More Indian!' (Grey 1925: 260).

The image of the vanishing American resembled the new technology of the films it so often appeared in: the individual frames of motion-picture film become 'moving' pictures only by their continual vanishing, reappearance and vanishing. Like painting and photography before it, but with a greater reality effect, cinema provided a visual experience for the 'witnessing' of a vanishing America which had been a hallmark of much cultural rhetoric and practice regarding the American West in the nineteenth century (Mitchell 1981). Indeed, some of the photographs of Edward Curtis, in his epic, ultimately twenty-volume collection, *The North American Indian* (1907–30), are re-enacted in 'real' time and on the stage of performed pre-history in *The Vanishing American*. Curtis's photographs of hundreds of Indians were no less staged than this film's early scenes with their authentically dressed native extras. It is probable that Zane Grey even had one of Curtis's first and still most famous photographs in mind when he wrote his novel. His 1904 photograph of Navajos, titled 'The Vanishing Race' (published three years later in the first volume of *The North American Indian*), could be a visual template for the last sentence of Grey's novel: Navajos on horses, backs to the viewer, are moving into the ever-darkening background of an already dim image, with only the closest of the Navajo riders delineable, and just barely. Their simulated presence in such images and ethnographic narratives makes their actual presence ironic, as the Native scholar Gerald Vizenor argues in his discussion of Curtis and ethnography (Vizenor 2004: 181). The thousands of Navajo and Hopi extras in *The Vanishing American* share an elaborately ironic presence also with the Indians who had previously participated in Buffalo Bill's touring show: actual Indians simulate their 'vanishing' for an American audience, who believe in their vanishing despite appearances.

Ambivalent Sympathies: Melodrama and Epic

In 1922, Grey wrote to the *Ladies Home Journal*, which was serializing his novel,

> I feel certain that the sympathy of all true Americans will go out to the redman in his trial. This novel is concerned with the soul of the Indian. The great mass of busy Americans do not know the beauty and nobility of the Indian as he exists still where unspoiled by contact with a materialist civilization. They do not realize that he has been cruelly wronged, that he will never be absorbed by the white race, tha[t] he is vanishing from the earth.

(quoted in Kant 1984: 85)

By 'true Americans', Grey means those whites who are sympathetic to the Indian (in telling contrast to 'first' Americans, which his Indian character calls himself).

It is not difficult to see why the figural identity of the Indian became more culturally important to and sympathetic for whites than actual Indians. More often, Indians became – in their literal incarnations though not their symbolic ones – inconvenient.

Since the Enlightenment, the liberal cultural imagination in America has been ambivalent about Native Americans: sympathetic to them yet wanting them to remain perpetually under the threat of disappearing, or to be kept alive in a mythic or prehistoric past – or, despite facts to the contrary and for reasons which have nothing to do with actual Indians (living or historical) guiltily and not quite past-perfectly assuming that 'we killed them off' (as Louis Ironson asserts in Tony Kushner's *Angels in America*, arguing that America is exceptional because it has 'no racial or spiritual past'). In grammatical terms, 'Indians' have especially been figured as a gerund to keep in motion a particular idea of, or screen for, the 'true' American who responds to them in a sympathetically correct, even pitying manner. 'Pitiful and tremendous – riding away to fight for the white man!' says a white sergeant in the film as Nophaie leaves to fight in the First World War (with the hope, as he says earlier, of becoming 'American – *me!*').

More the case than with any other film genre in the silent period, argues Richard Slotkin (1992), 'public response to Westerns was taken as a symptom of the state

Figure 2 The Vanishing American.

of American taste, morals, and self-image', in what he calls 'an active mythographic enterprise' between what lies on the screen and what occurs in the 'real' world. To borrow from Leo Braudy's distinction (2002: 44–51), as a genre the Western film is both 'closed' – centripetally self-referential in its codes and signs – and yet referentially 'wide open', for reasons having to do with much more than its framed, wide-open landscapes. To a significant extent, the simulated presence of the Indian made that negotiation between the screen and reality possible, iconically static yet historically charged as it was. What makes the 1925 film *The Vanishing American* remarkable, in part, is both how closed and how open it is, at a time before a more formulaic and dehumanizing caricature of Indians became the norm in the 1930s and 1940s. One reason for this is that the film situates its melodramatic story within an attempt at epic history-telling (the former derived from Zane Grey's novel, the latter original to the screen scenario).

A visceral sense of right and wrong drives melodrama, of which Grey's novel and its first film version are exemplars. When an author or film-maker wants to elicit sympathy for Indians and hence racializes these moral categories (Indians as rightfully the first Americans wronged by white Americans), further moral distinctions among whites need to be made if the melodrama is to work affectively on a white audience. Zane Grey's solution to these ambiguous distinctions was to make interracial love between an Indian hero and a white heroine triumph over what he saw as the false and destructive effects that Christian missionaries had been having on the Navajo (Grey's 'Nopah') and other Indians of the Southwest where he travelled.[3] One of the most dramatic changes to Grey's story in its film version is that the moral valence of Christianity in Grey's novel is reversed. Evil federal bureaucrats, rather than missionaries, serve as foils to both white and Indian virtue in the film, a virtue achieved not through interracial procreation but through Christian belief, non-sexual romance and a romanticized death. Given that a white actor (Richard Dix in Max Factor's Indian Tan) is cast in the role of Indian hero, while 'his people' are played by actual Indians, the effect of this transposition is to reinscribe melodramatic moral distinctions as racial ones, but in reverse: there may be whites who wrong Indians, but the truest Indian is the true American if he becomes Christian – a denomination in the film which is marked already as white.

Appearing first in serial form in 1922, Grey's novel was published in 1925 to coincide that year with the release of its first screen adaptation. Both the novel and the film end in the American Southwest just after the First World War, in which the Indian hero Nophaie has fought heroically for 'his' country and for his people. Nophaie returns to find that Booker (Noah Beery) – a corrupt federal bureaucrat of Indian affairs who is the film's main villain – has further abused, betrayed and displaced Nophaie's people by taking their land. In contrast to the film, Grey's novel begins with Nophaie as a boy and narrates his Christian education back East, where he becomes a star athlete. When he returns to his people, he desires to rid himself of what increasingly feels culturally false and to reacquaint himself with his Indian soul, a desire which is both complicated and answered by his love for Marian (Lois Wilson). The relation and fate of Nophaie and Marian vary between the film and the novel and between the novel's two endings: in the serialized version of 1922, the two marry. Because Harper Brothers objected to that ending, in the 1925 novel Nophaie dies of a plague. In the film, Nophaie is accidentally shot by another Indian who suffers shellshock from the war as Nophaie is trying to calm an insurrection against government officials.

The differences among these endings reveal the contradictions at the core of American figurations of a race imagined at once to be foundational to American history and identity (the 'Alpha' of its 'alphabet') and to be forever disappearing. As a solution to this temporal paradox, the film draws on the religion whose missionaries Grey had criticized – and the result is not just that the film takes out some of the historical context of Grey's plot (Presbyterian missionaries were indeed at work in the Indian lands Grey visited), it also aims to transcend history altogether in a conflation of beginnings and endings, as in the Christian conflation of 'the Alpha and the Omega'. Where Grey identified Christian missionaries as a causally destructive force for native peoples, the film version of his novel renders Christianity as something which both is prior to and transcends American colonial history, rather than something deeply entangled and complicit in it. This aim is evident in the screen scenario by Lillian Hubbard, who describes the image that would frame the film – of Monument Valley:

> There is no sign of life anywhere in the scene, just the great mass of mountain, which must look today as it looked in the time of Christ, and may still look ten thousand years from now. (We want the effect of a vast, silent spectator to the human drama we are to unfold, a brooding Presence that will almost seem alive.)
>
> (MHL 1925: 3)

What frames the film is thus anything but human melodrama: a silent spectator of a landscape which sublimely subsumes the drama within.[4] *The Vanishing American*'s particular iconography renders Christianity as the meaning of and source of consolation for the Indian hero's death, by means of an ending the film producers ordained could not include marriage with the white heroine, i.e., a generational future for Indians and Americans, even if the Indian would be absorbed, as Grey imagined it, by virtuous white Americans. More significantly, silent film in *The Vanishing American* suited and allegorized many Americans' desire to 'know' (by visualizing) 'their' distinctive, indigenous history while being permitted by a sublimely indifferent spectator (mute landscapes and actors, the invisible camera and the audience in the dark) to ignore actual history.

The film's contemporary melodrama is situated within an epic history with which the film begins. (Grey's novel takes place entirely in the twentieth century.) As few films have done, such as some science-fiction productions and, singularly, among films whose central narrative is about romantic sacrifice in their contemporary moment, *The Vanishing American* begins its first scene with actors tens of thousand years in the past: a man, woman and child, appearing as hairy cavemen, rise up from behind a rocky mound then descend it towards the camera, until they disappear below the bottom frame. Yet the film's opening nods to a far more ancient past and sets up the film's peculiarly American brew of the fatalistic sublime, sympathy-inducing melodrama and Christian transcendence: against a still image of mastodons and dinosaurs, Herbert Spencer's *First Principles* is quoted claiming 'unmistakeable proof that throughout all the past there has been a ceaseless devouring of the weak by the strong . . . a survival of the fittest'. The film's next 30 minutes take us through representational chapters of aboriginal history and of Spanish and American conquest, chapters found nowhere in the work of Zane Grey but which, as I will show and explore the reasons for, externalize, temporally extend and sequentially reverse the internal evolution his characters undergo.

The film's extended prologue gives a staged, visual 'reality' and sense of ethnographic authenticity to a racial past in the Southwest. Sandwiched between the chronology of dinosaurs and Early Man, however, is yet another still image which returns at the film's end and which remains among the film's most memorable, an iconographic stage of both the ancient past and future history of what the film introduces in its early scenes as this 'Western state far from the haunts of men'. One of many shots which aesthetically rival anything by John Ford, it discloses Monument Valley, devoid of inhabitants and without any movement in the scene or by the camera (except for the flickering light as the scene fades in and fades out). 'For men come and live their hour and go', the intertitle at the beginning states, 'but the mighty stage remains.' When the same scene reappears at the end, that sentence is repeated in an intertitle – with one addition: 'For *races* of men come and live their hour and go, but the mighty stage remains' (emphasis added). This small difference (from 'men' to 'races of men') marks a world of difference: the failure of universality, which melodrama pretends to presume in its sympathetic guise, even as it makes ambivalent distinctions among types.

The audience of the film is given the gaze of a vast, silent spectator of the 'mighty stage' and the 'human drama' played out on it, such that the film's sublimely dispassionate 'historical' frame subsumes the melancholy and sympathy that the contemporary melodrama is scripted to elicit. After the ravages of the First World War, which are compellingly depicted in the film and despite the somewhat-qualified assertion about the ephemeral nature of all racial groups and cultures, the American viewer is situated in a frame of implied temporal transcendence and sanctification, with the screenplay's Christianizing diegesis and its ancient, newly iconic Western stone monuments providing a cinematic conflation of both the ancient past and the original audience's American present: 'Through the ages', one of the first intertitles asks, 'since the Great Beginning of It All, how many races have crept within the shadows of the Monuments?' This would seem a rhetorical question, except that the film-makers spend nearly 30 minutes answering it. More effectively than any silent film and even most sound pictures shot on location in the American West, *The Vanishing American* situates its landscapes in the frame of epic, even geologic history. (An interesting contrast is the 1983 film *Koyaanisqatsi*, which adopts a Hopi perspective on this same region across vast time; American civilization is that film's tragedy.) Onto this recurring landscape, which remains visually the same as the historical actors and eras change, the film displaces and resolves Americans' anxieties about whether or not they are exceptionally different from all other nations and races in world history – and whether it is the Indians' presence or whether it is their absence (or both at the same time) which is integral to that difference.

White Americans' anxiety about having already depended on a vanishing race or a vanishing frontier to achieve a true American identity found an uneasy cinematic resolution by means of whites 'playing Indian', to use Philip Deloria's phrase (1998), and especially by having whites love and leave (or be left by) an Indian on screen. This role-playing would not achieve its melodramatic purpose without a tragic conduit to sympathy. Many of the early Indian silents convey a more domestic kind of tragedy which rendered Indians no less pitiable than the large historical question of 'vanishing' did. These films' representation of Indians are more positively human and nuanced than the degrading images that came to characterize many later Westerns; they have what Grey ascribes to his Indians in his letter to the *Ladies Home Journal*: 'soul', 'beauty', 'nobility'. Indians are assigned these qualities and are scripted to have intimate relationships with whites – and often at a severe cost. In one 1908 Biograph picture, *The Kentuckian*, 'a rich young man goes West and marries an Indian woman. As he is struggling whether to return to the East for his inheritance, his Indian wife understands his dilemma and solves his problem by committing suicide' (Hilger 1986: 11). In the 1912 Bison picture *At Old Fort Dearborn*, Singing Bird loves a white soldier and is killed by her tribe while helping him to escape. In another 1912 Bison picture, *The Red Man's Honor*, Red Hawk, though innocent, is convicted and sentenced to be executed by an Indian chief for killing Seated Bear. Red Hawk 'shows his honor by returning at the time appointed for his death and his beloved June Dew dies with him' (Hilger 1986: 22). Indian nobility often means to choose death, a formula in which the question of Indians' agency in choosing their fate is paramount.

The first feature-length film which could be called a Western was an Indian subject made when the First World War began, and that happened to be the first film shot in Los Angeles. This film was also the first Cecil B. DeMille (co)directed, having directed the play on Broadway. In *The Squaw Man*, Englishman James Wynnegate flees the corruption of the aristocracy he was born into and settles in the American West, where he has an affair with an Indian woman, Nat-U-Ritch ('Not too Rich'?), daughter of the local Indian chief. One day he spies her knitting little moccasins. . . and runs to a pastor, who at first refuses to marry the interracial couple. After their child has grown to be a boy, Jim gets word from a messenger that his brother has died in the Alps and bequeathed to him the English family estate. Jim realizes he cannot take his wife to his nation of birth and so the messenger urges him to send his half-Indian son, saying, 'He is the future Earl of Kerhill. He is entitled to the education of a gentleman.' Nat-U-Ritch opposes sending their son away, and Jim forcibly separates her from the boy. Jim tells his son, who wears a small soldier's outfit, to take off his moccasins in preparation for his new life. In grief, Nat-U-Ritch seizes the moccasins, surreptitiously goes to the back of the house and shoots herself. Joanna Hearne astutely observes that a mixed-blood child in this film's scenario, as in some others, is no object of shame but rather a 'prized figure', a promise, in the white imagination, 'of racial rejuvenation rather than racial taint, and of licit white inheritance rather than land theft' (Hearne 2003: 183).[5] But concerns about the illicit nature of interracial sex, overall, trumped the need to legitimate white land theft in such plots. The dominant impulse was the dramatization – and implicit naturalization – of Indian vanishing, despite how often Indians reappeared on screen. Plots which contained surviving mixed-blood families were outnumbered by those which figured no model of either assimilation or what Gerald Vizenor has coined Indian 'survivance'. Most were films about the failure of an Indian future, a failure upon which Americans depended to imagine their own.

With few exceptions among silent films, the continual appearance of the Indian can be understood as a repeated visual performance of the Indian's ideologically perpetual vanishing. As in the repetition of the word at the end of Grey's novel, once again is never enough. In a repetition compulsion exemplifying what Renato Rosaldo (1989) has called 'imperialist nostalgia' – a culture's 'mourning' of that which it is responsible for having irrevocably altered or destroyed and against which it had defined its mission – what is more accurately described as a melancholic, punishing cultural impulse towards Indians seems to say, 'They have been vanishing since time immemorial and they must continue to vanish until time immemorial.' This impulse shares with the Christian Passion Play a ritualistic performance of inflicted suffering, repeated sorrow and perpetual idealization and identification. The melancholy figure of the Indian, seen in this film's title frame with an Indian sitting on a stationary horse (both of them slumped with nodding heads, a posture possibly derived from the figure of Jesus on the cross) serves as a place-holder for a kind of American melancholy, as distinct from mourning, psychoanalytically understood, which is a completeable process having a real object. 'They' are an indeterminate object, in this narcissistic sense of loss, which seems to have been at any point in history forever lost and which the melancholic needs repetitively to continue to lose.

Adapting (in) Zane Grey's West

As the most popular writer in America in the first half of the twentieth century, Zane Grey's Western novels were adapted into about seventy films. No writer, while living, has had his work so frequently brought to the screen. Closely involved with many of the silent productions of his novels (less so with the sound pictures), he insisted on fidelity to his plots and characterizations and asked for location filming. While Grey had included a number of Indian characters in his novels before *The Vanishing American*, it was the first to focus primarily on the Indian question. It was also the only one he began to write with the understanding that it would be made into a film. The writer chose the subject, but it was adapted to the setting which inspired the film producer Jesse L. Lasky to shoot a picture there. In 1918, for a staggering $25,000, Lasky bought the rights to one of Grey's novels after adaptations of two others appeared that year. (Lasky had already acquired the rights to the Broadway play *The Squaw Man*.) In 1918, Zane Grey decided to move west from Pennsylvania to be closer to Arizona, where he had travelled frequently for several years. A year later, at a time when there were no large film production companies, he started his own, Zane Grey Productions. After only a few pictures, he sold the company to Jesse Lasky, whose company eventually merged with Adoph Zukor's Paramount.

In 1922, Grey invited Lasky on a two-week trip into the Hopi-Navajo lands of northern Arizona and southern Utah where Lasky was so overwhelmed by the scenery that he asked Grey to write a novel he could film there. It seems rather telling that Grey's first novel devoted to an Indian subject originated in the cinematic possibility that a film producer espied in the Southwestern lands of the Navajo and Hopi, a landscape which would become a globally recognizable, historically deracinated, usually vacant icon of an authentic America.

Though the location was meant to serve realism, the setting and the film would lose authenticity – in their evocation of first cultures for the sake of fashioning Americanness – if the mise-en-scène did not include real Indians. Thousands of Indians lived in the region; at least one out of ten of them (3,500) were employed as extras in the filming.[6] Mainly Navajos, Hopis and Paiutes, they probably formed the greatest number of Indian extras involved in any silent film. 'Producing Indian Film Was a Stupendous Task', announced the *New York Times* on 20 September 1925 in its headline of an interview with Lasky, which included a subheading about 'Teaching Indians to Act'. 'Making the thousands of Indians who appear in

The Vanishing American understand what was wanted of them (99 out of every 100 of whom had never heard of motion pictures) was also a job', Lasky said – unwittingly describing the ideological work his film promoted.

In the 1920s, Americans were just becoming familiar with the ruins of ancient cliff cities in the Southwest (physical testaments of a truly vanished people, the Anasazi). In Grey's most popular novel, the 1912 *Riders of the Purple Sage*, his character Venters climbs a 'weathered' ascent toward 'the great cavern of the cliff-dwellers'. He finally sees what he is looking for:

> It was a stupendous tomb. It had been a city [. . .] The little houses were there [. . .] and stone pestles and mealing stones lay beside round holes polished by years of grinding maize – lay there as if they had been carelessly dropped yesterday. But the cliff-dwellers were gone! [. . .] Venters felt the sublimity of that marvelous vaulted arch.

> (Grey 2002: 104, 105)

He wonders about the cause of their demise: 'Had an enemy destroyed them? Had disease destroyed them, or only that greatest destroyer – time?' (Today's leading theory is drought.) Willa Cather describes a similar scene in her novel *The Professor's House*, which appeared the same year as the novel and film of *The Vanishing American*. Tom Outland sees an ancient city, and Cather describes his sense of its transcendence over time: 'Such silence and stillness and repose – immortal repose. That village sat looking down into the canyon with the calmness of eternity' (Cather 1986: 201). Personified, the cliff city seems 'almost alive', as Lucien Hubbard had described the scene of Monument Valley in the screen synopsis for *The Vanishing American*, as if to animate the dead for the living in a landscape that yet permits 'no sign of life' (MHL 1925: 3).

For the film production of *The Vanishing American*, an entire cliff city populated with Navajo and Hopi extras was built and filmed for just a few minutes of screen-time in the film's pre-twentieth-century prologue, before a 'younger, fiercer, harder people' attacks and conquers the cliff dwellers and destroys the set. They are led by the first of the hereditary leaders named Nophaie (all of them played by white actors). Intertitles tell the viewer that the doomed dwellers with a 'pre-destined end' were an 'indolent, harmless' and 'drowsing' people whose religious sense had been dulled by priests who preferred to 'amuse' rather than 'awe' them (a possible reference to Lasky's own high cultural ambitions). With its Native extras, filmed on Native lands, seen building and sustaining a community, performing religious rituals, battling enemies and (despite all that) living their 'indolent' life, the production sought an authenticity effect which might fill in its ahistorical crevasses. The shunting of history for the sake of an 'authentic' image of the past was briefly threatened by that very desire. At one point during production, Lasky reported, 'the mistake was made of mixing two tribes who, scores of years ago, had been at war and who still remember it. The realism they put into their battle scenes was so remarkable that a halt was called' (*New York Times*, 20 September 1925).

The incompatibility between the drive to authenticity and the fabrication of history is most glaring in a scene during the prologue which reveals the film's larger ideological aims in revising Grey's script. An intertitle tells us that the cliff dwellers, who are clearly played by actual Indians, are not, historically speaking, Indians after all. The people who destroy the cliff city and their people are 'the first of the race we now call Indians'. Two hundred years before the Spanish will arrive, the 'first' Indians, led by the first of the hereditary leaders (played by white actors) named Nophaie, destroy the most visually elaborate civilization in the film. One might conclude that the film is eliding the Navajo ('Nopah') with 'Indian', while erasing the Anasazi. This apparent ethnographic mistake is more likely a choice: the Navajo stand in for the arrival of 'Indians' not only because the Navajo had come to stand in for Indians in the 1920s, but also because the film requires a precedent for the destruction of a race and civilization – by Indians, no less – to which the Spanish and American invasions are just another chapter in the predestined course of things. Like the white actors who play incarnations of Nophaie from this point, this episode of Indians conquering another 'race' enables an identification between white Americans and pre-Columbian indigenous peoples in a continuous history grounded in a common landscape. As a result, the landscapes of the increasingly photographed Southwest become both more American and more ancient within a 'natural' history.

History does not so much repeat as rapidly recapitulate itself in this film, as it does on Frederick Jackson Turner's hypothetical frontier. Turner had argued that Americans became American by having to shed the skin of civilization and move along an advancing frontier line, where American social development was 'continually beginning over again' as settlers repeatedly regressed to conditions of the wilderness and rapidly recapitulated the stages of civilization (Turner 1994: 32). This process was argued to leave Americans self-reliantly individualist, egalitarian and strong of character for better and worse. As if he were already on the set of an Indian or Western picture, Turner's settler finds on the frontier

the line of most rapid and effective Americanization. The wilderness masters the colonist. It finds him a European in dress . . . and thought. . . . It strips off the garments of civilization and arrays him in the hunting shirt and the moccasin. It puts him in the log cabin of the Cherokee and Iroquois and runs an Indian palisade around him. Before long he has gone to planting Indian corn and plowing with a sharp stick; he shouts the war cry and takes the scalp in the orthodox Indian fashion.

(Turner 1994: 33)

In short, the Indian (as 'wilderness') teaches the American to act like an Indian in order to become an American. In *The Vanishing American*, the American heroine

Christianizes the Indian character played by a white man and teaches him to act like a noble Indian in order to become American.

Turner literarily achieved for historiography what Emerson had described in 'The Poet' and what the technology of cinema later allowed *The Vanishing American* to make visual in rapid time in one setting: the process of history. 'The poet turns the world to glass', Emerson wrote, 'and shows us all things in their right order and procession . . . he stands one step nearer to things and sees the flowing or metamorphosis' (Emerson 1968: 329). Influenced early by Emerson's writing, Turner asks the reader to stand in a then well-known natural gateway for migrants, Cumberland Gap, 'and watch the procession of civilization', as he enumerates the Indians, traders, pioneers and so forth who pass through at one historical moment, just as they do in the 'same' way a century later further west, with different historical actors. The Emersonian ambition that Turner demonstrates here (like Walt Whitman before him), to achieve a sense of temporal condensation which poses as transcendence, is one that cinema would satisfy.

Through its prologue, the film aims to represent 'the right series or procession' of historical stages. ('Stages' were a long-standing paradigm for understanding cultural and ethnic differences.) In Grey's novel, however, these evolutionary stages are not found in one geographic scene, but in the self. Whether externally in history or internally in the self, each figuration is an attempt to explain how Americans became American – which is also to say, no less tautologically, why first Americans are doomed and true Americans are doomed to civilization. Grey's West is where everyone can get in touch with and recuperate the primal self – including the white heroine Marian, in a manner unthinkable for the 1925 film adaptation – with racialized stages of evolution recapitulated in reverse. As he contemplates marrying Marian before a massive wall of 'impenetrable' stone which instils 'terror' in him, 'suddenly Nophaie found himself stripped bare of all ideals, chivalries, duties, of the false sophistries of his [Christian American] education, of the useless fetters of his unbelief. Human being, man, Indian, savage, primitive beast – so he retrograded in the scale' (Grey 1925: 201; ellipses added). He becomes a rapist whom Marian has provoked: '[S]he awakened to a terrifying consciousness that she had inflamed the savage in Nophaie. . . . His mastery was that of the primal man denied; his brutality went to the verge of serious injury to her. . . . [He] flattened her body as might have a savage.' In other words, Nophaie becomes an Indian: '"White woman – you'll make – an *Indian* of me," he panted, in husky, spent passion.' Marian's seductive charms are to blame for his regression and her 'pain': 'It pierced Marian. . . . She – who had loved the nobility in him – to drag him from the heights! To use her physical charm, her power in supreme selfishness!' (Grey 1925: 278–9; original emphasis). Yet the regression to primal urges is mutual and mutually beneficial: Nophaie liberates something in her.

The film is chaste in a way Grey is not. Adapting the internal evolutionary regression of Grey's romantic protagonists to the screen required splitting the sentimental melodrama off from the atavistic terror of the sublimely epic and primal history it forestages. Civilization is not achieved, as Frederick Jackson Turner and Zane Grey would have it, by recapitulating briefly to more savage states and dialectically overcoming them to achieve a new synthesis; it is achieved by cinematic stages of dress, customs and manners. By the time we reach the latest incarnation of 'Nophaie', Richard Dix has no savagery or primal urges in him. Where Grey describes a nearly sadomasochistic scene of Nophaie's sexual domination of Marian, which brings her to figurative orgasm (Kimball 1993: 75), the film's Nophaie rescues Marian from Booker's attempt to rape her (in her classroom!) and is always gentlemanly and even shy around her. He is 'whiter' (in the culture's moral-racial sense) than the white villain. For Grey, recapitulation to earlier stages of evolution is ennobling for Indian and White alike, as long as they get to do it together – and as long as the Indian, before he is about to vanish, reverses the trajectory and becomes better than he was before. After Nophaie dies of a flu-like plague in the novel, Withers reports to Marian, 'I must tell you the strangest thing. Many of these Nopahs who died of this plague turned black. . . . Nophaie talked of turning *white!*' (Grey 1925: 286; original ellipses and emphasis).

The Indian as American Redeemer of Christianity

At the end of the first version of Grey's novel, the Indian hero is left alive and discovering redemption through sexual love with a white woman *as opposed to* organized Christianity. Conversely, the film leaves Nophaie dead, but as redeemed spirit: he dies with a beatific expression as he grasps the Christian scriptural paradox that 'he who loseth his life for my sake shall find it.' Viewers of the film in 1925 might have been hard-pressed to answer where the redemption of the tragedy with which they are meant to sympathize came from: whether Nophaie, the landscape, the Bible, Marian, Indians generally, virtuous white women generally, the spectacle of cinema, the expanse of history. In its ideological density, 'America' might have subsumed any or all of these answers in the experience of watching the picture.

Absolved of the responsibility Grey assigns it in his novel, Christianity is redeemed in the film by a transubstantiation of the Indian body into pure American soul – a soul which makes race malleable for its purposes, and that in turn is transubstantiated into the visualized American ground from which Indians had to be removed in order for it to be made American. For this to be accomplished ideologically in American culture, the Indian had to stay both in and out of the picture: neither to be fully visible nor to completely disappear but to be in a perpetual state of vanishing. In Grey's novel, Nophaie has a life and a personal evolution before he meets Marian. But on the screen, he arrives fully formed with only two things to discover, Christianity and Marian's love, and fully prepared for two things he has to do, risk death in the war to prove his Americanness and then die on his native ground prematurely. In these respects, the film's story of Nophaie has more striking similarities to that of Jesus than to Grey's original story of Nophaie, who will vanish by assimilation. In the novel, he says to Marian, '"In the end I shall be absorbed by you – by your love – by your children. . . . It is well!"' (Grey 1982: 342).

If white Christian Americans would not sympathize with (a white woman's sexual relation to) an Indian body in Grey's original ending, they would surely, Grey assumed, sympathize with the Indian's soul. The film aims to ensure this sympathy by rendering Nophaie as an *imitatio Christi* in more ways than one. Killed by (one of) his own people while trying to bring peace between them and the governing state, he atones, as a true American soldier in the First World War, for the sins of Booker, who in the picture stands in for the Christian missionaries and corrupt federal bureaucrats criticized in Grey's novel.

The extent of Grey's criticism of various white Americans had concerned the writers of the film scenario. In 1923, M. C. Lathrop submitted a synopsis of Grey's original serialized story to the producers:

> The story is one of heart-rending distress, in which injustice, greed, and the baser passions are invariably triumphant and *remain unpunished*. There is conflict – but the weak and the just always give way to the strong and the unjust . . . and the miscreants who are the authors of this misery and death, are smugly hale, hearty, and prosperous. If it is the intention of the story to make the White Race appear, in general, as a poor thing in comparison to the 'Noble Red Man,' the author has certainly succeeded. It is difficult to see how . . . it could be made available for pictures without radical revision.
>
> (MHL 1925)

The film's opening quotation of Spencer about the 'ceaseless devouring of the weak by the strong' is the one concern of Lathrop's which not only is not revised in the film, but which is given its own intertitle, with the question of the justice of this perpetual devouring unaddressed. The suffering of the weaker and just is, of course, another important Christian trope which could be implicitly made to support Spencerian assumptions.

Nophaie serves this trope in the film, with the tutorial assistance of the virgin Marian, who persuades him to go to war by saying, 'Oh, I know – you have been unjustly treated. But Booker and his men did that – not the Government. This is still your country. You are an American as much as any of us.' Nophaie exclaims, 'American – *me!*' 'Yes, Nophaie!' she responds; 'And this is a war for freedom, for the right. For oppressed people everywhere. Out of it will grow a new order

. . . a new justice.' To be accepted as true Americans, to serve the spirit (by deferring the realization) of American idealism, Indians need to risk death. But they can only serve to do so by being already named within a nationalist imaginary and through a Christian typology which gives eternal solace over a sacrificial death by making it cosmically teleological. In a pronominal contradiction that illuminates the elusive meaning of the vanishing American as the tautological 'ground' of American ideation, Nophaie responds, 'Since we are Americans, we go fight. Maybe if we fight . . . maybe if we die . . . our country will deal fairly with our people.'

Atoning for America's sins, Nophaie dies as a Christ figure, made American and authentic in a manner that atones for Grey's sins against Christianity for having criticized missionaries. As Nophaie lies dying in the angled posture of the crucified Jesus, Marian takes the little New Testament from his pocket and opens it to a close-up of the passage he is finally to understand. Christian allusion is visually reinforced when a real Indian extra lifts up Nophaie's slumped body and holds him in a manner that, with Marian to the right, renders the scene as sculpture: unmistakably choreographed as Michelangelo's Florentine Pietà. The Indian holding his body is in the position of Joseph of Arimethea (in Michelangelo's sculpture), who had given Jesus his tomb to be buried in. (Real Indian actors kill and show pity to an Indian played by a white man who had tried to save them – a mirror-image of the rhetoric that justified the Christianizing and Americanizing of Indians as 'killing the Indian to save the man'.) As Marian reads the passage which had made no sense to him before, Nophaie speaks his last words: 'I . . . think . . . I understand.'

Rendering the Indian hero's body as a static icon of divine sacrifice, this sculptural scene also makes sense within the medium of silent film. 'Characters in silent films could be iconographic', Leo Braudy writes, 'because they were like moving statues, with a solidity and visual continuity that somehow raised them out of their individuality into some timeless image of human nature.' This predilection for the sculptural rendered actors as statues, which tended at one extreme to shade 'into idealized images and at the other into caricature. . . . The passionate narcissism of the actor drew the audience into hypnotic complicity' (Braudy 2002: 187, 188). Watching the end of *The Vanishing American* with Braudy's comments in mind, one cannot help feeling that this film's figure of the vanishing Indian reaches towards both extremes at the same time, to the extent that a caricatured image *is* an idealized one, if by ideal we mean an Indian hero played by a white man within a narrative underwritten by Christian archetype. In that case, the 'passionate narcissism of the actor' is that of the complicit audience and producers. While the Indian may be the 'Alpha of the alphabet of American history', as the epigraph which began this chapter states, he is so only if he is the Omega at the same time: a timeless and transcendent object known primarily through his death for the atonement of everyone's sins. Like cinema, whose images survive actors' deaths, that vanishing figure triumphs not over death, but over historicity.

Notes

1   I have estimated a numerical range of silent Indian films, within which the actual number probably falls. I have done so based on the confirmed low end of more than 200 identified in its possession by the Library of Congress as having 'substantial' Indian content (Lund [undated]; Aleiss 1995: 34); on Hilger's estimate (1986: 9) of at least 300 such films made between 1910 and 1913; and on Spehr's representative listing (1977). From those sources, I inferred my estimate with these additional facts in mind:

1. Many of these films are lost.
2. The silent period was more concerned with Indians than any decade in US cinema since then, in part because it was trying to compete in the new technology against Pathé with a distinctively American product (Abel 1999).
3. Hilger's expressly non-exhaustive list of Indian films (through 1984) numbers 830.

Given that the silent period represented at least 200 of those and given that, according to Hilger, at least 300 appeared between 1910 and 1913 (one-tenth of the silent era's duration), one can say with some confidence that at least 500 such films were made in the silent era, and probably more.

2   For an excellent study of the Anglo literary interest in the Southwest during this period, see Audrey Goodman's *Translating Southwestern Landscapes* (2002).

3   In response to demands from Harper & Brothers to change the ending, Grey briefly considered withdrawing the manuscript (Jackson 1989: 80). Because the film was produced when the novel was published and because Christian groups had complained about the depiction of Christian missionaries in the serialized version, Grey wrote to his publisher, 25 May 1925, 'As to the motion picture, I have eliminated entirely the missionary element. This I was forced to do by the influence brought to bear upon the Will Hays office, by missionary powers' (Grey 1982: vi).

4   The enfolding of melodrama into epic can also be understood as a negotiation between 'the desire to tell a story' and 'the desire to display', between narrative and spectacle. Richard Abel (1999: 152) argues that the genre of the silent Western offered an exemplary model of that negotiation. Of *The Vanishing American*, Virginia Wright Wexman writes that the 'sharp contrast' between the two spectacles of a sublimely open, native landscape and the forbidden cross-racial love between the protagonists in the melodrama suggests fissures in nationalist ideology between the egalitarian and the hierarchical: the Indian is barred from realizing the scene of domesticity (Bernardi 1996: 147–51). While this reading of the divide is certainly apt for many silent Westerns as it is for this film, I argue that this divide in *The Vanishing American* functions more complexly: while the film is ostensibly about resistance against a corrupt official, that melodramatic resistance cannot resist what the landscape, the Indian hero and the domestic white woman are made collectively to embody: a Christian transcendence within a Spencerian model of evolution for the sake of a 'true' American identity. It is, in other words, less ambivalent (in choosing between equality and domination) than its sympathetic rendering might suggest.

5 Buttressing Hearne's interpretation indirectly is an argument (Abel 1999) that Hearne's reading of an earlier film in turn supports. American silent cinema was in competition with (the French) film-production company Pathé Frères for an audience; American cinema argued that French Westerns (with their actors, costumes and settings) were inauthentic. In response to that criticism, Pathé made a more-authentic-than-thou picture in 1910, *White Fawn's Devotion*, which is otherwise quite unusual among silent Indian films but whose plot is almost identical, as Hearne points out, to (the later) *The Squaw Man*. Unlike the latter film with which it shares the scenario of an Indian wife who is desperate when she realizes her child will be taken from her to receive an English inheritance, the French picture ends happily, despite the Indian wife's attempted suicide: her white husband decides to stay for the sake of their child and their family. This film was directed by the Native American (Winnebago) actor and director James Young Deer, who at one time managed Pathé's west-coast studio (Hearne 2003: 191–2).

6 One contemporary source states (without citation) 3,500; the *New York Times* wrote that 'thousands of Indians are said to have been employed'; in that same article, Jesse Lasky is quoted as saying, '10,000 Indians can consume a lot of groceries' (*New York Times*, 20 September 1925).

References

Abel, Richard (1999) *The Red Rooster Scare: Making Cinema American, 1900–1910*, Berkeley, Calif.: University of California Press.

Aleiss, Angela (1991) '*The Vanishing American*: Hollywood's Compromise to Indian Reform', *Journal of American Studies*, 25 (3): 467–72.

—— (1995) 'Native Americans: The Surprising Silents', *Cineaste*, 21(3): 34–5.

Bernardi, Daniel (ed.) (1996) *The Birth of Whiteness: Race and the Emergence of U.S. Cinema*, New Brunswick, NJ: Rutgers University.

Braudy, Leo (2002) *The World in a Frame: What We See in Films*, Twenty-Fifth Anniversary edition, Chicago, Ill.: University of Chicago Press.

Cather, Willa (1986) *The Professor's House*, London: Virago.

Collier, J. (1923) 'The Pueblo's Last Stand', *Sunset*. February, pp. 19–22.

Deloria, Philip J. (1998) *Playing Indian*, New Haven, Conn.: Yale University Press.

Dippie, Brian (1982) *The Vanishing American: White Attitudes and U.S. Indian Policy*, Middletown, Conn.: Wesleyan University Press.

Emerson, Ralph Waldo (1968) *The Selected Writings of Ralph Waldo Emerson*, ed. by Brooks Atkinson, New York: The Modern Library.

Goodman, Audrey (2002) *Translating Southwestern Landscapes: The Making of an Anglo Literary Region (1880–1930)*, Tucson, Ariz.: University of Arizona Press.

Grey, Zane (1925) *The Vanishing American*, New York: Grosset & Dunlap.

—— (1982) *The Vanishing American*, foreword by Loren Grey, New York: Pocket Books.

Grey, Zane (2002) *Riders of the Purple Sage*, introd. and notes by William R. Handley, New York: Random House.

Hearne, Joanna (2003) '"The Cross-Heart People": Race and Inheritance in the Silent Western', *Journal of Popular Film and Television*, 30 (4): 181–96.

Hilger, Michael (1986) *The American Indian in Film*, Metuchen, NJ: Scarecrow.

Jackson, Carlton (1989) *Zane Grey: A Biography*, Boston, Mass.: Twayne.

Kant, Candace C. (1984) *Zane Grey's Arizona*, foreword by Loren Grey, Flagstaff, Ariz.: Northland.

Kimball, Arthur G. (1993) *Ace of Hearts: The Westerns of Zane Grey*, Fort Worth, Tex.: Texas Christian University Press.

Lund, Karen C. (compiler) (undated) 'American Indians in Silent Film', The Library of Congress. HTTP: www.loc.gov//rr/mopic/findaid/indian1.html (accessed 31 July 2005).

MHL (Margaret Herrick Library of the Academy of American Motion Picture Arts and Sciences) (1925) *The Vanishing American*, production file.

Michaels, Walter Benn (1995) *Our America: Nativism, Modernism, and Pluralism*, Durham, NC: Duke University.

Mitchell, Lee Clark (1981) *Witnesses to a Vanishing America: The Nineteenth-Century Response*, Princeton, NJ: Princeton University.

Rosaldo, Renato (1989) *Culture and Truth: The Remaking of Social Analysis*, Boston, Mass.: Beacon.

Slotkin, Richard (1992) *Gunfighter Nation: The Myth of the Frontier in Twentieth-Century America*, New York: Atheneum.

Spehr, Paul C. (1977) *The Movies Begin: Making Movies in New Jersey, 1887–1920*, Newark, NJ: Newark Museum.

Turner, Frederick Jackson (1994) *Rereading Frederick Jackson Turner*, commentary by John Mack Farragher, New York: Henry Holt.

Vizenor, Gerald (2004) 'Edward Curtis: Pictorialist and Ethnographic Adventurist', in William R. Handley and Nathaniel Lewis (eds), *True West: Authenticity and the American West*, Lincoln, Nebr.: University of Nebraska Press, pp. 179–93.

Wilson, James (1998) *The Earth Shall Weep: A History of Native America*, New York: Grove.

Chapter 3

American Madness (1932)

Eric Smoodin

At least since the 1930s, film studies as practised in the USA typically has considered national cinema in fixed terms, with an untroubled understanding of what 'American' cinema might mean. We can get a sense of this from the titles of some of the founding texts of film studies from that era: Lewis Jacobs' *The Rise of the American Film* (1939) for example, or Margaret Farrand Thorp's *America at the Movies* (1939). When Robert Gessner began teaching his film-appreciation class at New York University in the late 1930s, he included such categories on his syllabus as 'The Early American Spectacle', 'Legend and Fantasy in Germany', and 'Contemporary Soviet Naturalism' (Smoodin 2004: 4, 6–7). Thirty years later, Andrew Sarris called his study of directors (including Jean Renoir, Fritz Lang, F. W. Murnau and other Europeans) *The American Cinema* (1968).

'America' or 'American' are used in these texts as adjectives that unproblem-atically identify the nation and imply the uniqueness of that nation's cinema and its difference from the cinemas of other countries. In part because of the publishing categories established for film studies at least three-quarters of a century ago and also because of the way film studies is taught in universities in the USA – usually with an emphasis on author and genre as well as nation – the sense of the national that we see in Jacobs, Sarris and others continues today. Some scholars, however, have begun to question this idea of the nation. Thomas Saunders' *Hollywood in Berlin*, on the significance of American cinema in Weimar Germany, clearly indicates this rethinking and the possibility of addressing a national cinema which is at least equal parts two countries (1994). Ruth Vasey has begun the project of historicizing and theorizing the international effects of censorship on American national cinema in *The World According to Hollywood, 1918–1939* (1997). The fullest attempts to deconstruct prevailing notions of the national have been produced in a series of essays and books by Andrew Higson, who has sought to 'revisit the idea that the modern nation, in Benedict Anderson's terms, is an imagined community', and who has reconsidered 'the traditional idea of the "national" as a self-contained and carefully demarcated experience' (Higson 2000: 63–64; 1995, 1999).

Higson, Saunders, Vasey and others have shown us that while 'the nation' comes to be thought of as a stable object, it is anything but. Further, the difference between national and international is, like most terms thought to be in binary opposition to each other, actually quite unstable; or, to put it another way, only as stable as the belief in the complete differences between them. We may tend to think that the cinema itself takes part in the practice of nation-building, through systems of representation, distribution and exhibition, for instance. But film scholarship might also take part in such a project. Certainly, the studies cited above try to produce a notion of 'America' through a consideration of its cinema, as do other works which do not necessarily stress the nation in their titles. Garth Jowett's *Film: The Democratic Art* (1976) for example, argues for something specifically American in the development of the cinema in the USA and for a unique relationship between that cinema and its American audiences. Much of the writing about cinema, then, takes part in reasserting and rebuilding that 'self-contained' idea of the nation that Higson talks about, and in smoothing over the tensions between one national cinema and another, or between the national and the international.

A purposely polemical point about the American film audience, rather than American films, extends the work of Saunders, Vasey and Higson. I would suggest that, at least during the 1920s and 1930s, 'average' American audiences understood that American cinema, and American film culture broadly, was international in scope. Viewers ranging from those who saw movies at the Museum of Modern Art in New York to the US equivalents of Kracauer's 'little shop girls' went to foreign films as well as Hollywood movies, appreciated the European (and even, occasionally, Asian) influences in those Hollywood films and understood the back-and-forth movement of stars, directors, writers and others from the USA to various countries.[1] I would further suggest that, given the period's sense of an internationalist national cinema, a film such as Frank Capra's *American Madness*, from 1932, with its implication of a specifically national hysteria embedded in the title, came to be understood as an especially significant and precise representation of purely domestic events.

It is through a reading of film culture from the period that I can make these claims, rather than through an interpretation of a film or group of films. Thus, I am proposing that we develop an understanding of national cinema based not so much at the point of production – through textual analyses of the movies that Hollywood turned out – but at the point of reception, the ways in which audiences at the time of production understood the movies they saw. And to come to such an understanding, we need to interpret a range of primary materials. I would, of course, include the movies themselves, but also fan magazines, newspapers, advertisements and publicity materials. These constitute the film culture which I mentioned above, the numerous ways in which fans interacted with and gained information about movies, stars, current gossip, product endorsements, critical judgements and much more relating to cinema. This formation of national cinema produced both a widespread understanding of its international scope and also a focused sense of how some films might generate hyper-nationalist readings.

The period from 1932 to 1933 serves as an interesting case study. Of course, we have Capra's film, which premiered in August 1932. But we also have the significant American debut of the German film *Mädchen in Uniform*, which serves as a test case of the era's fluidity between national cinemas. Leontine Sagan's movie, and its star Dorothea Wieck generated discourses of the international aspects of American film culture and seem to point clearly to a broad understanding, among a number of audiences, of the significant European, or at least German, influences on that culture.

American Madness and the National Audience

Before examining this notion of an international national cinema, we can ask, first, what we make of a film which audiences seemed to understand precisely as a national document, one which primarily addressed problems and events in the USA? This was indeed the case with Capra's *American Madness*. The film tells the story of a run on a bank and the attempts – eventually successful – of the bank's president to overcome a hostile board of directors and maintain his control of the institution and also to calm his panicky depositors. Walter Huston, as the bank president, believes in banks that help average people rather than giant corporations, and so his triumph, in the end, is for a small scale, 'mom and pop' capitalism.[2] Most of the writing about the film acknowledges the link between the narrative and actual events, the bank runs which were a feature of the early 1930s and which led Franklin Roosevelt, in one of his first acts as President in 1933, to declare a 'bank holiday', suspending business in order to prevent mass withdrawals of funds. But scholars have paid particular attention to *American Madness* because it seems to be the first Capra film in the sense that we understand the director's movies today. It marks Capra's first collaboration with screenwriter Robert Riskin, who would work with him on *It Happened One Night*, *Mr. Deeds Goes to Town*, *Meet John Doe*, and many other films, and it also serves as the template for such films as *Deeds*, *Doe*, *Mr. Smith Goes to Washington* and, especially, *It's a Wonderful Life*: the exemplary common man winning out against corporate and governmental cut-throats. The film is also something of a virtuoso directorial effort, with its rapid dialogue, impressive depth of focus and assured montage scenes, and so it stands out as one of the signs that Capra, who had been making films only since 1926, had fully finished his apprenticeship.

So most of the analyses of *American Madness* are concerned with the film's textual systems, either in auteurist terms, as possibly the first of many similar films that Capra would make, or as a way to understand one possible response to the excesses of Depression-era capitalism. It is this sense of the film's connection to certain political and cultural realities that we might take for granted. Especially from the early 1930s, we are used to stories of Warner Bros., for example, under the guidance of Daryl F. Zanuck, finding subject matter in newspaper headlines (*Public Enemy*, *I Am a Fugitive from a Chain Gang*, etc.). We are also familiar with foundational texts in film studies which assert the links between American films and American politics, for instance the *Cahiers du Cinéma* collective editorial from 1970 about *Young Mr. Lincoln*. In other words, it has become a cliché of film studies to assume a link between the typical Hollywood product, on the one hand, and a US-based socio-political context on the other. And this has seemed particularly true of films from the early 1930s, from an overdetermined era of national crisis, the Depression.

This may not have been so readily apparent during the period, however, given the evidence of an understanding of the international scope of American cinema. In fact, I would suggest that when an early 1930s Hollywood film came to be viewed as having a specific link to domestic events, it would stand out as a very special film indeed, rather than just another product from a studio's assembly line. Studied from the point of its reception, a film such as *American Madness* becomes extraordinary rather than routine.

We can chart at least three stages in the film's reception and entrance into film culture, stages that indicate the relation of *American Madness* to the period's discussions of the national but that also do not always fully remove the film from the internationalism of Hollywood production in the 1930s. In chronological order, first would come the regulatory practices which helped to craft the film. Commenting on its script, and then just after completion of filming, industry and also state censors debated the meaning of the film and the best ways of presenting it to the public. Next, Capra's studio Columbia Pictures attempted to shape the reception of *American Madness* through advertising campaigns. Third, audiences went to the film and responded to it, and while these responses might be hard to come by, they have not completely disappeared.

In an important essay on historiographic practice from 1975, 'Notes on Columbia Pictures Corporation, 1926–1941', Edward Buscombe produced the best analysis of Capra's film (see Buscombe 1998). Here Buscombe formulated a critique of textual analysis as a primary method of determining the 'meaning' of a film, and instead called for a more thorough examination of primary materials and, especially, industrial records. He used these records to investigate the possibility that *American Madness* expressed a broad policy during the Depression of producing films which might be called populist on the part of Columbia. Buscombe went on further to examine whether the banker played by Walter Huston in Capra's film was modelled after Columbia board member and Bank of America executive A. H. Giannini, one of the assumptions usually made about the movie. Buscombe concluded that while Giannini may well have served as inspiration, it is doubtful that Columbia had formulated 'any deliberate policy of favouritism to the New Deal or left causes' (Buscombe, 1998: 274).

Buscombe makes this assessment precisely by using extra-filmic categories, not so much the ones that I examine here, but rather through an analysis of industrial practice during the classical era. In trying to understand the links between American cinema and American political ideologies – New Deal liberalism, for instance – Buscombe explains that film studies in the US and the UK has tended to deal with films as found objects. The movie, accordingly, is that which 'mysteriously appears and having appeared is simply there, fixed and given.' In such a practice, the film industry, 'with its own history, specific practices, economic relationships, and technological and other material constraints', simply disappears (Buscombe 1998: 260). We are left, then, with a sense of a direct relationship between the American film and American society, with the films themselves mirroring dominant beliefs, while also embodying the more particular and cautious will of the corporations that made them. With *American Madness*, then, Capra and his screenwriter are seen as channelling, on the one hand, broad public discontent with American capitalism and, on the other, the attempt of the movie studio to restore some faith in existing American systems and in President Roosevelt's modifications of them. Thus we have the notion, in so many histories of American cinema, of the general conservatism of movies of the 1930s and of the films themselves telling us everything we need to know about American beliefs and opinions. Lawrence Levine, for instance, argued in 1993 that a film such as King Vidor's *Our Daily Bread*, from 1934, demonstrated a general 'enthusiasm for authoritarianism' on the part of the American public and a willingness on the part of American corporations to endorse solutions to the Depression which could be deemed fascist (Levine 1993: 238–9). Here, then, the cinema simply depicts the ideology of the masses and that of the culture industry, with these positions at times dovetailing and at times in opposition to each other.

But if we follow Buscombe and examine materials which have until fairly recently been ignored by most historians, we find much more in the way of mediation and contradiction. Exhibition reports, censorship materials and publicity, for instance, demonstrate a far more vexed relationship between the screen and the viewer. The significant efforts of the industry to link Capra's film to recent American history may indicate that *American Madness* did not simply 'speak' the will and belief of the public. And the film's audiences, whatever their ideological beliefs, may have rejected both the image of America that they saw in the film and the very form of American cinema – centred purely on the domestic – that the film represented.

Issues of publicity and reception, the second and third categories mentioned above, relate directly to the film's links to the national and seem to support Buscombe's claim that Columbia mostly considered the film's connection to the routine practices of American democracy rather than to any 1930s-style leftist politics. The censorship apparatus connected to *American Madness*, however, which I will consider later, shows the film's relation to the international, not so much textually, but in terms of an extra-filmic discourse of the benefits of the film.

Publicizing the National

Columbia's publicity for *American Madness* clearly stressed the domestic implications of Capra's film. Underscoring the references to the national in the very title of the film, trade ads called Capra's movie 'the great American picture of today', thereby emphasizing none of the international aspects of Hollywood film culture, but instead its absolute, homegrown specificity (*Motion Picture Herald*, 23 July 1932, p. 44). A publicity still which ran in the trade journal *Motion Picture Herald* saw the Americanness of the film in its depiction of the country's history and even more specifically in a mythological moment between economic euphoria and collapse (6 August 1932, p. 18). The film directly referred to a banking crisis which would only worsen into 1933, but the photo of Walter Huston in front of the mob of depositors is captioned, 'mad with prosperity before they became calm in adversity – such is the story that Columbia has wrought around those events of 1929, in *American Madness*.'[3] Thus the film represented recent American historical events – the disastrous decline of the banking industry – and also stood metaphorically for the Depression in general and for the strength of an American national character which would start to make sense of catastrophe.

Columbia also stressed a sort of metaphorical slippage between the subject matter of several of its films, including Capra's, and basic American democratic practices. In a 1932 issue of the *Motion Picture Herald*, Columbia's ad for *American Madness*, another political film called *Washington Merry Go Round* and other of the studio's releases for the season, proclaims 'The Winner!' The advertisement continues, 'Everybody votes for Columbia.' Here the studio evoked the discourse of a national election to promote its films and even came up with a campaign slogan worthy of a presidential candidate: 'Prosper with Columbia.' The advertisement's illustration shows a mob of men stuffing ballots into a box, with the conclusion of the advertising copy moving from the electoral to the martial, urging exhibitors to 'Fall in line!' and 'March to victory with Columbia' (23 July 1932, P. 43). *American Madness*, then, as well as other Columbia films themselves formed part of a national campaign to put the studio's films into movie theatres, and to produce a victory for the studio not unlike that of a candidate for national office.

Theatre owners and managers picked up on these advertising ideas and shifted them to their own needs. When the Polk Theatre in Lakeland Florida ran Capra's film for two days in December 1932, the theatre manager devised a tie-in with two local banks, and in its advertisement for the event emphasized the link between the film and the nation. Over the title of the film, the ad exhorted, 'we urge you to see this great American drama!' (*Motion Picture Herald*, 3 December 1932, p. 49) .

This understanding of Capra's film as 'American' depended, of course, on the subject matter. But it also had to do with the geography of film exhibition. One *Motion Picture Herald* advertisement for the film proclaimed that 'It will sweep the nation', and, alluding to the film's significance, called it 'the first great story of today' and 'greater than a motion picture'. Thus the *Motion Picture Herald* advertisement was well in keeping with other trade publicity, which stressed the film's timeliness for an entire nation. But this advertisement added that the film would soon be playing in 'every R.K.O. ace house from Maine to California' (30 July 1932, p. 47). We get a sense here of the interesting contractual arrangements between studios. Columbia, with relatively few important theatres, made deals to play its films in the first-run venues held by the other studios (many of Capra's films would open, in New York, in RKO.'s most famous theatre, the Radio City Music Hall). But there was also a slippage between a film that somehow represented a nation and a film noted for playing across the entire nation. The film's significance to America could be marked by its narrative and also by the seeming demand for the film from New England to the Pacific Ocean.

Responding to *American Madness*

At least some record exists of the responses to Capra's film by the audiences in these theatres across the country. Every week, the *Motion Picture Herald*, the trade journal aimed quite specifically at exhibitors, printed a column called 'What the Picture Did for Me'. As I have written elsewhere, in this column local exhibitors, often in small cities and towns and almost always representing subsequent, rather than first-run, theatres, sent in their opinions about the movies they had shown as a means of advising other exhibitors about films they might book and the best way to advertise them. The exhibitors who wrote in almost always included some indication of how a film performed at the box office and how their clientele responded to it. These descriptions might run about 100 words or so (Smoodin 2004: 110, 120–1).

One exhibitor wrote that the film 'is very timely in this era of bank failures', and others observed the obvious connection of the narrative of the film to national events (4 March 1933, p. 59). But exhibitors also wrote about this timeliness in relation to the exhibition context itself, noting that they had shown the film 'during the bank holiday period, and a rather appropriate subject' or had 'played this right in the midst of the bank holiday' (1 April 1933, p. 34; 15 April 1933, p. 45). In other words, they had shown *American Madness* during that period in March 1933 when President Roosevelt had closed the country's banks. During the early 1930s, exhibitors contributing to the column might occasionally mention cultural, political or social events, but I have found no other examples of a film's screening linked to a current event as specific as the bank holiday. For at least some exhibitors, then, the local showings of Capra's film about a bank crisis – Nashwauk, Minnesota and Mount Vernon, Kentucky, in the cases noted above – were closely connected to a national narrative about saving the country's financial institutions.

I have been unable to find box-office figures for *American Madness*. But the responses from many of the subsequent-run theatres reporting in to the *Motion Picture Herald* would indicate that, at least in smaller cities and towns, the film did not do well. From Harrisburg, Illinois, an exhibitor wrote that the film was 'one swell piece of entertainment . . . and it pleased all who saw it, but sorry to report that it failed to draw and did the smallest Wednesday and Thursday business in the past two months'. The mystified exhibitor then added, 'Cannot understand why' (10 December 1932, p. 59). Others echoed these sentiments, lamenting that the showings over two days, a standard small-town run in the 1930s, just failed to meet expectations, in spite of the quality of the film. From Cotter, Arkansas, for instance, an exhibitor wrote that 'here is one of the finest pictures I have ever shown, but barely made expenses'. He concluded that, sometimes, quality was more important than box-office receipts, writing that 'you may not make any money on this one, but you will have one of the best shows of the year' (6 May 1933, p. 41).[4] On the other hand, in some locations, *American Madness* appealed to audiences. An exhibitor in Exeter, New Hampshire claimed that the film 'will hold up two days anywhere', while in Selma, Louisiana, it 'drew well and gave satisfaction' (10 December 1932, p. 59).

How can we account for such a mixed reception? Certainly, these small-town audiences were the people celebrated in so many Capra films and they were the viewers for whom Capra himself, in his autobiography, claimed to be making movies (Capra 1971: 136). And they were the audiences who, in the Capra mythology (although not in actual fact) made a hit just two years later out of *It Happened One Night*.[5] In some places, the national events to which the film made reference seem to have kept people away. The Nashwauk, Minnesota exhibitor who played the film during the bank holiday did only 'average business', while the theatre manager in Mount Vernon, Kentucky, who also ran the film during the holiday, said about this timing, 'so you can realize what the receipts were' (1 April 1933, p. 34; 15 April 1933, p. 45). Thus, a film that called attention to a national banking crisis seems, at least in those small towns showing the film in March 1933, to have fallen victim at the box office to the crisis itself, one that made it much more difficult for anyone to spend money on such non-essential items as motion pictures.

For at least one exhibitor, the national trauma invoked by the film militated against the movie's success with audiences. From Lexingon, Nebraska, the exhibitor seemed to be scratching his head as he wrote that Capra's film 'drew less than normal and can't understand it'. He continued that the 'picture is everything the critics have lauded it with', and he went on to say that Walter Huston was 'great' in the film, that it had a 'different and new idea', and that the 'mob scenes are truly great'. He commented, as well, on the local rather than the national aspects of the movie. At a time when one of the perceived divides in the audience, at least among exhibitors, was that between an urban, cosmopolitan film viewer and a more rural, less worldly one, this exhibitor insisted that *American Madness* 'especially should be a small town type story'. He concluded by questioning any audience's readiness to be confronted by the country's crisis. 'Maybe', he wrote, 'folks don't like to be reminded of "madness" in the title' (4 February 1933, p. 51).

It is also possible that some audiences rejected not the 'madness' of the title, but rather the 'American' that modified it. In a return to the beginning of this essay, I would suggest that even those small-town viewers in Exeter, Selma and elsewhere understood and appreciated the international aspects of their cinema over and above the apparent overdetermined Americanness of a film such as Capra's. They experienced film culture as a broad mix of practices and influences, and so, on occasion, may have been disappointed in films that so clearly referenced domestic events.

The National and the International

A quick example from a different national cinema helps to explain what I mean by an international film culture and also the kinds of primary materials which help us determine this. Most film scholars understand that French audiences, or at least Parisian ones, from about the same period – the 1920s and 1930s – participated in, appreciated and perhaps also objected to an international film culture. We know from the various film quota and tariff laws passed by the French that government officials understood, principally, the American impact on domestic film culture. But there is also ample evidence that 'typical' audiences of film enthusiasts, and particularly in major urban areas, experienced French cinema as fully international in scope.

For example, the front page of the 9 March 1928 edition of the weekly fan magazine *Ciné-Miroir* presents a large photo of George O'Brien and Janet Gaynor in F. W. Murnau's *Sunrise*, which was just opening in Paris, with that film alone, coming from a Hollywood studio and made by an émigré director, demonstrating the American-German aspect of cinema in France. The caption for the photo made it clear that the film was 'presented' ('edité') by 'la Société Fox-Film', the French subsidiary of the American studio. And above the photo, the magazine promised a story on 'the private life of Charlie Chaplin' ('la vie intime de Charlie Chaplin'). So, if headlines are to be believed, the French, like so many movie audiences of the time, were interested in gossip about a great American star. Inside the magazine, along with stories about Chaplin and *Sunrise*, there were features on French stars (Édith Jehanne and Charles Vanel), on American films (one of which starred Charlie's brother Sydney Chaplin) and on French films, in this case one called *Paris-New York-Paris*, which themselves signified the internationalism of a national cinema (9 March 1928, pp. 163–4, 166, 168–9, 170, 173).

Other materials from the same period give us the same proof that French film audiences fully understood that their national cinema was, at the very least, a Franco-American one. *Mon Film* was a fan magazine produced by an American studio, Paramount, for French film fans, and it routinely acquainted those fans with films that Paramount produced in French at the Joinville studio outside Paris. Those films might feature only French stars (*Le Secret du docteur*, with Marcelle Chantal and Jean Bradin), or a combination of international celebrities (*L'Enigmatique Monsieur Parks*, with two Hollywood stars fluent in French, Adolphe Menjou and Claudette Colbert, and also Emile Chautara and Adrienne d'Ambricourt, under the direction of a French film-maker, Louis Gasnier). Maurice Chevalier figured prominently in *Mon Film* gossip, with the great French celebrity described as the star attraction in 'the marvelous French production program instituted by Paramount', the American studio. Chevalier himself was named in a *Mon Film* fan poll as the 'king' of stars in France, with this international performer outranking such actors in French films as Jean Dehelly and Albert Préjean (*Mon Film*, Vacances 1930: pp. 8–9).

Another French fan magazine from the period, *Pour Vous*, provided a directory of all the films playing during the week in Paris – in this case, 13–19 October 1933. The two films appearing at the most theatres were from Hollywood: *The Man I Killed* and *I am a Fugitive from a Chain Gang*. But the film enthusiasts who read this issue of *Pour Vous*, which featured a photo of Jean Harlow in Frank Capra's *Platinum Blonde* on its cover, could also make plans to see such German productions as Fritz Lang's *The Testament of Dr Mabuse* and Max Ophuls' *Liebelei*, *Cavalcade* and *The Private Life of Henry VIII*, both from the UK, and American-German productions such as *The Blue Angel*, along with any number of French films (*Pour Vous*, 12 October 1933, p. 15).

In other words, examined at the point of reception, in terms of what fans were reading about movies, their favourites among stars and their options for seeing films, French cinema was indeed an international one. But this is usually seen as a

European phenomenon rather than an American one. That is, European audiences were deemed cosmopolitan enough to demand films from France, Germany, Italy and elsewhere and sufficiently colonized to have their viewing dominated by Hollywood films. Conversely, US historians typically believe that American national cinema was fully American, with an often-repeated anecdote from the Second World War apparently exemplifying the average American fan's view of any film not made in Hollywood. As the story goes, when American troops arrested Leni Riefensthal in Austria in 1945, she complained that she deserved better, because she was a famous film-maker. The GI in charge of the arrest ended the argument quickly. 'Baby', he told her, 'I've been going to the movies a long time and I never heard of you.'[6]

Hollywood and International Film Culture

There may well have been a number of long-time moviegoers in the USA, however, who did know about Riefensthal, or, at least, about important German films and film-makers. As early as 1921, the *Literary Digest*, a highbrow, weekly magazine of 'literature, drama, music, fine-arts, education, [and] culture', claimed the need for protective measures and warned readers against the 'menace of German films'. Citing a piece from the *New York Herald Tribune*, the article noted that 'there are at times 300 German pictures on the American market', which might lead to the 'displacement' of American films and a consequent loss to American prestige. The *Literary Digest* mentioned that Congress was considering taking measures to protect the American film industry (14 May 1921, p. 28). Ten years later, in 1931, the *Nation*, then as now the liberal, intellectual magazine of record, noted a new 'German invasion' endangering, if not the country, then at least New York. Recently, 'one German talkie after another [has] found its way into the smaller movie houses of New York', the magazine reported, 'and today, if we glance at the list of films current in this city, the number of German films . . . is likely to give us quite a surprise.' The invasion was of such significance that, 'out of the twenty-one first run films shown in New York, fifteen are American films and six are German'. The *Nation* nevertheless questioned the fan support of these imports, guessing that the 'entire daily audience' for the theatres showing German movies probably did 'not reach a quarter of the number visiting the Roxy [theatre] alone' (13 May 1931, p. 538).

In 1932, the *Nation* seemed more grateful for the German films playing in the city (12 October 1932, p. 338). *Mädchen in Uniform* had opened there, and the magazine's reviewer, Alexander Bakshy, exclaimed that 'when a moving picture breaks away from the time-worn clichés of Hollywood, our hearts leap with joy and we feel like acclaiming the courageous piece of work as a masterpiece of art'. (In the same review, Bakshy also wrote about the French comedy *Le Bal*, a French fantasy about Bali called *Goona Goona* and a Paramount film, *The Night of June 13th*.) Other New York-based magazines took note of Leontine Sagan's film about a girl's boarding school. *The Commonweal*, a liberal, Catholic weekly, after distressing over Cecil B. DeMille's most recent epic, *The Sign of the Cross*, enthusiastically endorsed *Mädchen in Uniform* (21 December 1932, p. 216). The *Literary Digest*, gathering received wisdom about the film, cited the positive review in the *New York Herald Tribune*, and also quoted at length from documentary film-maker Pare Lorentz's analysis in *Vanity Fair*, in which Lorentz likened the movie to 'most post-war European literature', and especially to other 'German writings'. Moving from explication to economics, the *Literary Digest* then noted that the movie was 'breaking all box-office records at the Criterion Theater', and that a play called *Girls in Uniform* had just been announced (26 November 1932, p. 13).

Of course, we might read these reviews as indicative of a narrow, highbrow, New York-based reception of the film. *Mädchen in Uniform* certainly has come down to us as an art film, one which we might guess was more suited to museum screenings than to popular theatres. The film also faced significant censorship problems before it ever played in New York, and so it is also difficult to know precisely which version of the film these critics saw and also which versions played in other parts of the country. In other words, it is conceivable that some of the work attempted by the New York Board of Censors, whether successfully or not, was to make the film somehow more 'American' and less 'European'. In particular, according to the *New York Times*, the New York Board of Censors concerned itself with scenes of the young student Manuela's infatuation with her teacher, Fraulein von Bernberg, although clearly enough of her fixation remained to be fully commented on by reviewers, and critics such as Bakshy and Lorentz certainly appreciated what they saw as the Germanic, anti-Hollywood sensibility of the film (29 October 1933, p. X4).[7] And, indeed, a variety of primary materials exist that suggest the possibility that the film, so celebrated by critics, also had a much wider audience in the USA, or was at least well known among 'average' film viewers, and that its star, Dorothea Wieck, had become something of a sensation, especially among female fans.

Trade journals from the period, for example, give an indication that *Mädchen in Uniform* had achieved an extremely popular audience. The *Motion Picture Herald*, the journal for exhibitors in smaller cities and towns, serves as a case in point. The exhibitors who read the *Motion Picture Herald* were looking for tips on what films to show, how to advertise them and what kinds of audiences to expect. In the 29 July 1933 issue of the *Motion Picture Herald*, an article ran detailing the 'Box Office Champions: First Half of 1933' (29 July 1933, pp. 14–15). The list included films that we would expect: *Forty-Second Street*, for instance, and also two other films with Busby Berkeley musical numbers, *Gold Diggers of 1933* and *The Kid From Spain*; *King Kong* as well as the DeMille film maligned in *Commonweal*, *The Sign of the Cross*; and such star vehicles as the Norma Shearer–Clark Gable adaptation of Eugene O'Neill's *Strange Interlude* and the Will Rogers–Janet Gaynor small-town family romance, *State Fair*. This seems like fairly typical Hollywood stuff. But one of the fifteen films mentioned in the list might be somewhat more surprising as a 'box-office champion': *Mädchen in Uniform*.

Apparently because of this success, Paramount signed the star of the film Dorothea Wieck to a contract and ran a vigorous ad campaign for her based largely on the public's knowledge of *Mädchen in Uniform*. For two weeks, the movie studio placed an advertisement on the back cover of the *Herald* announcing Wieck's soon-to-be-released American film debut, *Cradle Song*. In at least one ad, Paramount stressed her particular appeal to women, at least implying that they were the most significant fans of the German film. Over a photo of Wieck with her eyes closed, the caption on the ad exclaimed, 'When her eyes open, ten million women will be thrilled!' (14 October 1933). In another ad, her appeal was somewhat less gendered. Here, her eyes are indeed open, and under the heading 'Star Gazing' the caption reads, 'When you look at her lovely face you are gazing on a great future star' (21 October 1933). In each instance, the ad remarked upon Wieck's German film and used that film as a means of generating interest in the Hollywood movie. 'Paramount brings to the screen Dorothea Wieck, star of *Maedchen in Uniform*, in *Cradle Song*', the first ad says, while the next reminds viewers that Wieck had scored 'an instant hit in *Maedchen in Uniform*'.

The example of *Mädchen in Uniform* argues for the possibility of an internationalist American cinema. Historians often speak of that internationalism in aesthetic terms and probably assume that viewers would not notice or hardly care, for instance, that German émigrés influenced American film noir, or that Ernst Lubitsch brought a new sophistication to American cinema or that, much later, the French New Wave taught young American directors entirely new ways to make films. I would argue, however, that 'average' audiences typically understood the importance of European cinema and might well have appreciated the American cinema as an interesting mixture of different national cultures.

Censoring *American Madness*

Through an examination of certain primary materials, we may indeed be able to place even *American Madness* well within this international American cinema, in spite of the seeming national fixedness of its title and subject matter. In Edward Buscombe's essay, mentioned above, one of the central problems became whether we can find the banker and Columbia board member A. H. Giannini in the text of Capra's film. Buscombe, finally, felt that this was possible, although not certain. But if we consider now the first category in the film's reception, the regulatory apparatus that took part in its censorship, we can clearly note the presence of Giannini, and he himself serves to complicate the film's relationship to the America of the movie's title and to the representation of the nation.

In 1932, before the strengthening of the Production Code Administration in 1934, the Hays Office examined films in script form and also after production, suggesting alterations that would make movies conform to the code and also ease their way through the tangle of state and local censorship policies. In the instance of *American Madness*, principally after filming was complete, code administrators worked hard to ensure that the film would be understood not only as a compelling national document but also as a useful one and invoked Giannini to make their case. In fact, Giannini, who exercised significant control in Columbia Pictures' affairs, wrote a letter about the film to Columbia President Harry Cohn, a letter which Cohn then sent on to Jason Joy, the Chief Administrator of the Production Code.

'I have just had the pleasure of seeing your *American Madness*', Giannini wrote, and he continued that 'I believe that this photoplay, which should be exploited by the leading theatres of this country, will do more than any other single agency to stop runs on banks which are started by false or malicious rumors' (28 May 1932).[8] The Hays Office seems to have distributed the letter to various state censorship boards. On 6 June 1932, for instance, the Chairman of the Kansas State Board of Review wrote to Joy that 'I read with a great deal of interest the copy of the letter from Dr. A. H. Giannini', and then added that, because of the letter, 'I will look forward with a new interest and I hope, a better appreciation of *American Madness*, when it reaches this office.' Other censorship board members, from the USA and Canada, also wrote to Joy about the usefulness of Giannini's letter. Joy himself, in a note to Will Hays, explained his use of the letter, saying that he was sending it to state censors 'just to give them a feeling of constructive things going on' (4 June 1932). In other words, Columbia and Joy hoped to use Giannini's letter to assert a reading of the film as a reassuring national document during perilous times, as a film that, in dealing with bank runs, referred directly to American current events and also as a movie that demonstrated the benefits – those 'constructive things going on' – of the American film industry to national recovery.

Giannini himself, the movie-studio financier and banker, stands out as something of a signifier of the fluidity between the international and the national. The son of Italian immigrants, Giannini and his brother, while in California, formed the Bank of Italy in 1904. The Gianninis pioneered branch banking and by 1930 the Bank of Italy had been transformed into the Bank of America (Buscombe 1998: 265–6). This overdetermined title of national affiliation, then, displaced the company's original reference to its European beginnings. And Giannini, the exemplar of the relationship between the international and the national in terms of financial institutions, came to be used to assert the national significance of Capra's film, despite a title, *American Madness*, which would seem to need no further effort to link it to the USA.

From the work of Richard Maltby and others, we know that sex and violence were, of course, highly censorable during this period (Maltby 1993; Jacobs 1991; Black 1994). And from Ruth Vasey, we understand that Hollywood's representations of other countries and their citizens would frequently raise concerns in the film industry's overseas markets (1997). The Hays Office file on *American Madness*, however, indicates that, at least at the state and local levels during the early 1930s, representations of the national – of an American body politic or character or corporate practices – were also high on the list of censorable offences.

In fact, Giannini's letter seemed designed to quiet the concerns of censors who doubted the film's depiction of the nation and, in particular, national banking practices. Any number of state censors asked for deletions of questionable language; the Pennsylvania board, for example, objected to 'lousy' and 'nerts' (26 August 1932). Dubious behaviour that might inspire imitation also raised the eyebrows of censors. From Ontario, the censorship board asked that Columbia eliminate the dialogue which explained the ease with which criminals in the film arranged to break into a vault: 'All that I had to do was turn off the alarm and fix the time clock' (26 September 1932). But the most extensive concerns came in relation to the representation of an industry and the practices of the collective.

Ohio rejected the film outright in July 1932, and then reconsidered two months later, while asking for significant deletions in prints that played in the state. None of the state board's concerns, however, focused on language or criminal behaviour. Instead, the Ohio censor objected to the film's representation of American banking and bankers and, even, of a bank's customers during dangerous economic times. In particular, the scene of the bank run seemed the most problematic. Ohio requested that Columbia eliminate Walter Huston's explanation of his attempts to end the run: 'Listen', the banker says, 'go back and tell the boys to stall as much as possible.' He continues, 'Get nothing but ones and fives . . . Tell them [the tellers] to take their time', and then, again, 'stall as much as possible.' Huston's assistant seconded his boss, and with dialogue just as objectionable: 'We haven't cash enough to last an hour . . . Stall! Stall!' Among other things, the Ohio censor also requested the elimination of 'all scenes of tellers closing windows and mob of people rushing to other windows' (19 July 1932; 8 August 1932). The panicky tactics of the bankers in the film seemed to make the Ohio board believe that the film would lower the national audience's confidence in the banking industry; Huston's altruism in the film could not be coupled with a rapidly improvised response to a bank run or any effort to deceive anxious depositors. But those depositors themselves, the film's depiction of an excited crowd possibly matching the one in movie theatres, also must not be seen to act irresponsibly. The film needed to depict the nation as both rational and orderly.

Of course, Giannini's presence in the discourses surrounding the film, available to the historian with access to certain materials, was far less so to audiences of the 1930s, audiences which, in some places, were possibly distressed by the very title of Capra's film and by its purely American emphasis. And this returns us, in a manner of speaking, to the concerns of the first part of this essay and the effort to break down the uncomplicated formulation of the nation in film studies in the USA over the past seventy years. There is ample evidence that US audiences in the early 1930s understood the international elements of the films on the nation's screens. Even if they hadn't seen *Mädchen in Uniform*, for instance, it is altogether likely that they were reading about its star, Dorothea Wieck, in fan magazines and that they also knew about other German films. But given this understanding, a movie, like Capra's, of such self-evident Americanness, took on great significance as a national object.

The fully national object, however, might not always be the film that audiences wanted to see. Of course, it is far too easy to say that audiences sought escape, and there is certainly evidence from various periods in US film history of many audiences looking for films which were fully engaged with issues and politics (Smoodin 2004: 139–59). Nevertheless, we might ask, somewhat perversely, whether the apparently European sensibility of *Mädchen in Uniform* might not have appeared, to many American viewers, comfortingly international, while the representation of domestic crisis in *American Madness* might have seemed both compelling and offputting.

This significance of the emphatically national film within an international film culture might not even be primarily textual. Here we can fully see the importance of Buscombe's article, calling as it did for a rethinking of the discipline's dependence on textual analysis, or at least extending that analysis to a variety of different texts. From these texts, we can see that the special status of a film such as Capra's, one so tied to the national context, may have been especially apparent in the attempts of regulatory bodies to control the national aspects of the film or the efforts of a studio to publicize them. Most importantly, we may have to look to the evidence of the movie audience and to the viewing choices that they made. Methodologically, this means looking at materials other than the films themselves. Historiographically, this means rethinking our understanding of the 'national' in relation to national cinema. The evidence from *American Madness* and other films from the period indicates that, in many instances, audiences, critics and members of the film industry understood that American cinema might not really be fully national at all, and so such films as Capra's would be seen as exceptions in a filmmaking system that stressed fluidity between countries and cultures. Within this system, movies which were indeed understood as narratives of the nation created very special challenges, in terms of their presentation to the public, the perceived dangers they might pose to their audiences and in the public's very response to Hollywood's representations of American life and politics.

Notes

1 There is relatively little evidence of this Asian influence, but it does exist. For information about the apparent Japanese influence in American cinema before 1920, see 'Hayakawa, Japanese Screen Star', *Literary Digest*, 3 November 1917, pp. 70, 72.

2 The film tells the story of bank president Henry Dickson, played by Walter Huston, who, according to Columbia publicity, 'defies his directorate and makes loans to worthy enterprises at a time when other bankers are hoarding their gold.' When the bank is robbed, 'a run on the bank is [the] inevitable result and Huston is left alone and without support.' See the castlist and plot summary distributed by Columbia, 19 July 1932. For a more detailed summary, see Charles J. Maland, *Frank Capra* (1995), pp. 70–2: After the bank run, Dickson learns that his wife has been unfaithful, although this is really a rumour started by one of the robbers to establish an alibi. As a result, 'Dickson loses his desire to save the bank . . . Matt [a faithful employee] calls the small businessmen to whom Dickson lent money, and they come to his rescue in the nick of time. As the shocked mob looks on, the businessmen rush into the bank to deposit money, showing their confidence in the bank and their gratitude to Dickson. Reinvigorated by his wife's assurance [that she had never been unfaithful], Dickson shames the board of directors into depositing some of their funds and saves his bank.'

3 For a brief chronology of the banking crisis, see Robert S. McElvaine, *The Great Depression: America 1929–1941*, p. 137. Here McElvaine claims that, 'by the beginning of 1933 the American banking structure was tottering more ominously than ever', although the problems depicted in *American Madness* can certainly be traced to the bank failures of the 1920s.

4 For other reports of bad box office, see *Motion Picture Herald*, 17 December 1932, p. 48; 24 December 1932, p. 40; 31 December 1932, p. 50; and 28 January 1933, p. 41; 4 February 1933, p. 51.

5 Even an historian as thorough and nuanced as Richard Maltby accepts the standard mythology about *It Happened One Night*. He has written that 'the film received only moderate attention and did satisfactory but unremarkable business at its New York opening. Its big box-office success was in the neighborhood theatres, where it attracted repeat bookings all year' (Maltby 1998: 148). Actually, the film did very well in its first run, both in New York and in other cities. At the Palace Theatre in New York, for example, Capra's film was held over a second week (unusual enough at the time) and in that second week came within $120 of making more money than any film, for any single week, shown in that theatre (through 24 March 1934). For first-run receipts, see, for example, *Motion Picture Herald*, 24 March 1934, pp. 54, 56.

6 The story about Riefensthal can be found in the 28 May 1945 issue of *Time* magazine. See the *Time* web site, <http://www.time.com/time/archive/preview/0,10987, 775650,00.html>.

7 The *New York Times* reported the following elimination of one of Manuela's lines about her teacher: 'In the evening when you say good night to me and go away from my bed and close the door, I must always stare at the door through the darkness, and then I would like to get up and come across to you, and yet I know that I am not allowed to, and then I think that I will grow older and will have to leave school and that you will remain here, and every night you will kiss other children good night.' The *Times*

also noted that 'all views of Manuela's face as she looks at Miss von Bernberg in the classroom were barred.'

8   This letter, and all of the regulatory material on *American Madness* cited here, can be found in the Production Code Administration collection at the Margaret Herrick Library at the Academy of Motion Picture Arts and Sciences in Los Angeles.

References

Black, G. (1994) *Hollywood Censored: Morality Codes, Catholics and the Movies*, Cambridge, Mass.: Cambridge University Press.

Buscombe, E. (1998) 'Notes on Columbia Pictures Corporation 1926–1941', in R. Sklar and V. Zagarrio (eds), *Frank Capra: Authorship and the Studio System*, Philadelphia, Pa.: Temple University Press, pp. 255–81.

Capra, F. (1971) *The Name Above the Title*, New York: Macmillan.

Editorial Collective (1976) 'John Ford's Young Mr. Lincoln', in B. Nichols (ed.), *Movies and Methods.*, Berkeley, Calif.: University of California Press, pp. 493–529.

Higson, A. (1995) *Waving the Flag: Constructing a National Cinema in Britain*, Oxford: Oxford University Press.

—— (2000) 'The Limiting Imagination of National Cinema,' in M. Hjort and S. Mackenzie (eds), *Cinema and Nation*, London: Routledge, pp. 63–74.

Higson, A. and Maltby, Richard (eds) (1999) *Film Europe and Film America:Cinema, Commerce and Cultural Exchange 1920–1939*, Exeter: University of Exeter Press.

Jacobs, L. (1991) *The Wages of Sin: Censorship and the Fallen Woman Film*, Madison, Wisc.: University of Wisconsin Press.

—— (1939) *The Rise of the American Film*, New York: Teachers College Press.

Jowett, G. (1976) *Film: The Democratic Art*, Boston, Mass.: Little, Brown.

Levine, L. (1993) *The Unpredictable Past: Explorations in American Cultural History*, New York: Oxford University Press.

McElvaine, R. (1984) *The Great Depression*, New York: Times Books.

Maland, C. (1995) *Frank Capra*, New York: Twayne Publishers.

Maltby, R. (1993) 'The Production Code and the Hays Office', in T. Balio (ed.), *Grand Design: Hollywood as a Modern Business Enterprise, 1930–1939*, Berkeley, Calif.: University of California Press, pp. 37–72.

—— (1998) 'The Recreation of the Patriarch', in R. Sklar and V. Zagarrio (eds), *Frank Capra: Authorship and the Studio System*, Philadelphia, Pa.: Temple University Press, pp. 130–63.

Sarris, A. (1968) *The American Cinema: Directors and Directions, 1929–1968*, New York: Dutton.

Saunders, T. (1994) *Hollywood in Berlin: American Cinema and Weimar Germany*, Berkeley, Calif.: University of California Press.

Smoodin, E. (2004) *Regarding Frank Capra: Audience, Celebrity, and American Film Studies, 1930–1960*, Durham, NC: Duke University Press.

Thorp, M. (1939) *America at the Movies*, New Haven, Conn.: Yale University Press.

Vasey, R. (1997) *The World according to Hollywood, 1918–1939*, Madison, Wisc.: University of Wisconsin Press.

Chapter 4

An American Romance (1944)

Rembert Hüser

It takes 151 minutes from the arrival of the ship until the first birds promising the land of rescue can be seen. With this, the film ends. Our romance with America can now begin.

The birds of King Vidor's series of V-formations are made of steel. We have seen the big star on the side of each plane before; now, with countless stars flying over our heads, we are reassured. The future is in good hands. The patriotic pattern which is drawn in the sky – the lines of stars moving forward, building a spiritual roof – combines the principle of the carrier pigeon and its good news with the air-force bomber and its power to deliver the message. The notice it sends to the enemy is 'The End'.

King Vidor cheated a little with his montage to emphasize the immediacy of production. The four-engined B17 Flying Fortress bombers roll out of the production plant and take off in five-minute intervals.[1] By the end of this film, there is no longer any difference between the military and the factory.[2] The smoothness of the operation, the trouble-free accomplishment of the giant task (to initiate the beehive of home-front production) celebrates the master trope of US productivity and industrial organization: the 'assembly belt', and the vision of (entrepreneur) father, mother and youngest son (corporate chief executive officer) who first brought this spectacle into being and who are shown proudly watching it. A nuclear family comprised of two men – a first generation Czech and his son, born in Chicago – and an American-born woman from Hibbing, Minnesota. Blending the values from somewhere which is referred to as the 'old country'[3] is decisive for the new world of unmatched national achievements. Standing on their ('our') soil, looking into the sky and seeing the (fuel-burning) planes flying overseas is fundamental in another respect: it brings the four elements of earth, water, air and fire together in one image. What we are supposed to have witnessed in this film is the formation of the American character.

An American Romance starts as a fable of creation. The background image for the title sequence provides the metaphor of materiality that prevails throughout the film. This time it is not clay which is the raw material of human creation. What we see is a close-up of iron ore. The names of the actors are inscribed against the texture of one of the major mineral resources of the country. The subject of the film which we are about to see is revealed to us by the title sequence: iron and men, our nation's treasures. But it is not just iron ore and the names of the cast and crew which we see. It is iron ore which is at the same time also an image of iron ore. In the close-up, the mineral is itself enclosed in a metal frame that emphasizes the margins of the shot. Like an exhibit in a natural-history museum, the iron ore is put on display, its metal frame asserting its status as a symbolic object. This film is about how to make cutting-edge technology from what we find in our earth.[4] It is also about how a particular soil shapes a victorious character and, last but not least, as a frame within the frame, as a meta(l)filmic construction, about how that ground shapes the very structure of the image itself.

> One day I had a talk with Irving Thalberg and told him I was weary of making ephemeral films. They came to town, played a week or so, then went their way to comparative obscurity or complete oblivion. I pointed out that only half the American population went to movies and not more than half of these saw any one film because their runs ended so quickly. If I were to work on something that I felt had a chance at long runs throughout the country or the world, I would put much more effort, and love, into its creation. Thalberg replied that my wishes were certainly in line with his own. Then he asked if I had any ideas commensurate with this ambitious goal. I said I had. I would like to make a film about any one of three subjects: steel, wheat, or war.
>
> (Vidor 1953: 111–12)

It is matter that matters. Twenty years later, adding a cornerstone per decade, King Vidor's architecture of national love – *The Big Parade* (1925), *Our Daily Bread* (1934), *An American Romance* (1944) – is completed. The 'or' in Vidor's initial enumeration of probable success stories to the mastermind of MGM is misleading. The three subjects are facets of a single theme and still firmly rooted in the experience of the First World War, which, in view of the new type of modern military success, is critically dependent on a country's ability to produce a continuous supply of goods for its armies. However, the economic rationale is not sufficient to explain the necessity of mobilizing the cinemagoer. Working for the nation guarantees not only survival – films that last – but also love. Film has become a national resource in itself. 'The picture wouldn't have one iota of obvious propaganda, flag-waving, or "Star Spangle Bannering," but I would hope to have everyone thinking, as they left the theatre, "I am glad to be living in the same sort of town where the same things occur," in other words, "I'm damn glad I am an American."' (Vidor to E. J. Mannix, inter-office communication, 16 December 1939).

One is tempted to boil down the three themes of Vidor's national narrative to the guiding principle which appears at the end of *An American Romance*, and which is already indicated by the title of this film. The movement of the trilogy – from one world war to the next, from the rich son in *The Big Parade* and the girl he loves in Europe, to the poor father from Europe and the American woman he loves in *An American Romance*, with the woman-at-the-side-of-the-man as the core of the modern workforce in *Our Daily Bread* – is unthinkable without the model of the reproductive unit of the heterosexual couple at the very core of the war effort. The parade of children – four boys and one girl in 1944 ('Some girls must be born, too' says a disappointed Steve Dangos [Brian Donlevy], the film's protagonist, when he realizes that his first-born is a girl) – in the national economy of love adds one more component to the parades of the military, industry and the cinema.

Unlike *The Big Parade*, *An American Romance* did not provide the 'long runs' Vidor had sought. Designed to conquer world markets, it even failed in Los Angeles. 'For any number of reasons the picture was not the big box-office success we had hoped for. Many of the inhabitants of Beverly Hills and Hollywood have never seen the film and many do not even know it was made' (Vidor 1953: 259). In the end, the film's only extensive audience was the military.[5] Today, it remains in comparative obscurity.[6]

The journey of *An American Romance* into 'what America was really about' (Vidor 1988: 194) begins in biblical terms. The earth of the title sequence yields to water. Feeling its way through the foggy darkness, the contours of a ship can be be made out. Next to it, at first just a glowing spot, a rainbow emerges. The biblical image establishes the land that we are about to see as a chosen one, founded through a covenant with God (Genesis 9: 8–13). The rainbow is a beacon of hope, a pledge against death and destruction. The steamer's cargo is passenger, all diligently typified as they stand on the weather deck looking ahead. It is by their clothes (predominantly their headgear), that their national character is constructed. Some of them wear national costumes, some are equipped with ethnic accessories. All are white Caucasians, most come in pairs. As they do not move within the shot, they give the impression of a series of tableaux. Here is a picture gallery of the New Americans. There are the two prototypical Spanish women with headscarves in the crowd; there is the exemplary large German family; there are two nuns, two Dutch women, a young girl holding her brother and a young Scandinavian couple – he dressed in a business suit, she holding a bundle with a newborn. The final gesture of this sequence is left to her: the young mother is pointing ahead. As the fog parts like a secondary cinematic curtain, revealing the promised land of

Manhattan in glimmering sunlight, an instrumental version of 'My Country 'Tis of Thee', already established in the title sequence as the film's musical leitmotif, can be heard. That this popular song is set to the melody of the British national anthem, an issue of considerable controversy over the years,[7] adds still another connotation to the founding myth of the USA. The covenant with God indicated by the rainbow is historically contextualized with the evocation of the Pilgrim Fathers, the English Puritans who came to America in 1620 in search of religious freedom.

That it is a series of paintings which is landing in America is not accidental. MGM's marketing campaign for *An American Romance* showcased one of the biggest productions of its twentieth anniversary year by hiring American illustrators to present the film in various drawings. 'On these pages the story of An American Romance is told in illustrations by a number of well-known artists who set down their conceptions of the film for M-G-M' (*Life*, 2 October 1944, pp. 75–7). Invoking fine art is part of a strategy that seeks not only to make *An American Romance* an instant classic but also to compete with the museum in representing the history of the nation. Film alone seems insufficient for this task.

The immigration complex of Ellis Island is then shown from inside as a gate swings open. As the camera pans across the excited newcomers streaming into the building, an off-screen narrator gives us the official criteria for the admission, the first words of the film: 'The admittant to this country had to be of sound mind, without a criminal record and not be a polygamist', and the camera stops at the protagonist being interviewed with the help of a translator. We learn that he is from Moravia, born on 5 June 1873 (he must be in his early twenties now). Asked whether he is married, he has to laugh: 'O no, no.' It will be in the future that he will join with what he is looking for. We also come to know from his interpreter that he wants to go 'to Mesabi, Minnesota', the only American word he recognizes and enthusiastically repeats: 'Yo, yo, Minesoty'. Going to Minnesota, one of the most ethnically diverse regions in the USA at that time, would not have been a very surprising move. 'The decades between 1890 and 1910 had witnessed the transformation of the Mesabi from a frontier wilderness to the world's leading producer of high-quality iron ore' (Walker 1979: 231). In particular, the so-called newer immigration of Slavs and Finns came in large numbers to the Mesabi range to work in the mines.

For our protagonist, this almost does not happen. The immigration officer rules that he does not fulfil the requirements for immigration and has him accompanied to a detention area behind a fence, to be sent back to Europe. The young, optimistic hero suddenly finds himself in the category of the elderly, sick, female. (We see Asian women entering this area; an old Turkish man with spectacles and a red fez stands in the middle of the crowd.) What follows is the crucial scene of the movie, introduced by the identification of the off-screen narrator as a voice of the family:

'You also had to have the equivalent of 25 dollars. My father had 21 kronas, about four dollars and 28 cents.' (Later in the film, this voice is revealed as that of his youngest son and future partner, who tells us the story of his family.) As the hero realizes that his money won't buy him the entrance to the USA, he stakes everything on a single ploy. He pushes the officer at the gate of the detention-room aside, rushes back to the immigration officers, takes a piece of iron ore out of his pocket and places it on the same spot in front of them on which he had previously placed his inadequate currency. The narrator mimics the volubility of the excitement he is describing: 'He told the interpreter he was very young and strong and he had come to this country to work. He had a cousin in the iron range in Minnesota and if they only let him through the gates, he would get there somehow and get immediately to work.'

The piece of ore left with the officers is several things in one: talisman, translation device, universal language of signs, memory aid, memento, wager, sign of expertise, 'mother earth', and a part of the old country. Most of all, however, it is something else: a gift. Stefan Dangosbiblichek makes a gift to the United States of America. With this act, he brings an entirely different logic into the immigration process. The gift, as we know from Marcel Mauss's classic anthropological study, has to be reciprocated. In an ingenious move that inverts the hierarchy of the power structure, the immigrant forces the USA to return the gift on an even bigger scale. What Stefan gives away with the iron ore is not just something of his belongings, but a part of himself. '[I]n this system of ideas one gives away what is in reality a part of one's own nature and substance, while to receive something is to receive a part of someone's spiritual essence. [. . .] Whatever it is, [. . .] it retains a magical and religious hold over the recipient' (Mauss 1967: 10). Stefan throws the iron dice and wins. The immigration officers, who have to smile in the face of this unexpected outbreak of energy, cannot but let him in.

> I guess the immigration inspectors realized that with a man like my father 25 dollars more or less would not make any difference. They figured that if he can take a chance on the United States sight unseen, why the United States can certainly take a chance on him. 'Good luck! Go Ahead!'

The immigrant and the iron ore are seen as parallel in *An American Romance*. 'This is what I believe has made America strong, this constant process of rebirth and refining of its cruder basic ores. I would attempt to make metal and men analoguous' (Vidor 1953: 258). The equation motivates the topographical model of the film. Two kinds of raw material are shipped all over the map.

> Steve's emotional life would be contemporaneous and analogous with the various evolutionary stages of transforming the basic crude ore into metal and then on into successive refinements. We would follow the iron ore and Steve as they

came from Mesabi by rail to St. Paul where the ore is loaded into lake steamers; through the Soo Canals to Lake Michigan and the steel mills at South Chicago, Illinois, and Gary, Indiana. Here we would show the whole business of making iron and steel, open hearth, Bessemer, and rolling mill methods would all be shown. Then as the metal became more refined and assumed more subtle and intricate shapes we would move with our principal character on to Detroit and go with him through each step of one of our amazing automobile plants and assembly lines. For the last act of the drama we would, at the inception of World War II, yank our protagonist from retirement in California and put him in charge of a big bomber plant like Douglas, Lockheed, or Consolidated, have him install assembly-like methods and turn out bombers at a rate of speed that would satisfy the most pessimistic of our production planners.

(Vidor 1953: 254)

What makes the immigrant and the iron ore not only comparable for Vidor but also embodiments of the essence of America is the idea of 'refinement', a version of the utopian concept of perfectibility updated for the industrial age. For man and nature, America is a giant refinery. When we watch the iron ore, we

Figure 3 An American Romance.

watch Steve. As Steve acquires stature, the iron acquires shape. Steve becomes an entrepreneur when the rolled steel becomes a car. Steve is melted down, becomes harder, gets formed, is a winner in the end. What *An American Romance* attempts is to film the metaphor of the melting pot, to take it literally.

Paralleling the refinement of the immigrant with the refinement of iron ore results in the formal division which is partly responsible for the film's failure. As a review in the *New York Times* on 24 November 1944 remarks:

> Mr. Vidor made a great big color picture with an abundance of vivid American scenes but with a story so banal and tedious that the whole film seems one massive platitude. [. . .] There are wonderful scenes in this picture of Steve mining in the Mesabi Range, wandering about the towering steel mills and working with molten steel. There are also fascinating glimpses of an automobile assembly line and, at the end, a colorful sequence showing a huge aircraft plant at work. Yet these are but objective pictures, made on locations by camera crews, and the relation of the leading character to them is purely coincidental.
> (Crowther 1944: 19)

In order to combine the story of the immigrant and the story of steel, *An American Romance* is punctuated almost every ten minutes with a documentary sequence which informs us about the respective stage of industrial production. There are ten of those sequences in the film, mostly about 1 to 2 minutes in length. Three dealing with major technological achievements – the Bessemer converter, the car assembly line and the plane assembly line – are double that size. The longer sequences are autonomous and are only connected to the rest of the film through the voice of the off-screen narrator. In the shorter ones, the protagonist is either shown acting in front of a rear projection, watching the scene from the margins, or walking through it. To insert these documentary sequences into the film was a risky move. Unlike most other films about mining and the steel industry – one could compare *An American Romance* to other home-front propaganda films such as Tay Garnett's *Valley of Decision* (1945) or Lewis Seiler's *Pittsburgh* (1942) – a great deal of work is actually seen in this film, however idealized it may be.[8] On the other hand, the constant alternation of the two filmic modes makes it difficult for the film to find its rhythm.

To make matters worse, the studio heads decided at exactly the time when *An American Romance* was scheduled for release that the length of a feature film should not exceed 2 hours, a restriction from which this prestigious production was at first explicitly exempted. But in the end, the film, which still had a running time of 151 minutes when it premiered, was cut to 125 minutes.[9] The final editing, at the dead of night, was done so unprofessionally that Vidor left MGM. Ironically, the long documentary sequences were left intact in the re-editing process, due to the difficulty of cutting their orchestral accompaniments.

It would be misleading, however, to simply bill the excess of the film's documentary scenes to MGM's sophisticated art directors' inability to restage industrial production in the studio.[10] To better understand Vidor's radical combination of documentary and fictional narrative, it is necessary to take account of developments in the 1930s that had blurred the boundaries between two modes of storytelling. A new type of industrial film had emerged in Europe. With respect to representations of the steel industry, one might mention, for instance, the two Nazi propaganda films by Walter Ruttmann, *Metall des Himmels* (*Heavenly Metal*, 1935) and *Mannesmann* (1937), which gained a good deal of international recognition by winning both the prize of the Fifth Biennale in Venice and the Grand Prix of the World Fair in Paris in the same year, or Victor Turin's 1929 Soviet railway film *Turksib*. Vidor, who was an avid collector of all kinds of materials relating to the steel industry, was well aware of these developments.

In the USA the documentary films of Vidor's friend Pare Lorentz had particular impact on the conception of *An American Romance*. In July 1938, shortly before accompanying Vidor to the shooting of *The Citadel* in England, Lorentz wrote an enthusiastic film review which was later included in an anthology prefaced by Vidor. The text reads almost as a programmatic prologue to *An American Romance*:

The most exciting picture I have seen in many weeks is neither a short nor a feature; there are no stars, and there is no plot or romance in the production. It was produced for the U.S. Steel Corporation by Roland Reed and photographed in Technicolor, and is called, none too aptly, *Men Make Steel*. [. . .] In a country built of steel, living in an economy that is governed by steel, few of you have an idea of the labor, the skill, or the gigantic equipment that is incorporated in the structure of Big Steel. Here is a picture that will explain many headlines to you – headlines about Aliquippa and the Mahoning Valley, and Pittsburgh, Steubenville, Wheeling, and Weirton. It is an advertising picture, or, if you will, a propaganda movie. But you can take from the movie exactly what you bring to it: you can marvel at the intelligence that went into the conception of such an industry; you can wonder how men can work so placidly with red-hot metal; you can wonder why so many of the men are under forty and worry about old-age employment – you can, in short, build a left-wing, a center, or a right-wing philosophy from the picture. [. . .] As far as Hollywood is concerned, the producers will say, 'It's an advertising picture and has no box office worth,' and let it go at that – that is, they will say that if they continue the policy they have maintained for years in the movie industry. But whatever they say, within the year these so-called industrial pictures are going to have significant effect on the entire movie world. There is visible proof that by their own limitations Hollywood producers have lost millions of potential customers. For the past ten years we have been thinking a great deal about the facts of this country – of its land, its social and economic problems, and about its great factories. Yet in the last decade no movie company has even attempted to use the actual drama of our national life as photographic material.

(Lorentz 1938: 154–5)

King Vidor undertakes the enterprise of filming the actual drama of national life in America by inserting a documentary logic into the Hollywood feature film. Similarly to the way Lorentz evokes the magical names of towns and landscapes in the review and in his own films, Vidor also develops his teleological plot (from humble origins to unprecedented power) along road-movie-like stops throughout the country, carefully introduced by signs with the name of the respective place. The problem that he underestimates, though, is that the images of the various stages of steel production, with their switch from the almost archaic pathos of bare-chested men handling the giant fires at the beginning to the more modern one of highly skilled women working at high-tech assembly belts in complementary industries, are not easily matched with a narrative. Characteristic of Vidor's often merely additive montage, and at the same time almost an admission of its failure, is the formulaic introduction to one of the documentary sequences: 'It might interest you to know . . .'

The title of Vidor's first story outline for this film was *Man of Tomorrow*. After six revisions by various writers (by the final version, there had been a total of fifteen different authors who had worked in various phases on this script[11]), it was changed to *The Magic Land*. Two drafts and several title suggestions and discussions later,[12] Vidor retitled the project *America* and submitted it to the Office of War Information (OWI). That there had already been a film with that title twenty years earlier, one of the most popular films of 1924 and, on top of everything, one by D. W. Griffith, whom Vidor admired, did not stand in the way. The OWI objected to it nevertheless: 'no one movie could encompass all of America' (Koppes and Black 1990: 147). (The response makes Vidor's choice seem almost blasphemous in retrospect. In times of war, *nation* has to be *surplus*. The *whole of a nation* is not allowed to be grasped in any respect.) The title was changed again, this time with the man of tomorrow and the magic land America brought together in the proven formula of *An American Romance*.[13] "'It seemed to tell better what the picture was about," says Vidor. "*America* might have indicated to many people that the picture was a straight documentary presentation, which it is not. The story of America is a romantic story, and that is what we wanted the title to say"' (Wilson 1944: 35).

The posters for the film translate the national romance into the convention of 'a man loves a woman', with America as the woman. Painted close-ups show the protagonists embracing in a pastoral idyll with tiny factory chimneys in the distance or, with glowing beams of light behind them, looking with fascination at a best-of-Steve's life montage of images. The absence of any depiction of commercial industry on many of these posters is striking.

Anna, the woman in Steve's background, does indeed share some features of this new archetypal America, and this not only because she is the only 'pure' American in the family. Above all, Anne is a refinement specialist. She is a schoolteacher, one of those classical pioneer figures who help convey the nation from wilderness to civilization. Steve meets her after walking into a schoolhouse to inquire about how the nail that he brought along is made out of the piece of iron ore that he holds in his other hand. With the nail becoming a question, it is evident that our main character is someone who is willing to learn how to build (machines, families, the nation). His inquiry varies the which-came-first?-the-chicken-or-the-egg conundrum along the lines of matter and tool, and it also has a sexual undertone. His insistence on an answer to this question triggers the relationship and leads to marriage. Steve is nailing the teacher. Anne takes care of the half-man half-schoolboy in front of her and shows him how to move from A to B.

The figure of the teacher is especially crucial for the semiological journey of *An American Romance*. In order to provide both a crash course in industrial steel production and in American landscapes, the film needs to instruct its audience without appearing to be too didactic. Steve, the immigrant, is new to this world. He is tagged by the immigration officers with a big note on his sleeve: '[I come from the] old country. I speak no English. I am walking to the iron range in Minnesota. Please point the way. Thank you.' We, the audience, have to point out the way to Steve. Consequentially, the film starts with situations in which we know better.

The tagged immigrant begins the experiment of adaptation by walking west. He repeats the expeditions of American explorers, discoverers and pioneers in changed terms. The itinerary begins, highly symbolically, along a railroad in construction. Stefan walks and sees smoking chimneys, fields with harvest, a dog behind a fence. He chops wood behind a house and is offered a sandwich and a glass of milk. He encounters industry, agriculture, property, hospitality and work.

> The original film included almost every state between New York and California. When the man is making his walk, I had signs of towns in practically every state that he went through, or was supposed to go through during the story. We had signs for places like Gary, Indiana, Chicago; towns in Minnesota; the Rushmore Monument; all kinds of places. [. . .] [A]ll those were removed. The important points were from New York to California, so I went through, and decided which ones were the most important and left those in.
>
> (Vidor 1988: 196)

The three singposts the film gives the hero and us to read are: Punxsutawney, Wapakoneta and Kankakee. At first sight, America is just incomprehensible! The three names mimic the wilderness, they are all Native American, unfamiliar to 'us', difficult to pronounce and to keep in mind. Steve (who cannot read at all, as we come to know later) is shown trying to sound out the names that he mistakenly takes for the first words of his new language. We know better: this is not the language which counts in this country. The transatlantic newcomer is confronted with what is visibly left of the indigenous Americans who had to go. Later in the film, Steve is already so Americanized that he mimics the hackneyed battle cry of Native Americans when confronted with a wooden chief in front of a cigar store.

But what is particular about Punxsutawney, Wapakoneta and Kankakee besides their being names without Indo-European pedigree? These names are not just seemingly incomprehensible, adapted names of another culture; they are also utterly familiar at the same time, even self-evident. Apparently randomly chosen, average, they are all names of 'small towns', an integral part of American national ideology. It is no surprise that the idealizing portrayal of American small towns, with its celebration of the traditional values of family love, personal interaction and a sense of community, reached its peak in the US films of the 1940s. Four years before *An American Romance*, *Our Town* (Sam Wood, 1940) had been released, situating its story at the turn of the century, when the introduction of the car seems to threaten the cohesion of community (Levy 1991: 72). *An American Romance* faces a far more difficult task. It has to reconcile the war effort with radical changes in the workforce and the one-dimensionality of production with the philosophy of family life and the community, while also 'stimulating interest in the postwar world' (Winkler 1978: 41).

Although it is part of the very concept of the small town, that nothing really important takes place over there, it is in their very choice (by Vidor) that one is tempted to play the game of deciphering what the invocation of these particular names might have to offer to the film on a symbolic level. Punxsutawney, Pennsylvania is the home of Punxsutawney Phil, the groundhog that, since 1841, has predicted the length of winter on Groundhog Day (or the arrival of spring, to put it in more appropriate metaphoric terms for times of war). Kankakee, Illinois is the birthplace both of the soft-frozen dairy products of Dairy Queen, a family favourite and one of the first American food franchises in 1938, and of Harold Lincoln Gray, the creator of one the most popular comic strips of the time, *Little Orphan Annie*, which tackled the Depression and the Nazis, and which, by this time, had already been adapted for film several times by Hollywood. Of course, these are just contingent contexts which conjure up elements of America's popular culture, but trying to construct these connections is exactly what the logic of the national ideology of the small town demands, a logic which still operates today.[14]

Stefan Dangosbiblichek finally arrives in Hibbing, Minnesota and starts working in the open-pit iron-ore mines. Entry into its industrial logic results in his baptism. Stefan Dangosbiblichek picks up an American name. '"D-A-N-G-O-S-B . . ." "That's enough. We make it Dangos. Steve Dangos."' It is telling that in this film it is not Ellis Island which is responsible for the abbreviation and Americanizing of the immigrant's name, but the foreman who takes him on. His cousin confirms the pace of the success story: 'How you like this country? So quick! A new name, a new job.' It is the industry that makes heroes.

But Steve Dangos is a name which is not easy to keep in mind either. At least not for King Vidor. 'I determined to tell the story of steel from the viewpoint of an eager immigrant, [. . .] Stephan Danahos of Czechoslovakia' (Vidor 1953: 253). As artificial as the Czech name 'Dangosbiblichek' already is, it is that much more irritating that in his autobiography Vidor does not even recall its abbreviated final form and constantly refers to the protagonist of his film incorrectly. The slip is telling, because it helps to make more clear what the fantasy is behind the entire project. Transcribing 'Steve Dangos' into 'Stephan Danahos' recalls 'Stevan Dohanos', the name behind the most popular depictions of American everyday life in the 1940s, the covers of the *Saturday Evening Post*.[15] The name of a second-generation male immigrant of East European descent, born in Ohio, who worked in the steel mills before he became one of the most famous US illustrators of his time. (Stevan Dohanos' framed portrait of Steve and Anna is also the first in the series of illustrations for the marketing campaign of *An American Romance*.) By mixing up the two names, in retrospect, Vidor displays the underlying aesthetics of his film as one that is eager to claim a kinship between film and painting, and to erase the borders between high and low culture. It is not by chance that in Vidor's recollections the making of *An American Romance* parallels his start as a painter whose work is exhibited. In March 1943, even before the film had been released, the Museum of Modern Art in New York made *An American Romance* the subject of its 'Bringing a Picture to the Screen' exhibition series.

To play Dangos, his wife and his friend, King Vidor sought some of the most famous contract stars with MGM at that time: 'The perfect casting for me was Spencer Tracy in the part of the immigrant Steve Dangos, Ingrid Bergman for the role of his wife, and Joseph Cotten as his friend' (Vidor 1988: 199). All three were unavailable for his film. Tracy played in *A Guy Named Joe*, and Bergman and Cotten in *Gaslight*, both of which turned out to be far more successful than *An American Romance*. After considering Joel McCrea and James Cagney, Vidor had to go with Brian Donlevy instead, Ann Richards (who was supposed to become the studio's 'next Greer Garson') and Walter Abel. Stephen McNally played the youngest son. Donlevy was a particularly surprising choice, having become famous in 1940 in the leading role of Preston Sturges's *The Great McGinty*, which told the story of the success of a social climber in almost exactly the reverse terms of Vidor's patriotic epic, with Donlevy playing a bum who rises to Governor of Illinois via a corrupt political machine. Despite studio publicity about Donlevy's own mining interests, the patriotic phrase 'your son can become president', voiced twice in the film, had been thoroughly discredited by his role of four years earlier. Vidor later blamed the film's lack of success to a large extent on its casting (Vidor 1972: 44).

In the film, all four sons of Steve Dangos[16] actually become American presidents. Steve names them: George Washington Dangos, Thomas Jefferson Dangos, Abraham Lincoln Dangos and Theodore Roosevelt Dangos '– a living Mount Rushmore' (Koppes and Black 1990: 151). The symbolic reference to the four presidents carved on Mount Rushmore, after planned footage of it had not been inserted into the film, is significant. The other heroic national monument that celebrates America's achievements by placing an object formed out of its earth and stone 'as close to heaven as we can' (Borglum 1941: 2) had just opened three years before. Both the frontier and the immigrant are mythologized in these four faces carved into the mountain, 'celebrating the accomplishments of the Old World radicals who shook the shackles of oppression from their light feet and fled despotism to people a continent; who built an empire and rewrote the history of freedom and compelled the world to accept its wiser, happier form of government' (Borglum 1941: 2).

Vidor repeats the sculptor's gesture of an 'absolute mastery over the frontier, subjugating it in the act of carving the mountain' (Marling 1984: 88), by making the American presidency a consequence of immigrant production and reproduction, of steel and sons.

With so much grandeur in the air in 1944, in what way might a product of the motion-picture industry of America seriously compete with the products of the American steel industry? The headline of the film's posters gives the answer: 'M.G.M.s Mighty Technicolor Drama'. Mighty in Hollywood in those years is colour. The epic drama of the aspiring painter on three-strip Technicolor starts from its dull, foggy beginning with a display of the chromatic scale, the painter's palette. As so often with images of creation in motion pictures, the rainbow which breaks through the almost black-and-white image and promises a bright colourful future stems quite unromantically from the miniature department of the studio (Vidor 1988: 201).

> For my second Technicolor film American Romance (1944) I planned an epic story of the European immigrant in America [. . .] – all the while thinking in color as well as in pictures and words. For the iron-mining episodes at Mesabi we would confine ourselves to the earth colors: browns, Indian reds, blacks, heavy grays, and earthy greens. The light, bright blue of a clear sky would be avoided at all costs. Blue skies would be used at the finish of the film in conjunction with the gray-blues of airplanes and the lemon-yellows and brilliant orange shades of California, which would serve to give an emotional color lift at the end of the picture.
>
> (Vidor 1972: 171–2)

The use of Technicolor has always been considered one of the major achievements of *An American Romance*. One has to be careful though not to credit too much of the colour composition to Vidor, as much of it is in line with the principles of Technicolor's Advisory Service as advocated by Natalie Kalmus, the colour consultant for the film:

> color should be natural, color should be built upon conventional standards of harmony, contrast and cultural connotations, and color should add to the story without distracting the audience [. . .]Kalmus [. . .] belongs to a long line of color practitioners who accept as fairly natural that color's meanings are fixed and definable. As such, she had great faith in anticipating the meanings 'determined' by certain colors.
>
> (Neupert 1990: 24–6)

By attaching the fixed colour meanings of Technicolor's company philosophy to certain American landscapes – the Mesabi is brown, Chicago is sparkling red, Detroit is blue, California bright orange – and subordinating this to a teleological ascent into the light, Vidor translates the historical westward expansion of America into a spatial structure which has as its destiny at the coast both the aircraft factory and Hollywood.

What a 'true' panorama of America was supposed to look like was highly disputed in Hollywood at that time. That the OWI, which called for a sympathetic treatment of the goals of the New Deal, and King Vidor, who, in 1944, along with Gary Cooper, Walt Disney, Victor Fleming, John Wayne and others had founded the new Motion Picture Alliance for the Preservation of American Ideals, would clash over the concept of the film did not come as a surprise. It was not just the title 'America' in the first script to which the OWI objected.

> In keeping with the idea of a 'people's war,' she [Thorson, the reviewer of the OWI] suggested some drastic changes to moderate the glorification of management and to enhance the role of workers. 'Implicit in the story,' Thorson pointed out, 'are many leaves from the classic but discredited American myth' that anybody with ability and determination can become an executive. The depression should at least be recognized. Equally serious was the treatment of labor unions. Dangos' first job in the steel industry appeared to be as a scab. Later, when workers staged a sit-down strike at his auto plant, Dangos dispersed them with armed guards and tear gas. Here were echoes not only of Henry Ford but of the Hollywood brass as well. The studios fought unions bitterly in the 1930's, though not as violently as Ford, and returned to the offensive after the war. As OWI feared, these scenes encouraged lurking suspicions that labor was radical, violent, and untrustworthy. 'This is a fascist tactic pure and simple, tending to divide one group of Americans from the others,' Thorson said. OWI insisted that labor be treated more sympathetically. A more general anxiety for OWI was that Dangos seemed unaware of American values, or

unimpressed by them. [. . .] The studio realized that the harsh treatment of labor had to be changed. Screenwriter Kahn wrote a scene in which Dangos returned to his factory as a 76-cent an-hour lathe operator and joined the union, but only when it signed a no-strike pledge for the duration. This was too improbable even for Hollywood. Instead, Vidor decided to have Dangos leave the company after his entire board of directors turned against his anti-union policy.

(Koppes and Black 1990: 148–50)

The image of Steve Dangos defeated in his fight against the emerging unions and having to grant them power (but who later is asked to come back from retirement for the war effort, because without his energy and ideas the decisive entrepreneurial innovation cannot take place[17]) is the representation of work in the film that might have had the highest identificatory potential for Vidor himself. The various stages of our hero's refinement – from his Herculean confrontation with the monster 'giant steam shovel', to his patience as an avid reader, to the ballet of the workers shovelling in a circle, the rebuilding of the car in his garage and, finally, to the united-forces-of-the-family picture at the end, watching the Flying Fortresses take off – is conspicuously stylized, almost emblematic.[18] What they specify is the picture gallery of the New Americans that we have seen at the beginning. On land, we can witness the gradual formation of a prototype.

At a time when the leader of the other major ally of the nation had renamed himself the 'Man of Steel' (Stalin) and the two major European axis powers had agreed on a 'Pact of Steel', *An American Romance* was considered to be one of the most promising tools for the politics of post-war re-education, a model film that would be able to redefine the images of American culture that Hollywood had provided thus far:

the OWI feels that it has found the perfect picture to show the Fascist nations. This picture, more than any other in recent years, shows democracy really working – shows what the shouting's all about. An American Romance is one of the few films that will have a whole world for an audience. It will explain the American way to a bewildered Europe far more effectively than floods of words. It couldn't have better timing, even though the idea for it was conceived nineteen years ago.

(Wilson 1944: 34)

Since Vidor was primarily concerned in his heroic films with staging pathos and paid little attention to conflicting ideologies (Mund 1999: 716), the OWI, the Bureau of Motion Pictures and the Motion Picture Alliance for the Preservation of American Ideals could all be happy with the film in the end. While the one was content to see 'the celebration of management-labor cooperation' (Koppes and Black 1990: 154), the other could embrace the patriotic story of heroic individualism. Even Louis B. Mayer, the head of MGM, who considered OWI's suggestions to be 'politically tainted' (Koppes and Black 1990: 149), 'put his arm around [Vidor's] shoulders and said, "I've just seen the greatest picture our company has ever made"' (Vidor 1953: 258).

To understand the unifying idea of Americanness in *An American Romance*, one has to take a closer look at the very centre of the film, when Steve's son George Washington is giving the valedictorian speech on his graduation day. Historically accurate for 1944, it is the Class of 1918 that designates the 'deeper meaning of America,'[19] the year not of America's entrance into the war, but of its ending it and the beginning of both its stronger investment in Europe and the transformation of American society.[20]

> *George Washington Dangos*: My preceptors, parents, classmates and friends. On this graduation day, we stand upon the threshold of a new world. A world of strife and struggle. We are about to take our places in the world. The future belongs to us. The future of America that we are about to inherit. The right to be Americans was won for us by others. Most of us are sons and daughters of foreign born parents who came from distant lands to find opportunity and freedom. We must learn the deeper meaning of America [. . .].
>
> *Steve Dangos*: That's my son!
>
> *Anna O'Rourke Dangos*: Steve . . .
>
> *Steve Dangos*: What's wrong with that? I want everybody to know that Georgie is my son. Georgie is a smart fellow.

An American Romance is about Steve Dangos' sons, about the legacy of the immigrant for the first generation born in the USA or, in terms of the family, about the love of sons for their father, who embodies the deeper meaning of the nation. Immigration itself is not the everyday situation of the film. Contrary to the very first promotion shots for the film (when the project still had the name 'America') in which we see the figure of Steve, the immigrant, as the focus, emerging from behind a metal half-meridian formed out of the word 'AMERICA' on top of the globe, immigration is presented nostalgically, as a heroism of the past. One consequence of this is the complete exclusion of people of colour, even in the factory scenes. *An American Romance* is as white as it can get,[21] which finally gives a more precise meaning to the concept of 'refinement'. The concept of *race* is supplemented in the film by the concepts of *mobility* and *youth*. With his first salary cheque, Steve buys new yellow boots – not so much because he has walked so far to get here but to indicate that he intends to make a fresh start, to move on. He is the one who will send this generation that is writing the living present, i.e., fighting the war, on its way.

The four Dangos brothers are modelled on the folklore of the presidents whose names they bear. George Washington, the first son born at the very moment in the film when we see steel for the first time, which is also the very first year of the new century, is the son who talks his father into patriotism. The final stage of conversion takes place in Steve's garage.

If one had to decide on a single take that epitomizes the entire film, it would be the dismantling of a new car on the floor of Dangos' garage. The shot both restages a famous anecdote of the American self-made man: Walter Chrysler, taking apart his very first car (which is mentioned in many of his obituaries in 1940) and echoes the scrap metal drives which were popular in the propaganda of the US home front. The pieces of the car-to-be on the floor form the background for the patriotic talk between father and son concerning 'going to war' and what it means to be an American. What we see is both the trope and the hermeneutic principle of the whole and its parts. The body of the nation which is under the scrutiny of father and son is (quite fittingly for the USA) the body of a car. With this, the film promotes at the very same time the upward mobility of the self-made man, the nation, modernization and consumer society.

George Washington joins Steve in the garage and reveals to him that he intends to join the army.

Steve Dangos: Wait a minute. What about college?

George Washington Dangos: There is no time for college now. We've got a war to fight.

Steve Dangos: What have you got to fight? What have you got to do with the war, Georgie? You are not a Frenchman, an Englishman, a Russian. You are an American citizen, born right here in the U.S.A. Why?

George Washington Dangos: Maybe, I better make my speech all over again. Just for you.

The new American patriotism of the Class of 1918 is not dependent on the territory anymore. American democracy must also be defended by fighting abroad.

The next time we see George (the very next take), he is already in uniform, waiting outside. Steve takes him to the station.

Steve Dangos: I meant to get you a graduation present. At least I should buy you something.

George Washington Dangos: There is only one thing, I'd like, Dad.

Steve Dangos: I bet I know: a gold watch with your name on it.

George Washington Dangos: No, nothing like that. I want you to become an American citizen.

Father and son say goodbye to each other and head into the future. We see them walking to the train at the railway station (and into the camera, which slowly recedes, always keeping the same distance). This walk (as is true for all walks in this film) is highly overdetermined. On the one hand, one generation marches next to the other, the past next to the future. On the other hand, the civilian marches shoulder to shoulder with the soldier. Taking into account the rear-projection of a column of workers marching out of a steel factory right behind them, this final walk is also the family leading the industrial workforce in the war effort.

Of course, the son as the symbolic father (of the country) has to make way for his natural father and his brothers. Steve and Anna receive a telegram that Georgie has been killed in Europe just as they are preparing to go to his naturalization ceremony. Both continue practising the Pledge of Allegiance. To prepare for the ceremony, Anna becomes a teacher again, asking the questions that Steve will be asked and helping him to memorize the history of the nation and the formula of the oath. It is within the family that the pledge of allegiance is performed for the very first time. Anna, the American, is the one who is taking the oath from her husband. This very image is then repeated and projected into the public realm of the ceremony, with Steve standing in a row with several white men and a nun. Steve has made his dead son a graduation present. Thanks to George Washington's sacrifice, Steve has finally arrived in the USA. He is an American citizen now. At home, we see him again working to improve the car, when George's teacher stops by the house to bring a poem that George had written for school. The two men become friends and, after the teacher has quit his job, business partners in their new car enterprise. In the remaining 60 minutes, the necessary steps can be taken – 'all to add strength to a mighty nation growing mighty.'[22]

The world premiere of *An American Romance* was held on 12 October, the anniversary of Columbus arriving in the Americas. The press book suggested publicity topics and events to its exhibitors:

> invite representatives of every nationality and working class in your community – Europeans and their descendants who are now local bankers, war plant employers, housewives, electricians, plumbers, office workers etc. [. . .] *Special Screening for Chamber of Commerce*. Branches of the Chamber of Commerce, Rotarians and Lions are always interested in success stories and the propagandizing of America as the land of opportunity [. . .], particularly owners of stores who have valuable window space [. . .]. *Honor Successful Men Who Rose From Obscurity in America* [. . .]. *I AM AN AMERICAN . . . Patriotic Rally With Pledge of Allegiance to the Flag* [. . .]. *Stage a Real 'American Romance'*. Select a local couple to be married on the stage of your theatre [. . .].

How many of those suggestions were in fact realized is not known. *Variety* and the *Motion Picture Herald* do speak of *Essay Contests* in several states on 'The Romance of Living in America.' The entire campaign, however, was futile.

In the closing credits of *An American Romance*, the final images of US bombers flying in formation towards the theatre of war are accompanied by the melody of

'My Country 'Tis of Thee', aka 'America', which had become an integral part of the Americanization programme in US public schools. Having received the gift of labour from Europe, America reciprocates with its gift of steel. 'The gift is not inert and often personified and strives to bring to its original clan and homeland some equivalent to take its place' (Mauss 1967: 10).

Notes

1 The film is faster here than the official propaganda of the OWI founded in 1942: 'The first issue of *Victory* carried on the cover a color picture of an American bombardier at his controls. The caption underneath said that 'Two Million Men Will Fight in 185,000 US Planes.' A story inside pointed out that as many as twenty-five bombers a day were already being flown to England. One factory produced a four-engine bomber every hour' (Winkler 1978: 154–5).

2 'We'll turn out planes here faster than bullets coming out of a machine gun' (Steve Dangos, addressing his business partners after coming back from retirement).

3 'At the beginning of the picture the tramp across the country – should we indicate in our narration that the man came here full of hope but he never dreamt of the expense, the size, fertility, productivity of country? My reaction on return from first trip to Europe' (King Vidor, preview notes, America, 30 October 1943).

4 'By 1935 he [King Vidor] was expressing his ideas in four words: "Earth to the sky"' (Wilson 1944: 35).

5 'I was glad I made it for the war effort, but most of the reactions I got were through men in the service. There was hardly a man in the service who didn't see the film. It was used on all sorts of ships, in camps, and even in Europe' (Vidor 1988: 201).

6 The extensive production notes for this film are part of the The King Vidor Collection in the USC Cinema-Television Library in Los Angeles. Many thanks to Ned Comstock for his help!

7 'Congress selected the supposedly more authentic and original "Star-Spangled Banner" as the national anthem in 1931. While historians pointed out that its melody was equally British in origin, it at least had the virtue of being less well known' (Branham and Hartnett 2002: 14–15).

8 '"I read more than eighty scripts dealing with steel," says Vidor. "In every case there were light romantic stories with steelmaking merely a convenient background. When the hero entered a steel mill there was a fade-out. You never actually saw him inside the mill. Nothing I read caught the spirit and the tempo of steel and the men of America who make it."' (Wilson 1944: 34.)

9 Eliminated were Steve's first night after work in the dormitory, his purchase of shoes, a rail journey from Duluth, an encounter with a black American, the explanation of the names of his sons to the superintendent, Tina playing, working at the Bessemer converter, designing the car, the meeting of the workers, a discussion between father and son after the vote on the unions, a visit to Mount Rushmore, and showing the family album to pilots. The 'spectacular scenes (including one in which Dangloss [!]

slips down an ore chute into a ship's hold) as well as the incidental detail of his marriage to the schoolteacher Anna, the growth of his family, and his daughter's marriage which might have made it [the film] less of a stylized spectacular' (Baxter 1976: 66f.) had been cut previously.

10 'For the bomber assembly line, which must climax the whole industrial panorama of America, the technical department of the studio thought they could achieve a more spectacular result by constructing an imaginary airship of the future and building it all in miniature. [. . .] when the sequence was screened for the first time, it looked unreal in contrast to the rest of the film, and it was decided to remake the episode in an honest-to-goodness factory, using the actual detailed construction of a Flying Fortress' (Vidor 1953: 257–8).

11 'The writing credit on the film ("Screenplay by Herbert Dalmas and William Ludwig; based on a story by King Vidor") conceals a chaos of revisions, extreme even by Hollywood standards' (Durgnat and Simmon 1988: 223.) Durgnat and Simmon provide a list that reconstructs the various stages of the manuscript and its various collaborators.

12 'Dear King, I have given considerable thought to the suggested title, "American Miracle", and I very much fear that it would seriously impede the basic concept of the entire picture. [. . .] While the rise to eminence and success of a hardworking, honest and intelligent immigrant might be miraculous in other countries we have maintained that in our country it is a future open to any man who will grasp it' (William Ludwig, Inter-Office Communication, 16 February 1944).

13 The only American romance that had existed in the US Motion picture industry before did not refer to the territory of the USA: 'A Central American Romance", an Edison-production of 1910, directed by J. Searle Dawley.

14 'WAPAKONETA, Ohio [. . .] These are not the happiest days in the United States. What happened four weeks ago, on Sept. 11, threw us. [. . .] Sometimes hope comes in the form of a reminder. Sometimes you can find it by the side of the road. On my way through the middle of the country the other day, trying to take a look at America at ground level in the weeks after Sept. 11, the highway sign said the next exit was Wapakoneta. [. . .] You'll find places like Wapakoneta all across the United States. Nothing in common with New York or Los Angeles or Chicago, it seems. Not a capital of ambition, or of lofty dreams. Unless you know about this town, and what happened here. In the 1940s, a boy went to Blume High School here. [. . .] Who would ever expect to hear from a kid in an Ohio town with so few residents? Who would ever expect that a kid in a town like this – like any American town by the highway – would go anywhere, would do anything? [. . .] This kid did. This kid from the airstrip grew up, and on July 20, 1969, he became the first person in the history of the world to step on the moon. Neil Armstrong, of Wapakoneta, Ohio. Don't ever say anything is impossible. Don't ever – in this country – assume that if something is important enough, we can't find a way to do it' (Greene 2001).

15 'The principal function the covers would come to serve was the representation of America or, more precisely, of America's ideas about itself. Such representation did not take the form of realistic images of all the varieties of American experience; rather, it expressed images that stirred common feelings and appealed to shared ideals' (Cohn 1995: xii).

16 The sequences with Steve's only daughter get lost in the course of the studio's final cuts. One of the very few things we come to know about her in the film is that she is accompanying her husband to the oil fields.

17 *Howard Clinton*: They've raised our quota from a thousand planes a year to 4,500.
   Steve Dangos: So what? We used to make 4,500 automobiles a month.
   Howard Clinton: Yes, but planes are different. We can't meet that quota.
   Steve Dangos: What do you mean can't?
   George Washington Dangos: Well, you can't build any plane on an assembly line. Ask any airplane man.
   Steve Dangos: But how do they know? They told us, you couldn't build an automobile with a steel top, but we built it. Where would you and I be, if we listened to all the people who told us, what we couldn't do? This whole country was built by guys who were told that they couldn't.

18 '[T]his glorification of the American dream has the stiff unreality of a daguerreotype reproduced and brought to life in some of the finest Technicolor photography of U.S. industry yet filmed. [. . .] An American Romance is a cameraman's field day' (*Time*, 16 October 1944, p. 94).

19 'World War I transformed the federal Army into a strong, national institution, and these soldiers played a critical role in shaping it. As a result, they determined what mass military service would mean for the millions of American men who served throughout the rest of the twentieth century. This generation left its mark on domestic society as well. [. . .] [It] remade the economic and social landscape of America' (Keene 2001: x).

20 Initial objections to that year's choice after the first screenings – 'In the high school graduation scene, the class is established, in the principal's speech, as that of 1918. This leaves only four months for the son to enlist, be trained, shipped overseas and killed. It would time better if the year of graduation could be changed to 1917' (J. K. McGuiness, 7 February 1944, card, remarks on rough cut) – are overturned in order to establish a parallel between 1918 and 1944 (as, hopefully, the last year of the war).

21 The sequence of Steve Dangos' encounter with 'his first black American' on a boat on Lake Superior was eliminated when the film was shortened. 'Brief touches on face after the negro passes. Be careful to distinguish between fear and wonderment. Careful fear does not emerge as fear of the bundle' (Notes from Brian Donlevy, 8 March 1942).

22 Off-screen narrator earlier in the film, after Steve Dangos, encouraged by his wife, had decided to push ahead and to leave the mines for the steel industry.

References

Baxter, J. (1976) *King Vidor*, New York: Simon & Schuster.

Borglum, G. (1941) 'Foreword', in *Mount Rushmore National Memorial: Shrine of Democracy. A Monument Commemorating the Conception, Preservation, and Growth of the Great American Republic*, Mount Rushmore National Memorial Commission.

Branham, R. J. and Hartnett, S. J. (2002) *Sweet Freedom's Song: 'My Country 'Tis of Thee' and Democracy in America*, Oxford: Oxford University Press.

Chrysler, W. P. (1950) *Life of an American Workman*, New York: Dodd, Mean & Company.

Cohn, J. (1995) *Covers of The Saturday Evening Post: Seventy Years of Outstanding Illustration from America's Favorite Magazine*, London: Viking Penguin.

Crowther, B. (1944) '"American Romance," Big Scenic Film, with Brian Donlevy at Loew's State–Bill at Music Hall "Together Again"', *New York Times*, 24 November 1944: 19.

Durgnat, R. and Simmon, S. (1988) *King Vidor, American*, Berkeley, Calif.: University of California Press.

Greene, B. (2001) 'A Place That Reminds Us: We Can Do Anything', *Jewish World Review*, 18 October 2001, Online. Available HTTP: <http://www.jewishworldreview.com/bob/greene101801.asp> (accessed 1 September 2005).

Keene, J. D. (2001) *Doughboys, the Great War, and the Remaking of America*, Baltimore, Md.: The Johns Hopkins University Press.

Koppes, C. R. and Black, G. D. (1990) *Hollywood Goes to War: How Politics, Profits and Propaganda Shaped World War II Movies*, Berkeley, Calif.: University of California Press.

Levy, E. (1991) *Small Town America in Film: The Decline and Fall of Community*, New York: Continuum.

Lorentz, P. (1938) 'Men Make Steel', in P. Lorentz (1975) *Lorentz on Film: Movies 1927 to 1941*, New York: Hopkinson and Blake, pp. 154–7.

Marling, K. A. (1984) *The Colossus of Roads: Myth and Symbol along the American Highway*, Minneapolis, Minn.: The University of Minnesota Press.

Mauss, M. (1967) *The Gift: Forms and Functions of Exchange in Archaic Societies*, trans. Ian Cunnison, New York: W.W. Norton.

Mund, V. (1999) 'King Vidor', in T. Koebner (ed.) *Filmregisseure: Biographien, Werkbeschreibungen, Filmographien*, Stuttgart: Reclam, pp. 715–17.

Neupert, R. (1990) 'Technicolor and Hollywood: Exercising Color Restraint', *Post Script*, (1): 21–9.

Vidor, K. (1953) *A Tree is a Tree: An Autobiography*, Hollywood, Calif.: Samuel French.

—— (1972) *King Vidor on Film Making*, New York: McKay.

—— (1975) 'Prologue', in P. Lorentz, *Lorentz on Film: Movies 1927 to 1941*, New York: Hopkinson and Blake, pp. 1–3.

—— (1988) *King Vidor*. Interviewed by N. Dowd and D. Shepard, in D. Shepard (ed.) *The Directors Guild of America Oral History Series*, Vol. IV, Metuchen, NJ: Scarecrow.

Walker, D. A. (1979) *Iron Frontier: The Discovery and Early Development of Minnesota's Three Ranges*, St Paul, Minn.: Minnesota Historical Society Press.

Weiler, A. H. (1944) 'Donlevy, The Miner', *New York Times*, 20 August 1944, p. X3.

Wilson, E. (1944) 'An American Romance', *Liberty*, 11 November 1944, pp. 34–5 and 88–9.

Winkler, A. M. (1978) *The Politics of Propaganda: The Office of War Information 1942–1945*, New Haven, Conn.: Yale University Press.

—— (1986) *Home Front U.S.A.: America During World War II*, Arlington Heights, Ill.: Harlan Davidson.

Chapter 5

An American in Paris (1951)

Pam Cook

An American in Paris, directed by Vincente Minnelli and starring Gene Kelly and Leslie Caron, is widely celebrated as one of the high points of the golden era of MGM musicals in the 1940s and 1950s. Despite being perceived by some as less successful than *On the Town* (Stanley Donen and Gene Kelly, 1949) and *Singin' in the Rain* (Stanley Donen and Gene Kelly, 1952), the film retains a special place in the canons which have grown up around the production of the musical in this period: as a major success for the Arthur Freed unit (songwriter-turned-producer Freed received a Best Picture Academy Award for *An American in Paris*); as one of Minnelli's most sophisticated and stylish works; and as a demonstration of Gene Kelly's virtuosity as dancer, singer, choreographer and director at the peak of his career. *An American in Paris* was nominated for eight Academy Awards and gained six: Best Picture (against Elia Kazan's *A Streetcar Named Desire* and George Stevens' *A Place in the Sun*), Best Story and Screenplay, Best Music Score, Best Costume Design, Best Cinematography and Best Art Direction/Set Decoration (Robinson 2004). This list is significant for its validation of the film as a pinnacle of studio production, rather than an achievement by its director or star.[1] In emphasizing the creative contribution of teams of craftspeople, it asserts the status of the Hollywood studios at a time when the American film industry was under pressure from several directions.[2] The post-war period witnessed a series of far-reaching changes to the studio system that would transform 'old' into 'new', or 'classical' into 'post-classical' Hollywood.

An American in Paris, along with other MGM musicals of the time, can be seen as a bravura attempt to put on display the superior facilities and resources, creative talent and technical know-how of a major Hollywood studio at the height of its power. It exudes energy and optimism, affirming a national product to audiences at home and abroad. Technically challenging set pieces, complex choreography, innovative special effects, dazzling visual design and inventive interpretation of song-and-dance numbers are the hallmarks of the Hollywood studio musical, and *An American in Paris* has all these elements in abundance. Add to this the presence of Gene Kelly, a charismatic performer who combined athleticism and physical strength with graceful movement and the ability to push back the boundaries of American dance, and the package was complete. Despite his remarkable gifts, Kelly's image in films such as *For Me and My Gal* (Busby Berkeley, 1942), *Cover Girl* (Charles Vidor, 1944), *Anchors Aweigh* (George Sidney, 1945) and *On the Town* was that of an 'ordinary American guy'. His muscular physique and robust performance style epitomized the post-war American masculinity embodied in emerging stars such as Marlon Brando, and though he is usually perceived as confident and ebullient, his characters often had a darker side. Kelly's populist credentials, conflicted persona and reputation as an innovator were all at the heart of the 'Americanness' portrayed in *An American in Paris*.[3]

In this chapter, I shall explore how *An American in Paris* formulates and debates American national identity at a time when this identity was in question at home and in the rest of the world. The film does not consciously set out to present a treatise; rather, it negotiates a range of popular ideas of American and French culture in order to resolve perceived ideological conflicts between the two. In the process, it produces a relatively pessimistic view of the prospect of cultural exchange and reciprocity that appears to run counter to both Hollywood musical conventions and contemporary socio-political pressures. I have argued elsewhere that national identity cannot be viewed in terms of a stable set of core motifs or fixed stereotypes; I prefer to think of it as a dynamic relationship between the home nation and those it designates as foreign 'others', both internal and external (Cook 1996). The terms of this relationship are influenced by specific historical circumstances and are continually reinvented, a process that produces multiple, conflicting discursive ruminations emanating from different locations that, however apparently marginal, must play a part in the formations of national identity current at any given moment. I shall approach the film as an example of such discursive activity, exploring its cultural context and the social, political, economic and industrial factors which may have had an impact on its depiction of Americanness. That depiction is complex and contradictory, reflecting anxiety about the relationship between the US and France: on one hand, the film celebrates a romantic American dream of Paris, in which each nation finds common ground with the other; on the other, it portrays that dream as mere façade, fraught with doubt and deception. The title is equally ambiguous, confidently nominating its protagonist/star as both unique in terms of national origin and typical (representing every American), yet intimating his displacement. It affirms America's long-standing love affair with Paris, while simultaneously alluding to national alienation and exile. It could also be understood as hinting at the renewed US military presence in France following the signing of the NATO agreement in 1949 (Kuisel 1993: 21), and at the post-war aspirations of the United States to extend its global reach in western Europe.

An American in Paris participated in attempts by the American film industry to build bridges between itself and Europe (France was one of its biggest markets besides Britain) at a particularly difficult time in US–European relations. There is a discernible propaganda element to the film, part of its purpose being to promote greater understanding between the French and Americans in the interests of strengthening cultural links between western Europe and the USA.[4] This was a tricky project, since many Continental Europeans were suspicious of America's motives. *An American in Paris* addresses the business of seducing the French[5] at several levels, some more obvious than others. The plot itself revolves around the seduction of a young Parisian shop assistant, Lise Bouvier (Caron) by Jerry Mulligan (Kelly), an ex-GI leading a bohemian existence as a penniless artist in post-war Paris. The cross-cultural romance is a conventional vehicle for exploring national difference and conflict, and it also commonly features themes of tradition and modernity, the legacy of the past (perceived as an exotic and alluring realm) and moral questions of desire and self-sacrifice.[6] *An American in Paris* is no exception; as Jerry pursues Lise, his progress is impeded by her engagement to French music hall star Henri Baurel (Georges Guétary), a suave older man to whom she owes a debt for his protection during the war, and by the attentions of wealthy American art patron Milo Roberts (Nina Foch), who furthers her sexual interest in Jerry by sponsoring his painting career. When Henri is offered an opportunity to work in America, Lise agrees to go with him, despite being in love with Jerry. Desperately unhappy, Jerry turns to Milo for comfort, but finds he cannot forget Lise. On the night of their departure for America, Henri discovers that Lise loves Jerry, and gives her up in an act of self-sacrifice.

On the bare bones of this narrative, in which love overcomes obstacles such as cultural difference, duty and poverty, are hung spectacular song-and-dance numbers that foreground elements of visual design such as set decoration, costume and colour, as well as choreography, gesture and performance and music. These interludes are based on popular ditties written by George and Ira Gershwin in the 1920s and 1930s. Arthur Freed had bought the title 'An American in Paris' from his friend Ira Gershwin, along with the rights to the entire catalogue of George Gershwin's musical compositions, following the latter's death in 1937. Apparently, Alan Jay Lerner was presented with the title, hundreds of songs and six months to come up with a screenplay (Levinson, n.d.). The song-and-dance routines do not help to tell the story; rather, they provide a thematic commentary that operates on a different level than narrative or dialogue. The numbers deal with the interior, subjective world of the characters, providing visual and auditory clues about their state of mind, but they also deploy allusion to conjure another layer of meaning. The visual codes are not necessarily transparent, and they require the audience to engage in an activity of decipherment distinct from the business of reading the narrative. Some allusions are easier to interpret than others, and their meaning changes according to different reception contexts. There will always be a degree of openness (and therefore contestation) about the activity of interpretation, but I hope to establish that the visual components of *An American in Paris* play a vital role in the film's project of promoting cultural exchange and reciprocity between the USA and France. Those components are also employed to question the feasibility of such an enterprise, thus undermining the utopian resolution characteristic of the Hollywood musical.

Locating *An American in Paris* within the broad social context of US–European relations in the post-war period immediately raises the issue of the relationship of text to context. My aim is to trace some of the discourses in play at the time of the film's production and suggest the way they are re-presented and reinvented by the film text. Through this creative process, the text actively participates in the production and re-production of discourses, and my own reading, as well as those of others, contributes to this dynamic. *An American in Paris* lends itself to this approach: numbers such as 'Embraceable You' and 'I Got Rhythm' deal explicitly with cultural differences, translation and interpretation. Like other MGM musicals, it privileges fantasy over 'reality', at the same time as commenting on the limits of fantasy in providing an escape from reality.[7] The opening sequence, in which travelogue-style location footage of Paris is coupled with Jerry's voice-over explaining how he came to be living there, is a case in point. From the beginning, post-war Paris is explicitly presented as a fantasy escape route, filtered through Jerry's imagination: 'This is Paris. And I'm an American who lives here. [. . .] I'm an ex-GI. In 1945, when the army told me to find my own job, I stayed on, and I'll tell you why. I'm a painter. All my life, that's all I've ever wanted to do. [. . .] For a painter, the Mecca of the world for study, for inspiration, and for living is here on this star called Paris. [. . .] Back home everyone said I didn't have any talent. They might be saying the same thing over here, but it sounds better in French.'

Jerry's monologue, which reveals his disenchantment with America and infatuation with Paris, smooths the transition between the location footage, which features several of the tourist landmarks that figure in the closing 'American in Paris' ballet, and the studio recreation of the street on the Left Bank where he lives and works. The elision is deftly handled, and the set is a *tour de force* of meticulous reconstruction; nevertheless, it is clearly a painted set, reminiscent of the nostalgic pictures and prints sold as souvenirs to tourists, depicting Old Paris.[8] Indeed, were it not for the contemporary posters in the foreground, the scene could be set in any period. The quaint flower stall, cobbled street, pavement café and the priest riding a bicycle conjure up a community uncontaminated by the pressures of modern urban existence and apparently untouched by the ravages of the recent war. In these opening sequences, Paris, as seen through Jerry's expatriate eyes, offers an alternative to the productivity-centred, conspicuous consumption of the USA. The film does not recreate Paris as the progressive haven for freethinkers that drew many American artists and intellectuals in the 1920s and 1930s away from a puritanical, repressive homeland. Apart from references to surrealism in the design of the Beaux-Arts ball, it harks back to the impressionists and post-impressionists whose dramatic use of colour and light not only provided the film-makers' inspiration but also offered a repertoire of popular images of Paris in the late nineteenth and early twentieth centuries. This period, during which Paris was a centre for artistic and technological innovation, witnessed the convergence of modernism with mass culture, as painters chose to depict subjects taken from everyday life and burgeoning popular entertainment.

Jerry's identification with this vision of Paris as a hub of creative activity and his wish to find a 'home' there are questioned in the course of the film, as are the motives of other American characters living there. His disenchantment with US-style progress leads to a confrontation with the French past that threatens his American identity. Although the film does not refer directly to social context, its destabilization of Jerry's fantasy relationship with Paris can be seen as an allusion to the reality of US–French relations at this time. Following the Second World War, the traditional hostility of the French towards America was revived as the USA began its campaign to establish itself as a global superpower, and self-appointed guardian of world peace.[9] The nations of western Europe (among whom France was one of the most powerful) figured prominently in plans for the economic, military and political reconstruction of a continent devastated by war, using American methods of modernization as a model. The post-war swing to the left across most of Europe was a major cause for concern, as it fuelled resistance to capitalism as well as fascism in countries outside Soviet-aligned eastern Europe (Reynolds 1997). Indeed, many western European leaders regarded 'the red tooth and claw of American capitalism' with as much suspicion as they did 'the Communist dictatorship of Soviet Russia'.[10] With western Europe wishing to remain independent of both new superpowers, the USA found it difficult to establish the reciprocal trade and cultural agreements which it hoped would regenerate its markets and stem the tide of Communism. The solution to this precarious situation was an economic recovery programme proposed by Secretary George Marshall in 1947 in a speech delivered at Harvard, which invited Europeans to come up with their own ideas for American aid to the continent. Marshall's insistence that the initiative should come from Europe propelled Britain and France to lead the European response, paving the way for a period of intense debate and negotiation from 1947 to 1950 which laid the groundwork for the future shape of Europe and its relations with the USA.[11]

The significance of the Marshall Plan for my argument is that it was not simply an economic aid programme, but a major political and ideological offensive that recognised the importance of winning over the European sceptics. France was gradually won over and aligned itself politically with the USA in 1949.[12] However, the friction between the two countries continued into the late 1940s and early 1950s, when acrimonious quarrels over trade barriers led to recriminations on the part of the USA, and increased hostility from the French.[13] Thus the period in which *An American in Paris* was produced was characterized by conflict between the two countries, as well as major diplomatic initiatives on the part of the USA aimed at stabilizing this volatile situation and creating circumstances favourable to its perceived mission. The latter was to lead western Europe into a programme of technological and economic modernization aimed at increasing productivity and fostering the transition to a consumer economy.[14] Even those French people who welcomed American financial aid were often suspicious of the motives underlying this apparent generosity and concerned that Americanization would colonize and erode 'the French character'. Although these attitudes were most vocally expressed in official circles and by leading social commentators, there was evidence of debate among unions and ordinary people too. Public awareness of the issues was high, and national stereotypes, positive and negative, proliferated on both sides. The French favoured views of Americans as infantile, young, arrogant, optimistic, materialistic, wealthy, puritanical, conformist, pragmatic and addicted to popular culture, while Americans saw the French as, among other things, culturally superior, sophisticated, snobbish, backward-looking, intellectual, bohemian and dominated by tradition.[15]

Most significant for my analysis is the fact that the Americans believed that the success of the Marshall Plan, in its widest sense as an economic, political and ideological campaign, depended on persuasion at all levels, from the refined echelons of political diplomacy to the everyday experience of ordinary Europeans and Americans, who were invited to participate in a process of reassessment of traditional attitudes held by each towards the other. It is this context that helps to place *An American in Paris*, a Hollywood movie directed at European audiences as well as Americans, as a contribution to that process of reassessment.[16] It undertook this project via familiar images of national culture which would appeal to the public at large, and it is important to recognize that the film is a popular work primarily dedicated to entertaining audiences. Equally, however, it would be rash to assume that those who conceived and made *An American in Paris* were entirely innocent of the broader social circumstances.

It is frequently asserted that the film-makers (particularly Kelly, reputed to be a Francophile) initially wanted to shoot the film on location in Paris, to give it a more realistic aura. *On the Town* had been shot on location in New York and had been praised for its authenticity by reviewers.[17] However, the decision was taken to reconstruct the French city entirely in the studio, with forty-four specially built, elaborate sets and minimal use of location material.[18] According to Director of Photography Alfred Gilks, the avowed intention was 'to do a picture which would reflect the real heart and emotional appeal [. . .] of the city [. . .] regarded by travelers, painters and story tellers as the most romantic in the world'. Gilks's account reveals that, despite the deliberate choice to recreate Paris as a fiction through images borrowed from photographs, prints and impressionist paintings, the film-makers went to great lengths to achieve authenticity, defined as 'a higher and more artistic form of realism' in which the camera faithfully interpreted 'the sense of the young painter's inner vision' of the magical city (Gilks 1952: 39). The challenges of this task resulted in a development period extending over many months (Gilks 1952: 18). The US press book emphasized the six-month-long preparation period for the lavish ballet number and quoted Minnelli as describing this fantasy sequence as presenting 'the half-real world which makes things even more real'.[19] Despite the claims to realism, the film makes it clear that the Paris it recreates is an American dream, a fact that led some reviewers to condemn it as tasteless and patronizing.[20]

The choice to shoot the entire film in the studio had a number of advantages. It would be cheaper than transporting the crew, equipment and actors to the location, even if studio construction work was extensive. It also enabled the film-makers to plan in advance the lighting, colour and camerawork, as well as to control sound recording. The production design was crucial in presenting a painterly vision of Paris that would project the city through the imagination of an expatriate American would-be artist. Jerry identifies Paris with a tradition of high art which he aspires to yet finds daunting and overwhelming – an ambivalent perspective which would not necessarily be that of the everyday American tourist. Indeed, Jerry consciously distinguishes himself from American tourists in Paris: he has lived there for two years and is accepted by the locals, even speaking rudimentary French. He despises those Americans who come full of highbrow ideas and fail to understand the real heart of the city and the experience it offers. He is also suspicious of wealthy visitors like Milo Roberts who exploit local talent for selfish reasons, without appreciating the creative process. In an early scene without dialogue, his sympathy for French resistance to US-style modernization is intimated as, in a brilliant display of inventive choreography, he demonstrates the efficiency of his tiny studio apartment, with its foldaway bed and bathroom and drop-down table. The scene is reminiscent of a Chaplinesque lampoon of technological progress.

Jerry appears to be a displaced person, alienated from his home culture, yet not fully integrated into the one he has chosen to inhabit. His cynical friend Adam Cook (Oscar Levant) is similarly displaced, an aspiring concert pianist and composer who scrapes a living playing piano in local cafés and describes himself as 'the world's oldest child prodigy'. In a virtuoso comic set piece without dialogue,

Adam envisions himself in concert playing George Gershwin's 'Piano Concerto in F' with a large orchestra to an enthralled audience. In his imagination he is not only the pianist but also the conductor, and he plays several instruments as well as applauding himself enthusiastically from the audience. Adam's narcissism and egotism are masked by his sardonic wit, which enables him to live with failure. Jerry, on the other hand, is an eternal optimist, still hoping that his talent will be recognized, despite the fact that he does not really believe in himself. In both cases, the will to succeed artistically is seen to derive from a sense of insecurity, disguised by arrogance. In an early sequence in his studio, Jerry looks critically at the charcoal self-portrait he is working on, attempts to adjust it and then erases it in disgust. This small gesture expresses his wounded narcissism, and it was not unusual for Gene Kelly to play characters afflicted by self-doubt.[21] The 'ordinary American guy' represented by Kelly had more than one dimension. His brash persona was often a cover for his sensitive side, suggesting aspects of the national character which might be useful in persuading Europeans that Americans were not all bad. The darker, mordant character of Adam Cook provided the perfect foil, his morose pessimism acting as an ironic counterpoint to Jerry's native ebullience.

The dual aspects of Jerry's personality are worked through on the thematic level, via a tension between high art (associated with France) and popular culture (identified with America). This antithesis has been discussed by Jane Feuer as a basic motif of the Hollywood musical, where it is generally presented in terms of a conflict which is resolved in favour of the popular, often through the union of the romantic couple (Feuer 1978: 491–9). Some of the characteristics of the opposition described by Feuer are relevant to *An American in Paris*, though their resolution is not secure. The film negotiates the high-art–popular-culture divide through a set of oppositions between ballet and tap dance, classical and popular music, abstract and figurative art. The conflict is embodied in Gene Kelly/Jerry Mulligan himself, whose paintings are naturalistic, while the art he reveres is modernist and whose dancing style spans the vernacular and the balletic.[22] In musical terms, all Jerry's numbers are in popular mode, and the classical manifests itself only in Adam's imaginary concert scene described above, where his high art aspirations are parodied. However, in this case too the opposition is nuanced: Feuer points out that the composer of 'Piano Concerto in F', George Gershwin, was famed for combining the popular qualities of jazz with the status and respectability of classical music.[23] After his death in 1937, his influence on the Hollywood musical continued to be felt, and the presence of music and songs by George and Ira Gershwin in *An American in Paris* plays a significant role in defining and refining perceived cultural differences between France and America. The fusion of popular- and high-art traditions in the film provides a metaphor for *rapprochement* between the two nations, viewed in terms of their cultural compatibility rather than difference. Thus, the bias in favour of the popular that Feuer identifies in the

Hollywood musical is softened, if not reversed, in *An American in Paris*, due to the impact of its historical context and its project of promoting cultural exchange.

The problems of overcoming cultural differences feature prominently in numbers such as 'Embraceable You', where Henri attempts to describe Lise to Adam, only to find that his American friend misunderstands him. Of Lise's five 'moods' represented in this scene, four are interpreted through ballet and one in Charleston style, suggesting an element of versatility in her repertoire and the influence of American popular dance.[24] It is also implied that Henri constructs his own fantasy image of Lise, as the scene begins with a reflection of Henri and Adam in a mirror, which then provides the frame for Lise's vignettes. The mirror recalls the scene in which Henri is first introduced, as a travelling shot from his point of view through the street comes to rest on his reflection in a mirror in the wall. The narcissism that characterizes Jerry and Adam is thus seen to be a French trait too, one that inhibits mutual understanding. Sometimes, however, the possibility of rapport is presented more positively. The 'I Got Rhythm' number is preceded by Jerry's return to the Old Quarter after his first meeting with oil heiress Milo Roberts, who insists that he go home in her expensive limousine. His arrival in the narrow streets of Montmartre in Milo's flashy car, which he treats with irony, is greeted with excitement by the local children, who pester him for bubblegum. Jerry responds in French, and the children demand an English lesson, whereupon Jerry, who is dressed in baseball cap, sweater with sleeves rolled up, slacks and loafers, gives a rendition of 'I Got Rhythm' in which the children participate in English, while he sings in both English and French. He then performs 'le danse américain' (sic) in a dazzling exhibition of tap steps. This bilingual number foregrounds Kelly's genial persona as a regular American guy, while simultaneously suggesting his partial integration into French culture. Popular American song and dance provide the means to overcome language barriers, bringing the nations closer together. In another spectacular number, Henri sings 'Stairway to Paradise' in English in a French theatre reminiscent of both the Folies-Bergère and the Ziegfeld Follies, surrounded by statuesque showgirls in elaborate costumes. As he climbs the huge staircase, each step lights up beneath his feet, providing a visual realization of the confidence and optimism transmitted by the song.[25] Immediately after performing this tribute to cultural compatibility, Henri is offered the chance to go to the USA by an American impresario.

'Stairway to Paradise' presents a spatial metaphor for the opportunities offered by the USA, and visualizes the upward mobility of a modern utopia characterized by abundance and material success. Despite Jerry's romantic, bohemian vision of Paris, there are signs that the French are open to the attractions of consumerism. Paris is not only the Mecca of high culture but is also an exclusive shopping centre for tourists, as Jerry's encounter with the American woman who buys expensive perfume in the shop where Lise works testifies: a reminder, perhaps, of the value of the US market to France. The scene in which Henri and Jerry perform ''S Wonderful' together, unaware that they are in love with the same girl, takes place against a wall plastered with posters advertising luxury goods such as Perrier and Vittelloise mineral water, silk stockings and wine, intimating the sophisticated and exotic lifestyle that French commodities offered. However, the utopian vision of cultural reciprocity is shadowed by the past: by recent history, represented by the French experience of the Second World War; France's pride in its national traditions; and its past as a colonial power. The war is the major obstacle to Jerry and Lise's union, since Lise owes Henri a debt of gratitude linked to his role as her guardian when her parents were fighting with the Resistance. It is explicitly referred to several times: as Jerry bounds through the streets of Montmartre, he comes across a familiar figure sat at an easel who resembles British Conservative Prime Minister Winston Churchill, out of a job at that time and able to enjoy his favourite pastime. In a more sinister vein, as Adam, Henri and Jerry perform 'By Strauss' as a parody of Viennese-style operetta in the café, a poster advertising 'byrrh' in the foreground is a reminder of the German occupation.

The darkness shrouding Jerry and Lise's love is opposed in spatial terms to the 'Stairway to Paradise' imagery. They meet in secret by the mist-swathed banks of the Seine, descending a slippery staircase to the quayside, where they are surrounded by dank stone walls. The scenes that take place here are sombre and reflective, providing the backdrop for the bittersweet rendition of 'Our Love Is Here to Stay', in which they circle one another in a tentative expression of their blossoming romance, and for the traumatic episode in which Lise reveals her commitment to Henri, breaking Jerry's heart. The staircase here represents conflict and separation, as both Lise and Jerry use it to run away from each other. The sense that the legacy of the past will impede their union is reinforced at the carnivalesque Beaux-Arts ball, as Jerry and Lise say goodbye, looking out over the beautiful vista of Paris by night. Lise tells Jerry that Paris has ways of making people forget, but Jerry responds: 'Not this city. [. . .] It never lets you forget anything. It reaches in and opens you wide, and you stay that way.' In his bitterness, Jerry rips in half the black-and-white sketch of the Place de l'Étoile that he has drawn, and it drifts away, mingling with windswept scraps of paper in a visualization of his tattered dreams.

The ball itself is a riotous masquerade designed in black and white by Walter Plunkett and featuring outrageous costumes influenced by surrealism, with over-tones of travesty.[26] The ball sequence is a fitting prelude to the ballet, in which Jerry's fantasy of Paris is revealed as illusion. Here everyone is in disguise and nothing is as it seems, as Jerry confirms when he admits his unhappiness to Milo, confessing that his cheerful demeanour is fake. Jerry is dressed as Harlequin, with one half of his outfit decorated with black diamonds on white, while the other half is black. Lise's white tulle dress, its waistband motif tied at the back with a bow, suggesting an apron, evokes Columbine's costume. The references to *commedia dell'arte* are not incidental; the narrative of *An American in Paris*, with its love triangles and scenario of frustrated amorous entanglements, resembles the stock storylines found in this popular European theatrical tradition. Indeed, if Jerry can be seen as the irrepressible Harlequin to Lise's fickle Columbine, Adam's role as confidant to Henri and Jerry echoes that of the melancholy Pierrot, while Henri as Lise's older suitor compares to Pantalone and Milo relates to one of Harlequin's lustful upper-class female admirers. However, in a characteristic role-reversal, Jerry's two-sided masquerade costume fuses buoyant Harlequin and mournful Pierrot, symbolizing the dual aspects of his personality.[27] It also provides a visual link to the black outfit he wears at the beginning of the ballet sequence that follows.

This 17-minute extravaganza is the film's pièce de résistance, representing pictorially and through music and dance the enchantment and disillusionment of Jerry's encounter with French culture. The spectacular number was filmed after the rest of the production had finished shooting and is reputed to have taken six weeks to rehearse. Minnelli and Kelly collaborated on the libretto, while Irene Sharaff, who had studied art in Paris and New York and was renowned for her work on Broadway as well as film, designed the costumes.[28] The US press book acknowledged the debt of this sequence to the ambitious ballet staged in Powell and Pressburger's *The Red Shoes* (1948), whose American box-office success had lasted two years.[29] *The Red Shoes* concerned a young ballerina (Moira Shearer) forced to choose between her controlling mentor (Anton Walbrook) and the talented composer (Marius Goring) with whom she falls in love. The ballet sequence told the story and its tragic outcome through dance and music set against backdrops in modernist styles such as cubism and surrealism, using elaborate visual effects to depict the nightmarish experience of the heroine. The press book's tribute to this British film is suggestive: Powell and Pressburger were well known for their pan-European working methods and aesthetic heritage, so this may well have been a further attempt to forge cross-cultural links. However, *The Red Shoes* projected a darkly pessimistic view of British–European collaboration, and it is this influence which is visible in the ballet sequence of *An American in Paris*, as Jerry's love affair with Paris and Lise becomes a crisis of national identity for him. Portrayed as Jerry's subjective vision, with the camera closing in on his face at the end of the Beaux-Arts ball, the ballet dramatizes his passionate pursuit of the elusive Lise, who seems to embody the mercurial spirit of the city that enchants and intimidates him. They dance around sets painted in the style of the artists that Jerry admires: the Place de l'Étoile and the Place de la Concorde (Dufy), the Madeleine flower market (Renoir), a street scene (Utrillo), the Jardin des Plantes (Rousseau), the Place de l'Opéra (Van Gogh), and the Moulin Rouge (Toulouse-Lautrec).[30]

This is a modern piece that mixes music and dance styles from ballet to tap to jazz dance and appears to celebrate the fusion of popular forms with high art, and cultural connections between France and the USA. However, the colour design tells another story. Jerry, dressed in black with touches of white, pictures himself against a background of sets and costumes tinted red, white and blue, the colours of the French national flag. The film uses these colours more than once to foreground French national identity: the opening credits, for example, feature the revolutionary tricolour ribbon, overlaid with the heraldic fleur-de-lis, while Lise's Frenchness is marked in the scene where Jerry first meets her in the cellar bar by her red, white and blue outfit. These colours dominate the ballet until the penultimate scenes in the Place de l'Opéra and the Moulin Rouge and, indeed, the French flag itself is glimpsed for sale in the Jardin des Plantes. By contrast, the American flag is notably absent. Jerry's black costume suggests his lack of identity, and his attempts to adopt France as his 'home' are thwarted as he is persecuted by vengeful Furies and spurned by characters from France's cultural heritage. He appears overwhelmed as he chases and loses a capricious Lise against the background of the nation's military and colonial past.

Depressed by his failure, he gains temporary relief when he meets four GIs on leave and they unite to perform an exhilarating tap routine, dressed in colourful striped blazers, slacks and boaters evoking American jazz dance. This culminates in a face-off between Jerry's tap-dancing skills and Lise's ballet expertise which ends in *rapprochement*, with Jerry and Lise now partners as they move into the final scenes, which become increasingly sensual. In a seductive dance set in the fountain of the Place de la Concorde, the black of Jerry's costume is transformed by the lighting into a blue shade that matches Lise's dress. Following an exuberant interlude against the backdrop of the Place de l'Opéra in which the couple interact with a variety of French characters, Jerry's cultural integration is expressed in an extraordinary number in which he imitates the black clown Chocolat, celebrated in the famous Toulouse-Lautrec sketch 'Chocolat dansant dans un bar'. Jerry, dressed in a revealing, figure-hugging white costume and executing a suggestive jazz dance, becomes Chocolat to Lise's Jane Avril,[31] as she displays her underwear in a risqué rendition of the can-can at the Moulin Rouge. The connotations of this episode are complex: Jerry's adoption of Chocolat's identity can be seen as colonization of black artistic accomplishment by a white performer, an accusation which might also be levelled at Gene Kelly's appropriation of African-American dance. However, in the context of Jerry's dream, it represents affinity between American and French culture: Chocolat frequented the Irish and American Bar, a reference to Kelly's origins.[32] Jerry's impersonation does not qualify as mimicry, since he is not wearing blackface; rather, it can be understood as homage, albeit ambiguous. There is a further layer of ambiguity in the connections between Chocolat and Harlequin, whose use of a black mask has been construed as a play with racial stereotypes (Smalls 2003: 361). Thus, Jerry's masquerade could be interpreted as pointing to a fluidity of identity which would facilitate cross-cultural assimilation. At the same time, the Mardi Gras aspects of this section of the ballet allude to chaos and disorder, implying miscegenation rather than social harmony.

As the pace quickens, Lise and Jerry (dressed in black once more) gyrate with the other dancers in front of tall mirrors whose glancing reflections create a kaleidoscope of frenetic movement and colour. This scene is difficult to interpret; on one hand, it appears to affirm the meeting (mirroring) of cultures, on the other it seems fraught with the dangers of loss of identity, as the mobile mirrors fracture the space and the whirling dancers' bodies. The frenzied atmosphere borders on hysteria, evoking anxiety as well as euphoria. The sense of delirium continues as the wild dance segues into the red, white and blue tones of the final ecstatic number in the Place de la Concorde fountain, where Lise wears a white dress with a tri-colour ribbon around her waist. At the climax, Lise and the other dancers suddenly disappear and Jerry finds himself alone against the monochrome Place de l'Étoile backdrop, with the red rose which symbolizes his love for Lise and Paris the only remnant of his fantasy. As the screen fades to melancholy black, the camera irises in on the rose, which dissolves into a close-up of Jerry's grief-stricken face at the Beaux-Arts ball. Closing his eyes in a gesture of despair and resignation, Jerry turns to walk away, acknowledging that his dream is not to be. At that moment, a car horn sounds the return of Henri and Lise.

The film's final sequence, in which Henri gives up Lise to Jerry, can be interpreted as a utopian union of the romantic couple, made possible by the self-sacrifice of both Henri and Jerry. There is an implication that the French and Americans will have to meet halfway, visualized spatially when Jerry runs down the staircase outside as Lise climbs up it, and they embrace in the middle. However, it is striking that the couple, still decked out as Harlequin and Columbine, then descend together to the pavement in a movement opposite to the upward motion of the 'Stairway to Paradise' number. In a joyous gesture, the camera swoops up to reveal the Paris skyline, but their downward steps remain tentative, as if they are aware that their future relationship might encounter further obstacles. But if the film can be seen to recognize the existence of continuing difficulties in the process of cultural exchange, the US press book was oblivious to any problems, suggesting multiple tie-ins to tourism, men's and women's fashion, French lessons, dance and art classes, commodities such as perfume, jewellery, cars, records and even ideas to attract French war brides living in America, all of which emphasized potential cultural links rather than differences. The breezy optimism of the press book is only partly reflected in the film itself, which engages with a range of contradictory discourses on cultural relations between France and America, circulating around axes of high/low culture, tradition/modernity and progress/stasis in order to articulate its own hesitation about the prospect of cooperation between the nations.

Although this hint of darkness and doubt is not absent from other Hollywood musicals, it overshadows *An American in Paris* to the extent that the utopian resolution fails. The resulting modification of the musical's narrative conventions creates an ambivalent ending closer to European art cinema. The film's use of visual allusion displays a resistance to interpretation which is also associated with art cinema. While this may chime with the aim of promoting cultural collaboration, it implies a European stylistic appropriation of what was often perceived at home and abroad as an American national product.[33] Ambiguity at the level of the image is employed to point up the blurring of cultural boundaries and the consequent risk to US national identity. The American dream of Paris, the fantasy projection of its Francophile protagonist/star, is exposed as dangerous delusion; it is only after relinquishing his dream that Jerry is able to unite with Lise, and even then it is not clear what his future relationship with Paris will be. Indeed, the destabilizing of Jerry's fantasy relationship with Paris reveals a void at the heart of his American identity, underlined by his Harlequin costume in the final shot.

In so far as *An American in Paris* is concerned with the reassessment of cultural attitudes, it echoes the Marshall Plan's call for Europe to rethink its past and future and its resistance to America. By challenging its hero's wishful thinking, the film also highlights the need for Americans to revise their view of France. However, *An American in Paris* stops short of endorsing the Marshall Plan's agenda for western European modernization. Instead, it ends on a note of uncertainty, leaving open the issue of what it now means to be an American in Paris, or in Europe. In this light, the title's appellation of America first can be read as ironic, allowing a question about the superiority of America in relation to France to surface. Gene Kelly's divided persona, encapsulating confidence and insecurity, arrogance and sensitivity, idealism and pragmatism, light and dark, is mobilized in the interests of working through an ambivalent perspective, enabling an exploration of the boundaries of national identity which is never completely resolved.

Notes

1 Gene Kelly received an honorary award from the Academy in the same year, 'in appreciation of his versatility as an actor, singer, director and dancer, and specifically for his brilliant achievements in the art of choreography on film'. See T. Dirks, 'An American in Paris'. Online. Available HTTP: <http://www.filmsite.org/amer.html> (accessed 15 February 2005). Neither Minnelli nor Kelly received an award for *An American in Paris*.

2 Anti-trust legislation in the late 1940s and 1950s heralded a period of major reorganization of the Hollywood studio system and its methods of production, distribution and exhibition. At the same time, television and other leisure pursuits were poaching audiences from cinema, causing the industry to respond competitively with new kinds of product. Immediately following the Second World War, the House Un-American Activities Committee (HUAC) launched an assault on Communist activity

in Hollywood, forcing the industry to resort to defensive measures, among them self-censorship. In addition, the American film industry faced major problems in selling its product to European markets in the wake of the Second World War.

3 Examples of Kelly's inventiveness had been seen in 'Alter Ego', a double-exposure solo number in *Cover Girl*; a live action and animated sequence featuring Jerry the Mouse in *Anchors Aweigh*; and the 'Slaughter on 10th Avenue' ballet in *Words and Music* (1948). His roots were in vaudeville and Broadway, and he was known for his creative reinterpretation of African-American jazz dance.

4 Historian Ian Jarvie, writing about Hollywood's delicate relationship with the British and Canadian film industries between 1945 and 1950, offers primary evidence of the significance attached to ideological matters by the Americans, and the hostile reception to 'Hollywood's lying propaganda' on the part of those they hoped to win over (see Jarvie 1992: 415). Jarvie also offers comparative information on other film industries, including the French (1992: 409).

5 This phrase is borrowed from the title of Richard Kuisel's book (1993).

6 A comparable example is discussed in Cook (2002). Minnelli's 1954 film *Brigadoon* uses the same plot structure.

7 The relationship of fantasy to reality is also a primary theme in *Meet Me in St. Louis* (Vincente Minnelli, 1944) and *Brigadoon* (Vincente Minnelli, 1954), and in the more 'realist' musical *West Side Story* (Jerome Robbins and Robert Wise, 1961), where it is given a political edge in numbers such as 'America'.

8 During a holiday in Paris in the 1950s, my parents bought an original oil painting in this nostalgia genre from a local artist, which they kept for fifty years.

9 My analysis of the social and cultural background of US–French relations in the post-war period draws heavily on Kuisel's account in *Seducing the French* (1993). Kuisel examines a range of contemporary discourses, from official documents and opinion polls to newspapers and books, from which he pieces together the mixed response of the French to the American intervention in western European affairs. He acknowledges the limitations of his methodology, which focuses on particular strata of French society, but his fusion of political, economic and cultural analysis produces a richly textured picture of French attitudes towards America, which is particularly useful for my argument. Kuisel establishes that America was acutely aware of the resistance to its hegemony in Europe and mounted an extensive propaganda campaign to overcome negative perceptions of its economic and cultural aspirations.

10 British Foreign Secretary Ernest Bevin speaking in 1946, quoted by Reynolds (1997).

11 Reynolds (1997) sees the Marshall Plan as instrumental in the division of Europe into east and west, and thus as contributing substantially to increasing antagonism between the Soviet Union and America. He also sees the plan as a major force in defining post-war Europe.

12 In 1949, France and America signed a military alliance, the North Atlantic Treaty Organization, and were soon fighting a joint war in Indochina (Kuisel 1993: 19).

13 These disputes partly concerned reciprocity between the US and the French film industries. The Fourth Republic took protectionist measures to prevent American films from swamping the French market, whereupon the USA retaliated by insisting that as

a condition of the Blum–Byrnes loan, set up in 1946 as interim aid, the French should remove barriers to Hollywood imports. The French took exception to this demand, especially as the USA was not willing to relax its obstacles to French imports. The ensuing outcry led to the scrapping of the Blum–Byrnes agreement (Kuisel 1993: 19).

14 The USA invested a great deal in this modernization programme and went to great lengths to convince European workers, especially in France, West Germany and Italy, that the Marshall Plan was to their advantage. According to Reynolds (1997), 'By the end of 1950, 40 films had been made, shown in town cinemas and by mobile projection units, and 6.7 million Italians had visited ECA [Economic Co-operation Administra-tion] exhibitions' (<http://www.foreignaffairs.org/19970501faessay 3823-p0/david-reynolds/marshall-plan-commemorative-section-the-european-response-primacy-of-politics.html>, p. 5). Kuisel describes the French response to these tactics, and also outlines the cultural exchange programme by which teams of French businessmen, engineers and workers were sent to tour American plants in order to study the principles of US economic growth (1993: 70–102).

15 This is a necessarily schematic list of national stereotypes. Kuisel warns against ignoring the process whereby stereotypes are constantly in flux due to changing historical circumstances (1993: 9–10).

16 The release pattern of An American in Paris is interesting in this respect. According to the IMDB, it was first released in New York on 4 October 1951, and in Continental Europe some time later: 4 February 1952 in Denmark; 25 February 1952 in Sweden; 1 May 1952 in Finland; and 24 December 1952 in West Germany. Online. Available HTTP: <http://www.imdb.com/title/tt0043278/releaseinfo> (accessed 11 May 2004). According to the French database BiFi, it was first released in Paris on 13 June 1952 (Le Cid, on-line information service, by e-mail, 31 January 2005). The British release date is given by Kinematograph Yearbook 1952 (1952) as 22 October 1951. The film's release in Continental Europe appears to have been limited, but it was released in key Marshall Plan countries such as Britain, France and West Germany (the British Film Institute has copies of the British and West German press books, available on microfilm).

17 See IMDB, 'Trivia for American in Paris, An'. Online. Available HTTP: <http://www.imdb.com/title/tt0043278/trivia> (accessed 22 February 2005). There are conflicting accounts as to why the plan to film on location was abandoned. In his biography of Gene Kelly, Yudkoff claims that Freed resisted Kelly's wishes because of logistical problems and the difficulties of dealing with French bureaucracy (1999: 210). Minnelli puts the decision down to timetabling and technical constraints (in Minnelli 1974: 239–40).

18 Location footage was used only in the opening travelogue-style sequence, the scene in which Milo and Jerry go in her limousine to the Ritz hotel (for which doubles were used), and the rear projection when Jerry and Lise are travelling through Paris in a taxi.

19 US press campaign book, available on microfilm at the British Film Institute library.

20 See, for example, the Daily Worker review of 18 August 1951, available on microfiche at the BFI library. More recently, Julie Levinson in an undated National Film Theatre

(NFT) Programme Note described the film as an 'American's eye-view of life in gay Paree (. . .) garnished with several bromidic, self-consciously French touches of the ooh-la-la variety' (available on microfilm at the BFI library).

21 In *Cover Girl* (1944), Kelly executed a dance number in which his bravura performance is halted when he sees his reflection in a shop window. His reflection dances hesitantly, expressing his inner doubt, in contrast to the confident and expansive style of the 'real' character's body movements. The latter smashes the shop window with a brick in order to destroy his insecure alter ego.

22 Apparently Gene Kelly was chosen for the role of Jerry Mulligan because he had the dancing skills necessary for the ballet sequence (see Levinson, n.d.). However, the film showcases Kelly's versatility, and he demonstrates extraordinary skill in both tap- and ballet-dance numbers.

23 See Feuer 1978: 497. Feuer points out that the classical music performed in the Hollywood musical is already popular. The musical can therefore be seen as fusing elite and popular art, rather than maintaining the high/low culture divide.

24 Leslie Caron's background was in ballet. She was 'discovered' by Kelly when he saw her dance in the Ballet des Champs Elysées during one of his visits to France.

25 The 'Stairway to Paradise' number was difficult to stage, since it required careful timing and a complex lighting programme to ensure that the staircase lit up at the right moment under Guétary's feet. The number was held up as a feat of technological ingenuity on the part of the studio (see Gilks 1952).

26 The scene includes a cross-dressed male couple.

27 At the ball, Adam wears a white cowboy outfit which, apart from its colour, does not recall traditional Pierrot garb. During the scene, a character dressed as Pierrot follows Jerry closely as he descends the staircase to the dance floor. Although Pierrot is normally decked out predominantly in white, the black half of Jerry's costume provides a clear indicator of his depressed state. It might also allude to Harlequin's traditional use of a black mask.

28 See the US press book. Apart from the ballet sequence and the Beaux-Arts ball, the film's costume design is credited to Orry-Kelly.

29 Some sources claim that Gene Kelly screened *The Red Shoes* for sceptical studio bosses to convince them that the ballet sequence would work. For example, IMDB, 'Trivia for American in Paris, An'. Online. Available HTTP: <http://www.imdb.com/title/tt0043278/trivia> (accessed 28 February 2005).

30 This list of references to artists corresponds to that given in the US press book, and it does stand up to closer scrutiny of the ballet sequence. The references are to the artists' more popular works.

31 Jane Avril was a dancer at the Moulin Rouge and one of Toulouse-Lautrec's favourite subjects.

32 Chocolat was an Afro-Cuban whose performance derived from American minstrelsy, which became popular in late nineteenth-century France.

33 The roots of the Hollywood musical in Broadway, with its origins in popular European theatrical traditions, indicate the permeability of boundaries between European and American cultural forms.

References

Cook, P. (1996) *Fashioning the Nation: Costume and Identity in British Cinema*, London: BFI Publishing.

—— (2002) *I Know Where I'm Going!*, London: BFI Publishing.

Feuer, J. (1978) 'The Theme of Popular vs. Elite Art In The Hollywood Musical', *Journal of Popular Culture* 12 (3), pp. 491–9.

Gilks, A. (1952) 'Some Highlights in the Filming of "An American in Paris"', *American Cinematographer*, January, pp.18–19, 36–9.

Jarvie, I. (1992) *Hollywood's Overseas Campaign: The North Atlantic Movie Trade, 1920–1950*, Cambridge: Cambridge University Press.

Kuisel, R. (1993) *Seducing the French: The Dilemma of Americanization*, Berkeley, Calif.: University of California Press.

Levinson, J. (n.d.) 'NFT Programme Note for An American in Paris'. Available on microfiche from the British Film Institute Library.

Minnelli, V. with Arce, H. (1974) *I Remember It Well*, London: Angus and Robertson.

Reynolds, D. (1997) 'Marshall Plan Commemorative Section: The European Response: Primacy of Politics', *Foreign Affairs*, May/June. On-line. Available HTTP: <http://www.foreignaffairs.org/19970501faessay3823-p0/david-reynolds/marshall-plan-commemorative-section-the-european-response-primacy-of-politics.html> (accessed 10 February 2005).

Robinson, D. (2004) 'An American in Paris: Oscar Stories', Supplement to *Sight and Sound*, 14 (2), February, n. p.

Smalls, J. (2003) '"Race" As Spectacle in Late-Nineteenth-Century French Arts and Popular Culture', *French Historical Studies*, 26 (2), pp. 351–82.

Yudkoff, A. (1999) *Gene Kelly: A Life of Dance and Dreams*, New York: Back Stage Books.

Chapter 6

The Quiet American (1958 and 2002)

Peter William Evans

'The Quiet American' seems like an oxymoron. Aren't Americans supposed to be loud? The title reflects Graham Greene's anti-Americanism, aimed above all at Monroe-doctrine foreign policy and the stealthy off-stage involvements in the affairs of other nations. 'Quiet' here means more than personal qualities of reserve or modesty, suggested for instance by John Wayne's 'quiet' man, and points in all three versions (novel and two films) to political strategies of interference and manipulation. Fowler, the English journalist soon to be embroiled in the 'quiet American's' political meddling, describes him in a way that underlines his superficial deviation from stereotype, but the reader is intended to look ahead beyond stereotype towards political meaning: 'He's a good chap in his way. Serious. Not one of those noisy bastards at the Continental. A quiet American' (Greene 2001: 17). The novel carried in their pockets by every journalist covering the Vietnam war (French 2002: 9), met with predictably negative reviews in the USA on its publication in 1955. The release of the first film version (Mankiewicz, 1958) fared little better, though Bosley Crowther, noting its moderation of the American's 'villainy', finds reasons for approval (1970: 3042). Even more recently, Andrew Sarris continues to dismiss it as a 'movie with a message' (2002: 13). Although Godard thought it was the best film of the year (Lower and Palmer 2001: 17), and Eric Rohmer considered it 'admirable' (1958: 46), British reviewers of the time tended to be uncomplimentary, especially over its reformulation of the ending, absolving the American from any involvement as a covert CIA agent in the political fortunes of a country facing a communist challenge to French colonial rule in the early 1950s.

Both 2002 and 1958 versions were made in difficult times. They are also key films about America, above all serving as invitations to American audiences for self-reflection. The Mankiewicz version asks awkward questions about self and nation as America disentangled itself from one war, Korea, only to prepare for a longer engagement in Vietnam. Noyce's *The Quiet American*, post-9/11, is brave enough to follow suit in even more difficult times, addressing key issues when 'anti-Americanism had gone out of fashion in the United States' (Queenan 2002: 8–9). By 2001, the rights to the novel were jointly owned by the Swedish producer Staffan Ahrenberg and Sydney Pollack. Their production company, Mirage Enterprises, had already been attempting to remake the film. Following a visit to the 1945 Vietnam training ground, Philip Noyce, an Australian film director with a history of politicized, socially conscious films made in Australia, such as *Newsfront* (1977), *Backroads* (1977) and *Heatwave* (1981), had also been drawn to the novel:

> I had spent time with these [US] veterans who were full of remorse about the way things had turned out subsequent to their adventures in Vietnam [. . .] They were training the Vietnamese to fight the Japanese, although eventually they trained them to fight themselves – the Americans. Everyone was full of regret, so reading *The Quiet American* again I thought 'wow, this is the novel that answers the questions that these 70 and 80 years old men have been perplexed by all these years – why? Why did this happen?'
>
> (Production Notes 2002:10)

A combination of motives, including the intrinsic merit of the Vietnam story itself, as well as an opportunity for an Australian growing up against the background of his own country's history of dependence, to expose the self-serving hypocrisies of colonialism (Morrow 2002: 10–11) led to a desire to remake *The Quiet American*. Clearly, as both Noyce and Christopher Hampton (along with Robert Schenkkan the scenarist) claimed that their version was not to be yet another film about the experience of Americans fighting the war in Vietnam, but 'why the fighting occurred, why the Americans prosecuted that war over such a long period with such vehemence' (Production Notes 2002: 10), the film appealed to a director like Sydney Pollack with a track record in socially conscious films.

If the official account of the film's origins are to be trusted, these were ultimately the reasons why Sydney Pollack, an American, agreed to work with Noyce: 'This really isn't about the Vietnam war, it's about how we got drawn into an impossible political situation which we totally underestimated and in many ways misunderstood' (Production Notes 2002: 11).

Nevertheless, Pollack's approval was countered by the dismay of others. The film was considered by Miramax too risky for exhibition. Its first run was delayed and only agreed – for a limited period – after a favourable reception at the 2002 Toronto Film Festival. The full release was only authorised in 2003, as the memories of 9/11 and the scathing reviews against what was considered its anti-Americanism (Queenan 2002: 8–9) began to fade.

The 1958 film also deserves credit for its reflections on the ambiguities of the 'Quiet American's motives in the context of the Eisenhower doctrine of the containment of Communism in the Middle and Far East. It remains true to the original narrative's account of two men: one, Fowler (Michael Redgrave), a cynical, quasi-autobiographical, married English journalist unable to secure a divorce from his wife, the other, Pyle (Audie Murphy), a naïve American medical-aid worker. Their professional relations, determined by the politics of a country entering a period of sustained political turmoil, are complicated by rivalry over Phuong (Georgia Moll), Fowler's young Vietnamese mistress. The historical background in all three versions is the attempt by the French to recolonize the country in the wake of liberation from the Japanese. However, instead of retaining the American's role as a CIA agent, the Mankiewicz version transforms him into an innocent apologist of a so-called 'Third Way' political movement, a naïve moralist seeking to rescue Phuong from concubinage, offering her instead the security of the conventional marriage she does not enjoy with Fowler. Since in Mankiewicz, but not in Noyce, the narrative unravels against the background of the Chinese New Year, the original film's domestic mise-en-scène even includes the detail of the pussy-willow tree in the living room to symbolize not only renewal but also the wealth and long life of the happy couple. Phuong – her name means 'phoenix' – is awaiting rebirth as a woman married to a westerner – with all the attached material benefits – but she is also appropriately a symbol of the New Year celebrations that foretell, ironically, the changing fortunes of a country soon to be convulsed by a war in which America was to become so fatally involved. The end of the film shows us Fowler's living room again, with the dying buds of the pussy willow falling off the tree of life. The tree had presaged not regeneration but havoc, self-interest not fair play. Trusting too much in the Englishman's sense of fair play, Pyle fails to see that his rival's mixed motives will eventually lead indirectly to his death. In the novel and Noyce versions, Fowler is reunited with Phuong; in the Mankiewicz he is isolated – abandoned by Phuong, condemned by Vigot, the French Chief of Police – left alone to struggle with the pangs of conscience.

In line with familiar Greene patterns, *The Quiet American* presents us with a pair of characters: to some extent, Fowler and Pyle are the equivalents of Harry Lime and Holly Martins in *The Third Man* (1949), Scobie and Wilson in *The Heart of the Matter* (1948), or Bendrix and Miles in *The End of the Affair* (1951). One is a naïve meddler, determined to pursue a doctrinaire ambition, a stranger to ambiguity, his convictions a blend of moral and political certainty; the other, a relativist, devoid of faith, untroubled by the nuances of sexual morality and yet in whom still flicker the embers of a journalist's dispassionate even-handedness and decency which prioritize a nation's prospects of self-determination over dependency on an emerging superpower. Like the novel, both films dramatize the action through the eyes of Fowler, the latest in a string of unreliable Greene narrators. The role in the Mankiewicz was originally earmarked for Laurence Olivier who, on learning that ill health forced Montgomery Clift to turn down the part of Pyle, backed out of the project, no doubt further discomfited by the thought that Clift's role was to be offered to Audie Murphy. Fowler was eventually handed to Michael Redgrave who, according to his biographer Alan Strachan, was absorbed by the role, leading him to engage in many discussions with Mankiewicz over the screenplay. The end result, however, was a disappointment to Redgrave, who wrote in a letter to Robert Lantz, Mankiewicz's partner in Figaro, the independent production company responsible for the film, 'I was, frankly, very disappointed at the general diminution of character all round. What could have been a great picture has missed its mark by a mile' (Strachan 2004: 324). In another letter, on this occasion to Dick Green, an old Cambridge friend, Redgrave commented: '*The Quiet American* was one of the biggest disappointments of my life. By hoping to present it as an action picture, they cut almost all that was not action or plot, and what should have been the stripping, by painful skin after skin, of a man's character, became – well, nothing much' (Strachan 2004: 324–5).

This is a curious observation, since various commentators attacked the film precisely for being too wordy – a common accusation against Mankiewicz's work as a director who began in films as a screenplay writer – and insufficiently concerned with plot and action. Redgrave's comments highlight the narrowness of vision of an actor too close to his own part to notice the overall patterns of the film. If his lament at the degradation of his role and what he obviously considered the story's true merit seems ill founded, his Fowler is a remarkable tour de force, projecting just the right blend of world-weariness and flagging idealism, selfishness and clarity of vision, jealousy and altruism, demanded by the part. Redgrave's skill at expressing the agonies of damaged losers – perhaps most poignantly exemplified in *Kipps* (Carol Reed, 1941), *Dead of Night* (Robert Hamer et al., 1945) and, above all, *The Browning Version* (Anthony Asquith, 1955), serves him well here. Something, too, of Crocker Harris's schoolmasterly air from the latter survives in his playing of Fowler. The European cynicism of Fowler's witty ripostes to the brash American acquires even more of a Jamesian resonance on the lips of Redgrave's patrician correspondent for *The Times*.

Michael Caine's *Times* man in the Far East, whose performance, finding favour with Alexander Walker (2002), but failing to convince all reviewers (Queenan 2002: 8–9), is less emotional than Redgrave's and acquires the merest hint of the tabloid hack – a variant of his *Little Voice* (Mark Herman, 1998) down-at-heel proletarian opportunist – a tribute perhaps to the rise of the yellow press in recent times and the decline in status of the broadsheet foreign correspondent. If Caine's Fowler is also, at some levels, a self-conscious commentary on the nemesis of the cheeky Cockney – whose apotheosis was, of course, *Alfie* (Lewis Gilbert, 1966) – Redgrave's jaundiced hack is further nuanced through his underlying nervousness, conveyed through the slightly edgy delivery, the economy of smiles and intense glare, all attributes given perhaps their most heightened expression in the behaviour of the mentally unstable ventriloquist in *Dead of Night*.

While Caine's Fowler demonstrates the growing demotic, more democratic tendencies of the post-Suez Englishman, as Continental and other fashion trends finally began to leave their mark on a nation up until the 1950s too inhibited by its 'island race' stuffiness, Redgrave's costumes offer a perfect example of pre-1960s style. In Mankiewicz, contrasts of costume draw attention to the reserve of the British and the informality of the Americans. Our first glimpse of Audie Murphy's Pyle, as Fowler begins his flashback, sees him in a dark suit with a characteristically buttoned-down shirt and neatly folded square in the breast pocket. Pyle's neatness speaks of American opulence. But American casualness, a style of dress which supposedly erases class distinction and acknowledges social mobility, is equally recognizable in scenes where Pyle trades the formality of business uniform for informal, sometimes even polka-dotted short-sleeved shirts. Fowler's suited appearances announce neither the tidy confidence nor the relaxed informality of his American counterpart. The suits are never crisply tailored and, in this most sweltering of climates, Fowler scrupulously avoids short-sleeved shirts. Sartorial clues to the Englishman's reserve are matched by contrasts of language.

Significantly, cutting so much else, the first film repeats the novel's fascination with discourse to provide markers of difference between two nations 'divided by a common language'. Alan Jay Lerner's Shavian comment on Professor Higgins's lips about English not having been spoken for years was yet to be heard on screen in *My Fair Lady* (Cukor, 1964). While the novel, true to Greene's characteristic self-consciousness, seems indeed to be ridiculing what it considers the degradation of the English language, the film is content to use Fowler's point-scoring against the solecisms of America's linguistic representative as a means of highlighting the wordsmith's desperate attempts to stave off the feared victory not only of an increasingly powerful and dangerous nation but also of a rival in love.

Fowler's superiority is expressed, for example, through cultural allusion, especially the many references to cricket and fair play. When Pyle tracks down Fowler in the north of the country to explain his feelings for Phuong, Fowler comments: 'How do we go about it? [i.e., the competition for Phuong] I assume it's my turn to bat [. . .] It's so long since I've played cricket. I have to see what I can do. It's only cricket if you have the first whack.' This is a more elaborate slight than the jibe with which he later greets Pyle, 'I was afraid you'd greet me, if you'd greet me at all, with "Hi"'. 'Hi', like the use of 'gasoline' for 'petrol' – for which he reprimands Vigot – is a perfect example, in Fowler's eyes, of linguistic degeneracy. No progressive theorist of philology, he matches his unbending defence of historic forms of discourse with reliance on metaphors that confirm his cultural imperialism. Cricket is the Old World's cultural reference, but both in Greene and in Mankiewicz its choice is laced with dramatic irony. After all, Pyle has trekked all the way through dangerous territory, risking life and limb in the cause of fairness and a desire to confess his passion for another man's mistress.

While Pyle strives to live by the ideals of what he considers fair play, Fowler has fair play only on his lips. Greene treats his characters with even-handedness, denying any particular sympathy towards his British anti-hero. As with all his protagonists, the virtues are balanced by failings: Harry Lime's debonair Miltonic charm is undermined by racketeering; Scobie's piety by adultery. Fowler's name is significantly pronounced 'Fowlair' by the French Chief of Police and, even though little is made in the films of this punning association with moral squalor, the name's resonances – including the link with foul or unsporting behaviour – seem irresistible. And yet, for all that, Greene redeems his flawed anti-hero from isolation by allowing him redemption through reunion with Phuong. This closure affirms Greene's anti-Americanism and Communist sympathies, tendencies which were forged as a student in Oxford, leading to deportation from Puerto Rico in 1954 (Falk 1990: 137), as well as to friendship with Castro and approval of the 1958 revolution, something that enabled Carol Reed to film *Our Man in Havana* (1959) in Cuba.

Significantly, the Noyce version is faithful to the original ending. In Noyce, as in Greene, Fowler – and for roughly comparable reasons – is not legally punished for his involvement in the assassination of an American. Noyce's audience remembers the horrors of the entire war in Vietnam, not just its start. The later film dramatizes what, in a general discussion, Marina Heung sees as the attempt to deal with the trauma to the collective psyche provoked by 'anxieties about military and masculine prowess' (1997: 161). As Heung further argues, the Noyce version can only be understood against the background of post-Vietnam shows and films such as *Miss Saigon, M. Butterfly* and *Indochine*. In other words, for all the implications for a film-maker directing a film about Vietnam at a time of post-9/11 anger and nervousness about foreign threats to homeland security (Morrow 2002: 11), fall-out from American foreign policy in the Far East was sufficient to make audiences at least feel remorse or guilt (Production Notes 2002: 10) for the mistakes of earlier generations of political leaders. Discussing *Rabbit-Proof Fence* (2002) and *The Quiet American* together, Noyce tellingly comments: 'I suppose both films have a little guilt in them' (Morrow 2002: 10). Beyond the complexities of inter-racial romance, the shifts of power in relations between the sexes and postcolonialist attitudes to world politics, the film addresses indirectly but firmly the implications of US involvement in the modern history of Vietnam, deconstructing the patriarchal bases of both the private and public structures of the USA.

Mankiewicz's hands are more tied. Even though produced by his own company, not a major studio, in the late 1950s, the film could hardly, in the context of

Eisenhower's return to office, appear to attack American foreign policy. For that reason, as contemporary reviewers noted, the film 'never fully adopts the caustic anti-American comment expressed by Greene' (Cutts 1958: 22). Even more, Mankiewicz obviously felt obliged to alter the political content of the original so that Pyle is discovered not to have been a CIA agent, after all, but an innocent victim of Fowler's, 'Old Europe's', misconception of the good intentions of the USA.

The contrasting representation of the American in Mankiewicz and Noyce offers a yardstick by which to measure changing perceptions of a powerful nation. Audie Murphy, the poor Texan who became America's most decorated Second World War hero, whose autobiography, *To Hell and Back* (Jesse Hibbs, 1955) – an instant best-seller – had already been screened in 1955, expresses the fresh-faced innocence of a conviction politician and an America whose overt intentions are undermined by the film's contradictory strategies to expose the dangers of a country blind to its own follies. Redgrave was uneasy in Murphy's company on set (Strachan 2004: 322), but Murphy's 'disconcertingly unvarying preppy smile and unblinking eyes' (also noticed by Leslie Mallory in *The News Chronicle*, 1958) proclaim the confidence of a nation not yet agonizing over failures in Vietnam. Audie Murphy seems ideally cast as the 1950s American abroad. In addition to his gung-ho heroics as the all-conquering hero of the Second World War, he had already appeared in a string of middle-order Westerns, such as *The Kid from Texas* (Kurt Neumann, 1950), *Kansas Raiders* (Ray Enright, 1951), *Duel at Silver Creek* (Don Siegel, 1952) and *Gunsmoke* (Nathan Juran, 1953). His own story of a country boy from a family of twelve children, abandoned by his father, orphaned at twelve, who went on to make such a success of his life, at first as a soldier and then as a Hollywood star, represents a classic rags-to-riches realization of the American Dream. That *To Hell and Back* was, until *Jaws* (Steven Spielberg, 1975), the highest-grossing film ever indicates the extent of Murphy's popularity as an example of all-American masculinity. Mankiewicz capitalizes on the meanings of 'Audie Murphy' in *The Quiet American*, but given the film's rhetoric of political ambiguity at all levels save, perhaps, its closure, the affirmative qualities are projected through occasionally negative perspectives, justifying Dilys Powell's view that his virtues are maddening enough to go some way towards explaining, if not excusing, Fowler's betrayal (Powell 1958: 8).

This seems a much more subtle and convincing assessment of Murphy's pocket-sized bundle of 1950s energetic American masculinity than C. A. Lejeune's failure to measure the full impact of his contribution, a blindness which leads to dismissal of the film's overall impact: 'nor do I think the producers had considered how poorly Audie Murphy, as an actor, might stand up to Michael Redgrave. Fortunately, for international relations, *The Quiet American* as a film is deadly dull' (1958). Lejeune is perhaps still too much in thrall to Redgrave, exaggeratedly respectful of his theatrical aura, to notice the significance of Murphy not only as a performer, but also as an icon of American masculinity. Fowler's constant attacks on Pyle's heroism and characteristic reliance on military allusions to undermine his adversary, serve the dual purpose of pinpointing the significance of character and performer: for example, 'Don't be a bloody hero . . . I don't want to be helped by you'; 'We're not a couple of movie Marines – you're not going to get the girl in the end'. In Fowler's voice-over, the point is further stressed: 'He moved like a hero in a boy's adventure story, his heroism like a scout's badge, and quite unaware of the absurdity and improbability of his adventure. But the absurd and the improbable, like the boy scout and Marines, win in the end more often than we like to think.'

Fowler's combined references to boyhood and to military values suggest the instabilities of 1950s American masculinities. Steven Cohan (1997) refers to the decade's predilection for a more youthful brand of male star – exemplified, above all, by Brando, Clift, Dean, Newman and Presley – whose boyishness appealed to post-war audiences in several ways. The issue is, of course, more complicated than Cohan's impression of a simple substitution of one kind of (ageing) star for a younger alternative, since 1950s films continued to couple young female stars (Sophia Loren, Leslie Caron, Audrey Hepburn) with older men (Cary Grant, Clark Gable, Gary Cooper, Humphrey Bogart, John Wayne), as if to affirm the surviving patriarchality of post-war America. Even so, the younger generation of actors emerged to question to some extent the values, especially the heroic ideals identified with their action-man roles, of a past associated with their precursors. Their characteristic dress – T-shirts, leather jackets, jeans – was a mark of difference and contempt both for the more rugged outdoors look of the classic Westerner and the elegant attire of the smart set. Their dialogue, too, and delivery were famously incoherent and introspective, their behaviour self-scrutinizing or tormented, signs of disaffection with what Connell (1995) termed a 'hegemonic' masculinity, embodying, as Cohan argues, a trend in deference to the non-conformist beat movements in 1950s America.

Audie Murphy was the exception to the rule: a combination of youth and – not dissidence or rebellion – the hegemonic masculinity which Wayne is said to have missed in the war hero's male contemporaries. The star's persona, which, to a degree, in a film of much self-conscious reference to the cinema, literature and the other arts, comes under scrutiny in *The Quiet American*, asserts a form of masculinity which brooks no alternative: physical superiority (like Alan Ladd, Murphy is not compromised by his five-foot-five-inch stature), patriarchality, heterosexuality. Interestingly, though, when early in the film, accompanied by Fowler, Pyle resists the charms of the professional hostesses who swarm around him at 'Le Rendez-Vous', one of the girls wonders 'Il n'aime pas les femmes?', a comment of sufficient ambiguity to open up the possibility of Pyle's homo- or bisexuality and, perhaps, to gesture ironically to the homoerotic appeal of the emergent 1950s boy stars of the Hollywood cinema. Overtly, though, Murphy's physical size and his humble origins declare both that hegemony is not the preserve of a certain class and that even the most physically and socially disadvantaged men can, by embracing it, earn the rewards of supremacist masculinity. Murphy, then, was the answer to Wayne's prayer, a traditional manhood reborn in a star who deplores the rise of the unmanly mumblers.

The political compromises of the Audie Murphy figure in *The Quiet American* exemplify John Tosh's point that 'nowhere is the potential for the application of a "masculinity" perspective more promising than in the realm of politics' (2004: 41). If, as Tosh argues, the political order is reflected in gender structures, Pyle's dual mission to rescue Vietnam from Communism and Phuong from a fate worse than death perfectly illustrates the point. Pyle's assumptions about Phuong – that she could not have been a 'Le Rendez-Vous' hostess herself – and his determination to make an honest woman of her, a condition over which Fowler has a more relaxed attitude, demonstrate his allegiance to heterosexual norms of love and marriage. 'We both have Phuong's interests at heart', Pyle remarks to Fowler, implying that these interests stretch beyond the laws of desire to the imperatives of ideology. Fowler's contemptuous riposte is predictable: 'I'm fed up to the teeth with your brothers-under-the-skin drivel about cellophane-wrapped security for the atomic future. I don't care that about Phuong's future. I want her. I want her with me.' Fowler's reaction may be confused but it is also honest. Unable, until too late in the Mankiewicz film (but not in the novel), to get the divorce from his English wife that would release him for marriage to Phuong, he finds no difficulty in frustrating the wishes of Phuong herself and those of her materialistic sister, to regularize their relationship. His domestic arrangements and relationship with Phuong are hardly radical: Phuong's position is scarcely different from the standard role of submissive female in 1950s Orientalist texts such as *Love Is a Many Splendored Thing* (Henry King, 1955) or *South Pacific* (Joshua Logan, 1958), even those, such as the former, where the female has a respectable profession.

Love Is a Many Splendored Thing, like *The Quiet American*, casts a white star in the role of an eastern character (Jennifer Jones in the former plays a Eurasian). While, after decades of racial and ethnic consciousness-raising, the second version of *The Quiet American* could not get away with this practice, Mankiewicz's version has no qualms about casting an Italian actress, Georgia Moll, as Phuong, maintaining a Hollywood tradition which lasted well into the 1960s.

By the time of the making of the Noyce version, even a Disney film, *Aladdin* (1995), had drawn its heroine, Jasmine, with more Semitic features than might have been possible in the 1950s. Such transformations in the racialized figuration of the Hollywood 'beauty', partly also driven by an eye for the Asian market in both the USA and abroad, enabled Asian actress Do Thi Hai Yen to be cast as Phuong, but the character retains in her demeanour, ambitions and behaviour that subordinated femininity traditionally prized by the western male in flight from the assertiveness of his female contemporaries.

Michael Caine's Fowler explains his love for Vietnam at the very beginning of the film, with its altered opening from the novel and Mankiewicz versions, through a fusion of space and femininity. 'I can't say what made me fall in love with Vietnam', he remarks, as we see Phuong's face superimposed on images of opium, fire, explosions and landscapes, still the object not the subject of history, the links between the troubled topography of a nation and its female representative simultaneously an identification of the latter with uncontrollable forces, and the former with exoticism and suffering but ultimately triumphant femininity. As ever, true to a classically Orientalist trope, femininity is defined as remoteness, an otherness at once alluring and threatening to the conformist male. The Armageddon-style aesthetics of this opening, identifying Phuong with a Saigon reduced to ashes provides an appropriate prelude to the film's subsequent visual fusion of glossy lyricism and unimaginable horror, the metaphor for the fatal attraction of the exoticized female and her alien native land. Greene's work often finds room for a young and innocent female in his many triangles of love – no more poignantly so than in the case of Helen Rolt in *The Heart of the Matter*. But Fowler's fantasy offers more than freshness and innocence. She provides unthreatening companionship and devotion. Whether supplying her lover with another opium pipe to soothe away the travails of the day or servicing him sexually, Phuong represents an opportunity to undo his failure, of which he is accused by his estranged wife, both as a man and husband. When Caine's Fowler asks Phuong, as he loosens her hair in one of the film's last scenes, whether she misses Pyle, her affirmative reply leaves the viewer, moved by her grief, divided between feelings of empathy and dismay. Little of the deliberately wrought feelings of regret that 1950s audiences would have had for the death of Audie Murphy survives here.

As Neil Sinyard notes (2003: 160), Brendan Fraser's 'Quiet American', 'who comes on like a Clark Kent innocent but, by his final scene, has revealed a self-righteousness and ruthless fanaticism that is truly dangerous', makes it difficult for anyone to feel anything more than sympathy for Phuong's dashed hopes of a more secure future. Though in Caine/Fowler's words, Fraser/Pyle has the 'face with no history and no problem', there is nevertheless something about his implacability that removes the character from Greene's anti-capitalist caricature and even makes Fowler recall his own idealistic past: 'He made me remember a time when I had wanted to make a difference.' In Brendan Fraser, in any case, the film relies on a star associated with successful box-office films in which, though no Harrison Ford or Tom Cruise, he is identified with positive, sometimes heroic characters. The gradual unwinding of the character is measured by the progressive informality of his clothes: from dark suit and tie, to the removal of his jacket, to white suit, to shirt-sleeve order. Admittedly his glasses and his pretence at being interested in eye disease in the Third World, emphasized in his speech to Fowler on trachoma, are ironic reminders of American short-sightedness. In the touching scene where he asks whether she misses Pyle, Caine's Fowler tells Phuong he is sorry Pyle is dead. But when she replies he has nothing to be sorry for, his rejoinder that he needs to apologize substitutes for the emphasis in the Greene–Mankiewicz concern with guilt the regret that Phuong has lost a lover for whom she cared, someone her own age, however misguided and catastrophic his political meddling.

Fowler and Phuong, whose many ties are even highlighted through alliteration, belong to different ages and seasons and are governed by ill-matched rhythms, however solemn the promise of the now-free westerner (finally granted a divorce by his wife) to remain henceforward beside her. Caine's Fowler is perhaps more self-aware than Redgrave's in this respect, and his overriding motive for betraying Pyle smacks less of loathing for a political creed than of jealousy. No one can forget that this is a film made long after the end of a bloody war, many of whose extras are played by its survivors, the latest in a line of anti-Vietnam films, less focused on the moral ambiguities or dilemmas or declarations and betrayals of love than on the origins and legacy of a tragic act of political folly. Significantly, the poem Fowler reads just prior to his signal to Pyle's assassins, waiting in the street below, reverts to the novel's original quotation from 'Dipsychus', by Clough (also used as one of the novel's epigraphs), rather than the speech from *Othello* that replaces it in Mankiewicz:

> I drive through the streets and I care not a damn
> The people they stare, and they ask who I am,
> And if I should chance to run over a cad,
> I can pay for the damage if ever so bad.
> So pleasant it is to have money, heigh ho!
> So pleasant it is to have money!

The Mankiewicz version resorts to one of Iago's speeches:

> Though I perchance am vicious in my guess
> As, I confess, it is my nature plague
> To spy into abuses and oft my jealousy
> Shapes faults that are not.

For all its scepticism about the propriety of American involvement in Vietnam, the Mankiewicz version, not complicated by Australian (Noyce) or British (Hampton) agendas, takes pleasure through appeal to the older culture's greatest cultural icon to make an unexpected alliance between Fowler and Iago, and, consequently, Pyle and Othello. The links between the former emphasize the negative eventualities of age, class, racial purity and jealousy; those between the latter highlight youth, classlessness and 'melting pot' racial hybridity. Fowler's revenge on Pyle is the act not only of a betrayed lover but also of a venerable nation against the emergence of a younger rival, perhaps more suitable for the aspirations of a Desdemona/Phuong/Vietnam ready for liberation from its colonial past. By 1958, of course, the horrors of this seemingly more natural liaison had not come fully into view, even though the allegory of Fowler's betrayal of Pyle seems now somewhat deserved, a comment on the self-serving policies of the new colonialists whose interests seem little different from those of the old.

While Mankiewicz's Fowler, whose flashback voice-over addresses the audience like the penitent in a confessional, is spurred predominantly by jealousy, Noyce's, reverting to the original Greene text, is driven above all by the desire to eliminate a 'cad'. Mankiewicz stresses Fowler's guilt, teasing out the moral and psychological implications, rescuing the American and condemning the European, whereas Noyce, true to his more critical attitude towards America, reverses the pattern. Ultimately, Fowler's role in Mankiewicz as an objective, sharp-eyed journalist is compromised by jealousy. Noyce's Fowler modifies guilt through a more committed politics. Aided by his scenarists Christopher Hampton and Robert Schenkkan, neither of whom is American, he defines the American's 'caddishness' not only as the meddling politics of a superpower but also as ignorance of foreign cultures, admiration mixed with arrogant disdain for Europe and an unshakeable belief in the material and moral superiority of America, to which the American is impatient to transport the disadvantaged foreigner, away from what he considers her private and public squalor. The American's ignorance is demonstrated through pretence, in an early encounter with Phuong, at knowledge of Vietnamese. His contempt for what his political heirs have referred to as 'Old Europe' is seen in its most virulent form in what is almost his parting shot to Fowler: 'The French aren't going to stop the Communists. They haven't got the brains, and they haven't got the guts [. . .] I don't think you see the big picture, Thomas.' Curiously, Mankiewicz's version, not Noyce's, emphasizes French civilization. In Noyce, the role of the French Chief of Police is minimal, reduced to only functional significance. In Mankiewicz, Vigot is not only civilized – admittedly no longer quoting the moralist Pascal, only the Romantic Lamartine – but also, as a contemporary reviewer noted (Dixon 1958: n.p.), the conscience of a flawed individual, the equivalent of Raskolnikov's nemesis in *Crime and Punishment*. The development of the character of the French Chief of Police in Mankiewicz could well be viewed as a balancing element in the film's eventual condemnation of the English. Spared the fraught Oedipal relationship between Britain and the USA – here replicated in the younger man's desire for the patriarch's concubine – France had always been for the USA a nation admired for its elegance and culture.

Both films have much to say about Vietnam, the old colonialists and the enigmas of human behaviour. Each, above all, encourages introspection in times when notions of self and national identity are increasingly at odds with the promotion of a tarnished American ideal.

Acknowledgement

I am indebted to Kelsey Thornton for identifying the poem by Clough, and to Tao Tao Chang for information about Chinese New Year festivities.

References

Cohan, Steven (1997) *Masked Men; Masculinity and the Movies in the Fifties*, Bloomington, Ind.: Indiana University Press.

Connell, R. W. (1995) *Masculinities*, Cambridge: Polity Press.

Crowther, Bosley (1970) 'The Quiet American', in *New York Times Film Reviews*, Vol. IV, 1949–1958, New York: New York Times and Arno Press, p. 3042.

Cutts, John (1958) 'The Quiet American', *Films and Filming*, May: 22.

Dixon, C. (1958) 'The Quiet American', *Daily Telegraph*, 29 March.

Falk, Quentin (1990) *Travels in Greeneland: The Cinema of Graham Greene*, London and New York: Quartet Books.

French, Philip (2002) 'Saigon? It's not too far from Ealing . . .', *Observer*, 11 August, p. 9.

Greene, Graham (2001) *The Quiet American*, London: Vintage.

Heung, Marina (1997) 'The Family Romance of Orientalism: From *Madame Butterfly* to *Indochine*', in Matthew Bernstein and Gaylyn Studlar (eds) *Visions of the East: Orientalism in Film*, London: I. B. Tauris, pp. 158–83.

Hibbs, Jesse (1955) *To Hell and Back*, New York: Henry Holt and Co.

Hillstrom, Kevin and Laurie Collier Hillstrom (1998) *The Vietnam Experience: A Concise Encyclopedia of American Literature, Songs and Films*, Westport, Conn.: Greenwood Press.

Lejeune, C. A. (1958) 'The Quiet American', *Observer*, 30 March.

Lower, Cheryl Bray and Palmer, R. Burton. (2001) *Joseph L. Mankiewicz: Critical Essays*, with an annotated bibliography and a filmography, Jefferson, NC: McFarland.

Mallory, Leslie (1958) 'Show Piece', in *News Chronicle*, 20 March.

Morrow, Fiona (2002) 'The Art of Noyce', *Independent*, 22 November, pp. 10–11.

Powell, D. (1958) 'The Quiet American', *Sunday Times*, 30 March, p. 8.

Production Notes (2002) *The Quiet American*.

Queenan, Joe (2002) 'Raising Caine', *Guardian, The Guide*, 30 November.

Rohmer, Eric (1958) 'Politique contre destin': *The Quiet American*', *Cahiers du Cinéma*, 86 (August): 46–51.

Sarris, Andrew (2002) 'Latest "Message" Movies: Anti-American but Entertaining', <http://www.nyobserver.com/pages/story.asp?ID:6682>. (Accessed 9 December.)

Sinyard, Neil (2003) *Graham Greene: A Literary Life*. London: Palgrave Macmillan.

Strachan, A. (2004) *Sweet Dreams: A Biography of Michael Redgrave*, London: Orion.

Tosh, John (2004) 'Hegemonic Masculinity and the History of Gender', in Stefan Dudink, Karen Hagemann and John Tosh (eds) *Masculinities in Politics and War; Gendering Modern History*, Manchester: Manchester University Press, pp. 41–58.

Walker, Alexander (2002) 'Reviving the True Spirit of Greene', *Evening Standard*, 28 November, pp. 50–1.

Chapter 7

The Americanization
of Emily (1964)

Sharon Willis

While *The Americanization of Emily* remembers both the Second World War and
the war movies it generated, this 1964 film also deftly delivers a picture of its own
period. The film captures the Cold War as cultural pressure articulated across
consumer society and media spectacle. And it reminds us that these were the vectors
not only of the Cold War's ideological discourse, but also of its determinants at
the level of everyday life.

A difficult film to summarize, *The Americanization of Emily* grafts together
a romantic comedy and a war plot. Lieutenant Commander Charlie Madison
(James Garner), an aide to Admiral William Jessup (Melvyn Douglas), falls for his
British driver, Emily Barham (Julie Andrews) in the weeks preceding the D-Day
invasion. Cultural difference seems to be the primary obstacle in the romance plot.
Entrepreneurial Charlie's commitment to 'cowardice' dramatically opposes the
prim, stiff-upper-lip philosophy of the war widow Emily. As the parallel war plot
unfolds, the film makes it clear that the invasion is as ancillary to its interests as it
is to Admiral Jessup's, whose main goal is to make a publicity film of the first dead
man on the beach, who must be a sailor. Increasingly unhinged in his obsession
with this project, the Admiral strategizes to produce a heroic portrait of the
Navy in order to compete for resources with the Army. As his obsession intensifies
and others endorse the project, the film's subject becomes military politics and
administration. In the defiles of this bureaucratic machine, Charlie navigates
clumsily, insisting on his cowardice and surviving his panicked Normandy landing
to proclaim the absurdity of glorifying war. Meanwhile, Emily comes to embrace
his commitment to cowardice over 'heroicized death'. She 'Americanizes' herself
in Charlie's image when she exclaims jubilantly, 'That's my Charlie, craven to the
end', upon hearing of his cowardly performance on the beach.

As this film opens with the indication, 'Hendon Airport, London, May 4, 1944', the soundtrack's march establishes its war theme. The camera closely follows Charlie Madison's energetic movements, often sweeping around his body, its motions creating a circle, rather than a rectangle, in a movement which will become characteristic of its assertive and inquisitive cinematography. But ironic notes intrude into the musical environment – quite literally. As Madison organizes the convoy leaving the airport, he pauses to greet the women drivers from the motor pool by patting their behinds. Each time he makes this gesture, a marked clang emphasizes it. More than anything else, this sequence establishes him as a smooth operator and ladies' man.

When Madison arrives at the hotel where his admiral and staff are lodging, he first rushes into the kitchen to report the inventory of supplies he has stocked – eggs, bacon, coffee, marmalade, butter and orange juice, all in prodigious quantities – and to order breakfast. After he dismisses his driver with a pat and gets dismissed himself with a slap, the film cuts to an establishing shot that characterizes his quarters. The bottom third of the frame is packed with goods: cartons of whiskey, champagne and Hershey bars. As the camera holds on the stock, a text scrolls down, establishing Charlie's position: 'In World War II, few men served their countries more ably than a small group of unheralded heroes known as "The Dog-Robbers." A Dog-Robber is the personal attendant of a general or an admiral and his job is to keep his general or admiral well-clothed, well-fed and well-loved during the battle. Every army and every navy in the world has its Dog-Robbers, but, needless to say, ours were the best.' As the text comes to an end, so does the musical march overture, and the camera backs away, framing these products like a landscape.

In the sequence that follows this one, we find Charlie and his colleague Bus Cummings (James Coburn) in their office, planning the Admiral's dinner party for a general. As they discuss the menu, 'steak, avocado salad, ice cream, appropriate wine', it becomes clear that they are responsible for a menu of women as well: for the bridge game to follow dinner, Charlie muses, 'the general likes a red-haired partner' suggesting that varieties of women are part of his inventory.

Madison's skills as a procurer become the explicit subject of the next sequence as well. Having learned that Lieutenant Wade, the Supply Master, is from Alabama, he puts on a marked Southern accent and offers his 'Southern kinsman' bottles of bourbon, a commodity Wade has thought impossible to obtain. In return for his own commodified good will, Charlie tells Wade in no uncertain terms that he requires 'the prime of everything' for his admiral. He acquires a prodigious inventory of products unavailable to British civilians. Emily is appalled, and she expatiates on this point, framed in medium close-up through the windshield, squeezed by a crate of oranges which takes up more than half of the front seat. Emphasizing an almost claustrophobic abundance, crates piled in the back seat squeeze Garner to the right of the screen. From this crowded frame, the film cuts to another frame also cluttered with products, as Charlie's colleague, Captain Harry Spaulding (William Windon) bustles into his room to talk about the Normandy invasion. As Charlie focuses on his own interests – finding a girl who is good at the dinner table and a sharp bridge player – Harry eyes and eventually pockets a bottle of perfume, helping to establish an equation between women and commodities.

The Americanization of Emily appears distinctly marked by the political and cultural pressures of its contemporary Cold War moment and by the post-war period more broadly. The Cold War turning points of the Berlin Wall (August/September 1961) and the Cuban Missile Crisis (18–29 October 1962) which brought the USA and the Soviet Union to the brink of nuclear war clearly contributed to the film's edginess and scepticism. In the anxious year after the Kennedy assassination, the USA intensified its activity in Vietnam, with Congress passing the Gulf of Tonkin Resolution, greatly expanding the President's war powers and allowing for the first air strikes against Vietnam.

Visual media took an unprecedented role in this period, as television not only reports but actively shapes news events. For example, Kennedy announced *and inaugurated* the Cuban Missile Crisis in a television address; subsequently, according to Mary Ann Watson, the media then became 'a willing partner in the administration's strategy' (Watson 1995: 79). As the Cuban crisis was the first international event to be started on television, so the Vietnam war was the first to be televized, and television certainly entered into the political fray on the domestic front, just as it had been doing in the civil-rights struggles (see Torres 2003: 13–35). In its pointed examination of the political and economic efficacies of the image, *The Americanization of Emily* clearly registers the effects of this new role for the media.

Notably, in this evolving media culture and the politics that attended it, Hollywood steered clear of Vietnam. According to Thomas Doherty, 'As *Variety* put it in 1965, "the war in Viet Nam is too hot for Hollywood"' (Doherty 1993: 283). Tellingly, he points out, 'the fear of being professionally burned by the land war in Asia extended to allegorical address. In 1964 Columbia bought the rights to Joseph Heller's *Catch 22* to "the accompaniment of much fanfare" only to sell it off at cost in 1966' (Doherty 1993: 283). In such a media landscape, it may not be surprising that *The Americanization of Emily*'s development culminates ironically with a botched attempt to film the invasion of Normandy and with the Navy's recuperation of this failure, as it immediately recasts a publicity campaign planned around the image of a dead hero by reshaping a cowardly survivor into the hero instead.

While this film resonates with the two nuclear-anxiety films released in 1964, *Dr. Strangelove; Or How I Stopped Worrying and Learned to Love the Bomb* (Stanley Kubrick) and Sidney Lumet's *Fail Safe*, it more forcefully echoes Darryl Zanuck's

The Longest Day (1962), the most expensive war movie to date. Made in cooperation with the US, British, French and German military authorities, Zanuck's production involved the military's participation in its own media representation. Zanuck set out to recreate the D-Day invasion and found himself obliged to restage battle scenes, since he found little usable footage shot at the time of the invasion. A film that aims to give an accurate depiction of the mistakes and the horrors of this event, *The Longest Day* also seeks to reconstruct it. In this connection, we might see *The Americanization of Emily* as a witty comment on this representation of the same invasion. Shot in black and white, like *The Longest Day*, this film reflects on cinema's place in the production of cultural identity, collective memory and rhetorics of political persuasion, but it also consistently explores its own status as a commodity in global exchange.

Despite its protestations to the contrary, from both its director and its main character, who claim not to be against war, but against the glorification of war, *The Americanization of Emily* is consistently appropriated as an anti-war film (see, for example: Crowther 1964: C2 and Wolcott 2005: 220–4). Some critics found it un-American. Military historian Lawrence Suid reports that

> One critic described the *The Americanization of Emily* as 'so hypocritical – because it dares to call itself funny – so callous, so cruel, and so crass, that it provokes a feeling of anger and resentment that we, as Americans, have allowed ourselves the luxury of permitting such an encroachment against our very heritage as it were.
>
> (2002: 206)

It's not hard to see how some might find this film 'un-American', since *The Americanization of Emily* does not quite feel like an 'American' movie. Its disjointed vignette structure, its preference for long speeches and prolonged and pointed dialogue over action, its narrative meanderings and sluggishness, its refusal to tie up loose ends and, above all, the ambivalence of its characters and its resolute and ironic ambiguity make this film feel somehow European. This is why James Wolcott calls it 'the greatest Billy Wilder film that Billy Wilder never made' (2005: 220).

But this film owes its shape, arguably, as much to television as to war movies or European cinematic influences. Both Paddy Chayefsky, the film's scriptwriter and its director, Arthur Hiller, had worked extensively in television during its 'Golden Age' (roughly 1948–58) of live drama.[1] This period was known for its interest in exploring the special properties of the medium in character (as opposed to plot) drama and for the unprecedented creative control it offered to writers. As Chayefsky himself recalled, 'Right at that time, it was a writer's medium. Think of all those shows that were done in New York – "Philco," "Studio One" . . . perfect for writers. If you could come in at the right time and do something that caught on, it was the beginning of a career' (Boddy 1990: 87).

The Cold War took its toll on this 'writer's paradise', however, as internal and external forces put pressure on 'controversial' material. Advertisers concerned about audience share pushed for a move away from the 'broad-minded' 'big-city sensibility' associated with New York, towards programming appropriate for broadcast to the entire nation, 'most of whom live in small towns and go to church on Sunday' (Carroll O'Meara, cited in Boddy 1990: 101–2). External pressures, as William Boddy details them, take the form of 'redbaiting and blacklisting that marked the industry during the 1950s' (1990: 100). These begin with the 1950 publication of *Red Channels: The Report on the Communist Influence in Radio and Television*, which charged that several programmes served 'as sounding boards' 'for communist propaganda purposes', 'particularly with reference to current issues on which the Party is critically interested; "academic freedom," "civil rights," "peace," the "H-bomb," etc.' (cited in Boddy 1990: 9). It is perhaps not surprising that the migrating writer slyly embeds a critique of commodified images and conservative propagandizing into a film whose drama is largely driven by his main characters' interrogation of each other's moral integrity.

Hershey Bars and Razor Blades

Several highly charged moments organized by superbly witty eloquence serve to shape the evolving romance between Charlie and Emily. Marked by stillness, which contrasts sharply with the fluid consistency of camera motion in the sequences that build the military story, these exchanges could be said to punctuate the war narrative, if they did not in fact ground it and provide its architecture. These speeches, however, do much more than structure the film; they frame its increasingly biting and bitter irony.

An early dialogue sets the stage for the love affair at the same time that it begins to establish the complex meanings this film assigns to 'Americanization'. Having decided to accept Charlie's invitation to dinner – what she fears might be a first step toward 'Americanization' – Emily arrives at the hotel. Madison, whose task as a 'dog-robber' includes arranging, organizing and procuring of all sorts, inspects the dinner table much as a maître d' might. Displaying his worldliness, he admires the crystal, 'Danish?', and the table linen, which he identifies as Italian. But, as we are soon to find, this knowingness and sophistication extends beyond commodities to cultural analysis.

As Emily enters Madison's suite, we take its inventory with her. 'Do you have chests of rubies in the bathroom?' Charlie's reply, 'Just perfumes and liquor', suggests that this suite is a sort of duty-free shop. 'All the girls talk about it', she continues. As the camera follows her across the screen, she browses the boxes piled high. We've already noted a crate marked 'Parfums Lanvin', before Emily has recited the names of New York department stores, 'Bergdorf Goodman, Saks Fifth Avenue, Lord and Taylor'. Concluding, 'it *is* the swankiest shop in town', she is struck by a final item: 'How did you manage Arpège with the Germans in Paris?' 'There *are* Germans in Paris', she asks snidely; 'there *is* a war on, I think. You Americans must have heard something about it, I'm sure.' Charlie's distance from the war will be emphasized repeatedly and never more pointedly than when he and his colleagues watch a film which is to serve as the model for their own. This is a newsreel of a training exercise for naval demolition engineers, a staged simulation. Their task will be to realize what this film rehearses. As the duty-free shop merges with the black market, Emily's crisp British attack provokes a speech from Madison.

'You American haters bore me to tears, Miss Barham', Charlie begins the first of the many rhetorically stunning speeches he delivers in the film.

> I've dealt with Europeans all my life. I know all about us parvenus from the States who come over here and race around your old cathedral towns with our cameras and our Coca-Cola bottles . . . and act like we own the world. We overtip, we talk too loud, we think we can buy anything we want with a Hershey Bar. I've had Germans and Italians tell me how politically ingenuous we are. Perhaps so, but we haven't managed a Hitler or a Mussolini yet . . . The most tedious of the lot are you British. We crass Americans didn't introduce war into your little island. This war, Miss Barham, to which we Americans are so insensitive, is the result of 2,000 years of European greed, barbarism, superstition, and stupidity. Don't blame it on our Coca-Cola bottles. Europe was a going brothel long before we came to town.

In conclusion, he adds, 'It's not my job to listen to your sentimental contempt.' The spectator may enjoy this pithy conclusion, but it still leaves open the question of just what his job *is*. And the whole speech demands some consideration of what his job as an *American* is. In a notable semiotic shift from the more explicitly Cold War-influenced 1959 novel on which it is based, the film renames the original protagonist, James Monroe Madison. That character's name evokes the nation's founding fathers, the Constitution, and its early foreign policy – the Monroe Doctrine. By contrast, Charlie Madison, in his opulent stockroom, evokes nothing so much as Madison Avenue.

However persuasive or pleasurable this rhetorical flight may be for the spectator, as we'll see it is for Emily, its visual setting marks a different emphasis. As Charlie and Emily back into their respective corners across the room from each other for this sparring match, the camera opens a wide space between them in a strongly horizontal picture plane, and a rack of dresses comes into view. This rack, along with the boxes of products that frame this whole encounter, make the scene feel as if it takes place in a retail outlet. Holding the characters and objects in the *plan américain*[2] (medium shot) which post-war French critics found to be predominant in American films and which recurs so consistently in this one, the camera isolates Madison throughout his speech. When it shifts to capture Emily's reaction, we see that she is 'framed' from below by a carton of Hershey Bars which appears on the bottom left-hand corner of the frame. When a reverse shot brings Madison back into view, we see a large box of Gillette razor blades interposed between him and the camera in the lower frame. This whole exchange has been mediated by commodities.

Commodities and the clutter of their accumulation, then, completely shape and mark Charlie's space. But they also put national identity in play as product or brand name, in this liminal zone between the military offices and the bedroom, which is entirely consigned to commerce. As obtrusive boxes and cartons block passage and encroach on the space, squeezing the figures into awkward positions and angles, so do product names mark and 'brand' the space. Interestingly, director Hiller remarks on the convenience of contemporary Motion Picture Association of America regulations that permitted the use of actual products, their brand names visible. More recently, such practices are considered 'product placement'; effectively, *advertising* (DVD director's commentary, Warner Home Video 2005).[3]

Though he trades in the most sophisticated international luxury commodities, it is the humbler and more iconic American products that come – and mediate – between the antagonists as they move towards seduction. And could there be more iconic American products? Emily declines Madison's offer of a dress, indicating that she has her own clothes: 'I'll do without your Hershey Bars.' Hershey Bars will become her metaphor for American 'favours' of all kinds, and especially for those for which she is expected to exchange *her* favours. But for the post-war viewer, whether in 1964 or today, the Hershey Bar remains the iconic token for expressions of American goodwill. Certainly, this modest candy is a staple of Second World War movies; standard issue for GIs, it becomes a kind of translinguistic – and ideological – currency in post-D-Day European territories, as represented both in the news media and in film.

But the commodities resonate as well with one of the meanings of 'Americanization' that play through this scene. As a result of the Marshall Plan for European recovery, in addition to interposing itself in inter-Europe trade relations, the USA positioned its capital and its products very favourably in western Europe's economies and markets. American investment in France peaked in the period 1962–5, accounting for over half of all foreign investment. In *Seducing the French: The Dilemma of Americanization*, historian Richard Kuisel provides an interesting inventory of sectors of US penetration in this period: 'Some industries where Americans acquired a dominant role during this period or several decades earlier were synthetic rubber, petroleum, office machines, tractors, photographic supplies, sewing machines, elevators, telegraph and telephone equipment, and computers.'

'From the perspective of national interest', he concludes, 'some of these sectors were strategic; others such as *razor blades*, were not' (Kuisel 1993: 160–1; my emphasis).

Kristin Ross notes the effect of this 'Americanization' on everyday life in the 'sudden descent of large appliances into war-torn French households and streets in the wake of the Marshall plan' (Ross 1995: 4). Radically shaping everyday life, of course, was the flood of Hollywood films which cascaded into France in the wake of 'the Franco-American credit agreement signed in 1946 by Leon Blum and American secretary of state James Byrnes', in which the French abandoned pre-war protective tariffs which had been especially important to the film industry (Ross 1995: 37).

Equally important as American exports to France under the Marshall Plan, however, were American management styles and the social-science expertise that helped to shape them. As the Marshall Plan supported a series of management exchanges, with French businessmen visiting the USA, and American consultants working in France, Americans were intent on promoting their ideas about management, productivity and marketing. According to Kuisel, 'It is no exaggeration to claim that the French discovered "management" during the Marshall Plan' (1993: 84). But along with management, the French modernization programme also emphasized marketing (Kuisel 1993: 88). In this context, American social science, management, marketing research and public relations revolutionized practices.[4] And, as Kuisel contends, not only were its methods new, but 'the goal of American marketing was new: it aimed at creating consumer society' (1993: 88). So reforms of corporate culture produce an enhanced realm of consumer desire – and significant American profits.

The Marshall Plan is thickly inscribed in *The Americanization of Emily*. Secretary of State George Marshall, the architect of the 'European Recovery Plan' better known by his name, had, as General Marshall, been the designer of Operation Overlord, the D-Day invasion, the ostensible subject of this film as well as of the film within it. During the war, he authored a famous remark whose significance is far-reaching. Thomas Doherty reminds us that, 'Marshall said that the war had seen the development of two new weapons, the airplane and the motion picture' (1993: 266).

Nowhere in Europe was the ideological weaponry of film more aggressively deployed, of course, than in Germany. In the post-war period, as Thomas Elsaesser puts it, 'American interests penetrate distribution and exhibition virtually without obstacle', as 'economic objectives complemented political goals' (Elsaesser 1989: 9). Elsaesser goes on to cite a speech by Spyros Skouros, then Head of 20th Century Fox, which argued, 'it is a solemn responsibility of our industry to increase motion picture outlets throughout the free world because it has been shown that no medium can play a greater part than the motion picture industry in indoctrinating people into the free way of life' (1989: 9). American films circulating in Europe functioned as advertising for the American 'way of life'.

In Wim Wenders' *Kings of the Road/Im Lauf der Zeit* (1976), Robert (Hans Zischler) reflects, in relation to both film and music, that 'the Yanks have even colonized our subconscious' (Corrigan 1983: 7). But in Britain, while less explicitly politically charged, the cinematic 'occupation' was equally overwhelming. American studios began investing in such volume that film scholars Marguerite Dickinson and Sarah Street contend, 'after 1961 it became increasingly difficult to define any part of the industry as British rather than Anglo-American' (cited in Petrie 1996: 607). Ultimately, 'the British industry became so dependent on American investment that by 1969, 90 per cent of investment in British cinema came from the United States' (Forbes and Street 2000: 21).

But in this film, the meaning of 'Americanization' as an occupation of consumer culture and popular media by US products lurks behind another meaning of this term, one that describes relations between US officers and their British female employees. In that sense, 'Americanization' refers to the exchange of luxury and consumer items largely unavailable in wartime Britain for companionship and sexual favours. One is struck by the connection between consumer goods and women, precisely the nexus around which operates the 'Americanization' which gives the novel and the film its name. Trading in branded products – from whiskey to Bergdorf's – Charlie Madison also seeks to 'brand' the British women around him as 'Americanized'.

At the level of the discursive sparring which gives this film its spark and its bite, 'Americanization' also means, for Emily, endorsing and embracing Charlie's celebration of cowardice and his critical position on war's glorification through a rhetoric of heroism, sacrifice and moral principle. Emily's Americanization, the film seems to argue, accomplishes itself when she speaks his language; that is, when, at the film's end, the two have reversed position, and she cites his previous remarks back to him.

Emily's first visit to Charlie's suite ends with evidence that she has found his diatribe somehow both persuasive and seductive, as she crosses the threshold and turns to ask him if he has a 'girl'. Charlie's bemused reaction to Emily's query abruptly gives way in a cut to a harshly lit, almost obscene close-up of a woman opening her mouth to taste the avocado salad which Admiral Jessup has had procured for his party. It's at this party that Emily seems quite visibly seduced by Charlie and very specifically through sight. We watch as she does while the camera follows him circulating through the room. Its smooth seamless flow here characterizes several sequences of Charlie 'at work'. The rhythm of long takes frequently inscribes a sequence within the sequence, emphasizing its sustained attention.[5] But, when Charlie is leading the camera, the long take visually inscribes his confidence, his smoothness in the fluidity of its own movement. We watch, with Emily, as Charlie 'works' the room, characteristically, he's 'arranging' things. And he will later tell us that in his previous civilian life, he worked as an 'assistant night manager' at a 'diplomatic hotel'. No doubt this is where he acquired his extensive experience with Europeans. His job there, he tells Emily and her mother at tea, was 'to arrange things for the many great historical figures who came to Washington on great historical missions'. Asked what exactly he 'arranged', he replies with suave knowingness, 'usually it was girls, but individual tastes varied, of course'. But it was also through this job that Charlie was able to 'arrange' his current commission so that he could avoid combat.

James Bond, Mary Poppins and Maverick

Released near the height of another invasion, the 'British invasion' (the Beatles attracted a record audience to *The Ed Sullivan Show* on 9 February 1964), *The Americanization of Emily*'s story of Anglo-American friction and *entente* inscribes significant contemporary cultural references that shape its period. Most notable among these are the unprecedented exchanges happening between Britain and the USA in musical and visual culture. The early 1960s saw a wave of 'Swinging London' films arrive in the USA (See Landy 2000: 63–79). And American directors emigrated into the British industry: Richard Lester brought out *A Hard Day's Night* in 1964; Kubrick made *Lolita* (1962) and *Dr. Strangelove* in England; Roger Corman, Joseph Losey and Fred Zinnemann (*A Man For All Seasons*, 1966) also worked there during the period (Petrie 1996: 604–13).

Fittingly enough, *The Americanization of Emily*, centrally concerned with consumer culture, itself consumes and condenses an eclectic variety of popular-culture icons. This film's web of intertextual resonances is anchored first in its stars, Julie Andrews and James Garner. Andrews is at this point freshly stamped by Walt Disney's *Mary Poppins* (which was released in July 1964), for which performance she would receive the Best Actress Oscar, and on her way to *The Sound of Music* (1965) – a very different war story. Unlike *Emily*, *Mary Poppins* seems intent on undermining the proverbial British 'stiff upper lip' of industry and imperial adventure. Interestingly enough, this film too stages an Anglo-American encounter: Bert, the chimney sweep who accompanies Mary and the children on many of their adventures, is played by Dick Van Dyke, star of the popular *Dick Van Dyke Show* (CBS, 1961–6).

Julie Andrews, we remember, had played Eliza Doolittle in the Broadway production of *My Fair Lady* (1956). The year 1964 also saw the release of George Cukor's *My Fair Lady* starring British stars Audrey Hepburn and Rex Harrison, which swept the Academy Awards (Best Picture, Best Actor, Best Director). These two films suggest that, despite the 'Swinging London' films, American culture remained fascinated with flattened nostalgic fantasies of a quaint and cosy pre-First

World War England. This fantasmatic Britain bears a curious resemblance to the striking flatness and unreality of the England we see in *The Americanization of Emily*.

For his part, in the witty, articulate cosmopolitanism of Charlie Madison, James Garner seems to condense his television character, Brett Maverick, with James Bond. *Maverick* propelled Garner to stardom, even as he propelled the show's success, and *The Americanization of Emily* seems marked by characteristics of both the character and the series. By his own account, Roy Huggins, *Maverick*'s creator, aimed to craft a hero 'capable of deflating the clichéd moral lessons that concluded most episodic Westerns' (Anderson 1994: 230). Brett Maverick, a suave, wily trickster, makes his living gambling. Unlike the conventional Western heroes who populate television in this period, he is rather self-serving, morally ambiguous, somewhat cowardly. An inept gunhand, he generally schemes and manipulates to avoid outright conflict. In short, he 'finds an angle'. He sounds very much like Charlie Madison. And, like Charlie Madison, both Huggins and Garner ran afoul of their superiors. Both left the show after contract disputes with Warner Brothers, whose drive for profit in the effort to save their foundering studio by tapping into the television market resulted in hyper-industrialized production, intense exploitation of actors and writers, breathless schedules, repetitiveness and recycling in the many series they were mounting simultaneously. As Christopher Anderson reports, 'relying on a limited supply of stock footage and one crowded backlot, Warner Bros. Series not only shared a striking visual resemblance but even recycled many of the same shots' (Anderson 1994: 268).

Interestingly, *Maverick* frequently produced ironic citations of 'straight' Westerns, offering episodes that spoofed *Gunsmoke* and *Bonanza*, for example. Writer Marion Hargrove described *Maverick* as 'engaged in satirical raids' on these Westerns, targets, which 'couldn't fight back' (Anderson 1994: 236). As he told *Life Magazine* in 1959, '*Gunsmoke* . . . cannot parody *Maverick* without endangering its own impressive dignity, and *Maverick* has no dignity to attack' (Anderson 1994: 236).

Maverick shares *Emily*'s pleasure in attacking its genre, but its pleasure in the spoof also makes it a comfortable inhabitant of James Bond's cultural moment. As Tony Bennett and Janet Woollacott indicate, the period of the early 1960s could be considered '*the* moment of Bond' (Bennett and Woollacott 1987: 236). In an enormously profitable cultural cross-pollination, backed by United Artists investments, the British industry produced a rapid output during the mid-1960s: *From Russia With Love* (Terence Young, 1963), *Goldfinger* (Guy Hamilton, 1964), *Thunderball* (Terence Young, 1965). At the same time, *Playboy* discovered Bond, and its interest in him coincides with his 'widespread use as a figure in advertising and commodity design' (Bennett and Woollacott 1987: 33).

In his exquisite and cosmopolitan tastes in women, food, cigarettes, liquor and clothes, and his love of technology, gadgets and cars, Bond is a likely hero for middle-class male consumers. Significantly, a good part of Bond's 'modernity' resides in the way he answers to a 'new, meritocratic style of cultural and political leadership, middle class and professional rather than aristocratic and amateur' (Bennett and Woollacott 1987: 34–5). This style, of course, contributes to his portability and his allure for the rising US professional managerial class, whose taste, culture and consumer habits resemble his.

Perhaps most strikingly, Bennett and Woollacott point out that Bond is ultimately a 'NATO' hero, 'adjusted to the prevailing climate of détente' (1987: 33). This means that his primary function comes down to averting the consequences of plots and manipulations aimed at creating catastrophic misunderstandings between the Soviet Union and the West (Bennett and Woollacott 1987: 33). A consummate crisis manager and diplomat, Bond navigates bureaucracy with aplomb. He thus shares Charlie Madison's most prominent characteristics; like Charlie, he's a middleman.

Airplanes and Motion Pictures

It is not surprising that images and story of *The Americanization of Emily* should be both enriched and destabilized by the pressure of the cross-cultural and generic exchanges its intertextual references bring to bear. At the film's heart is the Admiral's grandiose and delusional ambition to make a film that will help the Navy win out over the Army in the eyes of the Government. It is thus centrally concerned with the political and economic power of images.

At the Admiral's diplomatic dinner for the General, we learn his agenda: to take 'extreme measures' to 'publicize' the D-Day role of the Navy. From this point on, Jessup's machinations become increasingly baroque, maniacal and, eventually, insane. Admiral Jessup's agitated reflections on the means of raising the Navy's publicity profile culminate when he bursts in on Charlie and Emily with the excited announcement, 'The first dead man on Omaha Beach must be a sailor!' This is a visually stunning moment, since we have been watching the lovers in an atmosphere of inky shadow, and they are suddenly illuminated by a glaringly harsh frontal light which registers their astonishment. Framed in the doorway, with light shining through his rumpled nightshirt, the Admiral cuts a singularly bizarre figure.

His epiphany comes in the form of a slogan that will launch a publicity campaign: 'All of Washington is bug-eyed about this invasion . . . And the invasion is an all-Army show . . . That's why we're here. To remind Congress and the American public that this invasion of Europe is also a Navy show.' As the Admiral makes these remarks, the camera moves in to punctuate the words 'Navy show' with a tight close-up on his bowed head as he collapses in wicked laughter. This is a key scene, because it propels the rest of the film, which unfolds the Admiral's efforts to literalize the metaphor of the 'show'. In the segments that frame Charlie's tea with Emily and her mother, where he delivers the film's central 'anti-war' speech, the Admiral obsessively repeats his campaign slogan and aggressively pursues his efforts to guarantee that the first dead man on Omaha beach is a sailor whose death can be documented on film.

Far from focusing on the D-Day invasion itself, then, the Admiral is already anxiously projecting the ascendancy of the Army as the 'dominant service' in its aftermath. His expressed fear is that the Army's 'new bomber programme' will establish its dominance, leaving the Navy shrunken, 'scrapped', 'the runt of the litter'. Thus, in his breathless ambition, he aims to challenge the Army's *airplanes* with his *motion picture*.

As the Admiral addresses his staff who are lined up across the screen, he announces, 'I want a movie made that shows the Navy's contribution to D-Day.' While he develops his idea, waxing on about the number and type of vessels that will make up the 'largest armada ever assembled', the camera pans around the heads of the officers and circles back to frame them in medium shot as he speaks. Thus, we inevitably become aware of the cinematic artifice that attends the fictional conception of a documentary film. From this point forward, the status of the film we are watching is inextricably implicated in the one the Admiral aims – or projects? – to have his staff make.

In the sequences that bracket Charlie's critique of the rhetoric of heroism, sacrifice and commemoration that perpetuate war, he rapidly becomes more deeply implicated in the Admiral's schemes. Immediately following the tea, we follow the Admiral from a day-long D-Day briefing with his colleague, Admiral Thomas Healy (Ed Binns).[6] To let off steam, the officers propose to spend the evening getting drunk, which they do in a frenzied and chaotic sequence which makes clear that Admiral Jessup is becoming mentally unbalanced and that ends with his literal loss of balance in a collapse.

This sequence concludes with another shot of the Admiral's bowed head, starkly lit, as he collapses in Charlie's arms, assigning responsibility for making the movie to him before he passes out. In one of the many dissolves[7] that link sequences in this film, the image of the inert Admiral blends into Charlie's purposeful walk as he rejoins his fellow officers in the morning. He finds Bus and Captain Marvin Ellender (Douglas Henderson) in what appears to be a commercial movie theatre, complete with drapes and full-size screen, as well as a deep auditorium. We watch the three men, their faces illuminated by the light of the screen against the darkened depths of the auditorium. They watch the film which is to be the model for theirs; this is a documentary about the training exercises naval demolition engineers perform as preparation for clearing mines in the invasion. So this film is the 'rehearsal' of the 'real' one that Charlie is expected to make. As the film cuts back and forth between the screen they are watching, which coincides almost exactly with the film frame, we hear a voice whose hollow, metallic authority and vague sense of urgency is generic to the Second World War documentary, familiar to the post-war generations from its appropriations in fiction film. Likewise, the images appear to be stock footage of the sort with which Second World War films often filled out battle scenes. This practice accounts for the striking homogeneity and near abstraction of scenes and locales of combat as they recur across the genre.

When Jessup arrives, he enthuses that this is just what he wants his film to be like, except that he wants Charlie and crew to get right into the water with the engineers and follow them to the beach. Charlie confronts him as they stand before the screen on which the film continues to roll, held in medium close-up, squeezed to opposite sides of the frame. When Charlie asserts that he gets 'the feeling a man could get killed making this movie', the screen between their heads fills with explosions. He objects to taking a 'lot of risk' 'for no particular reason', concluding that 'It seems to me the only thing at stake here is a matter of naval public relations.' As the Admiral switches the terms, asserting that what is at stake is the inviolability of the order he has given, he avoids the central question of *public relations* which will drive the film to its conclusion.

Locked in their central dispute over the purpose of the cinematic representation, Charlie and Jessup are visually superimposed upon the film within the film. As the men stand weirdly flattened against the screen, we are reminded that, up to this point, arguably, the war has been a kind of movie for Charlie. He has seemed a distant, distracted spectator, who just now is about to be absorbed into that film.

Of course, in the sequence when Charlie meets Emily's 'dotty' mother, a war widow who denies the deaths of her husband and son, he gives the speech that earned it contemporary praise from Bosley Crowther, as 'slashing irreverence', that 'says more for pacifism than a fistful of intellectual tracts' (1964: C2). And as compelling as this speech is, it only gathers force from the moments that frame it. When Charlie arrives bearing a gift of Hershey's chocolates, Emily declines this 'small token of opulence'. 'Don't Americanize me', she enjoins him. 'I think it's profane to enjoy this war.' But this sequence is punctuated by Emily's exhibiting family photographs and portraits. A portrait of her uniformed father, who lost a leg in the First World War, presides over the small salon; it was painted, we learn, just before he died in an air raid. Indicating her brother's photograph, and her husband's, Emily recounts their deaths. Charlie responds to this memorial gallery by observing, 'I never realized what a sensual satisfaction grieving is for women.' But his subsequent speech will help to clarify this brutal quip.

Addressing Mrs Barham (Joyce Grenfell), Charlie declares 'cowardice' to be his new religion, his conversion to which allowed him to accept his job as the Admiral's aide to escape the combat in Guadalcanal, where his ill-conceived enlistment had landed him. 'Have you noticed that war is the only chance a man gets to do something redeeming? That's why war is so attractive', he tells the women, describing all the men 'screaming in agony' and dying around him as 'brave men', who 'in peacetime' had been 'normal, decent, cowards, frightened of their wives, trembling before their bosses, terrified of the passing of the years.' 'But war had made them gallant', he continues. 'They had been greedy men; now they were self-sacrificing. They had been selfish; now they were generous.' Before war ennobled them, each had been, in short, post-war America's dreaded 'man in the grey flannel suit', an emasculated corporate conformist. As Steven Cohan puts it, this figure 'exemplified the average white collar worker', who 'was no paragon of integrity, but a man who had sold out for a buck' (Cohan 1997: 72).

Charlie concludes his meditations, pronouncing, 'It's not war that's unnatural to us, you see; it's the morality of it. Wars are always fought for the best of reasons . . . always against tyranny and always in the interests of humanity . . . As long as valour remains a virtue, we shall have soldiers.' At this point, however, Mrs Barham offers some reflections of her own:

> After every war we always find out how unnecessary it was. And after this one I'm sure all the generals will dash off and write books about the blunders made by other generals, and statesmen will publish their secret diaries and it will show that war could easily have been avoided in the first place. And the rest of us will be left with the job of bandaging the wounded and burying the dead.

To this, Charlie replies by attacking precisely the memorializing impulses that characterize both mother and daughter. 'It's the rest of us who build statues to those generals . . . the rest of us who make heroes of our dead and shrines of our battlefields, who perpetuate war by exalting sacrifice'.

As he and Emily rise to leave, Mrs Barham, apparently having found his words therapeutic, admits that her husband and son are dead and, what's more, relinquishes any glorious image of those deaths. Significantly, as she speaks, we see Charlie against a backdrop of terraced houses, clearly a back projection – a film – which serves to flatten and denaturalize the space.[8] London, in the views that frame this sequence, looks like a billboard, a flattened abstraction.

Finding an Angle

When the film aggressively calls our attention to its own *images* as they frame this remarkable critique of the vocabulary of heroism, sacrifice and redemption, it also highlights Charlie's own emphasis, while pressuring it to shift slightly. Rather than morality and virtue, perhaps what is most centrally at stake here is representation and image. But this sequence also lays out the stakes the rest of this story – along with Charlie – must negotiate. In the course of making this dangerous film, he risks becoming the very image of heroism and sacrifice that he challenges. When this scenario doesn't play out, and he survives, the Admiral and Bus struggle to adjust by marketing a survivor in place of a dead hero. But the film produces

Charlie's return as anti-climax. Its flatness serves the film's often deadpan ironic tone admirably, hollowing out any possibility for triumph and, no doubt, more closely approximating the feeling tone of the traumatized combat survivor's actual experience than conventional Second World War movies produced from 1949 to 1964.

At a pivotal moment, when the Admiral's mental instability has become glaringly obvious – he falls into a trance and ends up hospitalized – Bus and Healy suddenly embrace the project that Charlie characterizes as insane. Bus has done an about-face when he learns that the President has shown interest in the film. So the Admiral's delusional plan becomes enmeshed in the machinations of naval bureaucracy, as Bus issues orders to himself and Madison, obliging them to accompany the D-Day landing boats. Struggling to avert the mortal consequences he anticipates, Charlie threatens what amounts to a 'public relations' solution, reminding Bus of the scandal produced when newspapers reported General Patton's striking a soldier hospitalized with 'combat fatigue'. After Bus strikes him in rage and storms out of Charlie's room – but not before tripping over a pile of his stock – Marv points out to Charlie that he won't follow through and expose the Admiral to the press. 'You're going to have to find a better angle out of this', Marv tells him.

'Finding an angle', if we think about it, aptly describes the Admiral's machinations to advance the Navy's case in the inter-service competition with which he is preoccupied. That angle involves making sure a sailor is the first to die on the beach so that his death can be filmed, thus providing him a favourable 'angle' for his pitch to Congress on behalf of the Navy's importance. Certainly, 'finding an angle' effectively characterizes most of Charlie Madison's professional activity. And, thus, his position curiously comes around to meet the Admiral's. They are both good public-relations men at heart; we can surely regard the Admiral's film and his campaign for the Navy's profile as pure public relations and product differentiation.

In one of the film's many ironic moments, Charlie has learned that he will miss what the Admiral calls 'the big show', since the invasion force will depart at 9:30 p.m. that night. 'Now *that's* an angle!' Charlie's plane leaves at 9 p.m., so he misses the boat. Emily sees Charlie off in a scene that condenses all their differences into their competing angles of view on the war. While Charlie cheerfully reports his expectation to be back in London for lunch the next day, as if he were on an overnight business trip, Emily accuses him of making a 'private joke' of the invasion and announces that she will not marry him, because she 'despises cowardice, detests selfish people, and loathes ruthlessness', her inventory of his main traits. Invoking cultural difference, she tells him: 'I believe in honour, and service, and courage, and fair play, and cricket, and all the other symbols of the British character which only civilized half the world.' He quips, 'You British plundered half the world for your own profit. Let's not pass it off as the Age of Enlightenment.'

But he insists that her reluctance to marry has nothing to do with cultural differences but with cowardice masquerading as moral principle: 'You've done the morally right thing. God save us all from people who do the morally right thing. It's the rest of us who get broken in half.' He concludes, having effectively demolished the cultural and moral 'angles': 'I want you to remember that the last time you saw me, I was unregenerately eating a Hershey Bar.'

But angles suggest photography and film as well. The Admiral's movie constitutes his 'angle' in the public-relations battle against the Army's air corps, its planes. Charlie's scheduling 'angle' fails him, as the invasion turns back in bad weather, leaving him right on time for the next night's launch. After a drunken Charlie and his two 'cameramen' mess mates commandeered for this job, are ignominiously hoisted in a net and dumped into the landing craft, the film proceeds to construct the invasion sequence through parallel editing. Alternating close-ups of the men in the boat with long shots of ships and, eventually, explosions, the sequence is markedly disjunctive. A man vomiting into his helmet produces a citation of *The Longest Day*,[9] which is intercut with the snippets of stock footage. Their content and their widely varying film stocks make the most generic of references to Second World War films. This deliberately clumsy, disjointed editing emphasizes the friction and collision of cinematic images.

When Charlie and Bus and the professional cinematographer who has finally been assigned to them 'land', the film offers no continuity whatsoever. After a cut, we see bodies catapulted into the water. As Charlie struggles clumsily in the surf, he quickly abandons his 'character', since he turns to run away from the beach, his camera angled up toward the sky. Bus keeps shouting to 'take pictures'. When he finally shoots Charlie in the leg to force him back to the beach, he succeeds in putting him 'back in character'. Or, he frames him: we watch with Bus and the cameraman, who is filming this, as Charlie lurches and scrambles amid the beach's fortifications. And we notice that not only is he the *first* man on the beach, but he is also – impossibly – the *only* man on the beach. When he finally falls, apparently dead, the cameraman remarks, 'Well, he's the first dead man on Omaha Beach, if *that* means anything.' This sequence closes on an image of his body at the frame's horizon line, and the rest of the film will be preoccupied with the meanings and interpretation of the still images captured here. Significantly, the Admiral's motion picture has failed; it has given way to the photograph.

In the sequence that immediately follows the image of Charlie's still body on the beach, we see Bus paying a condolence visit to Emily and her mother. As this scene unfolds, the camera repeatedly captures the enshrined images of the family's war dead. Bus proudly displays Charlie's picture on the front page of *the New York Globe* and carries on about how widely the photograph has circulated (in 200 newspapers in the USA alone). He marvels that this was just a 'standard release' from the press office; 'we didn't expect it to catch on this big'. Mrs Barham cannily remarks that it's not a very good likeness; 'it's mostly his back'. Bus continues recounting that the Public Relations office is talking about a big ceremony and a monument. One might conclude from this scene that the public-relations 'angle' of such broad dissemination and such grandiose consequences relates directly to the image's anonymity: the specific individual framed as a cipher, as in the Tomb of the Unknown Sailor.

Managing Memory

At this point, the film begins to elaborate its ironies, for this sequence dissolves to a scene in the Admiral's bathroom. As he stands framed in his mirror, he asks Bus how Charlie happened even to be on Omaha Beach, and what movie he was making. When Bus tries to jog his memory, it dawns on the Admiral to ask, 'Was this some idea I conceived when I was cracking up?' But just as the machinery of navy public relations picked up the Admiral's crazy idea when he became too crazy to cancel it, so Bus entwines Charlie's death in the ongoing publicity campaign: 'We wanted a hero. Now we've got one.' But when Bus mentions the idea of a monument on Omaha Beach, the Admiral overcomes his concern for Charlie and gets back in the game. If they want to 'catch the eye of the Joint Committee on Military Affairs', he asserts, they'll need 'something much more *immediate* than that' – a commemoration in Washington.

Abruptly, the film cuts to a startling image of Charlie in tight close-up, looking haggard and irritated as he lands back in England. In this strangely anticlimactic scene, the camera leads us through the disorienting and disoriented crowd of military men to focus on a newsstand, where a repeated image of Charlie running on the beach seems to march from cover to cover, across *Life*, *Newsweek*, *Yank*. After Charlie jadedly turns down an offer of a copy of *Life*, the next sequence shows Bus and the Admiral about to board their plane for Washington when the news of Charlie's survival arrives. Bus is incredulous and appalled at the public-relations disaster: '200 newspapers in the US alone . . . every newsreel in the world.' 'We had a nice dead hero', he snarls, 'now we've got a lousy live coward!' But the Admiral is far more sanguine; he already has a strategy for managing this crisis and turning it around: 'We're going to bring your first dead man on Omaha Beach right into Room # 610 of the Senate Office Building.' He projects bringing Charlie with him as a special aide for senate hearings on military appropriations, mounting a brass parade, 'using every coarse theatricality the public relations office is overpaid to think up'. Despite his expressed contempt for public relations, Jessup repeatedly demonstrates his expertise in packaging and pitching whatever product fate deals him. Significantly, Steven Cohan reminds us that the quintessential 'Man in the Gray Flannel Suit', depicted by Gregory Peck in the film of the same name (Nunnally

Johnson, 1956) was not only a Second World War veteran, but he was employed in public relations (Cohan 1997: 70, 76). It seems that the military – far from redeeming the man in the grey flannel suit – has become his ideal environment.

Bus, who has been dispatched to Southampton, is once again outraged to learn that one of his colleagues has already alerted the public-relations office to this reversal of fortune and that the press is flocking to the site. But he immediately moves to spin the occasion and begins to offer the heroic story he wants told. Only Charlie resists, insisting he wants to tell the truth, that 'a deranged Admiral had a demented idea for a lunatic movie whose only purpose was to juice up the Navy's bid for military appropriations'. 'I won't contribute to your wretched hoax', he asserts. 'I won't help you preserve the wonder of war . . . I want people to know . . . the whole shabby story about my heroism'. As this dispute escalates, Emily intervenes to ask why Charlie would persist in 'this futile gesture of virtue', which can lead to serious consequences for both of them. She sets about convincing him to chuck the principle and play the role of the hero. And in so doing, she ventriloquizes his speeches to her: 'It's the virtue of war that's a fraud, not war itself . . . And here you are, being brave, self-sacrificing and absolutely clanking with moral fervour, perpetuating the very things you detest, merely to do the right thing . . . All this time I've been terrified of becoming Americanized, and you, you silly ass, have turned into a bloody Englishman.'

Persuaded by this performance of the cultural chiasmas that confronts them, Charlie agrees to face the journalists, asking Bus, 'How do you want me to play it? Modest and self-effacing?' As a military march comes up on the soundtrack, the film cuts to its final image: a laughably crude and awkward bronze figure that approximates Charlie's running figure. This craven little image is rendered all the more pathetic and fragile as the camera wavers slightly as it pulls away from close-up range. This is a shaky hero indeed. But it reminds us that this film has been less about war than about the stories we tell ourselves about it and, more important, about the stories we tolerate which are routinely peddled to the very young who constitute our reservoir of sacrificial bodies.

In the image of Charlie lurching toward his putative death which emerges serially on magazine covers as well as in the tawdry little statue with which the film closes, we see the 'heroic death' sloganized. Abstracted as it is, just like the Normandy landing that the film renders schematically on a California beach, it resembles a slogan. Charlie's final position cancels the British one at the film's end, but we are struck by the way his position has somehow been cancelled as well, once he has submitted to the Navy's repackaging. Is 'finding an angle' the fundamental image of Americanness? In this film's sharp terms, 'Americanization' seems at first to mean managing and arranging, functioning as a middleman, like Charlie. But that image, in its mediocrity, is darkly overshadowed by the image of 'Americanization' as a public-relations project. For this film, to be 'American' is to turn history, politics and diplomacy into public relations. This biting conclusion seems especially timely as we are daily dunned by the platitudinous rhetoric of sacrifice in which every war death is a sacrifice and yet every sacrifice always demands justification by *yet another* sacrifice.

Notes

1   Interestingly, Hiller went on to direct *The Rifleman* (1958) and *Gunsmoke* (1959–60), contemporaries of Garner's popular *Maverick*.
2   More commonly known as a medium shot, post-war French critics dubbed it the 'American shot'. The medium shot frames the human body approximately from the upper thigh or waist up.
3   Significantly, Huie's novel makes much of brand names as well. See, for example: 'So our store offered every luxury in short supply: cigarettes, candy, soap, vitamins, nylon stockings, girdles, black nightgowns, cosmetics, lipstick, nail varnish, perfumes, champagne, and many cases of Johnny Walker Black Label and I.W. Harper whiskey' (Huie 1959: 15).
4   Kristin Ross goes so far as to contend that 'the foremost American export of the period was . . . the supremacy of the social sciences' (Ross 1995: 186). And she is quick to emphasize that these are of the empirical or quantitative type, tending towards the statistical models compatible with business.
5   Significantly, director Arthur Hiller comments on DVD that he relied rather heavily on long takes (shots sustained for unusually long periods before a cut) in order to discourage the studio from re-editing his film.
6   The actor introduces a jarring echo here, since he played Colonel Grady, the pilot who actually drops the nuclear bomb in *Fail Safe*.
7   'A dissolve briefly superimposes one shot over the next, which takes its place: one image fades out as another fades in' (Corrigan and White 2004: 114).
8   Rear projection is a form of 'projection process work', which involves 'placing the actors against a translucent screen and projecting a film of the setting from behind the screen. The whole ensemble could then be filmed from the front.' This technique 'was widely used well into the 1960s, but it does not create a very convincing set of depth cues' (Bordwell and Thompson 1986: 160).
9   In another deliberate irony, he vomits as the officer reads the official slogan-ridden message to the troops: 'You are about to embark on a great crusade. The hopes and prayers of liberty loving people everywhere go with you.'

References

Anderson, C. (1994) *Hollywood TV: The Studio System in the Fifties*, Austin, Tex.: University of Texas Press.

Ashby, J. and Higson, A. (eds) (2000) *British Cinema, Past and Present*, London and New York: Routledge.

Bennett, T. and Woollacott, J. (1987) *Bond and Beyond: The Political Career of a Popular Hero*, New York: Methuen.

Boddy, W. (1990) *Fifties Television: The Industry and Its Critics*, Urbana, Ill.:University of Illinois Press.

Bordwell, D. and Thompson, K. (eds) (1986) *Film Art: An Introduction*, New York: Alfred Knopf.

Cohan, S. (1997) *Masked Men: Masculinity and the Movies in the Fifties*, Bloomington, Ind.: Indiana University Press.

Corrigan, T. (1983) *New German Film: The Displaced Image*, Austin, Tex.: University of Texas Press.

Corrigan, T. and White, P. (eds) (2004) *The Film Experience: An Introduction*, Boston, Mass.: Bedford/St. Martin's.

Crowther, B. (1964) *New York Times*, 28 October, p. C2.

Dickinson, M. and Street, S. (1985) *Cinema and State: The Film Industry and the Government, 1927–1985*, London: BFI.

Doherty, T. (1993) *Projections of War: Hollywood, American Culture, and World War II*, New York: Columbia University Press.

Elsaesser, T. (1989) *New German Cinema: A History*, New Brunswick, NJ: Rutgers University Press.

Forbes, J. and Street, S. (2000) *European Cinema: An Introduction*, London: Palgrave.

Huie, W. B. (1959) *The Americanization of Emily*, New York: E. P. Dutton.

Kuisel, R. (1993) *Seducing the French: The Dilemma of Americanization*, Berkeley, Calif.: University of California Press.

Landy, M. (2000) 'The Other Side of Paradise: British Cinema from an American Perspective', in J. Ashby and A. Higson (eds) *British Cinema, Past and Present*, London and New York: Routledge, pp. 63–79.

Nowell-Smith, G. (ed.) (1996) *The Oxford History of World Cinema*, Oxford: Oxford University Press.

Petrie, D. (1996) 'British Cinema: The Search for Identity', in G. Nowell-Smith (ed.) *The Oxford History of World Cinema*, Oxford: Oxford University Press, pp. 604–13.

Ross, K. (1995) *Fast Cars, Clean Bodies: Decolonization and the Reordering of French Culture*, Cambridge, Mass.: MIT Press.

Suid, L. (2002) *Guts and Glory: The Making of the American Military Image in Film*, Lexington, Ky.: University Press of Kentucky.

Torres, S. (2003) *Black, White, and In Color: Television and Black Civil Rights*, Princeton, NJ: Princeton University Press.

Watson, E. (1995) *The Expanding Vista: American Television in the Kennedy Years*, Durham, NC.: Duke University Press.

Wolcott, J. (2005) 'From Fear to Eternity', *Vanity Fair*, March, pp. 220–4.

Chapter 8

American Graffiti (1973)

Barry Langford

At one level, George Lucas's *American Graffiti* (1973) is a representative example of a widespread preoccupation with defining – and recovering – 'Americanness' in the immediate aftermath of the social and political crisis of the late 1960s. Nostalgic, eulogistic, often cynical, sometimes plain maudlin, *American Graffiti* also recognizably foreshadows the reaffirmation of a transvalued Americanism that would characterize US culture under the New Right. In fact, the film elaborates key terms in the establishment of a new historical imaginary as a point of departure/point of return for a disenchanted present. A concern, even an obsession, with the images and meanings of 'America' typifies many of the films of the Hollywood New Wave, or Hollywood Renaissance, of the late 1960s and 1970s – the period of stylistic experimentation Geoff King (2001) has termed 'New Hollywood, Version I' to differentiate this first post-classical era of American cinema from the blockbuster-driven multiplex-orientation contemporary corporate Hollywood. By setting *American Graffiti* in the context of the 'critical Americanism' practised in many of the other most highly regarded New Hollywood films of the 1970s, we can identify both those elements the film shares with its contemporaries, and those it importantly – and influentially – does not.

Losing America

'This used to be a hell of a country . . . I can't imagine what's happened to it.'
George Hanson (Jack Nicholson), *Easy Rider*

Ambivalent and conflictual representations of American national identity are a central dimension of the 'New Hollywood' throughout its peak years from 1967 to 1977. It would take considerable ingenuity and imaginative elasticity to argue that these constitute anything like an elaborated ideological critique or even a coherent political position – all too often, New Hollywood films trade in less-than-subtle state-of-the-nation metaphors which are purely gestural: typically symbolic force substitutes for argument. In a few important cases, however, the sub- or paratextual political reference is indeed brought to the fore. One film in which the styles of tension that characterize Hollywood films in this decade are unusually starkly displayed – because they are presented in a non-narrative, and nakedly ideological, fashion – is Alan J. Pakula's classic conspiracy thriller *The Parallax View* (1974), which offers one of the New Hollywood's most striking and unsettling perspectives on film, ideology and nationhood.

The film's hero, reporter Joe Frady (Warren Beatty), having assumed the identity of an unstable loner in order to penetrate the Parallax Corporation – a shadowy para-governmental organization Frady suspects of engineering and covering up Kennedy-style political assassinations – subjects himself to the Parallax 'entry test'. This comprises a five-minute non-narrative film montage designed to elicit an identificatory response from the Oswald-types Parallax suborns as fall guys for its labyrinthine conspiracies: it's an audio-visual Rorschach for lone nuts. As we watch alongside Beatty, the test montage morphs reassuring, affirmative signifiers of individuality, family and country into pathologically disturbing tropes of violence, oppression and exclusion. Images of beneficent fatherhood and the consoling, inclusive embrace of the idealized American community, scored to tinkling muzak, darken into images of familial abuse and the coercive state (Hitler, Selma, Daley cops, Vietnam, etc.), the impact intensified by a relentless, discordant electronic soundtrack. The conceit of the Parallax test is that it is beyond conventional politics: its vision of the American inferno will draw a matching violence from subjects of the requisite pathology, regardless of their ideology. Rightists can react against the sequence's images of the permissive society and leftists embrace the implicit quasi-Laingian critique of the family and the state, but it is their common locus of exclusion and rage, not their specific value systems, that will qualify them as Parallax operatives.[1] The direct implication of the Parallax test sequence is that the traditional tropes of American values have been evacuated of meaning beyond even cliché, become empty vessels exploited indifferently by a corporate Moloch impervious to conventional political critique or opposition: a claim entirely congruent with the widespread mood of disaffection with the democratic process as a whole that exercised political commentators in the mid-1970s (and which Beatty's subsequent film, *Shampoo* [1975] would neatly encapsulate). Equally, Pakula uses the unusual (for Hollywood) and highly self-conscious device of the film-within-a-film to direct his audience to reflect on the role of cinema itself in sustaining such relations of manipulation and domination in contemporary America.

The Parallax View is organized thematically around a frequently ironic treatment of insight and blindness – of 'views'. The Parallax test redirects the general thematic preoccupation with vision specifically towards the vision of film itself – confirming the suggestion of the title, which alludes to the problems posed by the differential perspectives of viewfinder and lens for the framing and hence the legibility of the filmed image. Although the didactic montage style of the Parallax test stands at a clear remove from standard Hollywood practice, this very didacticism enables the sequence to present in stark, even reductive form many of the same preoccupations, insights and intuitions that typify the 1970s New Hollywood as a whole. Just as the Parallax test 'refunctions' traditional American iconography, many other New Hollywood films deploy Americana to ironic and/or critical purpose.[2] In a number of 1970s films, profuse displays of Americana – flags, parades, anthems, pastimes, all the regalia of disenchanted nationhood – advertise a critical project animated by a sceptical, recognizably Brechtian self-consciousness.

The most blatant example is the Stars and Stripes itself – ubiquitous in New Hollywood films, from the emblazoned petrol tank in *Easy Rider* (Dennis Hopper, 1969) onwards – which during the Parallax test is 'refunctioned' from a banner of transcendent freedom into an emblem of historically locatable oppression. Traditionally, Hollywood had used the US flag – especially during and after the Second World War – in the straightforward patriotic spirit of Iwo Jima.[3] When, on the other hand, the flag provides the backdrop for a federal judge's hackneyed, self-regarding tirade in the Jules Feiffer-scripted *Little Murders* (Alan Arkin, 1971), the scene sums up the contrasting spirit of 1970s Hollywood – characterized by Pauline Kael (1975: 256) as 'part of the new retroactive anti-Americanism'. Hanging flaccid and defeated or flapping with ironic confidence, flags lend a suggestion of political and social allegory or at least a wider frame of historical reference to films including *Joe* (John G. Avildsen, 1970), Arthur Penn's *Alice's Restaurant* (1970), both *Godfather* films, Hal Ashby's *Shampoo* (1975), Michael Ritchie's 'American trilogy' of *The Candidate* (1972), *Smile* (1975), and *The Bad News Bears* (1976), Robert Altman's *Nashville* (1976) and *Buffalo Bill and the Indians* (1977), and many others, including naturally *All the President's Men* (Alan J. Pakula, 1976). The iconoclastic trend runs the gamut from satiric diminution – the tiny flag planted on the indifferent desert soil of a distant planet which provokes Charlton Heston's caustic laughter in *Planet of the Apes* (Franklin J. Schaffner, 1968) – to burlesque excess – the storeys-high banner that corrupt patriarch John Huston rips apart as he tumbles to his death at the end of William Richert's anarchic conspiracy fantasy *Winter Kills* (1980). *Nashville* famously concludes with an extended zoom-out from another giant flag, beneath which the film's atomized communities briefly connect to sing along that, in the words of the film's Me-generation idiots' anthem, 'It Don't Worry Me'.

Westerns of the 1970s mine a particularly rich seam of ironized regalia. The community, culture- and country-building vignettes beloved of John Ford are replayed as charades masking self-interested venality (the downbeat climax of Altman's *McCabe and Mrs. Miller* [1971] parodically restages the celebrated church dedication scene from Ford's *My Darling Clementine* [1947]) or outright brutality – borne by the US cavalry, Old Glory flutters gaily over My-Lai-style atrocities in Penn's *Little Big Man* (1970) and *Soldier Blue* (Ralph Nelson, 1970). Coppola's later depiction of the flag-waving, Wagner-blasting, gook-annihilating Airborne Cavalry in *Apocalypse Now* (1979) in turn draws on these revisionist Western images as much as on memories of Vietnam itself. As manifestly ambivalent (or simply ambiguous) as it is, the symbolic presence of yet another outsize standard behind the eponymous Patton (George C. Scott) in the famous direct-to-camera address that opens Franklin J. Schaffner's Coppola-scripted 1970 biopic is about as close as the New Hollywood gets to a traditionally affirmative flag-waving moment.[4]

Francis Ford Coppola's *The Godfather* (1972) opens with the line 'I believe in America' – declared by an undertaker, who then refutes those convictions to seek refuge and redress in the more primitive structures of loyalty and vengeance represented by the Mafia. Thereafter, through the saga of the Corleone family between the turn of the century and the Eisenhower years, from Sicily via Ellis Island to Lake Tahoe, the film and its first sequel (1974) develop the American cinema's most sustained and corrosive picture of the fatal allure of the American Dream since von Stroheim's *Greed* (1925). The two films are notable for not relying solely on symbolic tableaux like the child Vito Corleone's first glimpse of the Statue of Liberty (in *Part II*) to make their case; rather, through both detailed depictions of institutions and practices – the Mob, politics, neo-colonialism, immigrant communities – and reflection upon the part of the characters themselves about the nature of American identity and American success, they grow towards a measure of the kind of complex historicity achieved by Visconti in *The Leopard* (1962). Later in the decade, Michael Cimino controversially closed his Vietnam epic *The Deer Hunter* (1978) – a film of comparable epic ambition to Coppola's diptych – with a beleaguered round of 'America the Beautiful', a scene whose degree of ironization or endorsement of its characters' naïve residual patriotic conviction provoked furious debate on both left and right.

But even with such exceptions, if the New Hollywood's American vision amounted to no more than these mostly superficial gestures of disaffection, it would be hard to take issue with Pauline Kael's dismissive reference (somewhat prophetically, in 1967) to film-makers working strenuously to puncture 'the myths we never believed in anyhow' (1987: 45). In general, contemporary critics quickly identified the self-lacerating strain in the New Hollywood as crypto-politics and tended not to take it very seriously. Six years later, in the fall of 1973, as the Watergate hearings provided daily confirmation of the endemic corruption of the American political establishment, Kael developed her charge that American films were implicated in, not commenting on, the Zeitgeist: 'Today, movies say that the system is corrupt, that the whole thing stinks . . . in the convictionless atmosphere, the absence of shared values, the brutalities taken for granted, the glorification of loser-heroes' (1977: 161–3). This Kael identified as itself a cynical and shallow move, a symptom not a diagnosis, less an authentic reaction of disgust at Vietnam and Watergate than the glib exploitation of those sentiments:

> American movies didn't 'grow up'; they did a flipover from their prolonged age of innocence to this age of corruption. When Vietnam finished off the American hero as righter of wrongs, the movie industry embraced corruption greedily; formula movies could be energised by infusions of brutality, cynicism, and Naked Apism, which could all be explained by Vietnam and called realism.
>
> (1977: 161–3)

It is perfectly reasonable to observe that neither New Hollywood's scepticism about traditional American values nor its exploitation of the accumulated symbolic capital of national iconography to express it are noteworthy except in the context of the hitherto reliably affirmative American cinema. Even a more favourably inclined viewer than Kael might regard scepticism as – certainly compared to any other medium bar network television – a minimally responsive reaction to America's crisis years of the late 1960s and early 1970s, while symbolic appropriation has evident precedents in the largely apolitical pop gestures of Jasper Johns, Andy Warhol and Robert Rauschenberg. Yet if iconographic refunctioning is accepted as a purely superficial critical gesture, it remains significant in advertising a widespread unease and dissatisfaction in New Hollywood with traditional images and imaginings of America – images Classic Hollywood had played an important role in disseminating, both to the American nation and the world. In fact, it is precisely the (necessary and inevitable) absence of a fully-articulated political discourse or context for its inchoate dissatisfaction that paradoxically enables New Hollywood to evolve a distinctive critical perspective on contemporary American life.

Kael and others dismissed New Hollywood's deflationary impulses as purely exploitative, jumping on the bandwagon of the fashionable cynicism that swiftly established itself as the hallmark of the new decade, in the downdraught of the tumultuous, inspirational, catastrophic, idealistic 1960s. Yet, with hindsight, the first half of the 1970s in America appears less a reaction to the 1960s than its frequently tragic final act. At least until Watergate, the dominant emotions discernible in popular culture in particular are exhaustion, bewilderment, sometimes anger, frequently sadness, even hopelessness and despair: all feelings which may finally resign themselves to cynicism but which are quite distinct from cynicism themselves. The transformation of the utopianism of the nascent New Left, encapsulated in the Port Huron Statement of 1961, into violent disillusion and correspondingly extreme, violent and destructive expressions of hostility to most aspects of life in the USA – revealed as 'Amerika' – is a complex story in which both Vietnam and the failure of Johnson's Great Society programme to renovate US political and economic life to manifest the New Left ideas of participatory democracy as they initially promised. Put simply, however, the counterculture's ultimate rejection *of* America has its roots in a rage at rejection *by* America – that is, at mainstream white America's failure to recognize its own true nature in the New Left's redemptive American vision.[5]

Of course, the New Hollywood, no more than the old, was in any sense an extension of the New Left or the counterculture, and it would be absurd to argue otherwise. Yet the same structure of feeling, the same arc of disappointment, offers a key to understanding the major New Hollywood films of the 1970s. Internal upheavals in the institutions and structures of American film-making and exhibition in the 1960s had made Hollywood better placed to focus and express the energies of American society than at any time since the demise of the studio system. During the decade, most of the major studios were taken over and became strategic holdings in the business fad of the time, the diversified conglomerate. At the same time, however, a wave of box-office catastrophes afflicted the industry, notably a string of ultra-high-budget studio musicals (*Doctor Dolittle*, 1967; *Star!* 1968; *Hello, Dolly*, 1969), which sought but failed to capture the increasingly chimerical family audience that had made *The Sound of Music* the all-time box-office champion in 1965. These flops and the parlous fiscal position into which they helped cast the industry by the decade's end suddenly made the studios much less reliable contributors to their new corporate parents' balance sheets and, in turn, hastened the departure from the scene of the remaining studio-era dinosaurs.

The stolidly affirmative Americanism of the transitional (late studio) era proved unsustainable in the face of Vietnam, Watts and Watergate. Changing audience patterns – particularly the need to appeal to the youth market – encouraged commercial film-makers to take up, or to commission projects which seemed to them to take up, fashionable critical attitudes towards 'Establishment' values and mores. A small minority of New Hollywood film-makers at least partly shared the New Left's excoriating vision of Amerika, while a somewhat larger number felt a measure of affinity with some – usually the more sybaritic or broadly 'cultural' (as opposed to 'political') aspects – of the youth counterculture.[6]

Such cultural affinities ensured that cynicism pure and simple was by no means the dominant tone of American movies in the first half of the 1970s; nor are the elements Kael identified as cynically present in movies necessarily or uniformly inauthentic as responses to the socio-historical situation Hollywood found itself in. The abiding preoccupation of the American cinema of the 1970s is loss. It is, by contrast with any period of Hollywood film-making before or indeed since, a profoundly disenchanted and often outright pessimistic cinema. Even in the most nihilistically inclined films of the period – *Nashville*, or Penn's *The Missouri Breaks* (1975), there is as much anger as world-weariness or disaffection. Moreover, it is mourning that best models the psychological and emotional profile of 1970s Hollywood: in the end, what the left-liberal cynicism of *Nashville*, the self-pity of *Easy Rider* and the backlash conservative resentment of *Dirty Harry* (1971) all share is a sense of loss, an elegy for an 'America' invoked (depending on the perspective of the film) as something either lost or unrealized, a promise and prospect unfulfilled or an achievement betrayed. Mourning is a condition by no means obviously or straightforwardly compatible with cynicism, which is marked by a disconnection from its object. The films of New Hollywood for the most part remain strongly invested in theirs. That mourned object is not easily or simply stated: it is perhaps best designated *America* – where (italicized or bracketed) *America* is distinguished from the lived, material social/political/economic realities of life in the USA in this period, i.e., *America* ≠ America. In fact, *America* as constructed in and through the films of New Hollywood is best understood as an absence, or a negative presence: less a coherent set of meanings and values than a term defined by, precisely, its obsolescence. The American promise whose betrayal is so insistently lamented in American popular culture of the early 1970s ought not to be seen as a substantive or verifiable socio-historical entity, or one directly experienced by those who mourn its passing: it is rather a myth of an impossible unity whose apprehension is possible only at the cost of its irremediable loss. As in Althusser's rereading of Lacan's Mirror Stage, the lost, unbroken America invoked in 1970s Hollywood is a myth whose perfection, wholeness and plenitude functions as a rebuke to the inevitably inadequate, incomplete reality of the self that perceives it. Hence, the general absence of affirmative visions in the films of this period – neither the right (deploring the subversion of traditional values) not the liberal left (mourning the failure of the utopian dreams of the 1960s) can do more than insist on a vision of contemporary America as a black hole swallowing up hope and ambition.

American Graffiti stands at the epicentre of this complex (in all senses of the word) pattern of forces. *Graffiti* is at once a notable exception to this disaffected rule – in its fondly nostalgic gaze – and continuous with the spirit of mourning at work in US popular culture of the period.

'Where Were You in '62?'

We all know, as every movie in the last ten years has pointed out, how terrible we are, how wrong we were in Vietnam, how we have ruined the world, what schmucks we are and how rotten everything is. It had become depressing to go to the movies. I decided it was time to make a movie where people felt better coming out of the theatre than when they went in. I became really aware of the fact that the kids were really lost, the sort of heritage we built up since the war [i.e., Second World War] had been wiped out by the '60s, and it wasn't groovy to act that way anymore, now you just sort of sat there and got stoned. I wanted to preserve what a certain generation of Americans thought being a teenager was really about – from about 1945 to 1962.

(George Lucas, quoted in Biskind 1998: 235)

American Graffiti stands in a unique relation to the currents in early 1970s Hollywood summarized above. Unlike Lucas's commercially unsuccessful first film, the dystopic SF fantasy *THX 1138* (1970) – released through Warner Bros. but very much the progeny of American Zoetrope, Francis Ford Coppola's short-lived Bay Area-based attempt to establish a collective environment for 'personal' film-making – *American Graffiti* was not only deliberately populist but also a wholesale studio picture, albeit a cheap one. (Originally commissioned by United Artists who rejected the final screenplay, the film was eventually picked up by Universal Studios' 'youth' unit – set up like comparable units at other major studios in the attempt to emulate the success of the youth-oriented BBS at Columbia in capturing the youth/counterculture audience, but whose last – and, somewhat ironically, by a huge margin its most profitable – production *American Graffiti* would prove to be.) But the film's miniscule budget ($750,000) and breakneck shooting schedule (twenty-eight days), largely unknown cast, mildly unconventional multistrand narrative structure (modelled after Fellini's *I Vitelloni*), innovative use of sound and music, plus the imprimatur of Coppola, benevolent patriarch of Hollywood's Young Turks,[7] all differentiated *American Graffiti* from the year's Old Hollywood turkeys such as *Earthquake* and *The Train Robbers* and firmly identified it as a New Hollywood film. *American Graffiti* pursued a canny strategy of triangulation, its virtually adult-free, rock 'n' roll milieu directed at the youth market while wholesome sex and drugs-free high-school high jinks and its wistful yet affirmative tone commended the film to conservative critics and middle American audiences. The vicissitudes of the shoot – notably the emergency relocation to Petaluma after the city council at San Rafael, the original location, withdrew permission for filming on the second night of shooting, and Haskell Wexler's providential last-minute enlistment as 'visual consultant' – as well as Universal's initial hostility to the finished film have all entered Hollywood lore in light of the film's runaway box-office success (with domestic rentals of $58 million, *American Graffiti* has frequently been estimated the most profitable studio picture, assessed on box-office return on investment, ever made) and Lucas's subsequent career as the popcorn mythmaker of *Star Wars*.[8]

A similar triangulation is discernible at the ideological level. While *American Graffiti*, as we shall see, clearly partakes of the lament for *America*, the always-already-lost national imaginary, it also undertakes a project of restitution: as Lucas's comments quoted above indicate, *American Graffiti* – in this regard differing very significantly from the contemporary films of Altman, Penn, Ritchie et al. – ultimately seeks to resecure rather than to challenge or subvert normative American values. It combines a revisionist account of recent American history with a reorientation of the terms of ideological debate away from the real-world complexities of American economic and imperial retrenchment in the early 1970s towards a cultural politics worked through in relation to a partly fantasized national past and brackets 'authentic' American experience and 'inauthentic' forms of contemporary social and cultural practice – specifically, those that posed challenges to hegemonic models of gender, race and sexuality. Ryan and Kellner are no doubt correct to note the strongly regressive drive in the film, and the suggestion that the protagonists' unconsummated sexual desires (nobody gets laid in *American Graffiti*) is alloyed with the overhanging shadow of social fragmentation in the later 1960s to induce in the spectator an infantile desire for stasis and security, the impossibility of which in turn generates anxieties over separation and loss (1988: 228–9). We might, however, adjust their Freudian paradigm, by the parenthetical insertion of a definite article, to reveal the specifically national locus of the film's affective charge: 'the threat of modernity provokes in this instance a desire for restoration of an earlier state of [*the*] union with a maternal and gratifying source of care' (Ryan and Kellner 1988: 228–9). The (white, male) spectator of *American Graffiti* is solicited to seek both refuge from and redress for the injuries suffered by hegemonic American identity in the later 1960s and early 1970s. This project entails the rendering of a mythic racially and culturally homogeneous youth culture focused emphatically on private and personal issues (sex, career paths, young adulthood generally), rather than the public and political concerns which would come to dominate the decade.[9]

At a grade-school level, all of this is neatly summarized by the payoff of *MAD Magazine*'s pictorial satire of *American Graffiti*.[10] Departing from its original, *MAD* does not fade out with Curt (Richard Dreyfuss; 'Squirt', predictably, for *MAD* readers) pensively departing for his nameless eastern college, but allows him finally a face-to-face encounter with the elusive object of his last night in Modesto's desire: the mysterious blonde driver of the white T-Bird (in the film, an airborne Curt wryly spies her car, as untouchable as ever, on the freeway below). Spotting her parked alongside the runway, 'Squirt' deplanes, filled with delirious erotic anticipation – only to find, to his dismay, his *belle idéale* to be a male with shoulder-length blond hair. Crestfallen, 'Squirt' asks the obvious question, 'What's with the *long hair*??' Replies the hirsute driver – his face at last revealed in a 'reverse angle':

> You may not believe this, but rather soon, *all* you chaps will be wearing your hair *long* like this! . . . You see, I am the drummer of a rather obscure English Rock Group! [*sic*] But we will have quite an influence on the rest of the '60s! Perhaps you have heard of us already? '*The Beatles*'?!?

Set aside the sledgehammer irony, obvious anachronisms and satiric license[11] – and overlook for the moment too the wholly unintended confession of the film's strongly homosocial dimension – and *MAD* is perfectly faithful to *American Graffiti*'s thesis of a youth and broader popular culture on the cusp of irrevocable, profound – and traumatic – change. The year '1962', in the film's construction at least, stands for a last sun-drenched instant of 'American innocence' prior to Dallas, the March on Washington, the Gulf of Tonkin and the arrival of the Beatles; more generally, it marks a last (imaginary) moment before the onset of the violent intergenerational conflict, militant Black, Chicano and American Indian nationalisms and women's and gay liberation movements which would, in different ways, destabilize the domestic hegemony of the white male imaginary in which *American Graffiti* is so heavily invested. While none of these incipient traumas play any part in the action of the film or are ever prefigured therein, they are of course famously invoked by the metonymic allusion to Vietnam in the closing capsule biographies that figure the futures of the film's (male) protagonists, primarily in the destinies of Toad (missing in action in Vietnam) and Curt (a writer 'living in Canada' – presumably dodging the draft).[12]

American Graffiti is, of course, the most successful entry in the Hollywood nostalgia cycle of the early/mid-1970s,[13] in which earlier, less conflicted and more purposeful, passages of the 'American century' were reviewed from the perspective of the disenchanted 1970s – although in some quarters the notion that so relatively recent a period as the early 1960s could be viewed nostalgically was greeted with incredulity.[14] By comparison with the Depression years (*Paper Moon*, Peter Bogdanovich, 1973; *The Sting*, George Roy Hill, 1973), the war years (*Summer of '42*, Robert Mulligan, 1971; *The Way We Were*, Sydney Pollack, 1973) or even the early 1950s (*The Last Picture Show*, Bogdanovich, 1971), the doo-wop malt-shop period treated by *American Graffiti* seemed to lack either significant social or historical content or, perhaps more importantly, a notional consensual meaning. The film's overwhelmingly favourable contemporary critical response therefore rested in large part on reviewers' willingness to engage with and indeed subscribe to *American Graffiti*'s vision of American (teen) life in 1962 on something like the film's own terms.[15] For numerous reviewers, *American Graffiti*'s epilogue proffered an irresistible critical invitation that elevated the picture from a slice of historical teen anthropology to something like a statement of national destiny. John Simon in *Esquire* (1973: 46) thought that *American Graffiti* not only documented but explained (how exactly, he didn't say) 'the innocence, the almost guilty innocence, that led to our stumbling into Vietnam, the Pentagon Papers and Watergate'. The film's most enthusiastic reviewer, Stephen Farber (1973: II1) in the *New York Times*, declared that 'the film freezes the last moment of American innocence'. While distancing himself from 1950s nostalgia generally, Farber added that he found himself 'drawn to the world created in *American Graffiti*' because, while acknowledging 'the insularity of the fifties . . . it also recalls the innocence and the sense of community – the shared language, music and humour that contributed to the last authentic national folk culture'. Foreign critics, too, chimed in: Chris Hudson in the *Spectator* (1973: 28) mused on

> memories of a time when Kennedy was still President, the 'hard stuff' was whisky and all was well and moderately innocent in the world, and if the writing was on the wall, it would be nothing more ominous than graffiti . . . Only eleven years have passed, but it is as if they are viewed across a great divide

echoing Farber's reflection that 'the kids who left home in 1962 . . . were embarking on a journey across centuries' (1973: II, 3).

There is a marked asymmetry between the film's few snatched gestures in the direction of this large national narrative and the forcefulness with which (white, male) reviewers seized on them to elevate *American Graffiti* into a eulogy for 'lost American innocence', as if *Graffiti* had supplied the pretext for an effusion of poignant reflection just waiting to surge forth. Few lines of dialogue make any allusion whatsoever to the world beyond the immediate malt-shop, hot-rod and making-out preoccupations of Modesto's teens: Curt's Clintonesque desire to meet Kennedy and, in a different register, John Milner's dismissal of the Beach Boys as 'surfer crap' and his complaint that 'rock and roll's been going downhill ever since Buddy Holly died'. Michel Crisiola in the *Nouvel Observateur* remarked the film's cultural and historical *lacunae* (Cuba, Vietnam, the death of Marilyn Monroe) and compared the characters' hermetic indifference to the outside world unfavourably to the references to the Algerian War in Godard's *A bout de souffle* and other New Wave films.

The theme of 'lost innocence' is, of course, ubiquitous in modern American literature, from Daisy Miller[16] through Jay Gatsby[17] to Malamud's *The Natural* and Richard Ford's *The Sportswriter*. So a pre-existing interpretative lexicon awaited the emotional tug of war between adulthood's wider horizons and home's familiar yet constraining comforts, a bifurcation narratively enacted by having Steve remain behind while Curt leaves. The film's closing image – Curt airborne on 'Magic Carpet Airlines', Wolfman Jack's paternal voice on his treasured transistor fading gradually into static as the airplane climbs – plugs *American Graffiti* into an American *Bildungsroman* reaching back to Thomas Wolfe. *American Graffiti* also connects to the elegiac tradition of the Western (the ambivalent antinomies of East and West, replayed in *American Graffiti*, are structurally central to the genre[18]), with Milner again the principal spokesman. His lament for the shrinking of the cruiser's horizons – 'used to be you cruise the strip for hours . . . it was really something' – is an equally self-conscious variant of the 'closing of the frontier' theme, and his hot-shot character, a target for every aspiring hot-rodder riding into town (Falfa [Harrison Ford], the out-of-towner John faces down in the climactic drag race sports a cowboy hat) is by design a juvenile version of the ageing gunfighter of post-war Westerns.[19]

Few critics at the time of the film's release voiced what now seems very obvious: that the film's partial and rose-tinted eulogy of a white middle-class American past is sustainable only through a strenuous exclusion of those social and political dimensions of America in 1962 which were – already at the time, and not merely in the incipient dislocations of 'the Sixties' – either challenging the stable world Lucas invokes or whose suppression was precisely the price to be paid for that stability. Of mainstream American critics, only Pauline Kael – who penned a second *New Yorker* review of the film in the fall[20] – even noted the film's masculinist perspective or chose to wonder 'for whom was it "just like that"?' in 1962: 'Not for women, not for blacks or Orientals or Puerto Ricans, not for homosexuals, not for the poor. Only for white middle-class boys whose memories have turned into pop' (1977: 155). Although Lucas subsequently claimed to regret denying *American Graffiti*'s female characters the emblematic post-film trajectories mapped out for their boyfriends, the omission is of course not only telling but essential. Like its peers, *American Graffiti*'s assumed subject position – the identity centred in the text and proffered to the spectator as a site of empathetic identification – is emphatically white, straight and male: in so far as this subjecthood is framed by a retrospective melancholy, the film is heavily invested in the white male pathos which characterizes much early 1970s American cinema.

American Graffiti's nostalgic remembrance is thus structured on a strategic forgetting in which the public and political are necessarily bracketed wholesale from the diegesis. Michel Grisolia in the *Nouvel Observateur* commented acerbically, 'The heroes of *American Graffiti* don't bother themselves about all that. They're somewhere else. Dangerously apolitical. . . . Yesterday's children, today's silent majority. They are the ones who elected Nixon.'[21]

Yet this isn't quite right. *American Graffiti*'s teens – even Steve, the future insurance salesman – can't be straightforwardly identified with the hard-hat, middle-American 'silent majority' Nixon mobilized against the counterculture in his speeches of 1970–1.[22] *American Graffiti*'s revisionist Americanism chimes more clearly with the cultural politics of the New Right – and not simply because Ronald Reagan and the tax-limiting Proposition 18, whose passage onto the California statute book in 1978 heralded the new US political order, both hailed from southern California. As Grisolia perhaps understandably misses – since in 1973 the New Right was still regrouping after Goldwater's calamitous 1964 campaign – what makes *American Graffiti* not only a conservative film but also a harbinger of the cultural politics of the 1980s is its gearing of the ostensibly retrospective gaze of nostalgic fantasy towards a direct and transparent purchase on the present.

The deliberate ambiguity in the film's representation of the early 1960s as effectively an extension of the 1950s – producing in several reviews (for example,

Farber in the *New York Times*) a measure of temporal slippage – reflects the governing conception of 'the Sixties' as a period of American self-alienation. The film's suggested remedy to this is to sever the continuity of cultural experience between the youth cultures of a newly-conceived 'long' 1950s (1952–62) and those of 'the Sixties' proper – while at the same time foreclosing through nostalgia on the 1960s' destabilizing extension into the present (i.e., the 1970s). *American Graffiti*'s nostalgia is the more politically effective precisely because in key ways it deviates from the classic nostalgic mode. It lacks the endemic, intentional and specific intertextuality Jameson (1991: 20) identifies as a 'constitutive and essential' element of the 'nostalgia mode' (Haskell Wexler's innovative night photography ensures that the film's visual register is distant from the melodramatically saturated colour of 1950s classics such as *Rebel Without a Cause*), but it also substitutes for the 'pseudohistoricity' and timelessness of genre pastiches like *Body Heat* (Lawrence Kasdan, 1981), an apparently very exact, quasi-anthropological recovery of a rather particular subculture that – 'objectively' – should have no particular claim to stand as a generalized or generalizable American experience. This enables *American Graffiti* to mask its fictive aspect while constructing a novel narrative that resecures the American imaginary in a refurbished popular cultural history.

The novelty of *American Graffiti* consists less in the fond evocation of a vanished prelapsarian youth folk culture as such than in its reinscription of rock 'n' roll in support of its conservative imaginary. Although by 1973 Elvis had accepted a medal from Nixon, rock remained essentially identified with youth and, to a degree at least, with youthful rebellion. *American Graffiti* separates out 'youthful rebellion' – time-limited and essentially contentless – from the more extravagant forms of social deviance and politicized forms of resistance to authority with which later 1960s rock had become identified and capitalizes on the emergent generation gap *within* rock's own constituency. In so doing, it anticipates – indeed, given the runaway success of the soundtrack album, it may reasonably be said to have inaugurated – the commodification of the 'classic rock' tradition (not a term in current parlance in 1973) in the FM era. By playing the first trump of the rock era, Bill Haley's 'Rock Around the Clock' (originally released in 1952 but not a major hit until used as the credits number for *The Blackboard Jungle*, 1954) over the opening credits, *American Graffiti* proposes itself as a summary review of rock 'n' roll's Golden Age. Rather than a typical radio playlist in summer/fall 1962, continuous with the film's cultural politics generally, the version of rock 'n' roll championed by the film is both emphatically male and subtly nationalistic. Of the forty-two songs on the soundtrack, none features a lead female vocalist, while the 'softer' pop sound of the Beach Boys is dismissively rejected by John Milner, whose declaration that 'rock 'n' roll's been going downhill since Buddy Holly' goes unchallenged. Lucas himself has in several interviews confirmed his own sense of 1962 as a last moment of indigenous American rock culture prior to the transformative impact of the British invasion.[23]

As a condition of rock 'n' roll's 'integration' into a mainstream American imaginary, the music also has to undergo a process of racial homogenization. Although African-American performers outnumber white rockers on the soundtrack by almost two to one, people of colour are conspicuous by their absence from *American Graffiti*. A sole Black couple (and one Hispanic couple) can briefly be glimpsed at the Freshers' Hop, but the band is white, and the film's presiding musical genius, of course, is a middle-aged white man, Wolfman Jack, who organizes the Cleftones, the Clovers, Lee Dorsey, the Platters and the other classic rhythm-and-blues performers into what Lewis (1988: 136) calls 'an indisputable narrativizing and authorizing force' – which is to say, a soundtrack for white teen suburban *anomie*. Walter Murch's much-praised sound design – which rather than simply overlaying the soundtrack numbers onto the action *à la The Graduate* (Mike Nichols, 1967) or *Easy Rider*, engineered an integrated soundscape where the acoustic mass, audibility and distance of each number mimicked the environment of passing car radios, school gyms and the like[24] – might be seen as subtly enforcing the appropriation of Black culture into white lifestyle 'product'. At one level, this is simply record-industry reality; at another, it is another chapter in the mainstreaming of the kind of 'hip' cultural miscegenation Mailer anatomized in *The White Negro*; at still another, it can be seen as a kind of posthumous innoculation against the actual relationship of soul and rhythm and blues to Black experience in the later 1960s and their explicit identification with civil rights and Black nationalist agendas.

Thus, allegiance to particular forms of youth cultural participation is allied to an affirmative rather than oppositional stance in relation to mainstream American society. The exploitation of rock 'n' roll (as a figure of race) exemplifies the ways that potentially (and in historical fact, actually) disruptive alternative subjectivities are ideologically 'retrofitted' and mythically recontained in *American Graffiti*. In the film's conflicted representation of female sexuality, a similar strategy is clearly discernible. Notoriously, the film's principal female characters are excluded from the epilogue that so profoundly affected so many (white male) reviewers.[25] What becomes of Laurie, Debbie and, indeed, the bratty Carol – the losses and trans-formations they would experience in the ensuing decade – is effectively delegitimized in terms of the core narrative of 1960s affect as white male pathos. While both Laurie and Debbie are granted a degree of agency in the film, ultimately Laurie is portrayed as a smothering homebody who denies Steve his chance to grow by escaping (in the coda, Steve's Rabbit-like subsequent career as a Modesto insurance agent is engineered to provoke melancholic recognition in the audience); while the thrill-seeking Debbie, with her peculiar voyeuristic glee at vomiting and fighting, is simply too weird to be a figure of audience identification. As already noted, that nobody 'goes all the way' throughout *American Graffiti* – which conservative critics hailed as indicative of the film's wholesome appeal – locks the film's relationships into an infantile matrix: thirteen-year-old Carol, who wrecks

John's night with her unwanted and insistent presence, might indeed be seen as simultaneously embodying the threats of both domesticity – as a nagging child, she foreshadows the carefree teens' imminent domestic obligations – and threatening (because unformed, unpredictable and, in any case, taboo) female sexuality (her key stratagem for preventing John throwing her out of the car is threatening to cry rape). Alternatively, one might understand the female characters' combination of desirability and sexlessness as recoiling from autonomous female sexuality generally as a figure of the feminist challenge in the later 1960s to hegemonic patriarchal norms; hence, another example of how *American Graffiti* works to retrieve from the traumas of lived history an American imaginary centred on the American subject understood exclusively as white and male (and of course straight).

Conclusion: You Can Go Home Again

In the short term, *American Graffiti* launched – in addition to its direct spin-off, the hit ABC TV show *Happy Days* (1974–84) starring Ron Howard – a subcycle of 'doo-wop nostalgia' films including *American Hot Wax* (1978) and *The Buddy Holly Story* (1978), all of which mimicked Lucas's spectacularly successful technique of nostalgic evocation through constant citations of period fashions, slang and music. It also inspired several films that followed Lucas's lead in dis-/re-covering a lost American Eden in the specific and resonant cultural moment of 1962–3. These include *Big Wednesday* (John Milius, 1976), *The Wanderers* (Philip Kaufman, 1978) and *Animal House* (which parodies *American Graffiti*'s biographical postscripts). A particularly subtle and resonant later intertext of *American Graffiti* is Rob Reiner's *Stand by Me* (1986), yet another 1962 coming-of-age/loss-of-innocence parable whose retrospective narration is voiced by Richard Dreyfuss, as one of the film's four adolescent youthful protagonists now, like Curt in *American Graffiti* before him, a writer (and, in a sense, a figure too of the nostalgic film-maker himself).

As for the trajectory of Lucas's own career, that, of course, is common knowledge. It is, however, worth noting that, although *American Graffiti* (against the trend for the 'movie brat' generation) lacks thematically pointed direct citations of *hommages* to period genre films,[26] the film's regressive mode paved the way for *Star Wars*' creation of a dauntlessly heroic, simplistic and sexless world of the distant past; and in its wake, Hollywood's (relieved?) wholesale withdrawal from the complexities of contemporary social experience into fantasy realms where the cultural politics of the New Right could be reinscribed in archetypal form while simultaneously soliciting from their spectator no response more complex than an undifferentiated childlike awe. Pulp science fiction of the 1950s was the seedbed for the genre's modern Hollywood hegemony: the fond recollection of pulp serials and monster movies at Saturday matinees – followed by the assiduous recreation of favourite genre films in backyards and local parks and ingenious approximations of special-effects techniques – are familiar tropes of the biographies of key New Hollywood technophiles such as Lucas, Steven Spielberg and James Cameron. Their successful translation of adolescent generic tastes into solid platinum global brands – namely the heavy symbolism of the little boy fishing in the heavens in the logo for DreamWorks (the studio Spielberg co-founded in 1994) – has enabled them to revisit such juvenile pleasures, albeit on an incomparably more lavish and sophisticated scale.

This revival of an earlier era when American science-fiction film abjured *Metropolis*-style social speculation caught the political tide, with Ronald Reagan's election to the White House in 1980 on a platform of conservative populism and homely patriotic platitudes encouraging a wilful disengagement from the late-1970s 'malaise' of social and political complexities in favour of the appealing simplicities of a fantasy past. Confirming the sense tacitly expressed in *American Graffiti* of a nation alienated from its true self, Americans in these films often received an injection of authentic values from alien visitors, often depicted as galactic innocents abroad, all too human in their vulnerability to the violence and corruption of contemporary American civilization but ultimately capable of effecting a restoration of the very values from which their hosts had become estranged: ET's desire to 'phone home' is an assertion of galactic family values. Thus, these ostensibly optimistic alien encounters were underpinned by an *American Graffiti*-like desire for (here otherworldly) redemption from the disenchanted present. In fact, the close alliances forged against established (adult) authority between childlike aliens and human children (or childlike adults) in *Close Encounters of the Third Kind* (Steven Spielberg, 1977), *E.T.* (Spielberg, 1982), *Starman* (John Carpenter, 1984) and *Flight of the Navigator* (Randal Kleiser, 1986) seemed to propose the wholesale rejection of the intractable difficulties of contemporary familial and professional life in favour of a numinous enchantment strongly identified with pre-adult perspectives. In the era of Reagan, the pursuit of enchantment in these 'regressive texts' was anything but apolitical; on the contrary, it was consistent with the anti-rational appeal long associated with reactionary political tendencies (see Benjamin [1936] 1970). Their distinctive contribution was to stake out a terrain of *cultural* politics for 1980s science fiction – the politics of private life, of family, gender and sexuality – that marked a clear break with the public-policy preoccupations of their immediate precursors in the late 1960s and 1970s.[27]

The valences of *American Graffiti*'s 'Americanness', then, are apparent. But what exactly is the writing on the wall here? Why *American Graffiti* – Lucas's own title, on which he insisted over the objections of studio executives worried Middle American audiences would find it incomprehensible,[28] but whose specific meaning he has never explained? Spraying graffiti doesn't number amongst the characters' various adolescent rituals: indeed, Modesto as envisioned by the film is a spotlessly hygienic environment, devoid of the frescoed arabesques that by the early 1970s had become ubiquitous in America's declining metropolises, faced with the associated pressures of racial tension, rising crime, underinvestment and white flight. By the decade's end, graffiti had become the generalized, and intensely racialized, metonymic token and symptom of catastrophic urban failure and threat, used as a visual shorthand in such depictions of the urban wasteland as *The Warriors* (Walter Hill, 1979), *Cruising* (William Friedkin, 1980) and *Fort Apache, the Bronx* (Sidney J. Furie, 1981). Lucas's graffiti, by contrast, seems more to connote a form of informal, impromptu public discourse, reflective of the film's semi-improvised, unplotted feel and, in any event, devoid of urban art's typically threatening connotations. In so far as the most highly visible urban graffiti in the early 1970s were strongly associated with both ethnic and ideological resistance to hegemonic Americanism – whether in the Black nationalist murals of Oakland or Harlem, gang tags on subways and overpasses or student political sloganeering – Lucas's particular brand of very white suburban south Californian graffiti, like so much in the film, again redirects oppositional and socially explosive energies into a normative and undifferentiated 'Americanism' predicated on the recovery of a prelapsarian American idyll.

Notes

1 The covert, shadowy and unanswerable corporation itself, as far as anyone can tell, maintains a lofty Nietzschean indifference to inflections of political ideology – its final terroristic act in the film, the assassination of a conservative candidate, balances out the earlier murder of a liberal senator.

2 In Brecht's original usage, *Umfunktionierung* (refunctioning) referred to the appropriation of exhausted dramaturgic and theatrical conventions for the new epic or dialectical theatre. It implied, amongst other things, a properly dialectical and hence necessarily self-conscious relationship to the formal and representational practices of the past as well as a qualified rejection of the parthogenetic modernist ideology of the at-all-costs-new.

3 The Iwo Jima flag-raising photo is discussed in relation to its re-enactment in the John Wayne film *The Sands of Iwo Jima* (1948) in Wills (1997: 149–56).

4 Lev (2000) discusses the ambiguous address of the scene in detail, noting its very different receptions amongst elite critics – who found the flag scene clearly satirical, bordering on camp – and blue-collar 'silent majority' audiences, who gratefully received a reassuring confirmation of traditional American values.

5 Amongst the sizeable and growing historical literature on the 1960s, Isserman and Kazin (2000) is perhaps the best general introduction; Miller (1994) the most sympathetic account of the origins and peak of the New Left; and Ayers (2001) a remarkable memoir by a key participant which clearly and often movingly articulates many of the complex and conflicted attitudes summarized in this paragraph.

6 See, however, Schroeder (2003) on the relationship between the BBS production unit at Columbia and the movement.

7 Universal finally greenlighted *American Graffiti* on condition that Coppola – white-hot property in 1973 in the wake of his critical, commercial and Oscar successes with *The Godfather* and his *Patton* screenplay – enlist as Lucas's line producer.

8 *American Graffiti*'s production and release history are widely retold, with minimal significant variation, in the numerous biographies of Lucas and Coppola: see, for example, Schumacher 1999.

9 Huyck and Katz recused themselves from working on the Lucas-produced sequel, *More American Graffiti* (B. L. Norton, 1979) – which follows the characters into the later 1960s – on the grounds that the Vietnam 'era . . . was so unpleasant and sad. It would have been like destroying our wonderful characters'. See Baer 1999: 43.

10 *MAD*'s principal draughtsman, Mort Drücker, who drew the satire 'American Confetti', also supplied the poster art for *American Graffiti*.

11 By Labor Day 1962, Ringo had only been a Beatle for a fortnight, had yet to grow his hair out from his greasy rocker's quiff into the group's trademark moptop let alone down to his shoulders, and he was never ever blond.

12 The coda was Lucas's concept, strongly opposed by his co-scenarists Gloria Katz and Willard Huyck; see Baer 1999: 43.

13 Jameson (1991: 19) is certainly incorrect in identifying *Graffiti* as 'the inaugural film of this new aesthetic discourse [i.e., nostalgia]'.

14 The preamble to the *MAD* satire addresses itself to 'all you nostalgic 12-year-olds out there!'

15 The small number of negative reviews tended to indicate a judgement of the disposable mass culture represented in the film as much as, or more than, a judgement on the quality of the film itself. Thus Robert Hatch in the *Nation* observed that 'all the boys and girls are listening to the same crude disc jockey, all eating the same junk food, all seeking status and trying to invent excitement' (quoted in Lewis 1988: 134).

16 Filmed in 1973 by Peter Bogdanovich.

17 Filmed in 1974 by Jack Clayton, with a screenplay by Coppola.

18 See Kitses (2003).

19 See, for instance, *The Gunfighter* (Henry King, 1950). 'We always saw [the Milner character] as a cowboy who sees his era ending' Baer 1999.

20 The film was originally reviewed for the *New Yorker* by Penelope Gilliatt in the 13 August issue while Kael was on vacation.

21 This author's translation.

22 And ignores the suggestion that Curt, at least, would go on to oppose the war.

23 In fact, of course, although The Beatles' UK hits of 1963 were released in the USA – by minor labels VJ and Swan – it was not until January, 1964, in the wake of Kennedy's assassination (and boosted by a massive $55,000 publicity campaign from Capitol) that 'I Want to Hold Your Hand' unleashed Beatlemania on the USA.

24 Toad is alerted to the theft of Steve's car when he stops hearing the car radio from the field where he and Candy are making out. On Murch's sound design, see LoBrutto (1994: 83–100).

25 Lucas insists that this decision was taken on purely stylistic grounds – including the girls would have required a second card that he felt would have over-extended the coda and dissipated its effectiveness.

26 Except for the in-joke of the theatre marquee advertising Coppola's Corman-produced *Psycho* derivative, *Dementia 13* (actually released in 1963 and thus anachronistic).

27 For a more extended discussion of the politics of 1970s and 1980s science fiction, see Langford (2005: 188–93).

28 The 1967 edition of *Webster's* defines 'graffiti' only in its archaeological sense: 'an inscription, figure or design scratched on rocks or walls or on artefacts made of plaster, stone, or clay'.

References

Ayers, B. (2001) *Fugitive Days: A Memoir*, Boston, Mass.: Beacon Press.

Baer, W. (1999) '*American Graffiti*: An Interview with Willard Huyck and Gloria Katz', *Creative Screenwriting*, 6 (1): 38–43.

Benjamin, W. (1970) 'The Work of Art in the Age of Mechanical Reproduction', *Illuminations*, trans. and ed. by Harry Zohn, London: Jonathan Cape.

Biskind, P. (1998) *Easy Riders, Raging Bulls: How the Sex 'n' Drugs 'n' Rock 'n' Roll Generation Saved Hollywood*, London: Bloomsbury.

Farber, S. (1973) '*American Graffiti*', *New York Times*, 5 August, pp. II: 1–3.

Grisolia, M. (1974) 'Un été 1962', Nouvel Observateur, 18 March.

Hudson, C. (1974) 'At last the 1962 show', *Spectator*, 6 April.

Isserman, M. and Kazin, M. (2000) *America Divided: The Civil War of the 1960s*, New York: Oxford.

Jameson, F. (1991) *Postmodernism; or, the Cultural Logic of Late Capitalism*, London: Verso.

Kael, P. (1975) *Deeper into Movies*, London: Calder & Boyars.

—— (1977) 'After Innocence', *Reeling*, London: Marion Boyars.

—— (1987) *Kiss Kiss Bang Bang: Film Writings 1965–1967*, London: Arena.

King, G. (2001) *New Hollywood Cinema: An Introducion*, London: I.B.Tauris.

Kitses, J. (2003) *Horizons West*, 2nd edn, London: British Film Institute.

Klatch, R. E. (1999) *A Generation Divided: The New Left, the New Right, and the 1960s*, Berkeley, Calif.: University of California Press.

Langford, B. (2005) *Film Genre: Hollywood and Beyond*, Edinburgh: Edinburgh University Press.

Lev, P. (2000) *American Films of the 70s: Conflicting Visions*, Austin, Tex.: University of Texas Press.

Lewis, J. (1988) *The Road to Romance and Ruin*, New York: Routledge.

LoBrutto, V. (1994) *Sound-on-Film: Interviews with Creators of Film Sound*, New York: Praeger.

Miller, J. (1994) *Democracy is in the Streets: From Port Huron to the Siege of Chicago*, 2nd edn, Cambridge, Mass.: Harvard University Press.

Ryan, M., and Kellner, D. (1988) *Camera Politica: The Politics and Ideology of Contemporary Hollywood Film*, Bloomington, Ind.: Indiana University Press.

Schroeder, A. (2003) 'The Movement Inside: BBS Films and the Cultural Left in the New Hollywood', in V. Gosse and R. Moser (eds), *The World the Sixties Made*, Philadelphia, Pa.: Temple University Press.

Schumacher, M. (1999) *Francis Ford Coppola: A Filmmaker's Life*, London: Bloomsbury.

Shumway, D. (1999) 'Rock 'n' roll Sound Tracks and the Production of Nostalgia', *Cinema Journal*, 38 (2): 36–51.

Simon, J. (1973) '*American Graffiti*', *Esquire*, October, pp. 44–6.

Speed, L. (1998) 'Tuesday's Gone: The Nostalgic Teen Film', *Journal of Popular Film and Television*, 26 (1): 24–32.

Wills, G. (1997) *John Wayne: The Politics of Celebrity*, London: Faber.

Chapter 9

American Gigolo (1980)

H. N. Lukes

Paul Schrader's *American Gigolo* (1980) begins by making Julian Kay look irresistible. When the opening credits appear over Richard Gere's character driving down the Pacific Coast Highway in his Mercedes convertible, accompanied by Blondie's song 'Call Me', who wouldn't want to be him or have him? As Roger Angell states in his *New Yorker* review of the film, 'Inescapably, irresponsibly (we feel terrible about it, really), we find ourselves beginning to have the wrong thoughts about him: This cat has really got it made!' (Angell 1980: 107).[1] The impropriety of Angell's thoughts are ostensibly moral: Julian is a prostitute. Yet narrative focus on the hooker with the heart of gold is nearly as old as narrative itself and had, in fact, provided a touchstone of 1970s US cinema with the Academy Award winners *Midnight Cowboy* (1969) and *Klute* (1971). Rather, it is *American Gigolo*'s combination of this prostitute's affluence, heterosexuality and historical context which is wrong. Angell's anachronistic evocation of the 1950s and 1960s playboy, hailed under the aegis of 'this cat', signals that Hugh Hefner's idealized bachelor has disturbingly morphed into a paid playmate for women.

Lest the audience be seduced by his success, Julian is ripped almost immediately from his privilege and eventually cast into jail. The viewer's identification is correspondingly transferred from his role as entrepreneur of the flesh trade to his position as the wrongly accused dupe. The 'we' that Angell evokes is only too relieved to lament the arbitrary injustice brought upon 'Julie' while maintaining the initial attachment to the accoutrements of his lifestyle. As it turns out, the decline of *American Gigolo*'s protagonist has precious little to do with vice. Departing from the long tradition of prostitution narratives that create sympathy for the individual sinner overwhelmed by the evil of the dominant power structures, *American Gigolo* sacrifices its protagonist to the machinations of an underworld of homosexuals and people of colour. The film is thus a telling narrative about how the rise – or at least the representation – of minority populations in the 1970s inspired a reactionary backlash in the 1980s. *American Gigolo* ultimately gets at what was both inescapable and irresponsible about the American decade for which it was a harbinger by outlining the logic of what Wendy Brown calls a 'state of injury' that this backlash created for straight white American men.

American Gigolo commences with a portrait of a hustler who is perhaps overstepping his place, yet this appears as Julian's economic and narcissistic assertion rather than classical hubris, as the consummately shallow and opportunistic character demands a larger cut from his female pimp and then proceeds to cheat on her by tricking on his own in the Beverly Hills Hotel and by taking a Palm Springs 'kink' job from another pimp, the black and gay Leon. This sadomasochistic gig – he abuses the wife while the husband instructs and looks on – soon functions as evidence in the framing of Julian for murder when the woman turns up dead. Meanwhile, Julian has reluctantly become involved with Lauren Hutton's character Michelle, a discontented politician's wife who immediately falls for him even though she is far too attractive to require the prostitute she knows him to be.

These two plot arcs converge when Michelle belatedly decides to act as Julian's false alibi, saving him from a manslaughter conviction while ruining her marriage and possibly her husband's career. Yet her act of love is delayed until Julian has had time to investigate the murder case in the racially and sexually othered subcultures of 'the street'. He eventually discovers that Leon has fingered him in order to cover for his hustler boyfriend who actually killed the woman in a hired rough-sex scene. Julian's question 'why me?' is met simply with Leon's 'because you were framable'. Leon justifies this frame by claiming that Julian 'stepped on too many people's toes'; yet the film indicates that these toes are merely those of Leon and his other female pimp. *American Gigolo*, however, is not a film about betrayal in the business contract between whore and pimp. Rather, Schrader's comment that he imagined Julian as a 'Horatio Alger of sexual fantasy' suggests that *American Gigolo* is a parable of class ascent and the ways in which a white male's attempt to divorce himself from economic negotiations with blackness, gayness and femininity could only fail in the face of these forces' militancy in this era (Tuchman 1980: 50).[2]

There is something unsatisfying, something at once disconnected and too simple, about the trajectory of Julian's decline and salvation. Every element that drives *American Gigolo*'s plot seems arbitrary, from Michelle's initial cathexis and Leon's framing of Julian to the gigolo's final speech to Michelle, allegedly signifying his redemptive acceptance of love over sexual commerce and independence – 'it took me so long to come to you', a line lifted from Robert Bresson's conclusion to *Pickpocket* (1959) with its approximated *mise-en-scène* of lovers conversing through the bars (in this case, Plexiglas) of a prison. *American Gigolo*'s excessive attention to surfaces – of clothes, bodies, architecture, speech and film itself – has led most reviewers to conclude that the film is an interrogation of style over substance set historically in the transition from the flamboyant counterculture of the 1970s to the well-heeled swank of the 1980s. This assessment excuses the movie's failure as a compelling thriller because the plot itself functions merely as a prop on which to hang a spectacle of unredeeming façades.

Other commentators have noted that for Schrader, a film-maker emerging from a Calvinist upbringing (which legendarily prevented him from even seeing a film until he was seventeen years old), human redemption *is* arbitrary. While renouncing the doxa of his Calvinist past and its thesis that the grace of God is not earned but given to an 'elect', Schrader has nonetheless continually been fascinated with the topics of redemption and transcendence in both his criticism and film-making. Because it deals so overtly with a dichotomy between redemption and style, *American Gigolo* appears to some critics as one of Schrader's boldest experiments in what he dubbed 'transcendental style', a form of cinema that strives for a purification of self and relationality by systematically shedding the false identifications that film's intoxicating surfaces naturalize.

Part of *American Gigolo*'s fascination is that these seemingly shallow and deep readings of the film are by no means mutually exclusive. Rather than mediating between them, I want to place the political at the centre of this ostensibly apolitical film. Beyond unpacking the film's Zeitgeist, my engagement of cultural text and political culture seeks to explicate how their mutual implication in this particular historical moment complicates negotiations between real and imaginary structures of being. In particular, I am interested in how *American Gigolo*'s strategic deployment of style and redemption at the literal cusp of the 1970s and 1980s thematizes the decline of the New Left and the ascendance of the New Right in the USA.

Although this broad political shift from left to right has a complicated and deeper past in the USA, both sides of the American socio-political spectrum have produced a mythology around 1980 as the year in which the right overtook the left under the name of Reagan. Although it is a coincidence that *American Gigolo* was released the same year Ronald Reagan became the President of the USA, Schrader's consistent ability to cultivate timely political parables from individuals' narratives belies this happenstance and frames him as an uncannily prescient film-maker. In the context of 1980, both the pointed production of Reagan *qua* idea and the idea of such a thing as an American gigolo became plausible and convincing precisely by producing fantasy versions of white male subjects. And while each cultural product turned overtly to 'America' in order to ground its fantastic vision, both Schrader's film and Reagan's revolution utilized Hollywood, not just the tools of the film industry but also the place of southern California, to make their masculine fantasies seem real. *American Gigolo*'s 1980 release poster, with its film-noir light sliced by Venetian blinds hitting Gere's pose (an image which has more cultural valence than the film itself), is no more 'Hollywood' than Ronald Reagan's evocation of the Western in his framing of himself on horseback at his South Californian ranch in his political publicity photos of the same year.

Despite its heady nods to American film noir, Russian novels and European cinema, *American Gigolo* is mostly remembered as a quintessential 1980s lifestyle flick. Yet Schrader's film implicitly questions the effects of style on life and what lifestyle says about its socio-political era. *Webster's New World Dictionary* defines 'lifestyle' as an American neologism signifying 'the consistent, integrated way of life of an individual as typified by his or her manner, attitudes, possessions, etc.'. This conception of lifestyle suggests that surface attributes might become so consistent, so integrated, that the word 'integrity' could lose its ethical valence.

Michel Foucault got at this threat when he said, 'I think that what most bothers those who are not gay about gayness is the gay life-style, not sex acts themselves' (Kriszman 1988, 301). Indeed, the word 'lifestyle' in 1970s and 1980s America signified homosexuality among the moral majority and its fellow travellers, who were less concerned with saving sinners than with controlling a public circulation of contaminating cultures. If lifestyle was already posited as less an effect of material history than as a pernicious cause of social decay, then phobic responses to the AIDS epidemic would reify this misapprehension by conjoining 'lifestyle's' usage in epidemiology with implicit and explicit blaming of the disease's then largely gay male victims.[3]

On the eve of the AIDS crisis, *American Gigolo* at once reactively deploys gay lifestyle as a foil for Julian's class ascent while at the same time anticipating these travesties of causal logic that would attend the so-called 'gay plague' in the story of one man's descent. Julian's lifestyle – at once conspicuous in its consumption and inconspicuous inasmuch as he conforms with and thus passes in the stylistic formalisms of polite society – does not cause his downfall but rather makes him 'framable', a scapegoat. Just as the humanity of gay men was negated under the mutual forces of the US public-health system's neglectful construction of minority populations and the country's tendency toward punitive puritan moralism, Julian becomes an outsider only when his legal troubles reveal to both his clients and himself that his expendable human life is the noxious remainder of the improvisations of self that lifestyle afforded him.

Whereas reactive discourses about AIDS at once denied and insisted on the presence of a gay male lifestyle in accounting for the disease, Julian suffers no such containment. His eventual salvation in the hands of a good woman (untouchable as they are through the transparent plastic prison wall that divides them) is only made possible by stripping him of the effects that make up his lifestyle. Because both Julian's punishment and redemption (he hardly deserves her) are arbitrary, his prior self-fashioning also appears as arbitrary and thus liberated from the specificities of economics, identity or history – free to circulate as a commodity for the taking.

The history of lifestyle is deeply about southern California and the cinema. The American film industry's move from the east coast to Los Angeles in the early twentieth century signified a relocation of America to an elsewhere. This elsewhere was both the literal site of southern California and the virtual site of a global market, as '[m]ovies from Hollywood would become the first American cultural export to conquer the world' (Koszarski 1990: 100) According to film historian Richard Koszarski, the 'mythos of Hollywood' circulating by the 1920s justified Los Angeles's economic lures for the industry, including open-shop labour policies and cheap real estate, through myriad discourses 'of small-town boosterism, industry braggadocio, and occult transcendentalism' (Koszarski 1990: 100). At this incipient point of Hollywood's self-production, California was pitched mostly to film-makers and the economies they would support as a place of 'sun, space, and somnolence', but such lifestyle rarely appeared as a feature of films' content (Brownlow and Kobal 1979, quoted in Koszarski 1990: 100).

Paul Schrader's definition of film noir as less a genre than a mood that attends certain films could also define 'lifestyle' as a parasitical cinematic quality that infiltrates any standard film genre (Jackson 1990: 80). And its infection has tended historically to carry California with it. The production of California 'lifestyle movies' did not take off until Cold War paranoia produced films about recalcitrant teenagers as a metaphor for the unintended consequences of the nation's manifest destiny on the west coast. In the 1950s, films about dangerous youth culture functioned as at once cautionary tales and vehicles for hot masculinity in a fading Hollywood studio and star system. While it is all too easy to remember the sexy outsiders embodied by Marlon Brando as a biker punk and James Dean as wounded truth-speaker, it is even easier to forget that *The Wild One* (1953) memorialized the actual history of a motorcycle gang taking over a rural town in northern California (Hollister, to which many a Harley rider returns every year like the swallows to the no-less legendary Capistrano, California) and that *Rebel Without a Cause* (1955) made Los Angeles's Griffith Observatory an icon (now replete with a bronze bust of Dean at the entrance).

These teenage-exploitation movies were fundamentally addressed to parents and non-residents of California, but such spectacles of threatening lifestyle were easily contained in the 'clean teen' cultural phenomenon later in the decade, producing most notably the Beach Boys and *Gidget* (1959), wherein a good southern California girl (Sandra Dee) tames surfer boys, the very kind of risk-bound slacker male who had heretofore appeared as a menace (Ormrod 2005, 40). By the time the 'pure' surf documentary *Endless Summer* (1964) had become a high-school favourite, Russ Meyer's porn-theatre classic *Faster, Pussycat! Kill! Kill!* (1965) replied with a California distilled into a desert landscape, fast cars and faster women. By the late 1960s, the old real-estate adage 'location, location, location' had affected Hollywood producers such that all they needed to sell was images of their own backyard. California would thus function less as a destination, a state in the union or even a place with its own politics, people and geography than as a site over which the nation could play out its disparate fantasies.

The early 1970s vastly expanded cinematic presentations of California lifestyle less as an ideological vehicle than as a byproduct of Hollywood's financial problems. California's shooting became a virtue of necessity as sets and remote locations became too expensive. Moreover, the studios' near insolvency in the mid-1960s shifted resources from big costly productions to those of young independent film-makers in touch with 'the tastes of an underserved youth market', which at that point had been stirred by California-based countercultures popularized mostly through music (Jordan 2003: 30). Yet California in film more often than not functioned as a proxy for this era's changes in personal politics. While comedies like *Bob & Carol & Ted & Alice* (1969) and Woody Allen's *Annie Hall* (1977) mocked the state's lifestyle, the ostensible horror movie *Play Misty For Me* (1971) would find itself extra-diegetically lingering on California landscapes, architecture, outfits and cars. Ostensibly addressing the effects of feminism and the sexual revolution, these films' excessive attention to California lifestyle contained this change and diverted attention away from these movements' impact on the nation.

Reagan's deregulation of the Federal Communications Commission in the early 1980s would shift the control enjoyed by directors and producers in the post-studio era to newly formed media conglomerates and talent agencies. Film historian Chris Jordan claims that the advent of 'high concept' movies – in which cast, crew and content were prepackaged for box-office success – collapsed the genres of music, television and film in accordance with the mergers and acquisitions that brought these entertainment industries under the same roof. Studio films in the 1980s abandoned articulated narrative in favour of newly formed music video and advertising modes that 'seduce[d] viewers with a montage of lifestyle images, carefully timed with music, which [sold] feeling and emotion rather than direct appeals to logic' (Jordan 2003: 13). In other words, by this point all studio films had become virtual lifestyle movies.

While this huge economic change would eventually yield star and soundtrack vehicles such as *Beverly Hills Cop* (1984) and *Down and Out in Beverly Hills* (1986) produced over the very themes and places of *American Gigolo*, Schrader's film would function as a sign of US film's rough transition from the 1970s to the 1980s. Richard Gere accepted the role of Julian Kay only after it was passed over by John Travolta, for whom the part was designed after his 1977 success in *Saturday Night Fever*, and Christopher Reeve (despite a $1 million offer). Reeve's *Superman* (1978) status afforded him the latitude to take on a gay role in *Deathtrap* (1982), but Travolta's super-dancer reputation seemingly drove him to take the lead in *Urban Cowboy* (1980), released within months of *American Gigolo*, in which the actor's fabulous competition on the dance floor was replaced with a manlier contest on an electric bull.

While Travolta's rearrangement of masculine presentation is important, it is worth remembering that *Saturday Night Fever* actually tells a story of the late 1970s recession in the USA, the displacement of white working-class men from unionized factory jobs and their appropriation of the aesthetics of the gay and black sub-cultures of disco. Yet despite, or perhaps because of, this film's similarity to *American Gigolo*'s whitening and straightening of urban subcultures, *Saturday Night Fever* is memorialized mostly as an icon of lifestyle that popularized disco for the suburbs with its unprecedented fifteen-fold platinum soundtrack. Had Travolta's polyester suit become an Armani and his pleasure his profession instead of a weekend delight, *Saturday Night Fever* and *American Gigolo* together might now be remembered as crucial cinematic interventions in the sublimation of style over economic sustenance wrought by and over the bereft white American male on the eve the Reagan revolution.

American Gigolo's threat to American masculinity was retrospectively confirmed by the overcompensation taken to resuscitate Gere's career after he suffered a decade of rumours about his homosexuality. In the runaway success *Pretty Woman* (1990), Gere switches roles from a well-heeled gigolo to a rich 'john' who redeems Julia Roberts's golden-hearted hooker with extravagant shopping trips and tickets to *La traviata*. It is tempting to trace the complicated calculus of how a Hollywood star such as Gere rises and falls between his screen roles as a gigolo and an 'officer and a gentleman' and his tabloid role in spectacular rodent exploits supposedly associated with homosexuality. Yet negotiating this publicity phenomenon is less important than recognizing the economic aspects of *Pretty Woman*'s strategy of containment around American masculinity. The story of the 1980s conveniently bookended by *American Gigolo* and *Pretty Woman* is that of 1970s decadence returned to the privileged classes while men are returned to power and women to the familiar virgin/whore dichotomy.

Yet the real effect of *American Gigolo* is realized less in either the course of Richard Gere's career or the context of 1970s auteurism than in the context of television's wanton marketing of lifestyle in this era. Inasmuch as *Gigolo* is a cultural text about lifestyle, the film makes sense of a transition from such groovy 1970s television shows as *Love American Style* and *Three's Company* to the early 1980s proliferation of wealth-obsessed prime-time soap operas such as *Dallas* and *Dynasty*. In his recent study of how 'Reagan would attract blame and praise for ushering in this new era of greed and ostentation', historian Gil Troy links the President's opulent inauguration with the new television season: 'Americans wanted to return to glamour, evidenced by *Dynasty*'s premiere the week before the Reagans'. Eighty million people a week would soon be watching this *Dallas* knockoff as popular culture echoed, intensified, and mass-produced these themes of the Reagan inaugural' (Troy 2005: 51, 56). Troy goes on to complicate the political Zeitgeist reflected in these implicitly right-wing shows with a 'competing narrative of crime, social disorder, race, recession, and Reaganism' encapsulated in the parallel popular cop show *Hill Street Blues*.

The legendary story of the NBC network's thirty-three-year-old head Brandon Tartikoff pushing a slip of paper reading 'MTV cops' across a table to *Hill Street Blues* writer/producer Anthony Yerkovich would bring these disparate telenarratives together. Yet it was not until Executive Producer Michael Mann conveyed *American Gigolo*'s visual interventions to the small screen that *Miami Vice* sealed a compromise between style and justice.[4] By appropriating Schrader's techniques of evincing subjectivity obliquely through spectacles of fashion, mood and setting, Mann also transferred the personal problems of a hustler to the very vice cops who would bust him. Mann's 'Reaganistic' rearrangement of power was lost on the millions of viewers who watched *Miami Vice* weekly as opposed to the thousands who had seen *American Gigolo*. Yet what these fans of *Miami Vice* unconsciously responded to was how easily Sunbelt lifestyle – spanning from Miami to Dallas to, eventually, Melrose Place – corresponded with the New Right's Sunbelt politics that started in southern California.

American Gigolo reads as a lifestyle movie because it throws fancy cars, swanky clothes, avant-garde workout equipment and designer water in the face of an America that imagines itself otherwise. Thus Don DeLillo in *White Noise* could conflate the natural disasters of earthquake, flood and mudslide which continually plague California residents with the state's unnatural constructions of a livable life: 'Californians invented the concept of life-style. This alone warrants their doom' (DeLillo 1986: 66). The hostility of DeLillo's speaker derives not from his own lack of cultural capital – he is, in fact, a university professor – but from the notion that the term 'lifestyle' trumps the idea of life, that the very concept of style equates consumer acquisition with personal presentation and thereby makes the ostensibly simple American life appear impoverished or inadequate. California's historical fostering of lifestyle as self-assertion has removed the state from the rest of the country so thoroughly as to make it appear alien to America, as more a nation within a nation than a part of the whole.

American Gigolo's title suggests that embracing this kind of lifestyle would make Americans into virtual prostitutes. While the very term 'gigolo', not to mention this film's particular glorification of the role, functions as a poisonous presence next to the modifier 'American', the name of the nation manifests only as an absence in this film. Schrader's titling of his movie *American Gigolo* – instead of, say, *California Gigolo*, *Hollywood Gigolo* or *LA Gigolo* – at once circumscribes the American dream and implores the audience to determine its relevance to the decadent and specific world the film portrays. Schrader's Horatio Alger comment notwithstanding, the film's silence around why this gigolo is particularly American stages a perceived divide between the lives of real Americans and the fantastic lifestyles produced both by and in Hollywood.

In this volume's study of how 'America' has been produced by films naming the nation in their titles, Schrader's is one of the few set in the actual location of 'Hollywood'. Sharon Willis's feminist critique cites *American Gigolo*'s locale as central to its reproduction of dominant masculinity. Willis claims that *American Gigolo*'s implicit correspondence between its displays of lifestyle commodity and its 'framing [of] the male body as spectacle' is informed by Los Angeles's mutual status as the 'capital of postmodernism' and as 'a major production site for cinema and television [. . .] ideally suited to figure effects of endless reproducibility' (Willis 1989: 48–49). *American Gigolo*, however, is careful in its distinction between the dream machine of Hollywood studio production and its geographical location. In fact, none of the film's characters are involved in the movie business, and Schrader's avoidance of 'the industry' comes with good reason. If a US-produced film focuses on Hollywood in its content, it automatically suggests a self-reflexive metanarrative, as in such films as *The Stuntman* (1980) and *The Player* (1992). This sort of navel-gazing can only prove distracting from any film's intention of evoking a larger and iconographic sense of the nation.

American Gigolo's concentration on a specific Los Angeles milieu without direct reference to the film industry draws attention to southern California's historical attraction to spiritual, sexual, fashion and even dietary dissidents. This promise of lifestyle, however, cannot be separated from the state's political function across the American twentieth century. As Mike Davis charts in *City of Quartz*, Anglo-American Los Angeles was founded in the early twentieth century as a new conservative frontier through its union-busting port and domestic white flight from the urban, ethnic east coast (Davis 1990: chapter 1). Yet it was the outlying areas of the metropolis, Orange and San Diego counties, that later in the twentieth century framed the national emergence of the New Right. Diverging from the old, east coast, Rockefeller model of the Republican Party, California gave rise to Richard Nixon and Ronald Reagan and a new brand of Sunbelt conservatism. Beyond the movies, which have functioned more as a myth of industry than as a backbone of employment for the area, southern California has thrived on the economies of aerospace and land development which have ideologically supported its strange alchemy of new wealth organized in anti-urban planned communities and a transplantation of the values of Midwestern middle-class Protestantism.

California lifestyle continues to signify a separateness from American life, but it is worth remembering the political common wisdom that has operated since the 1970s: 'As goes California, so goes the nation.' This saying was originally coined to mark the state's predictive conservative trends, including its new breed of

Republican candidate and its exploitation of proposition politics, which in 1978 yielded both the tax revolt of Proposition 13 and the 'Briggs Initiative' seeking to ban homosexuals from teaching in public schools. As California in the late 1970s was forming itself as a battleground between progressive and reactionary 'personal' politics, Paul Schrader progressed from film critic to film writer and director, turning out his scripts for *Blue Collar*, *Hardcore* and *American Gigolo* in less than a year.

During this period, Schrader was also actively abandoning his Calvinist upbringing by accompanying his gay friends to discos where he 'could go dancing stripped to the waist, hugging and holding men, and feel completely released and liberated because . . . I knew in the end I was not going to have a sexual encounter' (Jackson 1990: 161). Gay Los Angeles certainly informs *American Gigolo*'s portrayal of a hustler underworld, but the film's liberation politics come from quite another place. While Schrader states that he intended the movie to be a Midwesterner's fantasy of southern California lifestyle, he also admits that '[t]here is no question but that [in *American Gigolo*] heterosexuality is equated with redemption' (Byron 1980: 72). Despite Schrader's personal lifestyle and politics, *American Gigolo*'s deployment of Los Angeles decadence as a negative catalyst for heterosexual redemption places the film's sense of liberation more in line with California's reactionary socio-political culture, which sought to release American men from what Susan Jeffords identifies as the sensitive but impotent 'soft masculinity' of the 1970s (Jeffords 1994: 7).

It would be easy to say that as goes Schrader, so goes the Democratic Party. His films' almost prurient attention to the failures of American liberalism in this era could position him as the quintessential Reagan Democrat, the voter who registered disillusion with the left-wing 1970s in the 1980s ballot box. While Elia Kazan's *On the Waterfront* (1954) had already made its populist point about the potential evils of trade unionism, Schrader's *Blue Collar* updated its vision with racial tension and economic recession, accounting for the Zeitgeist which would enable Reagan's first real presidential action in 1981, his firing of the air-traffic controllers striking under the direction of their union. Schrader's *Hardcore*, presenting a religious Midwestern father rescuing his daughter from the Los Angeles porn scene, would find its hysterical political parallel in the Meese Commission's 1986 conclusion that organized crime and pornography were in collusion to undermine family values. While not strictly reactionary, Schrader's films are discomfiting to liberalism because they stage the silent dichotomies that stir beneath both overt polemics and daily life. Given that Schrader wrote all three screenplays in the same year, *American Gigolo* might appear as a negotiation of these other films' sex and labour issues. Yet *American Gigolo* sublimates these problems into two themes central to Reagan's production of himself and reproduction of the nation: the ethic of success and a masculine state of injury.

In 1980 when *American Gigolo* debuted, the former California governor was elected president on a platform of national renewal. Reagan promised American redemption through an implicit return to traditional values, a restoration of global military might for the USA after the 'humiliation' of Vietnam and a renewed role for white straight men after the threat of Black Power, the women's movement, and gay liberation in the 1970s. Reagan's triumph hinged precisely on *not* mentioning either his reactionary partisan and identity-specific goals or the conflicts and progressive movements of the preceding decade. Rather, his transcendent vision of a new, whole America was offered to cleanse the nation of its troubling parts, be they of history or demographics. Reagan offered the individual American, simply, America, wherein the substitution of the citizen for the nation was successfully reversed, or rather, overwhelmed by the positing of whole for part.

Reagan's promise of a unified America is more complicated than John F. Kennedy's exhortation that citizens 'ask not what your country can do for you; ask what you can do for your country'. As historian Michael Rogin has observed, Reagan succeeded politically not by making a one-to-one correspondence between himself and the nation over the concept of strength and inherent unity but rather by producing himself and the nation in a twined imaginary of vulnerability which needed protection by any means necessary. Through his active conflation of his presidential politics and his prior cinematic roles, both damaged and heroic, Reagan manipulated a postmodern milieu of political performance with unprecedented subtlety and effectiveness. As Rogin states, 'Reagan's easy slippage between movies and reality is synecdochic for a political culture increasingly impervious to distinctions between fiction and history' (Rogin 1987: 9).

Fiction and history really did collapse in the attempted assassination of Reagan, thanks – as Rogin also notes – to Schrader's screenplay for *Taxi Driver* (1976). This film evokes the circumstances of presidential candidate George Wallace's shooting in 1972. Like Schrader's sociopathic character Travis Bickle, Wallace's would-be assassin Arthur Bremer took his frustrated relationship with an adolescent girl as the apolitical motivation for proving his masculinity by attempting to kill then President Nixon. Due to tight security, both Bickle and Bremer fail in their assassinations, yet while Bickle shifts his cause to killing the various pimps and johns surrounding Jodie Foster's fourteen-year-old prostitute, Bremer shifted from the Republican candidate to the Dixie Democrat Wallace, whom he shot and paralysed. In the years following this film's release, John Hinckley Jr. took *Taxi Driver* personally and literally. Hinckley's stalking of Jodie Foster when she was a student at Yale led him to attempt an attack on President Carter in 1980. When Nashville airport security found his guns and thwarted his plan to assassinate Carter at his re-election event in that city, Hinckley underwent psychiatric treatment only to emerge again a year later and shoot the then President Reagan in 1981.

This chain of filmic and historical events is more than uncanny; its sequence suggests that the very task of reading political ideology in cultural productions must take into account this ricochet of fiction to fact. Any attempt at historical contextualization or analogy flags before Reagan's own exploitation of this event that threatened his life. As Rogin points out, Reagan forged a new kind of American exceptionalism by analogizing 'the recovery of his mortal body with the health of the body politic, his own convalescence with his program to restore health to the nation' (1987: 4). He did so in part by deploying his *Knute Rockne* line 'win one for the Gipper' while campaigning for Republicans in the 1982 congressional mid-term elections, effectively asking voters not to win it for themselves or their nation but for him personally – as a film character.

Reagan's 1984 re-election campaign slogan 'Morning in America' could easily summarize the message of *American Gigolo*'s conclusion, and Schrader's critical term 'transcendental style' could just as easily define Reagan's effect of a renewal through prominent displays of affluent lifestyle. Schrader's scholarly volume *Transcendental Style in Film: Ozu, Bresson, Dreyer* (1972) posits, as he simplifies in interview, that 'if you reduce your sensual awareness rigorously and for long enough, the inner need will explode and it will be pure because it will not have been siphoned off by easy or exploitative identifications'. He goes on to say, 'it will have been refined and compressed to its true identity, what Calvin called *sensus divinitatus,* the divine sense' (Jackson 1990: 28–9). Given that Schrader floods *American Gigolo* with sound, colour and, indeed, fashion, the question then is whether this excessive style marks a divergence in his film-making ethos or an intentionally flimsy structure upon which this sensorium collapses at the last minute to reveal a *sensus divinitatus.*

Yet *American Gigolo* seems to test both redemption as a means of narrative conclusion and the ends of applying film theory and referential logic to actual films. The redemption of Bresson's *Pickpocket* appears as purely arbitrary – there is nothing that can save the protagonist – and, therefore, by Schrader's standards, transcendent. Julian's last-minute 'coming' to Michelle parts from its antecedent in that this prostitute has every worldly reason for accepting her love, since it is the very means of his legal exoneration. The question of *American Gigolo* is, then, what happens to the idea of redemption when one's spiritual saviour is also one's alibi before civic law? *American Gigolo*'s conclusion cannot be both pragmatic and redemptive, just as Julian's artisanal pride in his work cannot overcome the socio-economic circumstances that position him as a prostitute.

The plainly unconvincing nature of Julian's redemption demonstrates that this film is more centrally about the idea of *framing* which the character Leon evokes in accounting for the protagonist's fate. *American Gigolo* appears as one of Schrader's most metacinematic works in its conflation of disparate senses of the verb 'to frame'. The plot's framing of Julian as the fall guy for murder meets Schrader's framing of himself as *auteur* in keeping with the cinematic traditions he loves. In addition to his overt reference to Bresson, Schrader also references film noir, Bernardo Bertolucci's *The Conformist*, and Japanese samurai films, seemingly in a bid for prestigious, 'arty' ways of conceiving Americanness (Nichols 1981: 8–11). In another sense, framing is simply the function of what Schrader calls the 'floating rectangle' of the camera's eye (Jackson 1990: xii).

American Gigolo's relentless framing of Richard Gere as an object of sexual and filmic desire leads theorist Peter Lehman to see not a feminine reversal of Laura Mulvey's thesis on the male gaze but a reification of male dominance, as the focus on Julian's body highlights his phallic sexual competence. Yet Lehman then reads the movie's rare display of male frontal nudity as an insufferable spectacle which justifies Julian's eventual decline: 'His powerlessness is the price he pays for standing nude while a woman [Hutton] and we, the spectators, look at him' (Lehman 1993: 19). While Lehman is correct in identifying heterosexual male viewers' phobia around nude male bodies in American culture, both his causal thesis and his hailing of universal spectators ('we', marked by neither gender, sexuality, nor race) elide the film's productive uses of straight white male vulnerability.[5] *American Gigolo* at first forces the kind of spectator Julian embodies to disidentify with the character's excessively naked and dressed (i.e., feminine) states early in the film and then allows the straight white male viewer to reidentify with Julian once injustice has rendered him as a universal subject before the law.

This transcendence can only happen through injury. Wendy Brown's *States of Injury: Power and Freedom in Late Modernity* puns on the mutual reproduction of the nation-state and the state of the injured individual, who would seek recognition from the former through 'claims of rights, protections, regulations, and entitlements' (Brown 1995: 5). Categories as diverse as 'people of color, homosexuals, women, endangered species, threatened wetlands, ancient forests, the sick, and the homeless' have been rendered as *identities* in part through such pleas for state legitimation (Brown 1995: 5). White straight masculinity has traditionally maintained its status as *the* universal subjectivity precisely by remaining outside this juridical framing of specificity. Yet Lauren Berlant notes that, since Reagan, 'many formerly iconic citizens who used to feel undefensive and unfettered feel truly exposed and vulnerable [. . .] They sense that they now have *identities*, when it used to be just other people who had them' (Berlant 1997: 2).[6] *American Gigolo* charts the process of this exposure and shows how white masculinity recentres itself through a defensive protection against the 'special rights' of other minority identities.

While the film predicts Reagan's similar sublimation of injury in his 1982 analogy between his own recovering health and the nation's recovering economy, it actually looks backwards in time to find its injured antecedent. All aspects of framing in the film are filtered through the lens of film noir, evoked in its lighting through Venetian blinds and its thematic focus on the random nature of crime and justice. Yet this movie fails to produce the dark mood of film noir on either an ethical or aesthetic plane. In contrast to its general attention to Los Angeles's light-saturated landscape and sunny social milieu in the late 1970s, *American Gigolo*'s ostensibly dark socio-sexual depths and darkly lit scenes nevertheless present an asexual gestalt of fun and fashion. The Palm Springs scene provokes less the viewer's revulsion over 'kink' (mentioned in the dialogue but not portrayed) than a fascination with how exactly California modernist architecture allows reflections of exterior water to dance so engagingly on interior walls. Later, the allegedly edgy gay club which Julian must penetrate in order to find Leon seems a mere costume party of men mildly grooving in cowboy outfits. As one such denizen gleefully recognizes Julian, this scene's mood suggests a high-school 'homecoming' dance more than a lascivious underground.

If Schrader fails to reproduce the mood that dictates the genre he evokes, then his crossing of filmic and gender dichotomies may suggest an undoing of the symbolic systems of classic noir, which ostensibly offers correlations between lighting, ethics and sexual difference. Lawrence Russell complains about *American Gigolo*'s formulaic postmodernism and calls the film a 'neo-noir inversion [in which] chromatic detail replaces shadow [and] paint replaces light' (Russell 2000). *American Gigolo*'s translation of noir lighting is less an inversion than an osmosis of the chiaroscuro of black-and-white noir film into pastels and earth tones. Gere's Giorgio Armani wardrobe is framed precisely by its blending so successfully with the chromatic presentation of interior space. When a topless Julian struts around his apartment and displays his Armani clothing to himself and the audience in a prolonged scene, his chromatic arrangement of ties on shirts on slacks at once exaggerates the now-common practice of cinematic product placement and metadiegetically functions as a trailer for the film's art direction.[7]

This film's actual inversion of noir genre has much more to do with the fact that Julian takes on the role of the classic femme fatale, with Michelle as his gendered counterpart plunging herself into self-destruction before his ineluctable sexual appeal. Yet *American Gigolo*'s deployment of colour to diffuse literal chiaroscuro parallels its diffusion of noir gender codes. Much classic noir already complicates its own diametric presentation of the über-masculine hero and his hyper-feminine foil by framing these characters in identification with each other through their mutual socio-economic stultification, their paired innocence or guilt relative to a crime and the envy often suggested in longing for each other's gender-specific power.[8] Schrader further conflates male and female roles by producing both Michelle and Julian as beholden to their sponsors – whether a husband or a female 'john'. When Michelle tells Julian that her husband 'has this big political thing about having a family . . . he keeps wanting me . . . pregnant'. Julian posits the quasi-feminist question, 'We talkin' bout what he wants or you want?' She replies that she is not sure any more, signifying the occlusion of self before the marital contract. Julian offers, 'Take your pleasure where you can.'

On the one hand, this last line functions as a stagy manifesto about sexual freedom that the film's conclusion sabotages. Pragmatically, one cannot simply take pleasure if it involves losing one's income or being incarcerated. On the other hand, Julian's supportive communion with Michelle fails because his women's liberation language is betrayed by the fact that she goes to non-liberating extremes for sex – hiring a gigolo instead of deferring to the potential reciprocity of an affair or divorcing her husband and attempting sexual and economic autonomy. Likewise, Julian is hardly a convincing example of the inherently liberating qualities of sex, as he seems to have no relationship to his own pleasure except as a means to affluence and what he proudly construes as a community service for those women who cannot get pleasure any other way. If prostitution is the only means of Julian's financial success and Michelle's pleasure and neither character gains access to the other's privilege then there is certainly nothing revolutionary about sex in this film.

As with the tone-on-tone art direction, *American Gigolo*'s mixing of standard gender and sexual iconography produces a milieu less ethically grey than personally and politically beige. Unlike noir's violent collision of gendered opposites, Schrader's tepid blend of a structurally feminized, narcissistic man and a needy woman (more a bossy bottom than a sexual aggressor) *requires* the last-minute intervention of love. Love here neither redeems the characters' wayward lives nor contains their sexual fire but rather offers at least some modicum of tension between man and woman, self and other. Thus Schrader seems both to caution against the short-sightedness of the sexual revolutions of the 1960s and 1970s and to long for traditional social and gender stability, as did so many Reagan Democrats.

I would argue, however, that if *American Gigolo*'s symbolic gender order marks Schrader's critique of the inherent power of sex, then it is not his final point but rather a provisional structure that functions most saliently in its lack of relation to the crime plot. The audience's entrapment in this *homme fatale*'s decline has less to do with either Angell's sense of irresponsibility, Lehman's framing of repulsion or Russell's discomfort with *American Gigolo*'s flaccid postmodernism and more to do with the film's staging of a negative coincidence between this prostitute's sexual and legal potency. In this regard, *American Gigolo* reads not as a cautionary tale about valuing decadence over love or style over substance but rather as a display of the logic informing the conservative backlash to the sexual revolution that historically conflated economic, political and sexual power in a monolithic form of masculinity.

Inasmuch as Julian is 'framable', it is because he is at once a titillating and intolerable sexual and socio-economic anomaly who has shed the recognizable signifiers of male hustler culture in the late twentieth century. *American Gigolo* thus speaks as much through what it frames as by what it does not: namely, the realities of a predominantly homosexual male flesh trade in the USA and a genealogy of films that address male prostitution, ranging from early quasi-gigolo movies such as *Sunset Boulevard* (1950) to more overt mainstream films such as *The Roman Spring of Mrs. Stone* (1961), *Breakfast at Tiffany's* (1961) and *Midnight Cowboy* (1969) to Andy Warhol's and Paul Morrissey's art films. By divorcing prostitution from femininity, poverty, homosexuality and Europe (at one point Julian unconvincingly feigns Italian origins), Schrader's film performs a formal study of American, straight, white, affluent masculinity sequestered from its naturalized institutions of social privilege.

Given Julian's isolation from both the social realities of prostitution and the institutional imaginaries of white masculinity, what straight man, the figure always presumed to be the saviour of the whore, would save this character from his fate? Schrader seems to put this task of salvation in the hands of a woman, a strategy common for later twentieth-century American films and Westerns in particular. While indulging the socio-sexual independence of male outlaws, these films eventually contain their heroes in a feminine domestic sphere. This containment is necessarily provided at the eleventh hour, lest the audience either critique unfettered male autonomy or worry that its potency could trump the nation's familial-industrial complex.

In many ways, *American Gigolo* is nothing if not a neo-Western, but as Western movies go, this film nods more to the genre's trope of justice than domestic containment.[9] The central problem of redemption in *American Gigolo* has less to do with its chastening of Julian through female domestication than with the fact that Schrader cannot forward his redemption narrative without conflating prostitution and murder through a conversion of Julian's intolerable freedom as a gigolo into his victimization as the falsely accused. Schrader's film morphs legal and moral stipulations against prostitution into the fundamental Christian commandment against bearing false witness. When Julian inadvertently causes Leon's death in his moment of realization that this pimp has framed him, we realize that Julian will appear culpable for not one but two murders – as if Schrader's point would not be clear without such reiteration. Yet the very force of the film's suturing of the audience's gaze to Julian's body, if not also his empty subjectivity, has already led us to assume that he is innocent of murder. It is only the critical viewer who recognizes that 'our' outrage about the injustice 'Julie' suffers serves to distract us from the very idea of a male prostitute. Hence, this gigolo is American perhaps only inasmuch as his false accusation evokes a mythic American sense of justice which has been forged mostly through film.

Even as Julian's final confrontation with Leon makes clear that this gay pimp both made and undid Julian – that the gigolo worked his way up from homosexual hustling to 'rich pussy' and that Leon did, in fact, frame him for murder – this scene is not fundamentally about either class-climbing or justice. In his desperation, Julian offers first to pay Leon off in cash, then to 'break in' his new boys and, finally, to work only for him and 'do fag tricks for you, I'll do kink'. When these concessions fail, Julian pushes Leon, who falls over a balcony and teeters from its rail. As our hero desperately holds on to his cowboy boots, Leon slowly slips out of them to his death. Thankfully for Julian, there is a witness to his rescue attempt, which saves him eventually from a double-murder indictment.

On the one hand, this climactic death indicates *American Gigolo*'s most salient reference to classic noir: Julian is momentarily willing to kill Leon but does not literally intend to; as with the existential strain of film noir, it is the arbitrary nature of crime rather than justice that damns the protagonist. On the other hand, Schrader finally acknowledges the aesthetics of gay hustler culture which he has at once repressed in his film and obliquely evoked. The scene following Leon's death presents Julian sitting stunned on the pimp's couch, clutching a single boot of the villain's unmaking, with the muscular male buttocks of Andy Warhol's 'Torsos posters hovering as dark haloes over him in the upper reaches of the frame. Some critics read this film's evocation of Warhol's queerest work as an indication of Leon's homosexual abjection (Doyle et al. 1996: 15). Others read it as further evidence of Schrader's postmodern logic of arbitrary referentiality, as merely another example of the film-maker's drive-by garnering of cultural authenticity (Carrol 1982: 66; Russell 2000).[10]

Figure 4 American Gigolo.

By contrast, I read this scene as an instance of analogical collapse. Overlaying the noir ethical terrain and gay aesthetic of this penultimate scene is the film's use of Leon's boot to evoke both an American cowboy iconography and the Horatio Alger ethos of 'pulling yourself up by your own bootstraps', which become literal to the point of being camp. *American Gigolo*'s famous early scene of Julian working out upside down in gravity boots while cramming for fluency in Swedish to language tapes provides a literal reversal of supply-side, top-down 'Reaganomics' through the image of a prostitute developing his economic, cultural and physical capital in a gravity-defying ascent. By the time of Leon's death, the cowboy boot – an image Schrader has deployed not to indicate Reagan's rugged American individualism but as a sign of the gay underworld – manifests only as a failed metaphor, one whose meaning has fled only to leave a mute object. The empty boot tentatively implies that Julian's inadvertent but literal killing of its wearer is retribution, if not redemption. Yet what Julian's stricken embrace of Leon's boot after his death actually marks is not justice but the fact that, at this point in the film, a boot is a boot is a boot in both Schrader's and Julian's mind. *American Gigolo* thus suggests that the moral values it has questioned must be understood through the circulation of cultural commodities. Once the commodity of Western footwear has been drained of its cultural and economic value in the film's diegetic and symbolic landscape, we are left with only dead metaphors to explain this film's complicated ethical terrain to which America's received moral systems are unequal.

If the title '*American Gigolo*' is a cipher – wherein it is by no means obvious why or how Julian's character stands in for the nation – it is because the film can only discretely unveil what the nation's imaginary must obscure in order to continue functioning as a liberal patriarchy: that is, the conflation of masculinity and financial success. *American Gigolo*'s misremembrance in US popular culture (sexy Gere stands in for a changing nation) signifies a form of repression about how sex crucially informs mythologies of American nationhood. The power of the title resides in its status as misnomer, as a national concept which makes no sense outside Schrader's framing of his fictional character.

Yet Schrader's nomination of such a thing as an 'American gigolo' has provided an irresistible discursive touchstone in much the same way that the saying 'As goes California, so goes the nation' has. In the months leading up to George W. Bush's re-election as the President of the USA in 2004, right-wing commentators Ann Coulter and 'Taki' Theodoracopulos dubbed Bush's Democratic challenger, Senator John Kerry, the 'American gigolo' (Coulter 2004; Theodoracopulos 2004). This charge was derived from the fact that Kerry is married to Teresa Heinz Kerry, the heiress to the Heinz ketchup fortune, and that he was previously married to another woman wealthier than himself. In the promotion of her book *How to Talk to a Liberal (If You Must)* (2004), Coulter claimed that Kerry's Democratic convention entrée – wherein he referenced his decorated service as a soldier in Vietnam with 'I am John Kerry reporting for duty' – functions as 'the same thing he says when he goes into the bedroom' (Moore 2004). On the one hand, Kerry's education in Swiss boarding schools and Heinz's Portuguese Mozambiquean childhood produced them as sufficiently un-American in a contemporary right-leaning US political milieu. On the other hand, these neo-Conservatives' evocation of *American Gigolo* tells us just how far the USA has backtracked from a 1970s notion of a sexual revolution, in which a man's status in the socio-political world would not necessarily be diminished by the fact that his wife could make or have more money than her husband.

On an ostensibly less political and more popular level, the title *American Gigolo* has been evoked as the very absence that Schrader first socio-politically circumscribed in the series of films featuring the comic Rob Schneider – *Deuce Bigalow: Male Gigolo* (1999) and its sequel *Deuce Bigalow: European Gigolo* (2005). These comic films could not legally replicate the title of Schrader's picture, but their comedy depends on circumscribing the inherently contradictory idea of an American gigolo. The nervous redundancy in the titles of these latter-day films – the term 'gigolo' is inherently male and European – reveals the ways in which Schrader named an intolerable fantasy in the American imagination of nationhood.

American Gigolo excises and transplants the European model of the gigolo into an American mythos of immanent class ascent in order to interrogate the nation's promise of individual success. Schrader's hailing of both Calvinist, or 'Puritan', theology and bootstrap mythology marks the movie's most salient intervention in the America of its title, as their combination reveals the contradictions inherent to each foundational, national ideology. As one version of the founding fathers, New England's seventeenth-century Puritans paradoxically believed that no work in this world would secure one's entrance into Heaven and that economic success was a sign that one was already 'elect'. Horatio Alger's late nineteenth-century *Ragged Dick* and his series of boys' books which followed revised this ethos of economic predestination with the myth of pulling oneself up by one's own bootstraps. Yet in these stories, 'Dick's' ascent depends very much on the kindness of strangers who somehow recognize in his handsome face and sexy style his honesty, work ethic and general deservingness. The fact that Alger himself was defrocked as a minister for his inappropriate conduct with the boys of his congregation tells us more about masculinity and success than most Americans want to hear. In the end, this film's antecedents are only important inasmuch as America wilfully misunderstands them. And yet, *American Gigolo* itself seems likewise to have become a cultural phenomenon remembered only through a repression of its subversion of a national imaginary.

Notes

1 Rob Edelman's review (1980: 77) likewise notes that the movie initially presents 'a male's fantasy'. While each critic differently suggests that getting paid for having sex with women is a straight male fantasy, neither engages in the sociological reality of male prostitution.

2 Sharon Willis (1989) makes a similar argument about the film's negotiation of class and white straight masculinity but does not situate *Gigolo* in its political milieu.

3 For in-depth analysis of the representational logics of the AIDS crisis, see Bersani 1987 and Sontag 1988.

4 *Miami Vice* conforms to what film theorist Robert B. Ray identifies as the fundamentally conservative tendency of mainstream US cinema at once to indirectly glorify the law in the form of maverick cops and to convert innovative filmic devices into 'mere cosmetic flourishes assimilable by Hollywood's conventional forms' (Ray 1985: 294).

5 The 'we' that Lehman, like Angell before him, evokes is implicitly not female, even though *American Gigolo*'s box-office success was due largely to an unprecedented post-women's liberation female audience looking for beefcake.

6 Thomas DiPiero complicates Berlant's assertion by reading how a dialectic of 'hysteria and mastery' has defined white masculinity negatively against various sexual and ethnic others from the eighteenth century to the present (DiPiero 2002). Schrader's male sexual and economic mastery produces audience and critical hysteria at precisely the historical moment in which Reagan secured the power of redefinition that Berlant attributes to him. Susan Jeffords sees Reagan consequently ushering in an era of 'hard body' films following *American Gigolo*'s transitional dialectic of the male body's presence and absence.

7 Schrader implicitly acknowledges this metacinematic moment by referring to Julian in this scene as 'the artist at his palette' (Jackson 1990: 161).

8 In particular, the film adaptations of James M. Cain's *Double Indemnity* and *The Postman Always Rings Twice* as well as such classics as *Gilda* pose the male and female leads in mirrored situations that do more to deconstruct gender essentialism than reify it. For more on this topic, see Kaplan (1998).

9 Evidence forwarding a reading of *American Gigolo*'s redemption through the love of a good woman as ironic lies in Schrader's interest in John Ford's *The Searchers*. In Ford's divergence from his own œuvre and Westerns in general, Schrader sees 'the frailty of the great American hero' as well as actor John Wayne's 'playing with his persona; he hardly ever plays the outsider, but this is a man [Ethan Edwards] who is deprived of the pleasures of hearth and home because he has blood on his hands' (Jackson 1990: 155). Nichols notes that *American Gigolo* in particular but also all of Schrader's films, 'in fact, seem like a series of variations on . . . *The Searchers*' (Nichols 1981: 8). Whereas Ford's movie refuses the trappings of social redemption, *American Gigolo* questions the spiritual content of redemption on the threshold of his hero's recognition and acceptance of the hearth and home.

10 The introduction to *Pop Out: Queer Warhol* claims that Schrader's evocation of Warhol is 'a marker of toxicity, betrayal, and abjection' coded as queer via Leon's status as

both gay and black. Russell reads the Warhol posters as 'Schrader's slick homage to Billy Wilder's *Double Indemnity* – recall that the hero Walter Neff (Fred MacMurray) has three pictures of prize fighters on his wall' (2000). Russell's anti-postmodern thesis that 'Like the hero, [*Gigolo* is] a retrofit, a make-over of an old personality' (2000), which he sees as film noir, meets Noel Carroll's claim that *American Gigolo* is among a type of 'two-tiered allusionistic film' (1982: 75) prevalent in the 1970s and 1980s that pretends to meaning by arbitrary reference to other art films of the past.

References

Alger, H. (1990) *Ragged Dick, or Street Life in New York with the Boot Blacks*, New York: Signet.

Angell, R. (1980) 'Review of *American Gigolo*', *New Yorker*, 4 February, pp. 107–8.

Berlant, L. (1997) *The Queen of America Goes to Washington City: Essays on Sex and Citizenship*, Durham, NC: Duke University Press.

Bersani, L. (1988) 'Is the Rectum a Grave?', in Douglas Crimp (ed.) *AIDS: Cultural Analysis, Cultural Activism*, Cambridge, Mass.: MIT Press, pp. 197–222.

Brown, W. (1995) *States of Injury: Power and Freedom in Late Modernity*, Princeton, NJ: Princeton University Press.

Brownlow, K. and Kobal, J. (1979) *Hollywood: The Pioneers*, New York: Knopf.

Byron, S. (1980) 'The Rules of the Games', *Village Voice*, 10 March, p. 72.

Carroll, N. (1982) 'The Future of Allusion: Hollywood in the Seventies (and Beyond)', *October*, 20 (spring): pp. 51–81.

Coulter, A. (2004) *How to Talk Like a Liberal (If You Must)*, New York: Crown Forum.

Davis, M. (1990) *City of Quartz: Excavating the Future in Los Angeles*, London and New York: Verso.

DeLillo, D. (1984) *White Noise*, New York: Viking.

DiPiero, T. (2002) *White Men Aren't*, Durham, NC: Duke University Press.

Doyle, J., Flatley, J. and Muñoz, J. E. (eds) (1996) *Pop Out: Queer Warhol*, Durham, NC: Duke University Press.

Edelman, R. (1980) 'Review of *American Gigolo*', *Films in Review*, 31 (3): pp.177–8.

Jackson K. (ed.) (1990) *Schrader on Schrader*, London: Faber and Faber.

Jeffords, S. (1994) *Hard Bodies: Hollywood Masculinity in the Reagan Era*, New Brunswick, NJ: Rutgers University Press.

Jordan, C. (2003) *Movies and the Reagan Presidency: Success and Ethics*, Westport, Conn.: Praeger.

Kaplan, A. (ed.) (1998) *Women in Film Noir*, London: British Film Institute.

Koszarski, R. (1990) *An Evening's Entertainment: The Age of the Silent Feature Picture, 1915–1928*, Berkeley, Calif.: University of California Press.

Kriszman, D. (ed.) (1988) *Michel Foucault, Politics, Philosophy, Culture: Interviews and Other Writings*. New York: Routledge, 1993.

Lehman, P. (1993) *Running Scared: Masculinity and the Representation of the Male Body*, Philadelphia: Temple University Press.

Moore, J. (2004) 'Coulter Speech Incites Pie-Throwing from Kerry Supporters', *Talon News*, 25 October, p. 1.

Nichols, B. (1981) '*American Gigolo:* Transcendental Style and Narrative Form', *Film Quarterly*, 34 (4): pp. 8–11.

Ormrod, J. (2005) 'Endless Summer (1964): Consuming Waves and Surfing the Frontier', *Film and History: An Interdisciplinary Journal of Film and Television Studies*, 35 (1): pp. 39–51.

Ray, R. (1985) *A Certain Tendency of the Hollywood Cinema, 1930–1980*, Princeton, NJ: Princeton University Press.

Rogin, M. (1987) *Ronald Reagan, the Movie: and Other Episodes in Political Demonology*, Berkeley, Calif.: University of California Press.

Russell, L. (2000) 'Review of *American Gigolo*', *Culture Court* (June), <www.culturecourt. com/F/Noir/AMG.htm>.

Schrader, P. (1972) *Transcendental Style in Film: Ozu, Bresson, Dreyer*, Berkeley, Calif.: University of California Press.

Sontag, S. (1988) *AIDS and its Metaphors*, New York: Farrar, Straus, Giroux.

Theodoracpoulos, Taki (2004) *The American Conservative*, 24 May, www.amconmag.com.

Troy, G. (2005) *Morning in America: How Reagan Invented the 1980s*, Princeton, NJ: Princeton University Press.

Tuchman, M. (1980) 'Interview with Paul Schrader', *Film Comment*, 16 (2): pp. 49–52.

Willis, S. (1989) 'Seductive Spaces: Private Fascinations and Public Fantasies in Popular Cinema', in Dianne Hunter (ed.) *Seduction and Theory: Readings of Gender, Representation, and Rhetoric*, Urbana, Ill.: University of Illinois Press, pp. 47–70.

Chapter 10

An American Werewolf in London (1981)

Diane Negra

In a Southern Comfort ad which appeared in cinemas in the UK in 2005, a group of young Americans is portrayed anxiously scanning the departure screen at a European train station, running to catch their train and then celebrating narrowly having caught it by breaking open a bottle of whiskey. As they lift their paper cups to toast their journey 'To Prague', a conductor enters the train and announces he is collecting tickets for Barcelona. With this, the bemused group improvises a new toast 'To Barcelona' and quaff their whiskey. This ad for a brand that positions itself as quintessentially American draws upon notions of Americanness as both disoriented in unfamiliar surroundings yet cheerfully adaptive, and it does so, strikingly, in order to sell an American product to European consumers. In condensed form, the ad recapitulates many of the stock elements of the European misadventure narrative that has intermittently played through the teen film genre.

The teen film in the past twenty-five years has been particularly concerned with the prospects and limits of mobility. As Steve Bailey and James Hay have observed, there are generic rules in place about spatiality in the teen film, with, for example, a number of films centralizing a thrilling encounter by the suburban male teen with urbanity. The fascination with that which lies outside white suburbia displayed in aspirational capitalist fables such as *Ferris Bueller's Day Off* (1986) and *Risky Business* (1983) or teen road movies such as *Crossroads* (2002) is writ large in the European misadventure where protagonists are confronted with heightened experiences of spatial and cultural disorientation. As Bailey and Hay point out, teen films tend to designate key sites such as the school, the shopping mall or the city and then endow these locations with a sense 'both of possibility and of restriction' charged with 'an increasing personal autonomy' and 'a simultaneous conformity to social norms'

(Bailey and Hay 2002: 219). In the variant of the teen film I will be concerned with here, this liminality is most often vividly nationalized, with protagonists revelling in cultural difference while falling back on the culturally familiar.

A cult movie beloved by audiences for its dark humour, tongue-in-cheek dialogue and (for the time) state-of the-art horror effects, *An American Werewolf in London* (1981) may be classed among a set of early 1980s films that tie the experience of being young in America to a necessary encounter with some sort of world outside national/natural boundaries. As in *Stripes* (1981), *E.T.* (1982) and *Wargames* (1983), the film stages a coming-of-age experience which might be understood as counter-Reaganist in its refusal of a solipsistic national identity. As a European misadventure narrative, *An American Werewolf in London* strikingly reverses the historical figuring of Europe as a place where young, privileged Americans go to acquire culture; this film situates Europe as the site where New York University students David Kessler and Jack Goodman degenerate into primitivism.[1] In doing so, it establishes a gendered formulation that has become rather familiar in teen horror and comedy. According to this formulation, males tend to suffer trauma in Europe while females are more likely to be redeemed or socio-economically elevated, or both. If the European misadventure narrative highlights the ineptitude and fearfulness of young American males (most recently *Eurotrip* [2004] as I shall briefly discuss), Hollywood cinema most often places girls in Europe to feature in fantasies of aristocratization (*The Prince and Me* [2004], the *Princess Diaries* franchise [2001 and 2004], *What a Girl Wants* [2003]) and women to be redeemed from America (most recently *Nurse Betty* [2000] and *Under the Tuscan Sun* [2003]).[2]

In a period that saw very close ties between the USA and Britain and the simultaneous emergence of Reaganism and Thatcherism, *An American Werewolf in London* trades on an understanding of Europe as hostile to (male) Americans. In the film, lycanthropy is equated with various primordial Old World terrors, yet a vivid and unusually precise rendering of British culture sits alongside a generalized substitution of Britain for Europe at large. While the film makes references to the British Hammer films of the 1960s and demonstrates aware-ness of the heightened presence of international conglomerates in British life,[3] it also sentimentalizes Britain, most notably through a bizarre closing message of congratulations to the newly married Prince and Princess of Wales. That Britain operates as a point of engagement with the horrors of remembered European violence is illustrated most clearly in an extraordinary sequence in which a hospitalized David suffers a nightmare in which he imagines his suburban Long Island home destroyed by monstrous Nazi stormtroopers. Nationalized anxieties about the character and content of masculinity enter the film very early on, in part through a joke in which the valour and self-sacrifice of a Frenchman and a British man for national causes are compared to an American who chooses to sacrifice a Mexican in his stead.

Part of the importance of *An American Werewolf in London* lies in its interrogation of some of the ideological certainties of suburban American life and its inauguration of a pattern that persists up to the present in which Europe challenges and traumatizes American males in the teen film. In addition, this film is replete with anxieties and uncertainties about Americans drawn into international situations they don't understand and shows itself to be of two minds about whether Britain stands apart from the terrors of a primitive Europe or should be considered part of a Europe that operates as a traumatic proving ground for young American males. In these ways, the film offers a valuable case study of the power of cult films to function as potentially radical forms of social expression and the manner in which popular culture feeds and challenges the Anglo-American 'special relationship'.

In addition to its status as a youth-oriented European misadventure, *An American Werewolf in London*, of course, is first and foremost a horror film (though one with strong satiric elements). As such, the film draws upon and in some ways sustains the generic conventions of canonical monster fictions amidst a cycle of early 1980s horror production which was exhibiting new freedom to overplay, spoof and parody. As Joseph Maddrey has pointed out, the film emerged at a time when 'more and more films [were] adopting a lighthearted approach to the old horrors' and 'the genre entered its most commercially successful phase' (Maddrey 2004: 4). This essay directly responds to Gregory A. Waller who has urged critics to

> pay attention to films like *Dracula* (1979), *An American Werewolf in London*, *The Funhouse* (1981), and *Re-Animator* (1985) which in modernizing and commenting on classic monster movies prove that the relationship between contemporary and golden age horror involves much more than simply the distinction between the graphically direct and the atmospherically suggestive.
>
> (Waller 1987: 8)

Like the vampire, the werewolf is often a boundary figure, marking the anxiety of national and cultural transit. Moreover, its use in cinema has frequently pointed toward cultural flashpoints and national preoccupations. In the 1935 film *Werewolf of London*, a British botanist bitten by an animal in Tibet returns to London and attacks the populace as a werewolf, the plot of the film thus doubly engaging broadly post-imperial and decidedly of-the-moment political and foreign-policy concerns in the interregnum between the world wars. The 1957 low-budget teen film/horror hybrid *I Was a Teenage Werewolf* struck a chord with audiences at a time of post-war preoccupation with the prospects and limits of adolescent rebellion, with protagonist Tony Rivers the unwitting subject of a psychiatrist's regression experiments. Amidst heightened fears about governmental secrecy and the abuse of political power, the Watergate-era comedy *Werewolf of Washington* (1973) showcased the transformation of a journalist having an affair with the President's daughter, who is bitten by a werewolf on a trip to Hungary and returns to

Washington where he balances duties as the President's press secretary with certain nocturnal exploits. *An American Werewolf in London* sustains a continuity with these earlier films in its adaptation of the werewolf to the concerns of its social historical moment. The figure of the werewolf in the film marks the uncertainties and tensions attached not only to the film's conception of Europe but also to the security and stability of individual subjectivity itself as the coming-of-age moment veers into monstrous transformation.

Re-Generating Anglo-American Affinity

Reading *An American Werewolf in London* as (among other things) a commentary on the shifting character of Anglo-American relations at the time of its release entails some analysis of the precise economic, political and broadly cultural features of that relationship in the early 1980s. While various rhetorical configurations have long existed to privilege a sense of affinity between the USA and UK (defining the relationship as 'special' or 'natural', for example), by the late 1970s there were few incentives for Anglo-American alliance. David Dimbleby and David Reynolds (1988) broadly characterize the mid-1960s to mid-1970s as a period in which Anglo-American relations were marked by a drifting apart. Likewise, according to John Baylis, 'Although there were few serious frictions in Anglo-American relations in the early 1970s there was a growing divergence of interests and an increasing inequality of power which helped to slacken the bonds between the two states' (Baylis 1997: 168).

With British reluctance to become involved in Vietnam or Israel, debate over the status of American military bases in Britain and the protocols of consultation over their use, intermittent American concern about the conduct of the British Government in Northern Ireland and the involvement of Britain in the European Economic Community, which was emerging as a serious economic rival to the USA, diplomats on each side found few occasions on which they could synchronize their diplomatic, political and fiscal strategies and interests. Both national economies were struggling in the late 1970s, and those economic struggles were matched by cultural tensions tied to issues of race and class. In 1970s Britain, living standards fell for the first time since the end of the Second World War, inflation was extraordinarily high and basic social services were frequently going unmet. From an American vantage point, it appeared that not only were there increasingly separate interests and a fundamental imbalance of power in relations between the two countries/cultures, the historic ethnic/cultural affinity was less decisive than it had once been. In the postmodern ethnic revival of the 1960s and 1970s, concepts of Englishness played little part, and the notion of Britain as a national and ethnic category tended towards an association with a staid whiteness. 'New Americans', as Dimbleby and Reynolds put it, 'felt no special affinities with Britain' (Dimbleby and Reynolds 1988: 317). Moreover, they write, 'even those Americans who naturally looked across the Atlantic felt little but dismay at the state of Britain during the seventies' (Dimbleby and Reynolds 1988: 318). With the expansion of nationalist campaigns in Wales and Scotland, the escalation of sectarian violence in Northern Ireland, and the conspicuous emergence of labour struggles in Britain, an image of the United Kingdom as fractious, violent and disintegrating took hold. According to Dimbleby and Reynolds, 'By the mid-1970s Britain no longer mattered, even to Anglophile Americans, as a world power or as a political example' (Dimbleby and Reynolds 1988: 318).

The declining cultural influence of Britain was apparent as well in its diminishing representation in American film and television; on the whole, 1970s Hollywood favoured urban US locations far more than overseas ones. (The one exception here was public television. As Dimbleby and Reynolds observe, 'By the 1970s Britain was rarely mentioned at all by the American media, with the exception of the royal family. But upmarket American television was keenly interested in things British' [Dimbleby and Reynolds 1988: 321].) However, even amidst political and economic exigencies, the 1960s and 1970s had been marked by a high level of cultural transit between the USA and UK, particularly in rock and pop music, notably the phenomenal success of UK bands in America under the auspices of the 'British invasion'. There had also arguably been a recent precedent for Americans imagining England as a positive alternative to the USA with the emergence of 1960s 'Swinging London' grounding an image of Britain as a lighter, freer society at a time of domestic Cold War anxiety and moral approbation about US military policy in south-east Asia. However, the greatest shift in Anglo-American relations would be catalysed by a tourism boom fed by the greater availability of air travel. Like the sporadic television representations of Britain, tourist discourses 'perpetuated the image of Britain as a country that relished being behind the times, not one desperately trying to keep up with them' (Dimbleby and Reynolds 1988: 322). By the early 1980s, the saleability of a British association with the past increased as the tourism boom came to define Anglo-American relations fully as much as the ideological bond cemented by newly elected leaders Ronald Reagan and Margaret Thatcher. According to Dimbleby and Reynolds,

> Americans showed little interest in modern Britain, struggling to emerge from the ruins of the old. They came not to see new towns and new factories but to visit the relics of Britain's past: ancient cities, country houses, literary haunts. Above all, tourists were fascinated by the monarchy . . . The marketing of Britain as a tourist attraction, an increasingly slick business operation, deliberately concentrated on these past glories.
>
> (Dimbleby and Reynolds 1988: 320)[4]

The emphasis on historical Britain in the American imagination surely existed, but it was increasingly matched by more contemporary iconography which emerged as part of a 1980s increase in the importation of British products, notably the popularization of music video, with its need to visualize locations and scenarios consistent with the images of 'New Wave' (and largely British) popular music.[5] In 1981, the tremendous American public interest in the new royal couple, Prince Charles and Princess Diana, certified that a kind of American Anglophilia was on the rise.[6] By the time, then, of the release of *An American Werewolf in London*, images of Britain were being decisively re-generated, greater transit of both the literal and metaphorical kind was in operation between the two cultures and the premise of two middle-class American college kids choosing to visit England as the first stop on their European trip carried a high degree of verisimilitude. The film's horror satire thus fittingly emerges in a narrative about tourism gone seriously awry. Where the film deepens and complicates its notion of Anglo-American affinity, however, is in intermittent suggestions matching the undeadness of Britain in its imagination with a suspicion that similar conditions of alienation and isolation prevail at home.

An American Werewolf in London and the Anxieties of Arrival

A generic hybrid which is a great deal more interesting than it might at first appear, *An American Werewolf in London* establishes its mix of vivid horror and deadpan comedy early on. To the strains of 'Blue Moon', against an empty rural landscape, Jack and David are deposited by the side of the road in northern England. The two are all innocence, discussing Jack's unrequited crush on a girl back home and telling each other knock-knock jokes to pass the time. They have been sharing space in the back of a truck with a farmer's flock of sheep and, in case we miss the point that this young and guileless pair are at risk in their new surroundings, they shortly find themselves at the Slaughtered Lamb pub. An icy reception by local villagers and a sense of unease produced by the five-pointed star painted on one wall lead the pair to awkward joking and bravado attempts to engage the other patrons in conversation. Jack tells his friend that the star on the wall is a pentangle, 'it's used in witchcraft. Lon Chaney Jr. and Universal Studios maintain that's the mark of the Wolfman.' This observation marks the film's generic memory of classical horror (*The Wolfman* [1941] here, but as the narrative progresses, also teen horror texts such as *I Was A Teenage Werewolf*) and, strikingly, its industrial memory, since Universal Studios produced not only many of the film's intertexts but also *An American Werewolf in London* itself.[7]

It is in the Slaughtered Lamb that a patron's joke (one which seems momentarily to break the ice after David's and Jack's unwelcome arrival, but is in fact at their expense) sets in place one of the film's broader concerns with American character. The joke holds that four United Nations employees are in a plane flying over the Atlantic when they are forced to lighten their weight if they are to have sufficient fuel to make it to New York. A Frenchman sacrifices himself, saying 'Vive la France!' as he throws himself from the plane, then an Englishman does so, yelling 'God Save the Queen', whereupon the American in the group yells 'Remember the Alamo!' and tosses his Mexican colleague out the door. This joke (heartily enjoyed by all the pub patrons apart from David and Jack) introduces the idea that there is something distorted in the American conceptualization of honour and that Americans are characteristically unable to sacrifice themselves for the good of others. As the film develops, it is this very problem that comes to define David's predicament, as I shall shortly discuss.[8] When they leave the pub, Jack and David quickly become disoriented. Naïvely disregarding the advice they have been given to 'keep off the moors', they stumble about in the dark, growing increasingly anxious about the recurrent howls they hear in the distance. When Jack trips and falls to the ground, the two laugh for a moment at their own (they presume, unjustified) panic. As David goes to help his friend up, Jack is suddenly set upon by the werewolf, and we see him being brutally (and bloodily) devoured. David too is bitten, but the werewolf is prevented from going further when the pub patrons appear, shooting the werewolf to death.

Upon awakening three weeks later in a London hospital, David is told that he suffered his injuries when attacked by 'a lunatic'. An American Embassy official appears to reassure him that all the formalities of notification have been taken care of, and when David is less than appreciative (he has only moments before learned of Jack's death), the official grumbles that 'these dumbass kids never appreciate anything you do for them'. The official's presence is a marker of *An American Werewolf in London*'s adherence to some of the codes of the teen film, as is the 'sexy nurse' (Nurse Alex Price) who will shortly become a figure of erotic interest to David. A continued emphasis on David as a juvenile in this section of the film comes across in a scene where he refuses to eat his dinner and Alex feeds him like a child.[9]

David begins to have a series of terrifying dreams in which his own primitivization, monstrousness and vulnerability are showcased. In the first, he dreams he is running naked in the woods, preying on woodland creatures. In the second, he is again in the woods but finds his own hospital bed incongruously placed there. When Alex approaches his sleeping form in the bed, his eyes pop open and he has been monstrously transformed (via Rick Baker's celebrated special make-up effects) into a fiend. Here, again, the film's adherence to some of the codes of the teen pic is clear, notably its defining ambivalence about sexual desire.[10] *An American Werewolf in London* was released in the midst of a boom in youth horror production; the subgenre, of course, is defined by its habit of meting out gruesome punishment for the sexual activity of young people. As Timothy Shary points out, the teen horror subgenre that would thrive in the '80s relied upon classical notions of misfortune falling upon transgressors of purity, only now such 'transgressions' as premarital sex and youthful hedonism were resulting not in punishment by social institutions like parents, teachers, or the law but in death at the hands of a greater evil.

(Shary 2002: 140)

David associates the loss of control and descent into the primitive with sex, and this association is intermittently maintained through the film; later, after a night of carnage, he will pretend to sexually 'devour' Alex.

Just as striking in this section of the film is David's terror that the attack on the moors has linked him with a primordial European evil which threatens both him and his family. In an extraordinary sequence, he dreams he is at home on Long Island and his father's answer of a knock at the door admits entry to a terrifying band of skeleton stormtroopers. The family's evening at home by the fireside shockingly and graphically transforms into carnage as the stormtroopers brutally slay the entire family and set the house on fire. The recognizably Nazi figures of the sequence factor importantly in terms of the care the film takes to name both David and Jack as Jewish New Yorkers.[11] (Indeed, before David had regained consciousness in the hospital, Alex and a co-worker had speculated about him with Alex saying, 'The chart says he's from New York', and the other replying 'I think he's a Jew', in reference to his circumcised penis.)

Where *An American Werewolf in London* gains its depth is in its repurposing of the werewolf narrative to articulate not only teen sexual terrors but also an American imagination of Europe as simultaneously more prosaic and more dangerous than the USA. In purely logical terms, there is no clear connection between David's unconscious fears that he is transforming into a werewolf and his nightmare vision of his Jewish family being slaughtered by supernatural Nazi stormtroopers. The connection the film means to supply has much to do with the dynamics I suggest structure the European misadventure story: the attraction to a perceived European exoticism, essentialism and sexuality, on the one hand, and a historically rooted association of Europe with terror, danger and the unknown on the other. The dream sequence speaks simultaneously to David's sense of alienation and vulnerability as he lies hospitalized far from home and of his terror of Europe as a site of historical trauma, a place where the legacies of the past live on in the present (as in the werewolf curse). The theme of innocents unwittingly sacrificed to 'monstrous' aggressors is, of course, already at work in the film from the point at which the Slaughtered Lamb patrons knowingly turn Jack and David out on the moors with only a terse warning, seemingly in compliance with a long-established local custom of appeasing the beast on the moors.

David's dream richly bears out what some critics have deemed an Americanization effect around Holocaust memory. In this formulation, according to Ronald

J. Berger, 'the United States has turned an event that was not of its own making into an event of its own, a process by which the genocide has become popularized' and rendered more accessible (Berger 2002: 141). The trend towards Holocaust awareness, moreover, was peaking in the period immediately preceding *An American Werewolf in London*'s release. In 1978 alone for instance, Jimmy Carter established the President's Commission on the Holocaust (leading to the creation of the US Holocaust Memorial Museum), the four-part NBC mini-series *Holocaust* drew 120 million viewers, and a planned Nazi march in Illinois made headlines nationwide, while books, conferences and courses on the subject multiplied rapidly (Weissman 2004: 9). The large volume of media material (historical documentary, documentary reconstruction and fiction) dealing with the experience of the Holocaust frames this episode in the film in an equivalency by which for American audiences the Holocaust has come to be seen strangely as 'ours'. The quasi-proprietary relationship between US popular culture and the Holocaust does not particularize David's terror; instead it generalizes it, with the protagonist's Jewishness here effectively working to fortify his Americanness.

Although the film's conscious events are set entirely in Europe, the American home remains ideologically central (all the more so because of the emphasis placed early on upon the protagonists' distance from it and the keen vulnerability of these two young 'lambs' as they are figured in the opening sequence), and, in this respect, *An American Werewolf in London* bears out some of the representational tendencies of the period sketched by Vivian Sobchack. Sobchack analyses a turn in contemporary American cinema in which, 'The exotic, decadent European world of the traditional horror film, the wondrous, alien, outer space of the science fiction film, and the familiar, domestic and traditionally American space of the family melodrama become closely associated' (Sobchack 1996: 178). As part of this shift, formerly externalized threats, horrors and aspects of the supernatural are discovered to be intrinsic to domestic experience in a range of *An American Werewolf in London*'s contemporaries including *The Exorcist* (1973), *Carrie* (1976), *The Omen* (1976), *The Amityville Horror* (1979) and *Poltergeist* (1982). Through its inclusion of this vivid stand-out scene, *An American Werewolf in London* participates (on a small scale) in the representational trend toward conceptualizing American families as newly vulnerable to 'outside' terrors.

Just as David is beginning to physically and emotionally recover from the attack on the moors, he is visited by Jack in a scene which is played partly for laughs; despite his grisly (and as the film goes on, increasingly mouldering) appearance, Jack is relatively matter of fact about his death and maintains the same deadpan style and fatalist humour he had when he was alive. Jack says that until David kills himself, bringing to an end the werewolf curse, Jack is doomed to walk the Earth in limbo, killing innocent victims. Blithely urging his friend to commit suicide before the full moon, he leaves, and David, now discharged from the hospital goes to stay with Alex in her apartment in London.[12]

It is at this stage of *An American Werewolf in London* that the connection to the joke at the Slaughtered Lamb pub is most forcefully felt. David is in denial about Jack's warning; at Alex's apartment, the film surrounds him with objects that alternately reference an idealized American sense of duty and sacrifice (a *Casablanca* poster on one wall) and a banal American commercialized mass culture (the Muppets, a Mickey Mouse doll). This alternation contextualizes David's dilemma in national terms, suggesting that while honour and duty (in the form of suicide) are being urged upon him, he will abjure this option in favour of pleasure and self-indulgence (his developing romance with Alex). And indeed, despite Jack's warning and signs of an imminent transformation (in that horror-film cliché where animals instinctively recognize evil, David is barked at by a dog and hissed at by a cat), he spends an aimless day in the apartment and is calmly reading a book when with a yell he suddenly falls to the floor and begins a grotesque metamorphosis. Fully transformed into a werewolf, he goes hunting through London, killing and partially eating six victims[13] and awakening the next morning in the wolf cage at the zoo. Unaware of his transformation, he feels euphoric the next day until he hears about the killings and knows instinctively that he was responsible. In a vain effort to get himself arrested, he berates a police officer in Trafalgar Square and slanders Prince Charles and the Queen, but to no avail. Now clear in his mind about the necessity and inevitability of his death, David calls home to Long Island but finds only his young sister Rachel at home. The phone call renews the connection established in the dream sequence to a notion of familial vulnerability, and the dialogue here highlights both the petty habits of sibling interaction and the plaintive quality of this last exchange. Impatient to learn that his parents aren't at home for his final phone call, David asks, incredulously, 'You're all alone? Mom and Dad would never leave me alone when I was ten, no, not ten and a half, either.' Asking Rachel to tell his parents he loves them and not to fight with her brother, he is met with the typical emotional squeamishness of a little sister, and his professions of love and care wind up alternating with admonitions including 'No, I'm not being silly, you little creep.' Having, it appears, primed himself for the romance of a sacrificial death, David makes a half-hearted suicide attempt in the phone box, holding a Swiss army knife to his wrist but finding himself unable to cut.

Just at that moment, Jack beckons to him from across the street in Piccadilly Circus, and the two meet in a porn cinema where Jack reiterates the necessity for David to kill himself and introduces him to his six bloodied victims of the previous evening. This group, it is worth observing, maintain the same sort of straightforward acceptance of death displayed by Jack; their reactions to their own murders range from undisturbed to peevish, though they do seem to relish offering suggestions for the methods by which David might do himself in. It is typical of the film's macabre humour that when guns are discussed, David asks if he would need a silver bullet, and Jack replies scornfully, 'Oh, be serious, would you?' Meanwhile, throughout the introductions and discussion, the group are also spectators at a hilariously inept porn film.

Even after the strongest urging and ample evidence of his own murderous werewolf nature, David cannot sacrifice himself. He stays on at the porn cinema until darkness, when the inevitable transformation occurs again. Attempts to subdue him as he goes on the rampage through Piccadilly create mass havoc and numerous injuries until he is finally cornered and killed. As the credits roll, we hear again the rather cheerful 'Blue Moon' (this time in a more upbeat doo-wop version), sustaining the film's combination of horror and levity even after the narrative has come to an end.

In my reading of *An American Werewolf in London* I have suggested that the film's European misadventure narrative resonates particularly within a socio-historical context in which Anglo-American cultural and political bonds seemed to be strengthening, and yet the film registers a persistent crisis of confidence over American character and the (mis)use of allies. While 'special relationship' rhetoric often highlights an idealized concept of shared sacrifice, the film perverts that notion by emphasizing the randomness and inequity of sacrifice from its opening sequence at the Slaughtered Lamb through David's inability to kill himself in the middle of his first romance. While it would be wrong to claim that the film manifests a clear or sustained political subtext, it continually references connections to a real-world Britain in a way that may seem unlikely for a teen horror film. At the same time, *An American Werewolf in London* drew attention for the impact of its horrific special effects, and in this sense the film strikes an uneasy (though potentially ideologically and critically productive) balance between aspects of realism and aspects of fantastical horror. This balance is brought to fruition at the end of the film's credits where a message of 'heartfelt congratulations' from the film's production company, Lycanthrope Films Limited, is conveyed to Prince Charles and Princess Diana upon their wedding. This reference to the image of ceremonial and romantic Britain which enthralled so many Americans in the summer of the film's release is succeeded by a disclaimer noting that 'All characters and events in this film are fictitious. Any similarity to actual events or persons, living, dead, or undead, is purely coincidental.' The juxtaposition of these two closing statements invites us to contextualize the film in relation to 'reality' but then abruptly cautions us against doing so; in this sense, closure entails the fusion of a sharp awareness of current political and social elements with an insistence on fantasy, a fusion that, as I have shown, characterizes *An American Werewolf in London* more broadly.

Conclusion

This essay has examined *An American Werewolf in London* as a youth-oriented horror satire, as a fiction responding tentatively and sceptically to the renewal of

Anglo-American cultural and political alliance in the period of the film's release and as a prototypical European misadventure. It would be illuminating to comparatively assess this benchmark film in relation to some of its contemporary successors in an era that has seen a distinctive rewriting of the terms of US internationalism with a pronounced emphasis on defensive ideological insularity rationalized through homeland rhetoric. The post-9/11 culture has fostered military adventurism, a rise in governmental secrecy, domestic militarization and an erosion of civil liberties while generating unapologetic rationales for detention and torture and a 'war for profit' stance consistent with the triumph of a market culture and intensified conglomeration of industries. As the American–European dynamic has become ambivalent and uncertain, Britain is increasingly positioned as America's one reliable ally and mediating political partner. Britishness is thus construed as a tolerable version of foreignness, and the celebrated 'special relationship' has sparked a flurry of new Anglo-American fictions, particularly in the chick-flick category (*Love Actually*, *Wimbledon*, *Hope Springs*, *What a Girl Wants*, *Closer*, *The Wedding Date*). The same period has also witnessed a moderate re-energizing of the European caper movie with either a couple at the centre (*Just Married*) or a group of friends (*Eurotrip*). Such films suggest a new version of the American-odyssey-in-Europe formula, one which entails the remystification of Europe. I suggested earlier in this essay that *An American Werewolf in London* draws on horror codes to turn the coming-of-age story inside out. By contrast, a more recent teen film such as *Eurotrip* determinedly patches identity back together after the travails of a European misadventure, even if in a hollow and unconvincing fashion.

In considering these divergent examples of popular cinema focusing on the misadventures of Americans in Europe, it becomes clear that the significance of youthful haplessness shifts in accordance with generic and ideological mandates. Perhaps the most striking difference between *An American Werewolf in London* and its successors can be found in how differently such films figure the loss of control, bearing in mind that the former was produced at the start of a period of conservative cultural retrenchment and the more recent teen films at a moment in which the conservative imperatives over contemporary American social life seem seldom to have been more dominating. The teen protagonists of *An American Werewolf in London* never experience a moment of control in their overseas environment; disorientation and uncertainty predominate from start to finish throughout the film. A film like *Eurotrip* is far more reluctant to stage a loss of control and, particularly in its conclusion, insists that lapses of control should be repressed in favour of a return to the status quo.[14] Interestingly, *An American Werewolf in London* uses the notion of the Anglo-American 'special relationship' to begin to prise open concepts of national confidence, moral certainty and the virtue of alliance. These examples of teen horror and teen sex comedy hold in common an association between Europe and chaos which is complicit with ideologies of defensive nationalism. Yet *An*

American Werewolf in London formulates a horror satire that unsettles both individual psychology and patriotic complacency, in the process attaining a degree of depth and forcefulness far surpassing its contemporary successors.

Notes

1 Universal Studios' Production Notes for the film characterize it as the story of 'two young American students whose European tour comes to an abrupt end when they come up against the supernatural' (1981: 6).

2 For a more complete discussion of this last category see my 'Romance And/As Tourism: Heritage Whiteness and the (Inter)National Imaginary in the New Woman's Film', in *Keyframes: Popular Cinema and Cultural Studies*, Amy Villarejo and Matthew Tinkcom eds., London: Routledge, 2001. Another common form of the Hollywood European misadventure is the franchise sequel which is under obligation to strike a balance between maintaining and differentiating its approach from that of its predecessor. This kind of film sometimes finds 'Europeanization' a useful means to achieve this as may be seen in *National Lampoon's European Vacation* (1985) and, more recently, *Deuce Bigalow: European Gigolo* (2005).

3 It does this most notably in sequences at Piccadilly Circus which emphasize huge billboards for Coke, Sanyo and other international brands.

4 An interesting anecdote from Ronald Reagan's first term in office illustrates the political capital that could be attached to imaginary, historic Britain. Trying to substantiate the validity of a 'tough on crime' approach, Reagan told a group of Chicago schoolchildren that the British used to hang criminals for possessing guns. Despite the inaccuracy of this claim, Reagan's Deputy Press Secretary defended the President saying 'It made the point didn't it?' Gil Troy reveals this anecdote in *Morning in America: How Ronald Reagan Invented the 1980s* (2005: 8).

5 One can reasonably surmise, I think, that the audience for a teen horror film like *An American Werewolf in London* would have been particularly familiar with this set of images of Britain and Britishness.

6 Arguably, this Anglophilia is connected to a heightening of the enduring association between Britain and the mystical/supernatural which continues up to the present in the vast success of the global print/film franchise *Harry Potter*.

7 A more elaborated discussion of Universal's *The Wolfman* comes later when David sketches the plot of the film to Alex. Interestingly, Universal Studios' Production Notes for *An American Werewolf in London* seek to craft a narrative of an American film crew 'conquering' Europe for the sake of art, referring repeatedly to the 'location coups' scored when the production team was able to persuade British authorities to approve filming in Piccadilly Circus, the tube and the grounds of Windsor Castle.

8 In line with this is the regularity with which David is specifically referenced as American in contexts where such a reference would seem superfluous. For instance, when Alex brings David to her apartment, she tells him she is not in the habit of bringing home 'stray young American men'. Later, a young boy at the zoo (speaking of David) reports to his mother that 'a naked American man stole my balloons'.

9 She also reads him a story when he cannot sleep (from the highly appropriate *A Connecticut Yankee in King Arthur's Court* by Mark Twain).

10 The association between sexual desire, monstrous transformation and death is also at work in Jack's characterization. Shortly before he is killed, he talks about his long-time crush on a girl named Debbie Klein, and David responds saying 'What are you worried about Debbie Klein for anyway? We're going to meet plenty of girls on this trip.' When Jack reappears after his death, he reports bitterly that Debbie Klein 'cried a lot' at his funeral but 'found solace in Mark Levine's bed'.

11 For a survey of Nazi representation in American cinema, see Lester D. Friedman's 'Darkness Visible: Images of Nazis in American Film'. It could certainly be argued that David's nightmare is integrated into the rest of the film in the sense that Nazism represents for many the ultimate horror of a civilized society lapsing into barbarism, and, in this respect, there is a parallel to the lycanthropic transformations central to *An American Werewolf in London*. It is worth noting that 1981 was a year in which traumatic memory of the Second World War played some role in popular film: blockbuster *Raiders of the Lost Ark* featured a plot in which US intelligence agents learn that a team of Nazi archaeologists is searching for the lost Ark of the Covenant and Indiana Jones is discharged to find it first.

12 It is a mark of the film's unusual level of attention to some of the realities of early 1980s British culture that as David and Alex shop at a market and then ride the tube, they have a discussion about inflation and the high cost of food and find themselves surrounded by Mohawked punks.

13 In the most extended scene of David's hunting and killing of his victims, he preys on a posh couple who think it will be fun to give their host a scare by creeping up to the house where they are invited for dinner through a back garden. When the hostess hears noises (her guests are being gruesomely devoured) she tells her husband 'Sean, there's hooligans in the park again.' This reflexive explanation is interesting in light of the earlier account of David being attacked by a 'lunatic'. In these ways, the film manifests an apparent belief that in early 1980s Britain socially marginal and potentially violent people were ubiquitous.

14 The thematics of control might usefully be compared to *Slap Her She's French* (2002) in which the cultural transit works in the opposite direction to that of *An American Werewolf in London* and *Eurotrip*. *Slap Her She's French* centres on the impact of a deceitful French exchange student who creates havoc in the life of an American high-school student whose life she usurps. In ways that chime with familiar cultural themes of 'girl power', the teen female heroine is obliged to forcefully (re)claim her life.

References

Bailey, Steve and Hay, James (2002) 'Cinema and the Premises of Youth: "Teen Films" and Their Sites in the 1980s and 1990s', in Steve Neale (ed.) *Genre and Contemporary Hollywood*, London: British Film Institute, pp. 218–55.

Bartlett, C. J. (1992) '*The Special Relationship': A Political History of Anglo-American Relations Since 1945*, London and New York: Longman.

Baylis, John (ed.) (1997) *Anglo-American Relations since 1939: The Enduring Alliance*. Manchester: Manchester University Press.

Berger, Ronald J. (2002) *Fathoming the Holocaust: A Social Problems Approach*, New York: Aldine De Gruyter.

Dimbleby, David and Reynolds, David (1988) *An Ocean Apart: The Relationship between Britain and America in the Twentieth Century*, New York: Random House.

Flanzbaum, Hilene (ed.) (1999) *The Americanization of the Holocaust*, Baltimore, Md.: Johns Hopkins University Press.

Friedman, Lester D. (2004) 'Darkness Visible: Images of Nazis in American Film', in Murray Pomerance (ed.) *Bad: Infamy, Darkness, Evil and Slime on Screen*, Albany, NY: SUNY Press, pp. 254–71.

Jeffords, Susan (1994) *Hard Bodies: Hollywood Masculinity in the Reagan Era*, New Brunswick, NJ: Rutgers University Press.

Maddrey, Joseph (2004) *Nightmares in Red, White and Blue: The Evolution of the American Horror Film*, Jefferson, NC: McFarland & Co.

Markovitz, Jonathan (2004) 'Reel Terror Post 9/11', in Wheeler Winston Dixon (ed.) *Film and Television after 9/11*, Carbondale, Ill.: Southern Illinois University Press, pp. 201–25.

Maslin, Janet (1981) 'Yanks on the Moors', *New York Times*, 21 August, p. C12.

Negra, Diane (2007) '1981: Movies Look "Back to the Future"', in Stephen Prince (ed.) *American Cinema of the 1980s: Themes and Variations*, New Brunswick, NJ: Rutgers University Press.

'Production Notes: *An American Werewolf in London*', 1981 Universal Studios Press Department, Universal City, California, 15 July.

Sobchack, Vivian (1996) 'Bringing it All Back Home: Family Economy and Generic Exchange', in Barry Keith Grant (ed.) *The Dread of Difference: Gender and the Horror Film*, Austin, Tex.: University of Texas Press, pp. 143–63.

Shary, Timothy (2002) *Generation Multiplex: The Image of Youth in Contemporary American Cinema*, Austin, Tex.: University of Texas Press.

Troy, Gil (2005) *Morning in America: How Ronald Reagan Invented the 1980s*, Princeton, NJ: Princeton University Press.

Waller, Gregory A. (ed.) 'Introduction', *American Horrors: Essays on the Modern American Horror Film*, Urbana, Ill.: University of Illinois Press.

Weissman, Gary (2004) *Fantasies of Witnessing: Post-war Efforts to Experience the Holocaust*, Ithaca, NY: Cornell University Press.

Williams, Tony (1996) 'Trying to Survive on the Darker Side: 1980s Family Horror', in Barry Keith Grant (ed.) *The Dread of Difference: Gender and the Horror Film*, Austin, Tex.: University of Texas Press, pp. 164–80.

Wood, Robin (1996) 'Papering the Cracks: Fantasy and Ideology in the Reagan Era', in John Belton (ed.) *Movies and Mass Culture*, New Brunswick, NJ: Rutgers University Press, pp. 203–28.

Chapter 11

American Me (1992)

Ana María Dopico

In March 1992, US movie audiences could choose between two films featuring the ethnic colour of American identities: one was *The Mambo Kings Play Songs of Love*, the other, *American Me*. As one critic put it, these were two new movies 'about Hispanics looking for respect – bandleaders in one film, gang leaders in the other' (Johnson, 1992: 51). The films marked contrasting points of exemplarity and visibility which triangulated the assimilation of Latinos to American life through entertainment and criminalization. They also offered audiences familiar ways to understand how Hispanics both sustained and threatened American identity. *The Mambo Kings Play Songs of Love* achieved popular success and critical approval with its novelistic origins, its Latin lover protagonist, and its musical immigrant romance. *American Me*, in contrast, languished critically and at the box office, despite the celebrity of its star/director/producer, Edward James Olmos. *American Me*'s violent prison narrative, its machismo and its pessimistic realism were hard to swallow. But even as the film died at the box office, it gained an afterlife among viewers compelled by its dystopic parable about the American self. It is clear nearly fifteen years later that its unassimilable negativity about the limits of American identity retains its political relevance. More hauntingly, the film's internment of its characters and its focus on a penitentiary America offers, in retrospect, a prophetic message about the 'prison-industrial complex' which presently polices an internal border and which constrains and forecloses national identity in the USA.

American Me begins with a message against a blacked-out screen which warns the audience that the film they are about to see is inspired by a true story, that the events are 'strong and brutal, but they occur every day'. As the opening titles appear between pitch-black screens that usher the viewer into temporary blindness, a male voice commands invisible subjects to move from position to position in a prison strip-search. Emerging from the blacked-out screen and disembodied orders, Edward James Olmos's face appears, framed by bars and prison doors: as the film's protagonist, Santana, he begins narrating his story in a poetic voice-over, a poetic autobiography which serves as a spoken-word aesthetic counterpoint to the visual chronicle of the career of the Chicano gang lord. The film takes us through flashbacks of his origins and criminal adolescence, where he helps to found a local gang called La M ('La Eme')[1] at sixteen, and almost immediately ends up in Los Angeles's Juvenile Hall.

In its protagonist, Chicano gang lord Santana, the film offers a racial 'other' sequestered safely behind bars whose pathologies can be observed, diagnosed and analysed at close quarters, and then traced back, in an etiological search, to the neighbourhood that produced him and where his social disease continues to spread. As we follow Santana's criminal career from the 'inside' to the 'outside' and back again, we move from the dynamics of cinematic narrative to that of surveillance. In this carceral order, white American identity is perspectivally displaced from the gaze of the viewer, who is present, to the implied gaze of security cameras, wardens, guards, social workers, psychiatrists, parole officers or ethnographers who follow the imprisoned 'subjects' but who are almost entirely absent in the film. Regardless of his or her race, the viewer is put in the place of the gaze of power, perspectivally identified with the eye of the camera, which rarely coincides with the criminal's point of view. The film presents some choice regarding identity, identification and, therefore, sympathy, as we encounter the primary triangle of protagonists: Santana, his sidekick/lover J. T. (William Forsythe) and his female 'beloved' Julie (Dyana Ortelli). But the only practical choice for audience identification is Santana, who is present in nearly every scene, nearly every frame, and whose own violence, rarely visible, is justified by codes of honour or leadership. Santana's voice is also inescapable: his autobiographical voice intervenes to explain and speed along cinematic *mise-en-scènes*, and his spoken-word narrative provides a potent interpretive and aesthetic supplement to the film's visual surveillance of his prison life. In approaching and identifying with Santana, our cinematic life becomes impossible and our sympathy is inevitably held hostage, caught between the disturbing evidence of the image and the political appeal of the confessional word. Despite ourselves, we are forced by the film to relentlessly identify Santana as protagonist and primary object but, more provocatively, to identify with him and his distorted American *Bildungsroman*. From the film's opening scene in the penitentiary to its conclusion in a scene of street violence, Santana and his cohort struggle to separate their subjecthood from institutions and mechanisms of subjection – social and psychic – which produce and define their pathologies and which exclude them from the very norms of American identity that their deviance serves to delimit.[2]

The film's long second act, filmed in cold prison colours and contrasting shades of light and dark, offers the everyday atmosphere of *American Me*, showing us Santana's paradoxical 'emancipation' into carceral criminality in the 1960s. The scene moves from Juvenile Hall to Folsom Prison chronicling Santana's eighteen years of prison life and his ascendant prison career, as he directs La M's shift from a fraternity of protection and tribal mutualism to a corporate 'Mexican Mafia', running the secret economies of penitentiary life. With the help of two friends, his Anglo homeboy J. T. and his fellow Chicano, Mundo (Pepe Serna), Santana gains status and respect by protecting La M's monopoly on prison trade and exercising a ruthless control of murder and violence. Santana negotiates La M's profitable expansion into a booming drug traffic which allows him to profit from social pathologies in prison and assert control over heroin, refusing it as a habit but cannily exploiting it as a valuable commodity. In the process, Santana is becoming a businessman; he gains business respect and social dominance on the inside while gathering economic and criminal capital which will allow him to expand and diversify into criminal infrastructures and illicit economies on the outside.

When Santana is eventually paroled, the cinematographic style shifts to diffuse light, warm colours, and softened contours, and the voice-over autobiography stops. No longer narrating himself, Santana seems suddenly unsure and out of place as he explores the life of his community after eighteen years away. He begins a romance with a local woman called Julie, cements his ties with his brother and his partner, J. T., and tries to parlay prison's 'business experience' from inside to outside by muscling out his Italian competitor, who controls the drug trade in East Los Angeles. The carceral continuum which Santana expected to inhabit nevertheless fails him: step by step, Santana's adventure in American civic life begins to unravel. His heterosexual romance is betrayed by his inexperience, his prison habits and secret sexual life: the audience watches as a promising love scene is shattered by the intercut scenes of a brutal prison rape, wondering if perhaps Santana's failure lies in the repression of a homosexual desire that has been both liberated and tainted by its prison origins. Santana's attempt to take over the drug trade falters, and the neighbourhood is punished for his violent reprisal against the rival Italian kingpin when the 'don' floods the Chicano community, killing its addicts with uncut heroin. Seeing the death and destruction that implicate him, Santana appears to reassess his code of violence, retribution and parasitic capitalism, and his criticisms and ambivalence cause his loyal friends to doubt his resolve. Accusing him of showing weakness, his closest friend and ally (and possibly lover), J. T., ceases to trust him.[3] His would-be girlfriend accuses him of being a curse on the community, and as he responds to her moral indictment on a city street, he is arrested and returned to jail, accused of carrying drugs that belonged to a fellow gang member.

Finally back in prison in the film's last act, Santana seems to regain his quiet confidence and authority, but his peace, and his renewed confessional address to the audience, is short lived. Refusing to authorize a reprisal against a fellow gang member, 'Little Puppet', Santana confirms his weakness to J. T., who is still on the outside. During a laconic exchange between J. T. and Santana which is divided by a prison partition, Santana casts devastating doubt on the heroism and necessity of their violent code of honour and their life as partners in crime. His 'crime partner' and beloved friend bids Santana goodbye and then authorizes his murder with a gesture to an inmate as he walks away. As a host of his former underlings in La M stab him repeatedly in a scene that evokes the murder of Julius Caesar, Santana's execution as the failing leader of an alternate prison empire is intercut with scenes of the fratricidal hit which he tried to cancel. Gang claims of homicidal reprisal conquer long-time loyalties to a leader and annihilate blood ties between brothers; as Santana is stabbed we see 'Big Puppet' killing his little brother and cursing himself on a California roadside. The film cuts back to Santana's murder, and we watch as his bloody body falls to the ground towards the camera like a broken doll, another ruined puppet. With his death, the film returns us to East Los Angeles and we watch young *barrio* boys re-enacting the ritual gang initiation that Santana inaugurated years before. The film ends, as it began, with an initiation into blood loyalty and violence, this time in the film's temporal present. But this contemporary initiation is more dangerous and more deadly: it climaxes as the young initiate, huffing fumes from a bag, is ordered to prove his new allegiance to La M by taking aim in a drive-by shooting. As the boy leans out the window with a pistol in both hands, asking, 'Which one?' and blearily taking aim, we watch pedestrians and residents dive for cover. The boy shouts, 'Fuck it, holmes!'[4] and as we see the pistol fire, the screen goes black. Returning to its frame of social reference, the film closes with statistics about gang violence in 1992.

The Difficulties of *American Me*

Approaching *American Me* nearly fifteen years beyond its release is a difficult prospect for many reasons. The film is not an American classic, nor a mainstream hit, but that is not the difficulty. It is relentless, depressing, brutally violent and its cautionary parable competes with its despondent content; its cinematic aesthetics make imprisonment seem cool, clean, natural and relaxed, at times even spiritual, but that does not explain its troubling effects. It is a breakthrough film for Latino production, with a cultural protagonist as director, producer, star and promoter; it addresses Latino audiences with the 'truth' of a cultural emergency which is both communal and individualistic; thus the burden of representation it bears, and demands, is overwhelming. But the real difficulty of *American Me* lies in its political importance. For me, this means judging what the film means in the contemporary American political imaginary, how it splinters under its representational burden and reveals a schizoid truth.

When I realized that *American Me* offered a masculinist prison imaginary as a central interpretive trope for American identity, I thought this an insidious notion, since it seemed a radical circumscription of political metaphors for Latino American identity. At first glance, the film can seem simplistic, brutal and negative and caught in the panoptic cultural politics of immigrant phobia and border-policing that secured American identity during the first Bush presidency. But something else remained beyond this, a new negative imaginary for identity, a buzz of dissonance that belied the critical and criminal sentence that the film seemed to impose. The movie's agonistic social parable and documentary realism, its ethno-poetic analysis and dramatic autobiography, its celebrity *auteur* activism, its implied pop-sociology of underdevelopment and criminal pathology all offered familiar generic currencies for identifying and interpreting minority American communities. These recognizable currencies, devalued but still exchangeable against the currency of cinematic greatness, have eased the film's assimilation into a 'minor' or 'emergent' mainstream American canon: a canon that gathers socially important films which are commercially and aesthetically marginal, but which, alongside films such as *Scarface* (1983), *Carlito's Way* (1993) or, more recently, the NBC series *Kingpin* (2003), offer a new Latino face for the limits, the foreclosures and the racialized fantasies of an outlaw American identity.

In trying to account for the film's critical negations, I realized that its focus on a prison imaginary for American identity, especially as it is experienced by criminalized ethnic minorities, was not an accident of social realism but was in fact *the* primary critical and political significance of the film. And although I admit that such a pessimistic metaphor goes against the film's ultimate project of social rescue, and its last-minute attempts to offer alternative, redemptive models for aspirational identity and get-out-of the-*barrio* self-improvement, the message that *American Me* conveys is severely pessimistic and nevertheless severely political. The cultural significance and critical legacy of *American Me*, I would suggest, lie not only in its portrait of communal decimation and political abdication, nor in its prophetic analysis of ethnic masculinity, carceral minorities, prison capitalism and institutionalized criminal consciousness.

The film's power and its importance result from a dynamic interplay which is symptomatic in many minority self-representations across genres and disciplines, where American identity is the result not of hospitable assimilation but of a long parole under the eye of the law and the discourses of the state. Most potently, this dynamic interplay offers a devastating message which recedes from view behind familiar framing strategies for ethnic subjects.

We watch as Santana is inextricably linked to a tense interplay between Chicano and US cultural history through the violence of the Zoot Suit riots and to the current crises of drug-trade and gang wars, but his story and the film's narrative poetics also betray a longer trail communal segregation, brutality and fatalism.

I would contend that the film reflects a dynamic operation in minority representation, involving a historical or contemporary message of political foreclosure and social emergency and an eternal theme about the social death of minorities in American life. This devastating critical content relies on a politics and aesthetics of realism as a documentary and diagnostic style and on insider exposés of ethnic socio-pathology.

Such collective analysis is usually mediated by the generic appeal and accessibility of autobiographical narrative, where individual and communal destinies are condensed in the ethnographic authority of a native informant, who provokes the analysis and the diagnosis with his confessional. *American Me*'s fictive autobiographical prison drama is often enriched and guaranteed by the celebrity of Olmos as a minority protagonist or *auteur*, whose career, popularity and activism serve as legitimation and as a compensatory supplement to his film's radical critique of American identity at the end of the twentieth century.

Framing a Carceral American Identity

American Me takes us to prison to see an exposé about carceral life and to hear the poetic testimony of a hardened Chicano gang lord. We meet Santana in the film's first frame and from that moment he rarely escapes the camera's gaze. His is the first voice we hear, and his voice-over narration guides us through the film. Santana's monologue about his identity (as criminal, as convict, as leader, as drug-dealer – implicitly as an 'American me') proves by far the most compelling voice in the film and to be more riveting and artful than any dialogue. Because of its rhyme and its performance, his confessional both frames and speaks beyond the film, reserving for Santana a double role as participant and analyst. In this dynamic of confessional, the speaking Santana becomes separate from the ruthless or silent Santana of the movie's visual imaginary. His confessional offers an interpretive accounting which connects individuality and identity to prison's alien and hidden reality. His voice-over establishes a bridge between the carceral realm of the prison and that of the *barrio* – but there, on the outside, his ability to narrate himself fades and his voice-over is silenced. In the last scene, Santana's narration shifts from the rhyming couplets whose sing-song performance artfully justified his life of crime, and he shifts into a wistful and analytical prose. He speaks to us, or speaks through us, in order to make sense of his life for someone on the outside, whom he has lost and for whom he no longer exists.

The first movement of *American Me* thus invites us to read the film as a lesson in Michel Foucault's 'carceral order', the state machinery where punishment is rendered socially invisible even as it relies on systems of surveillance, exposure and the internalization of social discipline.[5] In his seminal study, *Discipline and Punish*,

Foucault considers how surveillance, examination and incarceration have shaped and defined modern societies and how a disciplinary logic rules our relation to ourselves, one another and the State, such that 'each subject finds himself in a punishable, punishing universality' (Foucault 1977a: 178). Foucault explains how a carceral continuum of disciplinary institutions, judicial punishment and confinement not only segregates, punishes and attempts to reconstruct the utility of criminal subjects but simultaneously constructs notions of normality, identity, citizenship, social value and political integration. Watching the film's Latino *Homo criminalis* and listening to his autobiographical confession as he moves through prison spaces, we respond to segregated and contradictory strategies of identification. We are granted a panoptic privilege which isolates, watches and identifies Santana as a delinquent and pathological *object* – a privilege wherein the gaze of the audience is in turn identified with the gaze of the State and its disciplinary functions.

In enjoying the dominance of Santana and the safety of his protection in our tour through the penitentiary world, we begin to discover how *American Me* mimics the exploitation of the criminal within the penal order. Our recognition that Santana is an instrument of a disciplinary narrative, the criminal motor of an urgent social warning, produces a dissonance in which we recognize how we, the viewers (and in particular, we, the Latino viewers) are implicated in 'the carceral continuum' between penitentiary and society, where the internalization of panoptic authority 'assures the automatic functioning of power' as we define ourselves in distinction to his criminality (Foucault 1977a: 180). Thus, our ambivalent identification with Santana, his criminal dominance and his status as a functional object of a punitive system must lead us to a disturbing recognition: that Latino American identity occupies a parallel but not identical position to mainstream Americanness within the carceral continuum and within the disciplinary logic of the American state. Santana's aberrance and monstrosity help us to secure the forced norm within American identity. Often mapped between the surveyed coordinates of illegal migrant, illiterate citizen, criminal subculture, atavistic machismo, redemptive femininity or assimilated exemplarity, the barred Latino subjects that the movie addresses are forced to both internalize this disciplinary knowledge and to learn to negotiate and exploit its real and symbolic economies.

Santana's interned and internal confession of his own American subjectivity is severed from the conventional foreclosures of American identity, and the everyday violence of American life is released as a narrative only at the moment of his extermination from both the civic and the penal world. Santana's confessional transmits a tale in extremis and just before the moment of death, and it includes regret and repentance as part of its generic dispensation, helping the viewer assimilate and then disavow the hidden and dystopic world that we briefly see. His voice creates a subjective counterpoint to the film's watchtower gaze, and he tries to account for himself as a self-made man even as we are discovering how the

Figure 5   American Me.

carceral world has produced him as a liminal being. Against his voice, the film makes us 'see' how in foreclosing the young Santana's existence as an American in the *barrio* and in prison, the State has created a version of national identity which is racialized, ruthlessly capitalist, apolitical, violently sociopathic. And while we might wish to turn away and disavow this penalized identity, Santana's voice and his intelligent analysis ultimately offers us a political critique, reminding us at key points how a carceral continuum binds the visible and excluded realms of American life, the exemplary and criminal subjects who try to lay claim to American selves.

Santana's voice refers us to a body 'totally imprinted by history' (Foucault 1977b: 148), and his autobiographical address, his politicized memories and his Chicano poetics invite us to recognize his individuality and, against panoptic logic, to identify *with him* as a besieged political subject. In trying to negotiate these simultaneous but contradictory positions – standing in the place of the law isolating a pathogenic object, or standing in the place of the other as a political subject – the viewer is pushed towards positions of rejection and disavowal. The film indoctrinates us in the schizoid identity of the modern penal order, where the processes that normally shape a subject's social identity – identification, internalization, resistance and individuation – are negotiated as claustrophobic exchange between the prisoner and the institutional machinery of the State. For any viewer versed in sociology, psychoanalysis, racial politics or identity formation, the film discloses provocative and perhaps unintended truths. As Santana remarks laconically in a meeting with his fellow gang members, 'Inside runs the show. If there's any problems with that just let us know.' The phrase signals not only the internalization of a disciplinary order but also the inmates' ability (trained to virtuoso levels within the penitentiary) to negotiate and even control markets for exploitation (be it racial segregation, black markets or the drug trade) which connect the prison-inside and the *barrio-*outside of the carceral continuum.

This Hispanicized prison exposé offers not only disturbing titillation of prison life, it yields cultural history, developmental sociology, diagnostic psychology and spiritual autobiography. Through it, the audience enters the prison system as the invisible, and undiscovered, country where the Hispanic, to his horror, discovers his true role in a violent American imaginary and discovers within the prison-industrial complex a grotesque version of the operations of discipline, disavowal and desire that sustain national identity. The film is unflinching in its revelation of the machinery of the prison-industrial complex, that obscure but profitable state machinery which has expanded phenomenally in the past thirty years, deployed as a new arrangement of the State and private capital, disciplining minority populations through arrest and incarceration while simultaneously amassing and exploiting surplus labour within American corporate capitalism.[6]

But beyond the realistic contest of the penitentiary setting, the film turns to a more profound 'carceral' meaning for American identity. The lessons and effects of the 'prison-industrial complex', of Chino and Folsom State Prison, once internalized, produce the film's fascinating criminal protagonist: in the process, the film offers an alternative for the 'inferiority complex' as an explanation of minority entanglements with American identity. The film discloses how the symbolic and criminal economies of the penitentiary produce a disciplined, aberrant and purely 'American me', whose racial hybridity is not exemplary but an exploitable asset in the penal order, and whose Americanness is rooted in surveillance, prosecution and incarceration. In the process of watching and assimilating the film's physical and psychic violence, and in discovering the carceral continuum between prison and *barrio* in its realistic morality tale, we recognize how American identity relies on devastating foreclosures and exclusions. As I will argue later, Santana emerges as a true American through a process of negation and foreclosure: he is conceived by an anonymous American father through rape and racial violence, segregated from full American identity and surveilled as a putative delinquent in his *barrio* youth, and as a criminal he is the negation of everything that is apparently positive in American identity, even as he succeeds wildly in its entrepreneurial economies. He is a being produced negatively as an American by penal institutions designed to abolish the privileges of social life, cancelling American citizenship and reinforcing the exclusion of their coloured inmates from claims to civic or political being. Santana's *American Me* is the pure product of a carceral American identity. The film's imaginary reveals how individuals, communities or races are not merely denied their signification or repressed from political consciousness, but that they seem never to have existed at all as subjects with a claim to that identity.

Edward James Olmos and the Agon of the *Americano*

The initial fame or legend of *American Me* reveals varied audiences, celebrity politics, historical crisis and disparate receptions. The film addressed a wider public with different messages, but also became a cultural flashpoint, a vivid moment of critique and crisis within Latino communities. As the state was re-evaluating their Americanness against new immigrants and urban violence, they measured their own status and value by negotiating American identity and politics through the cinema, television and the entertainment industry (Fregoso 1993: 122, Noriega 2000: 75, 131).

The movie is notable for its documentary verité and authentic location shots, its neo-realist blending of civilians and actors, and the journalism of the time exalted its art-meets-danger elements and celebrated its valence as a 'happening' that succeeded in realistically representing violence by actually negotiating a temporary cessation of hostility in a besieged community. The preponderance of press coverage of the time focused on the proselytizing zeal, activist commitment and heroic determination of Edward James Olmos and his devotion to the film as a chance to help save Latino communities from a scourge of violence.

The mixed success, notoriety and the enduring importance of *American Me* depends in part on this urgent appeal to the reality principle: the empirical frame of its documentary value, its gritty sociology, its project of cultural rescue, by the special screenings for gang youth that marked its debut, and the celebrity proselytizing of its Latino everyman director. Yet the film's historicity and realist intervention is overdetermined by its provocative content, by the celebrity exemplarity of Edward James Olmos as the great American Latino and by his furious determination to expose and reform the suicidal culture of gangs in the Chicano community. Just as potently the film is marked by its historical moment (on the quincentennial of both the 'discovery' of the Americas and the consequent inauguration of 'American' as subject) and by its attempt to intervene in the racial politics of the USA and in the institutional politics of law enforcement during the Clinton Administration.

Transformed into the character of prison gang lord Santana, Olmos gathers around him not only the power and brutality of his character but the sympathy, pathos and heroism of all his previous roles. The opening scene establishes the film's forced perspectives and also its multiple addresses to distinct American audiences. Olmos allows white viewers to approach his criminal character with some aesthetic curiosity, and he invites Latino viewers into a more complicated entanglement, negotiating his fame and heroic burden of representation against the accusation of ethnic degradation or political slander that a film about Chicano criminality might provoke in a national atmosphere charged with contests over immigration and American identity.

Indeed, the film's extraordinary negativity might not have been produced, or endured, without Olmos's compensatory and reassuring presence on the screen. Audiences could shield themselves from the brutality of the film, agree to endure its content and accept its message, in large part because Olmos was a political broker they knew and trusted. The project of the film is connected to his determination to save Chicanos as Latinos as the newest Americans – to prevent their extinction or mass suicide at the moment of their political emergence into American identity. For Latinos and Chicanos, and in the Hollywood community, Olmos was notable as a cultural activist, serving on foundations, visiting hundreds of high schools, intervening in public forums about the future of minority communities. He had played in important films where Mexican and Chicano dramas were marketed for mainstream cross-over – most famously in *Zoot Suit* (1981), *Seguín* (1982), and *The Ballad of Gregorio Cortez* (1984). Olmos had become a familiar and famous cross-over Latino through his role as Lieutenant Castillo on *Miami Vice* (1984). His greatest cross-over fame and box-office success came with *Stand and Deliver* (1988), the movie version of the story of Jaime Escalante, the high-school teacher who had excelled in turning disenfranchised and marginalized Chicano teenagers into calculus-proficient, culturally proud, committed students – in yoking his name with Escalante's, Olmos helped secure them both the status of cultural heroes. In the late 1990s he achieved new mainstream visibility in two projects that mark the prominence of American identity in his work, appearing widely as a cultural ambassador in the media and at Hispanic events, even authoring a prologue for a coffee-table photography book about 'Latino Life in the United States' called *Americanos* in 1999. Olmos's most recent role brought him a new audience and restored him to a patriarchal role that he occupies in the Latino ethnic imaginary; playing the domineering and history-laden '*papá*' in the *American Family* (2002–4) which he brought to PBS with director Gregory Nava. Olmos once again produced, starred in and occasionally directed series episodes, which explored the life of a Chicano family in Los Angeles and engaged themes ranging from community activism to addiction to machismo, free speech and the war on Iraq. As a law-abiding and conservative paterfamilias, Olmos reaffirmed Latinos' claims to both American identity and to the complicated bundle of Hispanic-American family values.

In many regards, however, *American Me* seemed to echo Olmos's debut as a cinematic Chicano, and the film can be read as a self-defensive response to his popular fame as a violent macho *pachuco* in Luis Valdez's *Zoot Suit*. His new prison film offered a devastating sequel to the tragic and redemptive heroisms of *Zoot*

Suit, 'a different, tragic view of machismo as an endless re-enactment of a system that gorges on its young' (Christon 1991: 18). *American Me* seemed to offer a corrective message to those who were exploiting his filmic persona and theatrical violence to justify the logic of gang life, the fortified masculinity and the apathetic violence of gang culture. By 1991, Olmos had secured a $16 million budget from Universal (which doubtless banked on his recent Latino celebrity and cross-over success) for the prison film whose script he had first read eighteen years earlier and acquired in 1982.[7] Lobbying California state officials and wardens at Chino and Folsom State Prison, he campaigned for access and shooting rights which would give his cautionary tale an urgent and gritty realism. Olmos gained unprecedented access, the participation of prisoners as extras in group scenes and even the right to shoot a riot scene within prison walls. The conditions of this official cooperation gives the film's production another unexpected – and emblematic – hallucinatory dimension: wardens authorized the staging and filming of the fictional riot only on the condition that it be acted out in pantomime, with one gunshot permitted (Christon 1991: 18). The silent riot, to which sound was later added, seems a strange and fitting scenario for a film whose hallucinatory prison clarity offers only a momentary visibility – a theatre of revolt where a disciplinary silencing controls the Latino voices and simulated violence that might spur real upheaval within the prison. With Los Angeles Juvenile Hall, Chino and Folsom State as 'sets' that were repainted for grit, chiaroscuro effects and sharper contrast, Olmos's vision of carceral life promised an aesthetic reality whose psychic contours exaggerated the banal institutionalization of everyday prison life.

When *American Me* was released in March 1992, the movie was promoted as Olmos's brave, hard-won political project, the victory of an 'angry activist' and 'hero' who fought to produce the film and make a scared-straight intervention that would shake America, Latino communities and help change the youth culture and gang violence of Los Angeles. While some California reviews recognized the ethnic codes and subtexts of the film, national reviews such as Janet Maslin's argued that the film's cinematic aesthetics did not live up to its moral ambitions.[8] Olmos was portrayed during production and after the film's release as an anguished, angry man 'carrying the weight of Latino community expectation . . . angrily taking a message back to the *barrio* that he claims it will not want to hear' (Christon 1991: 18). Although the film lost money, grossing just over only $13 million at the box office, the sensation around its release attracted media attention and gained it notoriety. Journalists chronicled the hiring of extra theatre security by Universal and compared the film's provocation to violence with previous 'urban' and gang films such as Universal's *Juice* (1992), Warner's *New Jack City* (1991) and Columbia's *Boyz N the Hood* (1991) (*UPI* Financial, 13 March 1992).

American Me was thus doubly criminalized in popular journalism, which described gang fights and unrest after screenings and chronicled Olmos's defence of the film's explicit content and its urgent 'warning to young people about the futility of gang life' (Landis 1992: 1D). The film gained further notoriety when two members of its production crew, community activist Ana Lizarraga and former gang member Charles Manriquez, were murdered in the year after the film's release, reportedly executed in reprisal for their participation on the film (Fregoso 1993: 155). In the year that followed, *American Me* stayed in the news as it spurred a gang documentary for NBC, *Lives in Hazard*. Produced by Olmos, it was shot in East Los Angeles during and after the making of the feature film. The spin-off project, which was praised as superior to the movie, nevertheless gave the *American Me* film a strong political afterlife. In the weeks and months that followed, Olmos was interviewed about the political mission and impact of his films, disclosing to journalists that 'President Bush has asked to see the movie. Also the heads of the FBI and other agencies' (Jolson-Colburn 1992). Olmos subsequently offered special screenings for Hispanic government officials, gang members and their families, asking them, 'How many people feel like going out and gangbanging?' (Kroll with Wright 1992: 66), inviting them to share their thoughts by telling them, 'I made my life out of studying human behavior. I know what you're going through right now . . . You can't hide it' (Mills 1992: B1). Olmos's activist celebrity and Latino exemplarity were deployed once more as he urged caution and calm on television during the 1992 Los Angeles riots when he seemed to be cloaked in the mantle of a statesman, and was later lauded as a 'hero' by the Hollywood stars at humanitarian awards ceremonies.

By 1993, Olmos had reached new heights as an endangered and heroic Latino activist, enduring a lawsuit brought against him by a former gang leader claiming that his life had been used as material for the film (*Daily Variety*, 1993) and, most urgently, announcing that he feared for his life after learning that a contract had been put on his life by offended Los Angeles gang leaders (*UPI*, 13 June 1993).

Lives in Hazard sealed the film's institutionalization when it helped launch an anti-gang educational project which Olmos headed with funding from the Clinton Justice Department.[9] Nevertheless, for the popular press, the film's cautionary reality principle was translated into disciplinary discourses that affirmed its criminality: its portrayal of American identity was buried in reporting that emphasized its Hispanic gang content as both artistically distasteful and socially dangerous. Its message was judged to be lost, interpreted instead as a predictable incitement to the film's youthful 'urban' audiences, whose reactions were read as reflexive and violent mimicry of *American Me*'s content and not seen for what they might have represented: a collective and uneasy expression of the disturbing political recognitions that the film invites.

The film's scholarly critics have rarely diverged from the reality principle of its content, message and public afterlife. *American Me*'s popular and media reception has been supplemented by its canonization in an archive of studies across several fields, chiefly Latino and Latin American cultural criticism. Most influentially, in appraisals led by Rosa Linda Fregoso's excellent political and historical reading, *American Me* is signalled as a threshold film which both represents and addresses Latinos and whose content, message and style refused the injunction to exemplarity or mythography and negotiated dangerously between the community and the law in its diagnosis of a social pathology threatening an emergent American minority identity. In such critiques, the heavy valence, credibility, aura and the ethnic filmography of 'Edward James Olmos' are weighed as a counterbalance which helped frame the production and reception of the film. The film has also been canonized with text, theatre and poetry, as an ethno-poetic and psychoanalytic 'text' which forms part of a tradition of interpretation tracing the pathologies of a Chicano-American identity to Mexican national character, collective myths of violation and performative postures of masculinist 'hardness' and violence such readings locate the film in a tradition whereby identity is formed as a survival strategy based on negating the negation of a racial subject. In a third trajectory, the most comparative, the film is read as part of a hemispheric cultural canon in Latin America, and it signals how the foreclosures of American identity which the film exposes are, in fact, part of a larger problematic involving neo-liberal politics, cultural loss and melancholic subjectivity in modern Latino subjects.

Scenes of Torture

American Me refuses us a safe point of identification through which to assimilate the film or to imagine sacrificial or redemptive trajectories for American identity. The film largely refuses (until the last forced instant) a sympathetic referent for identity – a subject embodying Latino virtues of stability, exemplarity, sacrifice or redemption. As the mechanisms for identification conflict or fail, the viewer must reject or disavow both the punitive strategies of the State and the criminal tactics of the resistant Latino. These collide in a series of scenes of torture at key historical moments in the film's narrative trajectory; these make the film both intensely difficult to watch and extraordinarily important as a political intervention.

Pushing us out of the penitentiary setting, the film's first historical flashback echoes the spectacular opening of Foucault's *Discipline and Punish*, exposing us to graphic scenes of public torture, rape and humiliation and then returns us to the contained, surveilled and confessional present of Santana's prison world. The first half hour of *American Me* manipulates the viewer from claustrophobic shock to relieved acceptance of Santana's 'safe' carceral status. Moving backwards into history with Santana's monologue, the audience witnesses not a family romance or a childhood memory but a hallucinatory vision: a primal scene of torture and public violence which literally produces Santana as subject but which also marks a turning point in Chicano cultural genealogy.[10] Santana's autobiographical narrative becomes identical with Chicano history as the audience's gaze is directed to the night of the 'Zoot Suit' riots in 1943, when young Chicanos and Chicanas were attacked, raped and tortured by rampaging US sailors and soldiers on the streets of East Los Angeles. The Zoot Suit riots remain unexplained here, and this is an important sign, since it reveals the film's address to a Latino audience familiar with this moment of violence and outrage.[11] The Chicano flashback and its details of youth culture, Zoot Suit flash, social gesture and Chicano slang also reveals the film's reliance on the literacy of audiences familiar with Chicano culture and film and, in particular, with Edward James Olmos's career as Chicano protagonist. As the film moves back from Santana's prison present to the public torture of the past in the 1943 Zoot Suit riots, we also move back into Olmos's filmography and his popular success as the *pachuco* consciousness of Luis Valdes's *Zoot Suit*.

In the historical flashback, filmed in soft tones and warm light, the love story between Santana's parents becomes a scene of shame, violation and torture. Soldiers rampage into the safe inside of a tattoo-parlour storefront, separating Santana's parents for punishment. As Santana's mother is held down and spreadeagled by the arms of several sailors, the film cuts away with a tracking shot out of the store. We follow onto the sidewalk street, pushed into the perspective of spectators among the chaos. We watch as Santana's father and a friend are dragged and carried toward a public theatre of punishment. Shorn, beaten and stripped on the street, they are left as public tokens of young Chicanos' outlaw identity. As the camera returns to the storefront, we return to see another site of torture and punishment. The sailors' rape of Santana's mother is hidden from view, and beneath the waist-high shot, we watch as they look down on an invisible victim, zipping or unzipping as they take turns and then walk away, avoiding the camera's gaze. In this scene, the allusion to a Mexican genealogy of cultural rape and its unrepresentability is linked to the general erasure or selective instrumentalization of women in the film's plot and in its dystopic realism which explores but does not condemn the structure of a defensively homosocial world. The exclusion of women as subjects and their function as thematic and plot devices also betrays their erasure as objects of desire in the film's homosexual libidinal relations, which emerge only by implication and are foreclosed under the sign of penal violence.[12] Among them is Santana's father, who authors his filial American identity but who is consigned to a criminal anonymity which his son will later embody.

The screen fades to black as Santana spins his autobiographical rhyme:

Zoot suit, new suit, it sounded all the same,
I had no clue what they'd been through . . .
To be sixteen in '59
Stayed way from home even if I didn't have a dime
Cause the old man was just waiting to give me a piece of his time
Drove me to the streets just to save my mind.

The audience's daylight vision begins with the rhyme, zooming in from across the street (perhaps from a patrol car's point of view) on the sixteen-year-old Santana outfitted not in *pachuco* garb but in the youthful 1950s uniform of khakis and white T-shirt. His assimilated persona is betrayed – most obviously by his neighbourhood, his Chicano diction and slang and, more subtly, by the detail of a homeboy shirt carefully folded and hanging from his belt. He is never permitted entry to the kind of nostalgic vision of the emerging 1960s youth culture celebrated in films such as George Lucas's *American Graffiti* (1973). His ethnic masculinity is exposed through the camera's surveillance, offering a case study of youth transgression and assimilation in the style of Beatrice Griffith's 1947 sociology of Chicano culture *American Me* (which provided the film with its title). In this film, the camera and its implied disciplinary function follows him as social problem, tracks his social trajectory, his rituals and transgressions, but never assumes his perspective.[13] Through cinematic allusion and disciplinary intertextuality, Santana's first entry as an innocent subject in the film is robbed of its autobiographical self-sufficiency.

Framed formally by a cinematic aesthetics of social surveillance and allusively by a historical corpus of diagnostic literature on juvenile delinquency, amoral familialism and tribal thinking, Santana's emergence as an emancipated adolescent is synchronous with his emergence as an object before the law. Ironically, his birth as a leader in the rituals of gang life and, therefore, his entry into the logic of the film takes place in a mausoleum, marking his adolescence as a threshold not into openness, freedom and citizenship but into enclosure, prison and social death. The film never gives him a break, obeying the ideological mapping of the Chicano *barrio* as a distinct social holding cell, a liminal native's town[14] of deprivation, criminality and underdevelopment that produces the content, the justification and the workforce for the state's penal economy.

The film's second scene of public torture takes place among youthful sleeping bodies in Los Angeles's Juvenile Hall. Young men wake and turn away as an inmate approaches the young Santana's bed in his first night in 'juvie'. Moving to pillow level just beyond Santana's head, the camera directs us to watch a rape we cannot see, and to notice chiefly the blade at Santana's throat, the reaction of the boys around him, the threat whispered in his ear at consummation. The camera then moves up as Santana fights back and, for the first time, we gaze from his perspective as he plunges the rapist's stiletto straight through his throat – it is one of the few times in the film when we see through Santana's eyes. Transferred from the perspective of spectator in the first scene from 1942, to the 1956 perspective of Santana as victim and then executioner, we experience several permutations, carefully selected, in a public theatre of punishment. Our spectatorship comes to rest in the perspective of Santana as just executioner, and, in that moment of perspectival identity, we assume the place of the subject who has internalized both the spectacular past and the carceral present of punishment, who has moved from being the watched to being the watcher and who can teach us to survive and negotiate the logic of the penitentiary in the execution of every gesture.

The relief that follows Santana's rape, the daylit scene and the uncanny but joyful 'Rockin' Robin' soundtrack that follows, reflects not just an aesthetic change in mood or a shift in the character's trajectory from submission to dominance.[15] From spectacles of violation, torture and humiliation, the film delivers us into the everyday business and ritualized negotiations of the prison world, and we breathe a sign of relief. We welcome the segregation of such violence within the penitentiary, knowing that its invisibility is only lifted momentarily by the film's documentary realism. So, with 'Rockin' Robin' segueing into 1970s funk (signalling the passage of time) and penitentiary handball games[16] (signalling pleasure even in prison), the spectator welcomes the white blue light of the prison scenes, the clear racial divides of the yard and the rare poetic privacy of darkened cells. The movie invites us to accept the perspectives and the conditions of the panoptic order: permanent visibility, internalization of surveillance, self-regulation within a disciplinary architecture, the exploitation of the 'utility' of Santana's criminality as Darwinian metaphor or moralistic fable. Feeling a relief which, as Foucault would warn us, is unwarranted, we settle into the clarity of a modernity which is entirely revealed, entirely understood, entirely contained and finally, merely a prison story. And therein lies the problem and the paradox of *American Me*.

The third climactic scene of torture in the film connects the two realms of the carceral continuum. In the film's most violent scene, a prisoner (the son of an Italian drug boss in Los Angeles who has refused to share his territory in the *barrio*) is punished by the Mexican Mafia and violently raped and murdered. This scene, which is jarringly intercut with Santana's climactic love scene with Julie, establishes parallelisms of seduction and enjoyment between prison and civic life, as the would-be victim enjoys La M's homosocial camaraderie while Santana is enjoying his first-ever heterosexual experience. As the love-making scene in the soft-focus world of the bedroom grows to a climax, so does the progress of prison vengeance, and the penetrative meeting of bodies 'on the outside' is interrupted by the forced violence of a gang rape 'on the inside'. Scenes of the young man's rape against bags of rice are intercut with visions of Santana becoming more violent in his love-making and then breaking the heterosexual ritual and turning Julie on her back, mounting her as she cries out for him to stop. As the young prisoner is finally and fatally penetrated by a knife, Julie breaks away, and Santana's romantic interlude is broken, leaving him defeated and face-down on the bed, betrayed by the homosexual habits and perhaps real desires which prison allowed him. Once again, the film affirms the penal order as the body of desire is confused with the body of violence – in both cases, uncovering practices which, no matter how private or criminal, are always under surveillance, and revealing the successful internalization of a panoptic regime that casts desire, agency and choice always into doubt. This time, as the two realms are literally articulated – logically and visually joined – the relief of this disciplinary order is abolished, and its guarantee of containment and civic privacy disintegrates.

American Foreclosures

In *American Me*, American identity is only gestured to by scenes and discourses that reveal it as something that is not over, or ruined, or cancelled, or even killed, but something that for Santana, has never been – because for the State he has never existed as an American. Among the film's minority subjects, American identity has always been foreclosed.[17] The carceral realm (outside and inside prison) is revealed as a repository of beings who are living a social death and building an order within it.[18] From the beginning to the hopeless end of Olmos's *American Me*, the liberatory promise inherent in this semantic integration of identity is literally annihilated, and the Me in *American Me* turns out to have been a murderous gang 'La M' all along. The relations of mutualism, substitution and compensation promised by the analogical projects of citizenship and subjectivity are liquidated, and the promise of their identity is radically demystified, revealed instead as antagonism, conquest, submission and violence between the State and the self.

Where negation involves the denial of 'something' whose existence has been registered, foreclosure is a process of exclusion with a different and more devastating dynamic. Within psychoanalytic thought, foreclosure is distinct from operations such as repression, negation and projection, each of which belong to the neurotic realm and help the subject manage, negotiate or deny dangerous elements in his or her relationship to the world and the State. By contrast, in Lacanian accounts, foreclosure constitutes psychosis and lies in a realm beyond the analysable transferences with which the neurotic negotiates his or her relationship to authority.[19] Unlike negation, foreclosure (whether it is financial, political or psychic) involves no initial judgement of existence. Its exclusion functions as though this 'something' ('American' identity for Latinos, minority 'Americans' for the State) had never existed at all. The film places Chicanos, Blacks, prisoners and civilians in realms where their Americanness is subject to an exclusion that exceeds disavowal, repression or other forms of negation. The only Americans in the film are the police, since the white Aryan prison gangs are only distantly glimpsed in the film and never speak. Chicanos are represented within the ghettos of prison and *barrio*, places of foreclosure, as figures that are socially dead and excluded from enfranchisement and civil rights. They never really exist in the eyes of the law, except in the moment of their exclusion to prison, where they literally disappear from sight and as subjects of American identity. The signifying logic of the world that Santana inhabits confirms the mechanism of foreclosure, where biographies, names, places of origin, marks of custom and class become unsignifiable because they no longer have any referential value in the world. References to human subjects and American citizens are suspended, and their reference is foreclosed by the State and substituted with numbers, codes. And although this foreclosure is attributed as fair punishment for crime, it becomes clear that in Santana's narrative, there was never anything to lose in terms of American identity.

With devastating irony, the 'me' in the film's title lays claim to the universalism of America's libidinal promises (to life, to liberty, to the pursuit of happiness) by literally embodying their negation. His American identity and his Latino genealogy are conceived in a gang rape, he achieves adolescent autonomy criminalized by patriarchy and the law. He finds filial affect and cultural redemption in homosocial delinquency, is broken open by anal rape and reintegrated by homicidal vengeance and is socialized into violence and criminality. He expresses political status and ethnic power through extreme masculinity, coercion, drug-dealing capitalism and murder. Santana's American identity can never be registered, not only because his American father is an unknown rapist and he is born into a criminalized urban subculture, but because he, like countless minority subjects, seems never to have existed at all as an American in the eyes of the State.

Santana's American 'Me' emerges as the disastrously modified pronoun, the penalized object of an identitarian grammar that forecloses a place of enunciation for the Latino subject's 'I'. It is only as a transgressive object, or as a murderous 'M' (or Spanish 'eMe') that Santana can survive in the American grammar – as he departs from its logic of domination, seizing for a moment the consciousness of a tragic minority subject tracing a genealogy of violation buried within national history, his annihilation is assured. In the cancelled translation from *American Me* to an American 'I', the transitive properties of American identity are also cancelled, and the promise of its assimilationist imaginary disappears. In this process of mutual liquidation, *American Me* reveals a dance of empty signifiers and the vacuum at the heart of its political promise. By the film's end, the American grammar for the minority self has moved from a logic of incarceration and individual foreclosure to a logic of death and cultural annihilation – the historical foreclosure of a new strain in American identity.

The foreclosures involved in producing American identity, or an American subject, I would argue, constitute another kind of psychosis – a political psychosis that threatens the coherence and symbolic logic of the State. I would suggest that through the disciplinary perspectives and panoptic logic of the film, the State is not merely an abstract notion or disembodied law but an implied protagonist of *American Me*. Throughout the film, in a dynamic of identification and internalization, we are invited to enjoy an identity with the State, to become the *American Me* through our identity with its operations, which forecloses the possibility of Santana as part of its consciousness. Identifying with the gaze of the State, we are invited to 'foreclose' the truth of Santana and to therefore foreclose the existence of an entire American community, to exclude it from consciousness as though it had never existed.

As psychoanalysis points out, these exclusions, however efficient, are not permanent, and foreclosed signifiers return through the mechanism of hallucinations. Like images in a film, psychotic hallucinations come 'from the outside' and their 'projection' reverses the neurotic mechanism that externalizes a repressed element. The hallucinatory quality of life on 'the inside', like Santana's laconic affirmation that 'Inside runs the show', reveals foreclosed truths about American identity, capitalism and political imaginaries – about the American 'show' whose true conditions the film's prison visions reveal. Santana's bragging affirmation that he can 'run the show' from solitary accords them an unreal clarity.

For all its surface realism, I would argue that the film thus reveals a hallucinatory visual style – a carceral clarity – where we can distinguish 'false perceptions', in the sensual deprivation of prison recollections, 'in the absence of external stimulus'. Although the scenes of *barrio* life – their diffuse yellow light, their blurred edges, their darkened rich colours – appear to deliver us from the violent prison imaginary to a dream world of Santana's brief romance with civic life, the film reminds us that the penal hallucination will return to destroy any possibility of rehabilitation. Santana's rehabilitation through heterosexual romance is betrayed not only by his sexual practices but by the intercutting return of the prison imaginary, which breaks the amorous sequences with 'visions' of a prison rape and murder carried out by Santana's gang. Here we may well consider the intercut visions as hallucinations that reveal another foreclosure, namely the foreclosure of Santana as a homosexual, doubly excluded by his American and Latino identities but viable within the carceral world.

Knowing himself to be a disavowed subject for American identity – cast out of any possible symbolic inclusion or political representation – and knowing American identity to be a foreclosed category of being for him as a subject, Santana's return to civic life is doomed to failure from the start. The lessons revealed by his failure in civic life push him to demand of Julie in a diner, that quintessential zone of Americana, 'What the fuck do you want from me? Do you want me to start over, get a job? How about become a citizen?' In that moment, the film acknowledges foreclosure as he betrays that, although he is American-born, his 'citizenship' has never existed. Moments after he asks this dangerous and revealing question, he is arrested and returned to jail, and his challenge is confirmed and erased in the State's policing gesture. Santana's foreclosure cannot be revealed as the failure of the State; it must be buried in the reassertion of the carceral order, where it seems as though the criminal's actions have led to the cancellation of his citizenship and his American identity.

Prison Breaks and Lines of Flight

American Me exposes not an exceptional deviation but a normality of violence, social death and political foreclosure as indispensable to the construction of American identity. Read against its moralizing grain, the film reveals a criminal line of flight from the foreclosures inherent in minority American identity. The movie briefly offers a 'revolutionary' but apolitical hero whose schizoid knowledge and psychotic challenges illuminate the prison logic to which minorities are subordinated within the American imaginary.[20] Like Deleuze and Guattari's 'schizo', Santana knows a way through the disciplinary order that lies beyond submission and opens paths to autonomy, knowledge and even libidinal satisfaction (Deleuze and Guattari 1983: 14–15). And although Santana's performative critique of politics, capital and the ethnic self is sequestered to the solitary confinement of criminal autobiography, although he is recuperated through last-minute regret and renunciation and politically assassinated in the film's prison frame, something unassimilable escapes, creating a 'prison break' from the disciplines of Latino subjectivity.

This unassimilable meaning can be experienced as a residue of despair, critical paralysis and negativity by the viewer. In recognizing Santana and his American 'double' J. T. as subjects and not merely objects of the prison machine, viewers are moved beyond a consideration of the film's panoptic performances and carceral Latino continuum: they have to make sense of their personae, agency and discourse beyond their pathologized, psychoanalysed, ethnographic and criminal identities. The viewers must account instead for their productive subjectivity, their violence, their desires and, most of all, their uninterpretable status. Although the film seems to disavow this by pathologizing the violent lives of its protagonists, it does not ultimately represent these men merely as sociopaths but as beings proficient in economies of power, capital, desire and race that the social world cannot acknowledge. Delivered in the spare economy and artificial syntax of prison couplets and gnomic utterances and ritualized in the gestures of *pinto* Chicano masculinity, the discourse and message of the criminal are not merely theatre, a deviation through which to plot normative standards for identity – but a schizoid meaning, a political critique of Latinos' American identity. As J. T. remarks to Santana as he is released to the outside: '*Somos pocos pero locos*' – 'We're few, but we're crazy'. His hearty assertion confirms the insurrectionist posture of their alliance, a one-against-many logic that gives their criminality political resonance.

Like Frantz Fanon's colonial subjects who harbour no Oedipal complexes, but whose encounter with political repression provokes psychic abnormality,[21] Santana's 'pathology' cannot be interpreted through psychoanalytic logic. Santana is presented as a subject with nothing to mourn, no lost object to internalize and grow melancholy around. The film presents him as a man without a childhood, whose prehistory is not infantile memory and Oedipal anxiety, but the violence of a historical event.

Like Freud's unconscious and Deleuze and Guattari's schizo, he is an orphan, and his memory takes the shape of historical delirium, racialized agon, segregated social worlds. His mother is a non-being, one content/symbol in the historical delirium that produced him. Asking his 'father' why he and his mother hated him, Santana discovers that the man is merely his stepfather and that he is the product of a violent rape by a Navy crewman, during the Zoot Suit riots. Thus Santana has no conventional familial triangle to regulate identification, except through his true father, an American rapist. Santana does not identify, with anyone or anything. His is not a depressed subjectivity wrestling with an unconscious theatre of loss, but a paranoid subjectivity, whose schizoid unconscious – living in the split, the fissure, the crack of American identity – produces value (figural and economic) beyond identification and identity, value that lies both within the rules of capitalism and beyond the neurotic discipline of subaltern citizenship.

American Me is so disturbing, I would argue, not because Santana is too full, too sick, too mournfully aggressive, but because he is empty, irredeemably functional, eminently capitalist and beyond the law of the symbolic. He, like East Los Angeles's violent culture, is 'hopeless', as Julie says, precisely because he lies beyond analysis, beyond talking cures, beyond therapy. Santana's schizoid American/Latino subject – relegated to the realm of social death, the non-citizenship of prison – is in direct contact with the violent productivity of American identity: state violence and market capitalism.

Schizoid Economies and Dangerous Renunciations

Prison capitalism affords the members of 'La M' the only viable economy where control and status can be achieved. In jail and illicit markets, the commodity capitalism of the drug industry offers what Santana describes to Julie as 'just a road', a business he must take care of or someone else will. Santana's entrepreneurial capitalism, disavowed by his would-be girlfriend, goes hand in hand with his self-education. It provides a vehicle for autonomy, agency and, above all, power, once it has become clear that legality, citizenship and exemplarity, all identitarian economies of exchange between self and nation, have been liquidated along with everyday life. Santana's ambivalent agency is an inevitable but unintended consequence of his relation to the power in capital and in the State.[22] The schizoid truth that *American Me* reveals is that the degree zero of American identity lies not within the law, but within the market, where every other iteration of identity – ethnic, political, racial, affective and intellectual – is instrumentalized and splintered in the service of capitalist survival. The self and all notions of origin, individuality and pride are redirected to support paranoia, strategic tribalisms, and violent discipline that help La M, not to become a conscientious alternative political community but to maintain a monopoly on the markets within the prison that contains their social world.

The film also makes brutally clear that capitalism offers the best response for a carceral American identity, revealing a place of agency where a functionally schizoid subject can retain a residue of Americanness – entrepreneurship and market monopoly. In the film's illuminating inside-the-walls second act, we watch drugs relayed between female and male couriers whose orifices have become desexualized and function only as carriers of commodities. We discover that racial killings are simply business reprisals, responses to the hijacking of precious commodities. We witness the flashpoint and critical negotiations that lie at the heart of a prison riot. While prisoners explode and guards with guns gather above them, Santana and a black gang leader, Doc, engage in a stand-off, defending their respective positions as businessman exercising his rights and ethnic leader avenging a murdered underling.

In this scene, Santana confronts the limits of his schizoid position as racial prisoner and market capitalist, encountering the dangers of the battle for markets and the battle for identitarian honour. The two practical leaders acknowledge another monopoly within the prison, the State's monopoly on legal violence and the suicide that would be involved in a self-destructive uprising which would result in their mutual annihilation. But Doc's practicality is attended by a warning that Santana must exercise a double vigilance when his capitalist ambitions clash with the prison's racialized segregations – Santana's moves, violent and entrepreneurial, will be watched. Doc's warning foreshadows the destruction that will follow when Santana's drug capitalism provokes a racial war where honour offers the excuse for the market moves of rival ethnic groups.

In *American Me*, the Latino's position of desire within American identity – desire for respect, desire for political autonomy, desire for ethnic dominance, desire for the male other – can only be rendered within a carceral world and as an inversion, perversion or suspension of the social order. Santana must be negated as a subject before his desire can be represented. Even then, the political truths of these desires must be cancelled, covered over, pathologized by his institutionalized penitentiary identity and by a forced confession that he is a double being. Neither he nor his desire can be granted integrity or expression within the social order. As Santana reflects to Julie during his brief sojourn on the outside: 'We made it better for our people in the joint. I fed myself history, biography, politics. I loved it in there, I did whatever I wanted.' Yet there is no place outside jail for his aspirations, and inside they produce dangerous results. And so Santana has eventually to be disavowed by the film through the words of Julie, the feminine assimilable Latina aspiring to American self-improvement. She dismisses his earlier confession of possibility and desire with a damning distinction that separates her identity from his: 'When I met you I was impressed. You talked about books and *la Raza* and the revolution. You don't care about any revolution, do you, you're just a fuckin' dope dealer . . . There's no fuckin' hope for our kind, for our *barrios*, with people like you around.'

The exchange reveals how Santana is deemed beyond redemption and immediately following it he is once more expelled from the civic world of the film. His American insurrections – his schizoid knowledge, his carceral expertise and his splintered desire – cannot be tolerated either by the state or by the community that aspires to a normative American identity. His revolutionary desires for love, friendship, safety, power, freedom of movement risk destroying the structures of 'exploitation, servitude, and hierarchy' (Deleuze and Guattari 1983: 116) and criminalization through which American Latinos are produced and contained within the law and inside the city. In fact, Santana's revolutionary desires, whose political expressions (in movements of ethnicity and labour, in the guarantees of citizenship, civil rights and assimilation) have been cancelled during his time in jail, are left with only one recourse: the economic expression of power in a capitalism that Chicanos addictively serve but cannot control.

Like Santana, who knows that the key is not to 'control the yard' but to control the economic exchanges within his carceral continuum, American Latinos of the early 1990s and of the early twenty-first century have, until recently, largely abandoned the territorial strategies of resistance movements in laying claim to national identity.[23] Recognizing their problematic positioning between the punishment of the State and the reward of the marketplace, and their political triangulation with black and white identity, Latinos encounter the problems of identity not only as a crisis of political identification but also as a crisis of market expediency. In sacrificing collective resistance by internalizing a panoptic racial logic, by disavowing their own criminalized populations and by negotiating their place within the market economies of American identity, where success and control yield social status, the Latino subject risks a dangerous political renunciation. As Santana remarks to J. T. with devastating clarity in their final encounter: 'A long time ago, two best homeboys went to prison. They did what they had to do. They thought they were doing it to get respect for their people . . . to show the world, that no one could take their class from them. No one had to take it from us. Whatever we had, we gave it away.'

This renunciation, I would suggest, both symbolizes and masks a dangerous fear. It symbolizes, politically, a loss that cannot be signified because it both refers to and lies beyond the negations of ethnic history and linguistic community. As J. T.'s homicidal reaction to Santana's final testament suggests, political renunciation also masks a fear, and this fear is what makes *American Me* so important. The film offers a symbolic frame for a fearful truth, revealing a carceral world where we can foreclose political and libidinal needs and consign them to a hallucinatory criminal realm.

In the film's final moral revision, this loss is represented in disavowal and renunciation, with Santana returning to jail and suspending his schizoid knowledge, his carceral ethnic paranoia and his violence, and approximating the contrite 'lawful' position of a melancholic or mournful subject, internalizing or grieving his losses. But the punitive morality of the ending offers Santana redemption only on the condition of his death. It results not in his rehabilitation, but in his destruction – in the annihilation of his history. His contrition is lost, but his criminal legacy survives in the senseless continuation of a social violence that has lost its value as political knowledge or transgressive resistance and instead leads to communal suicide. Because Santana's life can only be disavowed or renounced within the film's moral symbolic order, his loss is displaced. It is abolished again and anew to psychotic and hallucinatory realms: first to the memory of the carceral 'real' of the film's past, its psychotic logic and its paranoid subjects; and then to the hallucination of a sociopathic drive-by future, where children shoot down strangers from passing cars. But a residue of meaning escapes in the uncomfortable recognitions that it forces from its audience.

American Me offers us a 'prison break' – a psychic, social and critical opening – that resists interpretation and decimates disciplinary social discourse. But within it we recognize the continuum between the clarity of choices for individuality, identity, forced loyalty and agency within the prison and the more naturalized double binds that mark identity in civic life and connect it to the market value of American identity. In the uncomfortable length of that prison break, we can either take comfort in our distance from these violent wards of the State, or recognize within our discomfort resemblances, shared psychic colonizations, resistant and submissive postures. Most dangerously, we might discover that these real characters enact what we cannot express and that we share with them a schizoid consciousness about the punitive logic and capitalist compromises that shape American identity, simultaneously producing and annihilating the minority subject for an *American Me*.

Notes

1 'La M', which in Spanish is pronounced phonetically 'La Eme', shortens the reference to the 'Mexican Mafia'. Beyond its realist signification, the name and its phonetic variations inevitably call us back to the film's title *American Me* and the phonetic echo of *Me* and Eme *(in Spanish the phonetic spelling is Eme)* – an echo that reinforces the link between identitarian claim of an *American Me* and its criminal development in 'La M'.

2 'The psychic operation of the norm offers a more insidious route for regulatory power than explicit coercion, one whose success allows its tacit operation within the social. And yet, being psychic, the norm does not merely reinstate social power, it becomes formative and vulnerable in highly specific ways' (Butler 1997: 21).

3   Subtle signs that J. T. and Santana are or have been lovers are scattered throughout the film. This implication, intentional or unintentional, is nevertheless there and has been signalled by critics (Levison, Gutierrez-Jones). It offers an interesting angle through which to understand the outrage of Chicano youth and gang audiences who were offended by the film's indictment of their 'lifestyle', its explicit portrayal of anal rape suffered by Santana as gang leader and the violent pleasures involved in the anal rape of a prisoner by his underlings in La M.

4   The word 'holmes' is a colloquial expression in Chicano, black and white slang. It is commonly understood as a foreshortening of homeboy or a play on 'homie'. It is used for casual acquaintances or friends. In the final sentence of the film, 'Fuck it, holmes!' the word binds the violence of the drive-by shooting, its abdication of hope or responsibility to the gang's male fraternity, addressing the action and its meaning to the 'homeboy' or friend driving the car and urging his friend to violence.

5   Foucault develops his notion of the carceral and the panopticon in *Discipline and Punish* (1977).

6   While the term 'prison-industrial complex' mimicked the phraseology of the military-industrial complex and circulated publicly from the 1970s onward, it was officially 'coined' for mainstream readers by Eric Schlosser in 1998. In 'The Prison-Industrial Complex', *The Atlantic Monthly*, December 1998, pp. 54–5 (which opens with a description of Folsom State Prison, the setting of *American Me*), Schlosser described a growing agglomeration of state and private capital exploiting prison labour. 'The prison-industrial complex is not only a set of interest groups and institutions. It is also a state of mind. The lure of big money is corrupting the nation's criminal-justice system, replacing notions of safety and public service with a drive for higher profits. The eagerness of elected officials to pass tough-on-crime legislation – combined with their unwillingness to disclose the external and social costs of these laws – has encouraged all sorts of financial improprieties.'

7   Olmos assembled a notably diverse production team for *American Me*, with a screenplay by Floyd Mutrux and Desmond Nakano, and Reynaldo Villalobos as his cinematographer.

8   Critics emphasized the moral ambition of the movie they repeatedly referred to as a 'Hispanic gang film', and praised cinematographer Villalobos' visual style (Guthmann 1992: D3), but they largely dismissed what they saw as the film's explicit violence, its 'unsavoriness' and heavy-handed polemics (Arnold 1992: D5), and suggested that the film's 'dose of reality may be too strong to swallow' (Wloszczyna 1992: 5D). Janet Maslin found the film wanting aesthetically, arguing that the script was 'dark, slow and solemn', that the film was 'unduly bleak', 'seldom dramatic enough to bring its material to life', but that its ability to 'sound a warning' was its 'most valuable aspect' (Maslin 1991: C6).

9   Olmos's long fourth act with *American Me* extended well into the Clinton Administration, leading its director to appear in Public Service Announcements as he became Executive Director of the Lives in Hazard Educational Project, an anti-gang violence initiative funded by the Clinton Justice Department and celebrated by Attorney General Janet Reno and the President himself.

10 This genealogy, inaugurated in Octavio Paz's *The Labyrinth of Solitude* connects the performance and pathologies of Mexican national character to a founding moment of colonial rape and betrayal, where a female translator, *La malinche,* becomes a guilty mother to the nation in her forced relations, political and carnal, with Spanish invaders. Her penetration by Cortés and his men is extended into the mass experience of rape within colonialism and the burden of guilt and shame that haunts the Mexican political unconscious.

11 For an invaluable discussion of the political context and historical sources on the 1942 'Sleepy Lagoon' murder trial and the summer 1943 Los Angeles Zoot Suit riots, see Fregoso (1993: 141–2, note 7).

12 The gender politics of *American Me* and the conservative role of victim, mother and assimilable student of American culture which are assigned to women within the film is an important subject beyond the practical limits of this essay.

13 See Beatrice Griffith, *American Me* (1948). Beatrice Griffith wrote and published this text in the years following the Sleepy Lagoon murder trials. Griffith covered the trials as a journalist, became a member of the Sleepy Lagoon Defense Committee and through her work gained entry to the nascent Chicano youth culture of the defendants and their communities.

14 For Fanon's political analysis of the geographic mapping of power in colonial settings and the contrasting worlds of the 'settler's town' and the 'native's town', see Frantz Fanon, *The Wretched of the Earth*, 1961.

15 The style and lighting of the film's visual imaginary suggest this path from night-time penetration to daylight respect as the real birth of Santana: the carceral 'delivery' of his American identity.

16 The handball game inevitably reminds the viewer of Olmos's role in *Zoot Suit*, where the song 'Handball' signals boredom, play and the sexual practices of prison.

17 Throughout this essay, I use the term 'foreclosure' to refer to both psychic and ideological mechanisms of exclusion, cancellation and segregation, and my analysis is strongly rooted in the articulation of foreclosure articulated by Jacques Lacan (see note below).

18 For the seminal discussion of the negations of subjecthood and citizenship within slavery, see Orlando Patterson, *Slavery and Social Death: A Comparative Study*, 1982.

19 Jacques Lacan pursued his interest in psychosis from *Les Complexes familiaux dans la formation de l'individu* (1938) through his seminar, *The Psychoses* (1955–6), and across his *Écrits*. He adopted the term 'foreclosure' to translate Freud's concept of the psychic defence, *Verwerfung* (originally translated as 'repudiation' in the English Standard Edition). On foreclosure and its relation to psychic orders and psychosis, see Lacan, 'Response to Jean Hyppolite's Commentary on Freud's "Verneinung", (2006a); Lacan, 'On a Question Prior to Any Possible Treatment of Psychosis', (2006b); and Lacan (1993). See also the invaluable definitions and discussions in Jean Laplanche and J.B. Pontalis, 'Foreclosure (Repudiation)' , (1973) pp. 166–9, and Dylan Evans, *An Introductory Dictionary of Lacanian Psychoanalysis* (1996): 64–5, 154–7.

20 For Deleuze and Guattari's invaluable critique of the disciplinary norms of Freudian psychoanalysis, see their *Anti-Oedipus* (1983).

21 In *Black Skin, White Masks* Fanon establishes the critique of Oedipal logic within psychoanalysis that Deleuze and Guattari would later echo. Emphasizing that the pathologies of colonial subjects emerge from their contact with the state and its negations, Fanon explains '[A] normal Negro child, having grown up within a normal family will become abnormal on the slightest contact with the white world . . . Like it or not, the Oedipus complex is far from coming into being among Negroes . . . it would be relatively easy for me to show that in the French Antilles 97 percent of families cannot produce one Oedipal neurosis' (Fanon 1967: 141–4).

22 In *The Psychic Life of Power* (1997), Judith Butler analyses the relation of agency to power: 'Agency exceeds the power by which it is enabled. One might say that the purposes of power are not always the purposes of agency. To the extent that the latter diverge from the former, agency is the assumption of a purpose *unintended* by power, one that could not have been derived logically or historically, that operates in a relation of contingency and reversal to the power that makes it possible, to which it nevertheless belongs. This is, as it were, the ambivalent scene of agency, constrained by no teleological necessity' (Butler 1997:15).

23 Since this article was first written, the recent social movement and mobilization around Immigrants' Rights in the USA have emerged. It is still unclear how this movement by documented and undocumented workers will change the political and racial landscape. The refusal of invisibility and negation and the claim to American identity and citizenship status is just and also extraordinary, since it moves against the carceral continuum in which legal and illegal immigrants have heretofore operated. The appearance of millions of previously anonymous or invisible bodies foreclosed from legal American identity is precedented only by the civil-rights movement. The challenge by millions to their status as 'criminals' and 'aliens' and the claims by marchers and demonstrators to 'American' identity, family values, labour rights and social justice provoked media attention and congressional interest and debate. It was met, however, with an extension of carceral and military logic by the Bush Administration, who announced the extension of the walls being built on the border and the deployment of the National Guard along the border with Mexico. The liminal space of the border suddenly became not merely more fortified, but militarized, as the resources of the State seemed to defend both the buried economies and the punitive order of the carceral realm that guarantees the privileges of American identity.

References

Archerd, A. (1992) 'Just for Variety', *Daily Variety*, 15 March.

Arnold, G. (1992) 'Prison Drama Guilty of Preaching: *American Me* Violent, Turgid', *Washington Times*, 16 March.

Butler, J. (1997) *The Psychic Life of Power: Theories in Subjection*, Stanford, Calif.: Stanford University Press.

Christon, L. (1991) 'Gangway for Edward James Olmos: Angry Stand and Deliver Star Exposes Barrio Life in *American Me*', *Los Angeles Times*, 15 September.

Deleuze, G. and Guattari, F. (1983) *Anti-Oedipus. Capitalism and Schizophrenia*, trans. Robert Hurley, Mark Seem and Helen Lane, Minneapolis, Minn.: University of Minnesota Press.

Evans, D. (1996) *An Introductory Dictionary of Lacanian Psychoanalysis*, Hove: Brunner-Routledge.

Fanon, F. (1963) *The Wretched of the Earth,* trans. Constance Farrington, New York: Grove Weidenfeld.

—— (1967) *Black Skins, White Masks,* trans. Constance Farrington, New York: Grove Weidenfeld.

Foucault, M. (1977a) *Disicipline and Punish,* trans. Alan Sheridan, New York: Pantheon.

—— (1977b) 'Nietzsche, Genealogy, History', trans. D. F. Bouchard, in *Language, Counter-Memory, Practice*, Ithaca, NY: Cornell University Press.

Fregoso, R. L. (1993) *The Bronze Screen: Chicana and Chicano Film Culture*, Minneapolis, Minn.: University of Minnesota Press.

Freud, S. (1911) 'Psychoanalytic Notes on an Autobiographical Account of a Case of Paranoia (Dementia Paranoides)' , Vol. XII *Standard Edition of the Complete Psychological Works*, Vol. XII, London: Hogarth and the Institute of Psychoanalysis.

—— (1924) 'Neurosis and Psychosis', *Standard Edition of the Complete Psychological Works*, Vol. XIX, London: Hogarth and the Institute of Psychoanalysis.

Griffith, B. (1948) *American Me*, Boston, Mass.: Houghton-Mifflin.

Guthmann, E. (1992) '*American Me* Beats You Up: Olmos Directs, Stars in Unrelenting Portrait of Violence', *The San Francisco Chronicle*, 13 March.

Gutierrez-Jones, Carl (1995) *Rethinking the Borderlands: Between Chicano Culture and Legal Discourse*, Berkeley, Calif.: University of California Press.

Harari, R. (2001) *Lacan's Seminar on 'Anxiety': An Introduction*, trans. Jane Lamb-Ruiz, New York: The Other Press.

Johnson, B. (1992) 'Latin Lovers and Losers', *Macleans*, 23 March.

Jolson-Colburn, J. (1992) 'Olmos Plans Film in South-Central L.A.' , *Hollywood Reporter*, 13 May.

Kroll, G. with Wright, L. (1992) 'Eddie Olmos's East L.A. Story', *Newsweek*, 30 March, p. 66.

Lacan, J. (1993) *The Seminar. Book III: The Psychoses*, trans. Russell Grigg, London: Routledge.

—— (2004) *Le séminaire, Livre X: L'angoisse*, Paris: Seuil.

—— (2006a) 'Response to Jean Hyppolite's Commentary on Freud's "Verneinung"', *Écrits: The First Complete Edition in English*, trans. Bruce Fink, New York: W. W. Norton, pp. 318–33.

—— (2006b) 'On a Question Prior to Any Possible Treatment of Psychosis', *Écrits: First Complete Edition*, trans. Bruce Fink, New York: W. W. Norton, pp. 445–88.

Landis, D. (1992) 'Movie Violence', *USA Today*, 16 March.

Laplanche, J. and Pontalis, J. B. (1973) *The Language of Psychoanalysis*, trans. Donald Nicholson-Smith, New York: W. W. Norton.

Levinson, B. (2001) *The Ends of Literature: The Latin American 'Boom' in the Neoliberal Marketplace*, Stanford, Calif.: Stanford University Press.

Maslin, J. (1991) 'Charting the Generations of East Los Angeles Gangs', *New York Times*, 13 March.

Mills, D. (1992) 'The Last Hope of Eddie Olmos; He Wants to End Gang Violence and Thinks his Movie Is the Place to Start', *Washington Post*, 21 March.

Noriega, C. (2000) *Shot in America: Television, the State, and the Rise of Chicano Cinema*, Minneapolis, Minn.: University of Minnesota Press.

Patterson, O. (1982) *Slavery and Social Death: A Comparative Study*, Cambridge Mass.: Harvard University Press.

Paz, O. (1985) *The Labyrinth of Solitude*, trans. Lysander Kemp, Yara Milos, Rachel Phillips Belash, New York: Grove Press.

Schlosser, E. (1998) 'The Prison Industrial Complex', *Atlantic Monthly*, December, (pp. 51–77).

Wloszczyna, S. (1992) '*American Me*: Olmos' grueling gang chronicle', *USA Today*, 13 March.

Chapter 12

American History X (1998)

Paul Smith

The Gates of Time

Before the attacks of 9/11, the most significant terrorist event on American[1] soil arguably had been the bombing of the Federal Building in Oklahoma City in 1995, when 168 people died at the hands of right-wing extremists, notably Timothy McVeigh. The Oklahoma City National Memorial that opened in 2000 now commemorates that attack. It is an interestingly literal monument. Built on the exact site of the downed building, it features two large portals called The Gates of Time, one at each end of the site and serving as entrance and exit to a park and a reflecting pool. Over the bronze-clad granite mass of the gates are engraved the time before the bombing at one end – 9.01 – and at the other end 9.03, the time when (according to the National Park Service who run the monument) people's lives 'were changed forever'.[2]

The memorial shares something with many American monuments: it commemorates an important event without expending any effort to explain or even recount the history of that event. The bombing is treated as a punctual phenomenon – two minutes of history treated as if they had no causal roots and given no contextual clarification or analysis. The event simply happened, it would seem, killing scores of people and changing many other people's lives. Thus, the on-site museum begins its ten-chapter storyline of the bombing two minutes *after* it occurred, offering an account only of the aftermath and of the people who died, survived or were otherwise affected by the blast. The right-wing terrorist perpetrators are not mentioned, of course, and the nature of their cause is totally unacknowledged. An unknowing visitor could not, in other words, glean from the site any reason for the attack.

It would perhaps be overreaching to suggest that such a monument could be built only in America. But it is striking how consistently the nation's monuments are inflected by the same gesture – the shearing away of history in the very moment of memorialization. It will be interesting to see how the planned memorial at the site of the World Trade Center will compare in this regard, but the signs are not auspicious, and it seems likely that it will follow in the style of two of the more recent memorials on the Mall in Washington, DC – the Second World War and the Vietnam War memorials. The latter, however moving its meticulous roll-call of the names of the American dead might be, offers no sense at all of the history of the conflict. Similarly, the former – in my view, a frightening reminder of the architecture of the defeated enemy in the Second World War – fails to specify any important detail of the war. What we have in these and many other cases is, I think, a kind of contradictory exercise which suits the way in which American cultural life habitually proceeds: American culture is capable of remembering events and people without feeling the need to know history or context.

This contradiction in the culture could perhaps be explained away by the old saw that proposes that America actually has no history. Even if that statement is patently silly, it is nonetheless how Americans frequently understand themselves and their nation, broadly speaking. Something of how this works could clearly be seen in the aftermath of 9/11 when it was considered at best irrelevant or at worst unpatriotic to try to contextualize the attacks in any historicizing fashion. Such distaste for history and for historical analysis normally operates in America in such a way as to validate not just specific punctual moments, but equally importantly, individual experience of those moments. This is certainly true of the Oklahoma City monument I've been describing: the museum curators have painstakingly collected some piece of evidence or some small material token to represent each individual life lost, but the exhibit cannot admit the slightest sign of a broader historical stroke. This cultural habit is replicated daily in the mainstream media where the individual eyewitness account of this or that event is usually made to stand for the event itself; or where the meaning of events is reduced and limited to the affect of some observer or participant. Thus, the individual anecdote comes to stand in for historical analysis; collections of individual anecdotes take on the role of collective experience; and the Gates of Time can frame only two minutes of the duration of history.

American History X

History in America is, then, by and large withheld, elided or otherwise ignored, and in that sense it is true that America has no history. The quality and significance of events is assessed by their impact on individuals, and anecdotal individualism takes on a central explanatory function. With these general propositions about American cultural life in mind, I want to look at the film *American History X*, which was released in 1998, three years after the Oklahoma City bombings, and which tapped into what was then an active cultural and political anxiety about domestic right-wing terrorism.

American History X tells the story of a lower middle-class family in California, caught up in the racial antagonism and violence fostered by a local white supremacist gang. The eldest son of the family, Derek (Edward Norton), is a skinhead who has attained some importance in the gang. After his father, a fireman, is killed on the job by a black drug-dealer, Derek becomes an efficient recruiter and rabble-rouser for the white supremacists; he is shown, for example, instigating and leading a skinhead attack on a supermarket staffed primarily by immigrant workers; he also orchestrates a confrontation with a black gang, expelling them from his local basketball courts. Derek's younger brother, Daniel (Edward Furlong), is still at high school and seems to be about to follow in Derek's neo-fascist footsteps. Derek, however, goes to prison after brutally killing three black men who had tried to steal his car. In prison he undergoes a change of heart. He becomes disillusioned with the behaviour of the prison's white brotherhood and simultaneously learns to respect the black convict with whom he works in the prison laundry. His antagonism towards the Aryan brotherhood leads to his being punished by them – he is raped and beaten by the white supremacists and then ostracized. When he is released, he is ready to break all ties with his old neighbourhood gang. His efforts to do so, while also bringing his family back together and turning Daniel away from the gang, seem auspicious. But the film ends with Daniel being shot dead by a black kid at school. Derek, then, is 'saved', but his younger brother is not.

This rather simple narrative is complicated by a number of different devices. The film's diegetic present is the day of Derek's release from prison, up to the death of Daniel the next morning. This timeline is shot in colour, while the back story – the history of Derek's path to becoming a skinhead, his racist activity and violence and his time in prison – is shot in black-and-white sequences which are interspersed among the colour ones. The order of their interspersing is dictated by Daniel in a voice-over as he reads an essay he has been assigned by Sweeney (Avery Brooks), the school's black principal. Sweeney is a central character – he has been Derek's teacher as well as Daniel's and is determined to turn both the brothers away from their racism. Part of his effort is to make Daniel write an essay in which he will 'analyse and interpret all the events surrounding Derek's incarceration . . . how these events helped shape your present perspective concerning life in contemporary America, and their impact on your life and the life of your family'.

Daniel's essay assignment in fact gives the movie its name: this is a school course, a special topic class, or an independent study in American History, 'American

History X'. There are perhaps other ways of interpreting the 'X' here. Graphically, it has a rough resemblance to the swastikas that are tattooed on Derek's body. Or else, it could be a reference to the film's extremely graphic violence and excessive bad language – though in the US context, 'XXX' would be the more common designation for such features. Equally, the 'X' might be a reference to the unknown part of American history, in the way that the 'X' in Malcolm X's name was adopted to refer to his unknown non-white origin. But given that the film is structured around Daniel's special school assignment, and given the film's overt pedagogical intent, it seems more likely that 'X' marks the special course, a course that demands the production of Daniel's individualized sense of history.[3]

When it was released, the film was notable for a number of reasons. First, it had had a chequered production history, with its nominal director Tony Kaye causing a media stir by attempting to have his name taken off the final cut with which he was not content. Citing his right to free speech, he unsuccessfully sued New Line and the Director's Guild for not allowing him to do so. Kaye was a first-time director, who had made his name as a director of commercials in Britain (British readers might remember his sleeping penguin advert for British Rail, or his exploding bus in a well-known Volvo advert). It was perhaps his inexperience in Hollywood that had led him to assume that he would have final cut, but Kaye claimed that the film that New Line released did not represent his own vision of the story. Kaye described the final cut as 'nothing to me but an embarrassment. A total embarrassment.'[4] and claimed that the film had been weakened as a direct result of studio interference and Edward Norton's influence.

It is difficult to comment on the meaning of this controversy between Kaye and the Hollywood institution – except perhaps to note that Kaye has not made a general release movie since that time. Indeed, he has described himself as being sequestered in 'Hollywood jail' and prevented from making new films (although he is apparently now working on a new one, *Reaper*, for M8 Entertainment[5]). At the same time, it has been reported that New Line and Kaye intend to release a DVD set of *American History X* which would include Kaye's cut and also his own documentary about the making of the film. If and when such a product is available, it might become easier to discern what different kind of film Kaye had envisaged. In the few interviews he has given since the release of the film, he seems keen to avoid giving details of a film he says he 'found' only in the final stages of his own editing. He spends rather more time attacking the film that was actually released. Even then, his criticisms are largely unspecific about the film's content – though he has been quoted as deeming the final cut 'preachy'.[6] Rather, his complaints are more general and concern the fact that the film was taken out of his hands and given to Edward Norton for the final cut.

By all accounts, Norton was indeed largely responsible for the edit that New Line eventually released. This is the film's second notable feature, then: it constituted a major step forward for Norton's career. Before *American History X* he had not been well known (despite his Oscar nomination for a supporting part in *Primal Fear*, 1966). By Kaye's account at least, Norton also greatly enlarged his own role in the film when he was given control of the final editing, and one result was Norton's being nominated for a Best Actor Oscar.[7] As I've said, it is not easy to see what kind of film Kaye had imagined and equally unclear how Norton's intervention changed that. However, some sense of how Norton changed the film can be gleaned from a version of David McKenna's screenplay that has appeared online.[8] This version of the script varies in a number of important ways from New Line's final cut. It does use the device of Daniel's essay project, but the essay's content is scarcely quoted and, in any case, appears to differ in significant respects from the final cut. (I'll return to this below.) In the final cut, the essay and Daniel's voice-over are used to guide the dispersal of the flashbacks to Derek's racist career, but the script confines those flashbacks to one central and unified sequence.

The biggest discrepancy, beyond that different organization of the film's time frames, is that the script calls for much more attention to be paid to the events after Derek's release from prison. It projects an extended confrontation between Derek and his former colleagues in the gang, particularly Cameron Alexander (Stacy Keach), the group's sinister leader. Over the course of several scenes not included in the final cut,[9] the political beliefs and violent actions of the gang are explored and set against Derek's new-found anti-racism. This part of the script is radically truncated in the final cut, and the film thus forgoes the chance both to exhibit and critique the details of a racist organization. It is perhaps worth speculating, for the sake of my argument in this essay, that the way a British émigré and Jewish director might treat the topic of American racism would be somewhat different from the point of view of a white American actor – or, indeed, from what New Line might expect. This elided part of the film might well have given play to Kaye's different sense of history – a sense gained, as he has said, from both his own knowledge of the National Front in Britain and his willingness to be in direct contact with Tom Metzger, leader of the White Aryan Resistance group in the USA.[10] It is possible that Kaye's version of the film would have been less 'preachy' and more exploratory. As it was released, however, the film's narrative falls firmly within the parameters of a typically American structure of sin and redemption; it exhibits the kind of displacement of history into personal experience which I have talked about above; and it displays the structure of a consistently American liberal view of race issues which I will discuss later in this essay.

One way in which the film does arguably break the mould of the standard Hollywood product, however, is the third feature that garnered it a lot of attention on its release – its uncompromising representation of racial violence. It should be said that not all the violence is physical – an especially nasty sequence shows Derek in full racist flow when his mother invites her Jewish boyfriend (Elliot Gould) over to dinner. One of the most powerful sequences in the film is the attack on the supermarket. Derek has prepared his gang with a speech about the evil of immigrant workers and this is followed by a frightful assault in which the entire Latino and Asian staff is brutalized and humiliated. But the most harrowing scene depicts the crime for which Derek is imprisoned. When he shoots the black men who try to steal his car, Derek is shown almost naked in order to highlight his body, buffed and heavily tattooed with swastikas and white-power mottos and emblems. One of the victims he shoots remains alive until Derek kills him by setting his mouth on the curb of the pavement and stomping on the helpless man's neck. The violence is shocking in and of itself, but the spectacle of Derek's neo-Nazi body and his gloating reaction to his own violence – all in black and white of course – is particularly hard to watch.

That kind of violence perpetrated by that kind of body would have had a compelling effect in 1998 when the nation still had Timothy McVeigh and various right-wing groups and militias on its mind, and when that home-grown kind of terrorism was considered the main threat to America. *American History X* appeared at the right moment, then, midway between the Oklahoma City bombing and the 9/11 terrorist attacks. However, the initial thing to be said about the relation between the two events is that the second has superseded the first. Despite its rather clumsy memorial, the Oklahoma City bombing has probably faded from the memories of most Americans because now, of course, all terrorists are radical Muslims. The feared Aryan terrorists of the 1990s are forgotten, Timothy McVeigh has been executed, and his convicted collaborator Terry Nichols has been imprisoned. Nichols's sentencing for his part in the Oklahoma bombing took up only a few paragraphs of space in the *Washington Post* in 2002, and this was one of many signals that the various right-wing groups and militias that exercised the nation so fully just a little while before were no longer of interest. Those groups are scarcely to be heard from – perhaps they have been safely neutralized, or perhaps their racist desires have been satisfied by President Bush's murderous policies at home and abroad, or perhaps they simply cannot get the airtime any longer as the mainstream media have time for only the newest terrorists. In media representation, the white supremacists have been reduced to nothing, or less than nothing. Once mightily feared, domestic white supremacists now appear in *The Grid* (a film about international terrorism made by the BBC and TNT and aired as a mini-series in the USA in 2004) as nothing more than hapless and helpless yokels, around whom the real terrorists easily run rings.[11]

History Lessons

American History X, then, is already a kind of memento, a ghostly remnant of a pre-9/11 moment which has slipped into insignificance. Ironically enough, one of the more interesting – not to say laudable – efforts of the film is to counter this trend in American cultural life – the forgetting of history. Such a didactic project is announced clearly enough in the film's very title. But, in the end, the title itself also indicates a problem, a contradiction. While the film (nobly enough) wants to address American history and counter its forgetting, the title essentially admits that in American culture history can be addressed only as a special case – the independent study, the class with one student, American History X. That is, the intent of the story and the meaning of its title are set into a contradiction that the film can never resolve. The teaching of history can only be a one-on-one effort. Sweeney says of Daniel at one point, 'I will not give up on this child'; his determination, however benevolent, will condemn him to repeating the individualized gesture of the special course, one student at a time. That is, making Daniel remember and analyse his brother's story of violence and imprisonment specifically fails to break the cycle of racial violence that the film abhors, precisely because not everyone can be taught in this tailor-made fashion. To deliberately render the lesson of history an individual matter is to guarantee the limits of the lesson; it can only last for its allotted few minutes. Sweeney further compromises his project by granting access to such lessons to whites only: the black student who eventually shoots Daniel, Little Henry (Jason Bose Smith), is apparently never afforded the same exceptional treatment.

However, such a debilitating and inbuilt contradiction scarcely troubles this film, which appears to be completely unembarrassed by its own didactic stance. From the moment that Sweeney assigns Daniel the analytical essay, right up to the moment at the end when Daniel's voice dutifully announces that he has learned the lesson, someone somewhere is always trying to teach someone else something. Sweeney is the prime example here. He is the literal pedagogue, the strong and indomitable black teacher, evoking all the images we saw in the 1990s of the salvational minority father figure whose strictness and moralism were supposed to inspire minority kids to greater things. But even so, Sweeney is all wrong in this film: his energy is spent on the extremist white kids, and even the skinhead leader, Cameron, calls him an Uncle Tom. Certainly, we never see him dealing with a black student. In that simple fact, one of the film's central lapses begins to make itself apparent, namely that through its delimited, specialized, X approach to the history lesson, in the end the film cannot or will not address history as a black issue, but only as a white one.

I'll return to this point later on, but for now I want simply to stress that all the lessons in this film are learned by white people because it is they who are, to say it this way, the subjects of history. Certainly they are the mobile subjects of the film's drama while the black characters remain in a kind of stasis. Sweeney, despite his central role in the narrative, is stuck in an endless struggle with each generation of racists. Little Henry remains caught in the cycle of violence which is produced by the ethos of racism. Derek's black friend in prison, Lamont (Guy Torry) remains incarcerated for stealing a television even after Derek has been released from his punishment for a much more serious crime.

Among the film's white subjects, Derek is clearly the most progressive learner. He is the perfect subject for the tragic version of a 'sin and redemption' narrative whose simplistic moralism is then duly transmitted to his younger brother, albeit too late. The way in which he himself learns his lesson is the gist of the film's flashback sequences (and thus contrasted with Daniel learning his lessons in the colour sequences) and is scarcely very complicated – indeed, it is formulaic and unconvincing in the end. In prison, Derek sees how his supposed allies and compadres, the prison's white brotherhood, compromise their supposed racial superiority in the context of inmate politics: he is appalled, for instance, that these purist Aryans buy drugs from Latino prison dealers. His conclusion that 'they don't believe in anything' turns him away from them. Meanwhile, his work in the prison laundry brings him into permanent contact with Lamont, and the two develop a bond which ensures that Derek will be protected from potential harm at the hands of other African-American prisoners. His learning process is more or less completed when the Aryan group punish him by way of a brutal rape in the prison shower which leaves him badly injured.

Clearly there is almost nothing in this learning process that would absolutely require Derek's conversion from his white separatist convictions at the political level. In fact, the film struggles to render the conversion a matter of Derek's actual beliefs and politics; disapproval of the white prisoners is scarcely a compelling motive. Rather, Derek's conversion is given as a simple matter of personal choice. The choice is begun in his laundry-room conversations with Lamont and is later encouraged by a visit from his mother and a reminder of his obligations to his family. And the process is completed during a visit from Sweeney, who asks him to consider whether anything he has ever done has made his life any better. Derek concludes that it has not and his lesson, then, is that his political beliefs must yield to his self-interest, the conditions of his own existence. However obnoxious and dangerous the politics that Derek turns away from, the lesson the film ultimately offers is a repudiation of politics altogether: political views must be seen as separate from and ultimately secondary to one's own life and self-interest.

If this is the lesson Derek learns and that his story proffers, Daniel's lesson is, overtly at least, more profound and indeed is presented as the very structure of the film. Forced to write the essay for Sweeney, in the film's colour sequences, he dredges his memory to produce the black-and-white scenes of Derek's story. But there is little in his effort that could respond to Sweeney's instruction that he should 'analyse and interpret all the events surrounding Derek's incarceration'. Instead of analysis and interpretation, there is simply a narrated set of memories. The only analytical or explanatory part of those memories involves the brothers' father, whose death at the hands of a black drug-dealer had at first been given as the proximate cause of Derek's racial outrage and radicalization. But part of Daniel's lesson is his realization that his father had himself been an outspoken bigot. In a scene over the dinner table he is shown discouraging a younger Derek from taking seriously the 'bullshit' he is learning at school through Sweeney's curriculum.

More than even his memories of Derek's violent crimes, this memory of the father seems to be the crucial one in making Daniel realize his own lesson. But ultimately, his memory produces only the merest analysis in the form of an implied idea: namely, that Derek's racism has been inherited from his father more than it has been caused by Derek's own thought and experience. Daniel's childhood memory thus hypostatizes the issue of racism, removing it from its political context and locating it instead in the private realm of the family.

If the lesson that Daniel learns is that racism is passed on as a kind of patrilineal curse, then of course its solution will be less political than personal – a matter of individual responsibility and personal benevolence rather than anything more structural. Thus, in essence, Daniel's lesson is parallel to Derek's. The realization opens the way for Daniel to conclude his essay with some sententious, not to say sentimental, thoughts about the need us for us all to overcome anger and hostility and for the races to get along. And the film attempts to evoke some portentous irony by having Daniel's voice-over performance of his essay finish only after we have already seen him shot and killed. Addressing Sweeney directly, he thanks him for helping him and ends his essay with a quotation from 'someone you'll like'. This turns out to be Abraham Lincoln (although the reference is not actually made in the film) and Daniel quotes, almost accurately, from the final words of the 1861 Inaugural Address, which originally went as follows:

> We are not enemies, but friends. We must not be enemies. Though passion may have strained, it must not break our bonds of affection. The mystic chords of memory, stretching from every battlefield, and patriot grave, to every living heart and hearthstone, all over this broad land, will yet swell the chorus of the Union, when again touched, as surely they will be, by the better angels of our nature.

It may well be that Sweeney would indeed have approved of a quotation from Lincoln, the president routinely credited with having freed the slaves – but perhaps not this particular speech. Lincoln spoke on the eve of the Civil War, and his words are generally understood as a last-ditch effort to persuade the Confederate States to remain in the Union. Indeed, in exchange for Southern support of the Union, Lincoln actually offered the continuation of slavery, and his speech is a crucial part of the deal that white America attempted to broker over the bodies and beings of its slaves. Far from a call to unify the races, as the movie would have it sound,

Lincoln's speech intended to facilitate the continual subordination of the one to the other. Thus, in the context of this film and its didactic attempt to have history remembered, this is an egregiously inappropriate citation. As I've suggested, the lessons the two brothers learn in this film have something in common. Both lessons displace the politics and analysis of the central topic of race violence onto the scene of individual memory and personal narrative: the brothers' stories offer memory without history, narrative without analysis. And what we can call the historical misprision of Lincoln's speech finally emblematizes the film's loss of history.

In this regard, the film becomes an exceptional instance of the conventions and habits of the American media and, indeed, of the culture at large, where the difficult task of transforming memories into history and personal sentiment into analysis is continually foreclosed and where historical detail is effortlessly traduced. If these are generalized characteristics of American media products, the apology is often offered that film is 'just entertainment' and should not be held responsible for its politics. This excuse is no more than a reflection of the industry's vital interest in sustaining the fiction that its products and their provenance are not politically motivated in any way at all. But that kind of argument cannot be employed to defend a film like *American History X* which, as I've already indicated, avowedly sets out to be a pedagogical exercise, a didactic excursion into one of the most pressing social and political issues of its time. What I'm suggesting, then, is that the particular narrative and diegetic habits of the industry are incompatible with a didactic or political project; indeed, those habits actually negate the historicization and the political analysis that would be necessary for anything but the most atomized and individualized form of a history lesson.

Bodily Memory

So *American History X* signally flunks its assignment of analysis and interpretation as a direct result of its immersion in the narrative and ideological habits which seem to inflect (or infect) the whole of the American media. But this is a film that also exhibits in a spectacular fashion one of the chronic corollaries of those habits or of the tendency to displace history into individual experience. That is, one consequence of this displacement is that filmic narratives need to be written across the isolated and atomized bodies of the (preferably white) male actor. We are familiar with how this works in action movies, for instance, where the preparation, punishment, repair and final vindication of the action-hero body mark exactly the sequence of action-movie narrative – the body *is* the diegetic frame for such narratives.[12]

American History X indulges in this kind of diegetic habit in an astonishingly literal way. That is, Derek's body is spectacularly decorated with tattoos marking him indelibly as the neo-fascist. From the start, the film wastes no opportunity to show Derek stripped down – playing basketball, for instance, or being roused half-naked from sex with his girlfriend when he kills the black thieves. Some of the film's most disturbing and memorable shots picture this emblazoned body gloating and smirking under the police lights as they arrest him after the murder. When the Aryan gang assault and rape Derek's naked body in the prison showers, the spectacular markings on their bodies set up a striking visual trope: in each moment of their display the swastikas and white separatist emblems act as an obvious and literal displacement of politics onto the individual body.

There is, no doubt, some homoerotic aspect to the display of Derek's body. It has been reported that Norton went to some lengths to buff his physique for this movie, and the camera focuses on that physique remarkably often. The film is perhaps attempting to invoke some popular assumptions about the latent homosexuality of fascist groups by foregrounding Derek's muscular definition. But for the most part the significance of this body lies in its very whiteness (enhanced by being shot mostly in black and white) and in the tattoos and emblems that bespeak threat and violence more than sexuality. But the extravagant and frequent display of Derek's body eventually leaves the film with a problem. That is, even when Derek recants his extremist past, the tattoos remain as the mark and the memory of that past. Other signs can be removed: the neo-Nazi decorations in the family house can be taken down; Derek can grow his hair and dress more conventionally and smartly. But (unlike the body of the action hero) Derek's body itself cannot be recuperated, cannot erase the stigmatic marks. Thus, the film is caught between contradictory propositions: on the one hand, Derek's racist past can be redeemed in terms of the narrative, but on the diegetic level the very same violent politics cannot be forgotten. Those politics remain visible, written indelibly onto the body.

It could be claimed that the film does in fact resolve, or at least attempt to resolve, this contradiction. In one of the more interesting shots that underscore Derek's conversion and his new life after prison, he is dressing after a shower and catches sight of his own body in a mirror. His response to the sight of the now-offensive marks of his past is to place his hand over his heart, momentarily hiding the giant black swastika on his chest. The gesture is momentary, to be sure, but it is unmistakably what any American would recognize as that normally accompanying the Pledge of Allegiance. Thus, Derek's conversion is completed in the most hackneyed fashion, his redemption signalled by the one of the most evocative but sentimentalized signs in American cultural life. More importantly, for my purposes here, this is also the moment when the film itself confirms and guarantees its belonging, its own allegiance. That is, the case is closed on the politics and history of domestic fascism in the simple movement of the hand. But it is, of course, just a sleight of hand inasmuch as the swastika still remains beneath the gesture as a memory whose history has merely been foreclosed.

Figure 6 American History X.

Forgetting

In an interview with the *Guardian* in 1998, Edward Norton offered his own version of the way – or the reasons why – *American History X* follows the path it does in relation to race and racial violence in America:

> In America, racism is much more a gang phenomenon, growing out of a need for a sense of belonging. It does not have the political underpinnings it seems to have in Europe. So I felt like [*American History X*] was an American tragedy . . . Contemporary urban society breeds frustration, and often the snapping point becomes race.[13]
>
> (Gristwood 1999: 19)

One real American tragedy, perhaps, is that the poverty of mainstream analysis is such that Norton's words could easily pass for a thoughtful and even accurate view of the problem of race. Norton at least offers some sort of explanation, however avowedly apolitical it might be, and part of my point about the movie has been that it totally fails in this regard. But the implications of what Norton says do in fact find their way into the film in particular ways. First, it amplifies the idea that racial division is in some ways merely epiphenomenal and that the central issue is something more general in the constitution of contemporary society and the way it produces 'frustration'. Second, the film, like Norton himself, somehow manages to construe an absence of 'political underpinnings' to the question of race in America. The least that can be said, about Norton's statement or about the film itself, is that such suggestions should perhaps constitute the beginning of an analysis rather than be taken as conclusions. But the absence of serious analysis of conditions, and the absence of the historical consciousness that such analysis would necessarily involve, constitutes in large part the very 'American-ness' of this movie.

I want to claim, by way of a concluding provocation, that the absence of those things helps constitute the structure of contemporary racism in America. In the post-civil-rights era (and we should note how that phrase has by now become ambiguous), the epiphenomenal features of racism have evolved in such a way that a central fact about contemporary racism is that it is bound to deny itself. That is, racism exists alongside of, or covered over by, the claim that it in fact does not. We might see this development as part of what Carter Wilson calls the 'meta-racism' of our day, where all the functions of overt racism have been camouflaged. Or, with Steve Martinot, we might see this as a function of the contemporary 'rule of racialization', whereby race as a category is produced and bestowed upon people (rather than found on their bodies) and proceeds from hegemonic notions of whiteness which are granted universality.[14] What either of those terms attempts to point to is in part exemplified by exactly the enunciative position of *American History X*, where the question of race and the constitution of the racial other are construed a priori from a white perspective.

In America, this racialized perspective is crucially construed by the imputation of equality to all subjects in a 'colour-blind' way. America's 'rhetoric of equality',[15] as Manning Marable disparagingly calls it, has the aim of willing equality into existence or simply asserting its existence in the face of overwhelming evidence to the contrary. We have recently witnessed, in the aftermath of Hurricane Katrina, the fragility of that ideological structure – it temporarily fell apart at the point where the empirical conditions of racial inequality were exposed. But the mere fact that that exposure appeared to be so shocking to American culture underlines the hold that rhetoric of equality normally has.

While this structure of denial is probably operative to some degree in all racially mixed societies in the North, it has special force in the USA, I'd suggest, and it is clearly subvented by the ideology of personal freedom and responsibility that is so deeply embedded in and reliably reproduced by the culture. If all American subjects are assumed to be endowed with equality, then anything bad 'they' do is a result of their own choices, and the question of what structural or historical forces might make 'them' do those things need never be asked. The spurious presumption of equality allows the bases or causes of actual inequality to remain unacknowledged, and what is necessary for such an act of will is exactly the abrogation of any analytical view and the shearing away of history.

American History X certainly makes some attempt to address crucial questions of race in the USA, and the film's effort overtly invokes the crucial role of history in helping things change. But in the end, the film does little more than replicate the very conditions it hopes to ameliorate. Its vapid invocation of Lincoln's 'mystic chords of memory' – already a misprision of history – does not really help in a land where memory cannot become history and where the dramatic Gates of Time in Oklahoma City stand as entrances only to an absence of historical and political consciousness. Those gates are a reminder, so to speak, that their drama of eliding, withholding, and otherwise forgetting history plays to packed audiences every day in contemporary America.

Notes

1 I have to say, from the outset, that I am one of those who feel some discomfort with the chronic use of 'America' and 'American' to apply exclusively to the United States of America. In a slightly more ideal world it would be recognized that not all Americans are of the USA and not all of America is in the USA.

2 See <http://www.nps.gov/okci/home.htm>.

3 One contribution to an on-line discussion of the film notes the probable origin of the 'X': 'As a college student, I see this often. When the university starts a class and it is still in the experimental stage, it is given a course number followed by an X . . . for instance, CompSci403X. The X indicates that it is a new course and that changes are still being made. I think that Sweeney was thinking of this method when he named Danny's class "American History X". Danny's class was new, experimental, individualized, and certainly not a part of his original curriculum', see <http://www.geocities.com/SunsetStrip/Club/3036/faq.html>.

4 'The Fade-In Interview: Tony Kaye', *Fade-In*, fall 1998, p. 37.

5 See 'Reaper is Director's Ticket out of Hollywood Jail', *Entertainment News*, 6 November 2005, <http://www.entertainment-news.org/breaking/38528>.

6 R. Welkos, 'The Thin Line Between Fear and Hate', *Los Angeles Times*, 21 October 1998, <http://www.geocities.com/Sunset-Strip/Club/3036/analyse1.html>.

7 See M. Maurer, 'A Quick Chat with Tony Kaye', *kamera*, September 1998, <http://www.kamera.co.uk/interviews/kaye.html/>, and S. Gristwood, 'Edward Norton is up for an Oscar. But Who is He?', *Guardian*, March 19, 1999, <http://www.film.guardian.co.uk/The_Oscars_1999/story/0,,36397,00.html>. See also the web site, 'The First American History X Page', <http://www.geocities.com/Sunset Strip/Club/3036>.

8 See <http://www.geocities.com/SunsetStrip/Club/3036/script.html> . No details are given for the origin of these scripts, so their authenticity and status in relation to the film's shooting are unclear. The date given, 6 February 1997, is close to the beginning of shooting.

9 Excerpts from three of the extra scenes are included on the US DVD release of the film.

10 'The Fade-In Interview: Tony Kaye', *Fade-In*, fall 1998, p. 39. For the web site of Metzger's group, see <http://www.resist.com>.

11 Some white-supremacist groups did appear briefly during the aftermath to Hurricane Katrina in September 2005, conducting Internet aid and relief scams designed to help whites only. See the Anti Defamation League's report: <http://www.adl.org/main_Extremism/Hurricane_Katrina.htm>.

12 This point and several other aspects of my argument in this essay are dealt with at greater length in my *Clint Eastwood: A Cultural Production*, Minneapolis, Minn.: University of Minnesota Press, 1993.

13 S. Gristwood, 'Edward Norton is up for an Oscar. But Who is He?', *Guardian*, 19 March 1999.

14 C. Wilson, *Racism*, Thousand Oaks, Calif.: Sage, 1996; S. Martinot, *The Rule of Racialization*, Philadelphia, Pa.: Temple University Press, 2003. The latter is perhaps one of the most challenging books on race and US society to have appeared in the past few years.

15 M. Marable, *Speaking Truth to Power*, Boulder, Col.: Westview, 1996.

Chapter 13

American Pie (1999)

Mandy Merck

Whatever one thinks of 'gross-out' comedies, they are, doubtless, typically 'American'.

(Williams 2002: 18)

Opening at Number 1 in the US box office with a first weekend's takings of $18.1 million (Macauley 1999: 39), amassing some $102 million in its national theatrical release alone (Finler 2003: 269), the Universal film *American Pie* is the gross-out comedy that grossed large, reviving the fortunes of a subgenre with its roots in the remote 1970s and fattening up its studio for sale. In the inadvertent *entendre* of the venerable film scholar Robin Wood, it is 'one of those rare films where "everything came together"', his favourite in Hollywood's high-school cycle of the 1990s:

one has the impression that the actors really enjoyed themselves, that there was a constant sense of fun and pleasure in the making of the film, a communal creative engagement more pronounced than in any of the other films . . . The film is very funny, but also very *sweet*, generous to its characters and with a sort of seductive innocence.

(Wood 2002: 4)

Wood is not alone. Not only was *American Pie* voted sixth (between *Monty Python and the Holy Grail* and *Groundhog Day*) in the UK fan magazine *Total Film*'s 2000 readership survey of 'The 50 Greatest Comedies Ever' (Crook 2000: 69), but critics have also claimed that the film marks a major shift in contemporary teen culture. As I shall argue, what is – and isn't – contemporary in this film is fundamental to its national designation.

American Pie begins in the present-day bedroom of high-school senior Jim (Jason Biggs), masturbating to scrambled images of television cableporn. When his mother (Molly Cheek) enters to bid him goodnight, she finds her red-faced son watching 'one of those illegal channels' and summons Jim's father (Eugene Levy). The next day at school, Jim and his friends Oz the jock (Chris Klein), Finch the wannabee sophisticate (Eddie Kaye Thomas) and handsome smoothie Kevin (Thomas Ian Nicholas) are introduced making plans for their classmate Stifler's (Seann W. Scott) party. That evening, Oz's crude pass at an older college girl is scornfully refused with her advice that he 'be sensitive to her feelings. Relationships are reciprocal.' At the party, the obnoxious Stifler interrupts Kevin and his girlfriend Vicky (Tara Reid) after oral sex in an upstairs bedroom, unwittingly drinks a glass of beer spiked with Kevin's semen and vomits explosively. Downstairs, several of the boys enthuse over a sexy portrait of Stifler's absent mother. The next day, Kevin, Oz, Finch and Jim make a pact to lose their virginity before graduation. Subsequently, Jim attempts to find an internet date; Kevin seeks his brother's advice on sexually satisfying the reluctant Vicky; Finch spreads rumours of his immense genital endowment; and athletic Oz joins the despised jazz choir to pursue Heather (Mena Suvari). Then Jim, informed that the vagina is 'like warm apple pie', is discovered in coitus with a newly baked dessert by his appalled father.

Jim's luck seems to change, however, when the beautiful Czech exchange student Nadia (Shannon Elizabeth) proposes a study date at his house. But foolishly agreeing to webcast it to his friends, he is witnessed stripping for her and coming too soon – twice – by the entire school. Nadia is repatriated and Jim is reduced to asking the apparently naïve Michelle (Alyson Hannigan), the only girl in the school who seems to be unaware of his failure, to the prom. There Kevin insists that this is the final opportunity for them to get laid before graduation. At the post-prom overnight party, at another Stifler house on the lake, an ashamed Oz confesses their pact to Heather, inaugurating the film's sole episode of romantic love-making. Meanwhile, in the Stifler billiard room, Finch encounters his host's divorced mother (Jennifer Coolidge), who seductively offers him Scotch the way she likes it, 'aged 18 years'. As the two repair to the pool table, Kevin and Vicky finally consummate their relationship in an upstairs bedroom and Michelle takes the lead with Jim in another, ordering him to don two condoms to slow his notoriously premature orgasm. The next morning, the shocked Stifler walks in on his mother and Finch, Vicky breaks up with Kevin and Jim awakes to find that Michelle has 'used' and abandoned him. When the four meet later at the diner, Oz declares that he's fallen in love. Just before the credits roll, Jim's father discovers his son back in his bedroom performing a striptease on a webcast to Nadia.

In *Laughing Screaming*, his pioneering study of films that celebrate 'gross physical existence' (Paul 1994: 4), William Paul traces *American Pie*'s predecessors back to the paradigmatic comedies of male sexual experience *Porky's* (1982) and *National*

Lampoon's Animal House (1978). But its ensemble cast of high-school seniors on the cusp of college, as well as its national designation, suggest an even earlier (if less farcically physical) forebear in 1975's *American Graffiti*, despite evident 'differences in tone' (Paul 1994: 94). Although Paul offers an argument for the function of gross-out comedy in its national culture, one to which this essay will return, he does not analyse how it represents the nation itself. Then again, *Laughing Screaming* was published as a premature valedictory to what its author described as a doomed mode in 1994 – long after *American Graffiti*, but before the successive sex quests of *American Pie* (1999), *American Pie 2* (2001) and *American Wedding* (2003), as well as 2000's *American Virgin* (itself prefigured by the lesser known 1982 defloration saga, *The Last American Virgin*). The extent of this national nomination in films that purport to portray adolescent sexuality is such that Mena Suvari has long since made trivia-quiz history by featuring in four films with 'American' in their titles, including the grandiose *American Beauty* (1999), whose own combination of male misbehaviour, teen virginity and maternal denigration identifies it more closely with its eponymous coevals than its exponents might appreciate. Taking such titling seriously, this essay will consider how 'Americanness' (acknowledged and otherwise) is constituted in these national lampoons of sexual initiation.

According to Jonathan Bernstein, 'the basic construct of this subgenre seemed to have been carved in stone: a group of young males – stud, sensitive, blimp, blustering but inexperienced foul mouth – in feverish pursuit of sex' (Bernstein 1997: 8).[1] Identifying the predecessors of *American Pie*, no less an authority than the film's young screenwriter Adam Herz, twenty-six in the year of his film's release and the author of an undergraduate thesis on the gross-out cinema, names the legendary 1981 teen comedy *Porky's* as the subgenre's 'key movie' (Macaulay 1999: 38). Here it should be noted that *American Pie* was widely hailed on its opening as a political improvement on its generic predecessors, particularly its much-mentioned 1981 prototype. Comparing that product of the early Reagan era with its successor from the last year of Clinton's administration, both US and UK critics hailed a new sensitivity 'to a woman's needs' (Charity 1999: 38) with a 'sweetly emasculated tone' (Maher 1999: 38). 'The girls in *American Pie* are much more than life-support systems for breasts', enthused Jonathan Foreman in the *New York Post*, and *Entertainment Weekly*'s Owen Gliberman declared that their sexual sophistication marked 'a major shift in contemporary teen culture' (quoted in Shary 2002: 237–8). Not only do the girls of *American Pie* 'emerge as sensible, balanced and intelligent about sex and human fulfilment', said the London *Observer*, but 'the humour is almost entirely at the expense of the callow, preening boys' (French 1999: 8). Such impressions were entirely intended, according to the film's young makers, the brothers Paul and Chris Weitz, credited respectively as the film's director and (co-)producer. Where *Porky's* was 'full of terrifying instances of misogyny', their film sought – in Paul's description – 'a role, however tiny, in bringing American morality up to date' (Leigh 1999: 7).

Endorsing this claim to modernization, David Greven claims that *American Pie* and similar recent films, including the inevitable sequels, have absorbed the influence of feminism and gay rights to represent a new American masculinity, capable of exhibitionist display and desire for strong women if still compelled to performances of heterosexual virility. And where Stifler's nausea at drinking Kevin's 'pale ale' underscores such comedies' continued homophobia, the film's mention of such fluids, as well as Jim's mistimed climaxes, draws then-unusual attention to male sexual performance. Meanwhile, their female counterparts, led by the ascerbic Jessica (Natasha Lyonne), wearily scoff 'It's not a space shuttle launch, it's sex.' But the female self-possession praised by other critics worries Greven, who rightly observes that this renders the girls 'simultaneously powerful and unreal', raised from the narrative's rites of passage to the status of 'remote goddesses' (Greven 2002: 18) At its best, this permits Alyson Hannigan's Michelle to mount Jim and demand 'Say my name, bitch'. At its worst, it sanctions the pornographic display of Nadia (played by former *Playboy* model Shannon Elizabeth) – unwittingly webcast masturbating while browsing through Jim's porn magazines. Around such scenes, the film's homosocial foursome continually regroup at their favourite diner, ingesting pizzas, cokes, fries and, occasionally, mouthwash, and finally reuniting there after the prom to celebrate their sexual initiations.

The orality of their pleasures – in a film titled, after all, *American Pie*, whose signature scene equates pastry with pudenda and whose most graphic coupling involves fellatio – suggests an eroticism that is shamelessly infantile even by the standards of its genre. From the outset, Jim's erotic objects are not only comically mediated, like the scarcely visible woman in the scrambled cableporn, they approach – in the case of the Disney mermaid he declares 'really hot' – the irreality of fairy tale. The generational distance between his adolescent male milieu and the adult world is graphically demonstrated at Stifler's first party, when a scene cuts from a shot of its host with his head in a toilet to a glamorous portrait of his mother. The gilt-framed photograph of a woman with bared shoulders, artfully disarranged hair and a come-hither expression is significantly hung above the boys, and the camera tilts downward to pan across the admiring group, one of whom begins to lead a chant of 'MILF! Mom I'd like to fuck!' and then reaches up to kiss the image. (Later, the subject of the photograph will gratify the boys' fantasy and actually seduce one of them at the post-prom party, just as Shannon Elizabeth, the former soft porn model who plays Nadia, will – aroused by the very magazines for which the actress once posed – not only masturbate in Jim's webcast but attempt his actual defloration.) To the predictable strains of 'Here's to You, Mrs. Robinson', Stifler's mom will flirtatiously ask, 'Mr Finch, are you propositioning me?' in what is not the film's only allusion to its most famously Oedipal predecessor. When the statuesque and evidently experienced Nadia removes her underwear to join Jim in bed, her apprehensive partner is framed between her legs in another reprise of *The Graduate*. That its updated successor is yet to graduate from high school amplifies the immaturity in *American Pie*'s portrayal of male virginity.

Then there's the unmistakable import of Jim's intercourse with the dessert made by his mother, Mom's apple pie. The incestuous implication of this feat is multiply signalled – first by Jim's sitcom greeting 'Mom, I'm home!' as he enters the kitchen, and then by a close-up of the note awaiting him:

Jim –
Apple –
You're [*sic*] favorite
I'll be home later
Enjoy
Mom

Enjoy Mom indeed. If the heart drawn on this note is not indication enough, the subsequent arrival of Jim's father to end his son's forbidden union with his 'favourite' seals the scene's oedipal tenor. That the pie's filling is apple, hidden beneath its latticed crust and explicitly offered to gratify Jim's curiosity about the vagina, ensures its figuring as the fruit of the Tree of Knowledge – enticing and forbidden. (For the spectator, this tabooed knowledge continues to be withheld. Instead of pumping the pie horizontally on the table top, a shot that was cut to secure the film's 'R' rating admitting under-18s, Jim takes it up against the kitchen wall.)

Male sexual initiation by a maternally inflected older girl or woman is a venerable feature of teen comedies. It features in *American Graffiti*, and the paradigmatic *Porky's* opens with its cast's ill-fated visit to an older prostitute. But as the gross-out film gets grosser across the 1990s, its increasingly explicit physicality regresses its sexuality still more. The immaturity of *American Pie*'s protagonists, in a subgenre preoccupied with the bodily processes of ingestion and excretion, locates its comedy at the earliest stage of libidinal development, when sexual pleasure is predominantly oral and 'the love-relationship to the mother . . . is marked by the meanings of *eating* and *being eaten*' (Laplanche and Pontalis 1980: 287). 'We'll just tell your mother that we ate it', declares Jim's father of the shattered pie, verbalizing its synaesthetic elision of oral and genital sensation. And if greed is the sin of the mouth, masturbation has been traditionally understood as the greediest of genital pleasures – by nature compulsive, excessive, addictive – and thus the least mature. The connection the film draws between this libidinal intensity and the oral stage, with its attendant fantasies of absolute satisfaction and sadistic devouring would explain both its idealization of and violence towards the female love object, as well as its heroes' infantile passivity. Such a primitive orientation could make any girl a goddess, as tempting as our first mother's apple and as distant as paradise. It will also, of course, make the exemplary male subject a *boy*.

With a nod to Leslie Fieldler, Greven suggests that this arrested development is a comic version of the nineteenth-century American idealization of pubescent males, which romanticized their escape from both the domestic sphere of women and children and the commercial world of their fathers. (In a teen-film tradition dating back to the 1955 *Rebel without a Cause*, *American Pie* merges the gendered spheres of adulthood in its portrayal of its cloyingly domesticated dad, who always seems to be around the house. The fact that, aside from a brief appearance by Vicky's father, Jim's dad is the only one in a film that celebrates the erotic possibilities of the mother–son relation also makes him an abject figure with whom his son constantly attempts to disidentify.) Conversely, in making their protagonists adolescents, such comedies consign the threat of strong women and the lures of other boys to the mature man's past, rather, as I've argued elsewhere, as the British costume drama does with the white-flannelled homosexual idylls of its young Edwardians (Merck 1993: 112–13). But if that is what these gross-out films say about American manhood, what do they say about America?

American Pie's invitation to consider this question is almost irresistible. First, there is its title's puzzling allusion to Don McLean's elegaic drive to the levy in his Chevy, since it is nowhere heard on the soundtrack. And McLean bids 'bye bye' to Miss American Pie, whereas the Weitz brothers' pastry is clearly identified with the maternal figure who baked it and, through her, with the staple food of American tradition: pumpkin pie for Thanksgiving, humble pie for comeuppance, custard pie for comedy, 'hair pie' in 1930s slang for the female genitals. From there, it's no distance to the expression 'piece of ass' for sexual intercourse, which the film's publicity puns on with its slogan 'There's something about your first piece'. And, in a scenario in which the girls are clearly more mature than the boys, and one's first piece will be his friend's mother, the pie in question obscenely puns on the patriotic simile, 'as American as Mom's apple pie'.

But there is another pie in the traditional iconography of America, one whose rich depths suggest the temptations of wealth rather than women – the pie as economic unit, the pie of the pie chart, its wedge-shaped segments measuring percentage, profit, pie in the sky. Here the film's title echoes that of a 1935 MGM short based on the American humourist Ellis Parker Butler's 1904 story, 'The Great American Pie Company'. In Butler's satirical jibe at the 'trusts', two small-town daydreamers plan to corner the market in home-made pies. As the scheme develops in their ruminations, the American Pie Company grows to monopolize the nation's fruit, wheat, flour mills, cotton, timber and railroads – while laying off a third of these industries' workers in order to fund further growth. In the Depression-era film adaptation (directed by Nick Grinde), comedian Charles 'Chic' Sale, in his stock old-timer role, lazily contemplates a self-help guide to 'Power and Success' instead of selling his wife's baked goods. Encountering his rival Phineas, he proposes a merger – munching his way through three of Phin's wife's pies while explaining how they'll 'just gobble up all the pie business in this whole country'. As his scheme enlarges to include buying up Congress, the greedy pie man belches while declaring, 'What we want is power, so that when we say to this nation "Go", we want her to go. And when we say "Come", we want her to come.' His fantasies of dominion over the (indicatively feminine) nation are undermined, however, when he admits to Phin that they'll 'have to depend on our wives to do the baking until we make our first million or so'.

The financial aggrandizement imagined in *The Great American Pie Company* is an established fact in the prosperous precincts of East Great Falls. *American Pie*'s plotting depends upon not one but two conspicuously large houses in the single-parented Stifler family, the second with its own lakeside boathouse, the scene of Oz and Heather's post-prom idyll. (Stifler's Mom, we are told, got this house in her divorce settlement.) The sequels maintain this bourgeois setting in the luxurious beach house the boys rent in *American Pie 2*, as well as the resort hotel of *American Wedding*. Discussing *American Pie 2* in the user comment section (28 October 2003) of the Internet Movie Database, one Cincinnati contributor complains of its preoccupation with 'upper class white teens. These people have nice cars, friends, girls, huge houses, go to nice schools, a summer beach house, no job, and plenty of money, no problems, and so on.' When the commentator concludes with a religious condemnation of the film's portrayal of premarital sex, the perceptible connection between its sexual liberalism and its class context becomes clearer.

A historical survey of Hollywood film titles suggests that the adjective 'American' soon came to problematize the nation it identifies as well as the noun it modifies. As in the overarching trope of the American Dream, the national adjective can operate as both a patriotic and an ironic term, sometimes suggesting the failure of an American ideal, sometimes the Americanness of failure in a highly competitive society. In this vein, *American Pie*'s director Paul Weitz has declared his film's signature scene as 'an aggressively subversive image', challenging what he calls 'the apple pie family' and the national representation of sex as 'this malign, dangerous thing' (Leigh 1999: 7). Lauren Berlant discusses a similar tactic in her commentary on the 1934 production of *Imitation of Life*, whose 'antinationalist message', Berlant writes, 'is, paradoxically, brought to us by a national trademark' (Berlant 1993: 195). As Berlant points out, director John Stahl's adaptation of Fannie Hurst's novel follows its plot more closely than Douglas Sirk's better known 1959 version. In the novel and the earlier film, the central black character creates the wealth of her white woman employer by providing the recipe that the entrepreneur turns into a national brand. And the exploitation of this 'buxom figure of a woman with a round black moon face that shone above an Alps of bosom' (Hurst 2004: 75) is comprehensive: not only does she labour as a maid, caring for her boss's family as well as her own rebellious light-skinned daughter, but her popular pancake mix is marketed with a logo of her own visage, whose features are deliberately exaggerated in a 'blackface' smile.

The reference is to another American icon, Aunt Jemima's Pancakes, launched at the 1893 World's Columbian Exposition in Chicago. At this international trade fair, a black ex-slave named Nancy Green was employed by the Davis Milling Company to cook their processed pancake mix on a griddle while telling tales of her former life on a Louisiana plantation. Wearing a padded dress and a white bandana, Green performed the stock mammy character already established in post-Civil War America: the usually unpartnered black cook/domestic servant/childminder who happily worked for 'her' white family. The widespread appropriation of this plump but muscular figure to represent the restorative powers of American breakfast foods suggests this surrogate mother's sexual significance, a phallic maternity combining feminine flesh and nurturance with masculine strength and energy. With her magical labour power and multiple genders, the ultra-commodified mammy has been aptly described as a fetish object (Mulvey 1996: 35) who 'needs no other to complete her, yet many others in her orbit can be completed by her' (Deck 2000: 70). In the Hurst/Stahl fictionalization of this already fictional figure, she is renamed Delilah, commemorating the mythic powers that she will devote to her female employer. Freely giving the recipe that will make her boss a mogul, Delilah stands in her store window grilling pancakes and grins broadly to advertise them. So doing, she becomes a self-described 'walkin' trade-mark' (Hurst 2004: 105), and at her death in the Stahl film, her neon image casts its blinking halo over her funeral procession. *Imitation of Life*'s national branding of the all-providing mother as its totem meal is recapitulated in *American Pie*. In addition to its own baked goods and powerful moms, the film enjoys a literal inheritance from the texts that Berlant analyses. For its makers the Weitz brothers are the sons of Susan Kohner, the actress who played a major role in the 1959 Douglas Sirk remake.[2]

American Pie is also the inheritor of another national cinematic tradition, what Fredric Jameson refers to as the 'nostalgia film', whose inaugural title he gives as George Lucas's *American Graffiti*. In Jameson's assessment, Hollywood's attempts to recapture the 1950s (to which he wrongly attributes the 1962 setting of Lucas's film) represent the pre-Vietnam War decade as a 'privileged lost object of desire – not merely the stability and prosperity of a pax Americana but also the first naïve innocence of the countercultural impulses of early rock and roll and youth gangs' (Jameson 1991: 19). Unlike Jameson's examples, *American Pie* is set in the present rather than the past, but the 1972 song from which it derives its title remains popular culture's most nostalgic celebration of the era before 'the music died', including copious references to 1950s hits such as Marty Robbins' 1957 'A White Sport Coat (and a Pink Carnation)' and the Monotones' 1958 'The Book of Love', as well as to 'a coat . . . borrowed from James Dean'. The song's title combines with other elements to suspend the film in a peculiar atemporality which sent the critics back some eighteen years to *Porky's* – a film released in 1981 but set in 1954, with a disc jockey informing us that 'President Eisenhower is . . . running a tight ship of state' while Patti Page sings 'Mockingbird Hill'.

Like *American Pie*, *Porky's* is a story of a group of high-school boys, one of whom – the pint-sized PeeWee – is desperate for sexual experience. *Porky's* also opens in the bedroom of this embarrassed adolescent, into which his mother enters to summon him to school. Unlike *American Pie's* Jim, PeeWee (Dan Monahan) is measuring rather than pleasuring himself, but he too is interrupted in a state of sexual excitement. From this parental incursion into the always precarious purview of teen privacy, the two films diverge markedly. *Porky's* is set in pre-civil-rights Florida, and what strikes the contemporary spectator is not so much its sexism – mitigated as it is by the male belittling performed by the tall prostitute Cherry Forever (Susan Clark) and the knowing high-school girl Wendy (Kaki Hunter) – as its extensive narrative of and about racism. This commences almost immediately with one boy asking the others if they have successfully employed a 'nigger' for a practical joke. Although the other boys protest this word and suggest, in the language of the period, 'negro' or 'coloured man', the prank proceeds to plan. When PeeWee and his classmates are taken by the older boys for their backwoods deflowering by Cherry Forever, a large and apparently jealous black man bursts into her cabin brandishing a bloodied machete and terrifies them.

Having prefigured the film's gamut of threatening paternal figures, its sole black character simply disappears. Instead, the plot shifts to the barely articulate anti-Semitism of Tim (Cyril O'Reilly), who is flattened by an athletic Jewish classmate after calling him a 'kite' [*sic*] as well as a 'communist' and a 'spic'. Needless to say, handsome Brian Schwartz (Scott Colomby) triumphs to become his assailant's friend and the film's hero, planning and leading the boys' revenge on Porky the pimp (Chuck Mitchell) – an obese, club-wielding redneck in the style of the real-life segregationist 'Bull' Connor – for cheating them at his roadhouse brothel. This is indeed Eisenhower's America (a point underlined in a scene in which the camera closes in on Ike's flag-draped portrait in the Principal's office), but it is neither the utopia of postmodern retrospect nor the dystopian site of sexual subordination recalled by the brothers Weitz. Although the female characters are admittedly consigned to the background and made the object of locker-room voyeurism and the occasional dirty joke, much of the joking and even the physical scrutiny is reciprocal. Instead of gender antagonism, the boys of Angel Beach High oedipally bond against older men – violent, racist, white men: pimps, police and Tim's abusive parolee father – in a movie merger of *Grease* with *Deliverance*. The unusual attention to racism in a teen film might be explained by its place of origin, not Hollywood but Canada. From there, its producers would issue *Porky's 2*, in which the Angel Beach boys clash with local Christians, Klansmen and city councillors in defence of a Seminole Indian cast as Romeo in a school production.

If the Weitz brothers or their screenwriter Adam Herz remembered *Porky's* emphatic interest in race and ethnicity when they set out to modernize its sexual comedy, they certainly made no effort to address it – no conscious effort, anyway, for *American Pie* takes place in the monocultural Michigan town of East Great Falls – a synthetic Middle America of Californian exteriors and Eastern lacrosse players with a strangely dated feel. (The Weitz's DVD commentary stresses the film's intentionally 'retro' styling, avoiding conspicuous Steadicam shots and swish pans, as well as comic sound effects.) Here the only ethnically marked teen is the Czech exchange student Nadia, who is quickly returned to her European homeland. And yet, both comedies of adolescent male sexuality have a notable Jewish antecedent, a founding figure of the entire gross-out genre.

The adolescent scenes of Philip Roth's 1968 novel *Portnoy's Complaint* are also set in the mid-twentieth-century past and, like other Roth novels, including most recently *The Human Stain*, *Portnoy* has been filmed, in a 1982 Warner Brothers adaptation starring Richard Benjamin (who played another Roth anti-hero in the earlier *Goodbye, Columbus*). But the novel's graphic representations of the adolescent sexual exploits of Alex Portnoy had to wait for their cinematic realization. Recall the chapter in which the self-described 'Raskolnikov of jerking off' describes, in a very cinematic present tense, masturbating in the family bathroom:

> the trajectory of my ejaculation reaches startling new heights: leaving my joint like a rocket it makes right for the light bulb overhead, where to my wonderment and horror, it hits and hangs . . . I begin a scrupulous search of the shower curtain, the tub, the tile floor, the four toothbrushes – God forbid! – and just as I am about to unlock the door, imagining I have covered my tracks, my heart lurches at the sight of what is hanging like snot to the toe of my shoe . . . the sticky evidence is everywhere! Is it on my cuffs too? In my *hair*? my *ear*?
>
> (Roth 1969: 21)

Thirty years after its publication, this episode was appropriated for the 'hair gel' scene of another classic gross-out, the 1998 Farrelly Brothers' hit *There's Something about Mary*, which follows a high-school boy's passion for the girl he loves and meets again thirteen years later. In it, the perpetually awkward protagonist, counselled by a male friend to 'clean the pipes' before his long-awaited date with Mary, emerges from his bathroom with the sticky evidence clinging, just as Roth's hero feared, to his ear. Alex Portnoy's onanist adventures also offer a clear precedent for the food fuck in *American Pie*, the notorious scene in which he masturbates into a piece of liver – loathed staple of the Jewish supper.

But *Portnoy's Complaint* set a precedent for *American Pie* in more ways than these. Not only does Sophie Portnoy, the ultimate Jewish mother of comic fiction, continually intrude on her son's desperate attempts at sexual relief, but his perpetually constipated father Jack is – like Jim's desperately agreeable dad in *American Pie* – a classic *schlemiel*. And, where Alex is a classroom star, Jim is a computer geek who complains that his 720 Verbal SAT score has not enabled him to talk to girls. (Able on his Apple, he is starving for the fruit of a different knowledge.) The film retains the familial cast of the Jewish joke: 'the beleagured provider . . . the shatteringly attentive mother . . . that heavily funded Oedipal energy' (Solotaroff 1982: 144–5) as well as an Uncle Mort who, according to Jim's father, masturbated six times daily in his youth. Not preserved is *Portnoy's* setting, that of anxiously unassimilated second-generation immigrants.

In reviving this family comedy without acknowledging its Jewish roots, *American Pie* is far from contemporary. Indeed, it faithfully follows one of the oldest traditions of US popular culture. The New York novelist and screenwriter Fannie Hurst was the daughter of German Jews, and her early stories portray Jewish immigrant life. Yet she shared her assimilated family's anxiety about appearing Jewish and sought to present herself as 'simply a white American' (Itzkovitz 2004: xxvii), an impression she was accused of trying to enhance by contrast in her association with the Harlem Renaissance novelist Zora Neale Thurston. As Michael Rogin observes, Hurst effectively displaced her own desire to be taken as a Gentile into the theme of black passing in *Imitation of Life* (Rogin 1996: 123). (The youthful appearance of its white protagonist, her friendship with a cosmetics magnate and the love she develops for a man eight years her junior also raises the related issue of passing as younger, as anything but a mother.) In Hurst's novel, the Yiddishe Mamas of the author's early stories are condensed into the 'overembodied' (Berlant 1993: 195) black mammy whose daughter repudiates her, her racial identity and the maternity that could reveal it, disembodying herself via sterilization. In John Stahl's 1934 film adaptation, the daughter is played by Fredi Washington, a talented actress whose own career suffered for her refusal to deny her black parentage. In Douglas Sirk's 1959 remake, the suppressed similarity between African-American and Jewish 'passing' is literalized by the casting of a Jewish actress as the rebellious daughter – Susan Kohner, the mother of Chris and Paul Weitz. The progress could be said to come full circle in the Weitz brothers' updating of *Porky's*, wherein the 1981 film's extensive references to black and Jewish oppression are also expunged. And, in 2003, Hollywood released its adaptation of Philip Roth's *The Human Stain*, in which a college dean accused of racism is revealed to be himself an African American passing as white. The actor playing this role? The white Welshman Anthony Hopkins.

While the white world of the 1980s teen pic has been described as 'a triumph of ethnic cleansing' (Bernstein 1997: 32), this is less characteristic of its 1990s successors, which generally include black or Asian-American characters, albeit in secondary roles. Yet even Robin Wood complains that in *American Pie* 'there isn't a single memorable black or Asian presence' (Wood 2002: 4). Succumbing to Hollywood's historical inclination to suppress difference and subordination, the film offers a compensatory expression – of sexual rather than ethnic explicitness. *Portnoy's Complaint* had combined both modes to make the hero's graphically detailed sexual exploits his rebellion from the vividly drawn claustrophobia of the anxiously unassimilated Jewish family. For Alex, both his furtive masturbation and his ethnic identity are occasions of shame – a shame that he seeks to dissipate by sheer expression. (Thus the book's dictation by the adult Alex to his psychoanalyst.) Half this project is attempted by films like *American Pie*, which seek to release adolescent sexuality from embarrassed withdrawal to extrovert display. This is one appeal of the genre for the seventy-something Wood, a near contemporary of Roth's who recalls his own homosexual adolescence, 'riddled with guilt and self-disgust' (2002: 2), at a time when 'the word [sex] itself could not be spoken' (2002: 4).

Yet in severing sex (and only heterosexual sex) from stigma, *American Pie* also effectively cuts it off from history, setting its narrative in a timeless teen age. Commenting on Nabokov's *Lolita*, Fredric Jameson proclaims this is the very age that the 'brash and vulgar adolescent United States' imagines itself to be – 'land of the future . . . land of desire' in Hegel's description in *The Philosophy of History* (Jameson 2002: 201–202). But, as Oscar Wilde remarked over a century ago, 'The youth of America is their oldest tradition. It has been going on now for three hundred years' (Kadir 1986: 7). Indeed, *American Pie*'s comedy relies on a society that is both young and old, modern and traditional, impetuous and repressive. And, unlike *Lolita*, the film masculinizes its adolescent energy and innocence while feminizing the antique insignia of nationhood itself: 'Mom, the flag and apple pie'. Like the Western, with its patent pairing of the schoolmarm and the gunfighter, *American Pie* mates the lawless male with the civilizing woman to recreate the apple-pie family that it derides.

The misogyny consequent upon making mothers the bearer of the law is also a venerable American tradition, articulated in the 1940s by the novelist (and quondam screenwriter) Philip Wylie in his broadside against what quickly came to be understood as pathological mother-love or 'Momism'. Decrying in his 1942 *Generation of Vipers* a land with more 'apron strings crisscrossing it than railroads and telephone wires', Wylie complains that 'Mom is everywhere and everything and damned near everybody, and from her depends all the rest of the U.S. . . . I believe she has now achieved, in the hierarchy of miscellaneous articles, a spot next to the Bible and the Flag, being reckoned part of both in a way' (Wylie 1955: 185).

Although Wylie's diatribe against the country's economically parasitical mothers coincided with American women's mass entry into the labour force during wartime, his fulminations became popular wisdom, achieving twenty printings by the mid-1950s and their most explicit dramatization in the domineering mother of *Rebel without a Cause*. A half-century later, they would be reprised in Eugene Levy's comic revival of Jim Backus's deferential dad from the '50s film' and Jason Biggs's nomination – in *American Pie 2* – as 'Jimmy Dean'.

These attachments to the gender politics of a darker age are in studied contrast to *American Pie*'s ostensible project of bringing the nation's sexual morality up to date, a contradiction the film lucratively fails to resolve. As Roz Kaveney (2006) points out, the attraction for *American Pie*'s target male teen audience is precisely the sexual misbehaviour for which its central characters are punished. In marketing both the gross-out ethos and its feminist comeuppance, the film not only appeals to adolescent boys but also propitiates their female contemporaries, enabling it to cross over from farce to date movie. The trick, in what has rightly been called an age of conservative modernity (Osborne 1996), is to sell both – and get the biggest piece of the profits. For all its iconoclasm, this aptly titled film upholds an age-old American tradition in managing to fuck its pie – and have it.

American Pie: The Sequels

After slices in its signature scene permitting its reclassification from an initially disastrous rating admitting no one under the age of seventeen, *American Pie* became a huge hit, scoring Universal's second greatest North American theatrical rentals in 1999. Together with that of *The Mummy*, *Patch Adams* and *Notting Hill*, the comedy's success reversed the studio's poor performance in the 1990s. This enabled its parent company, the Canadian drinks corporation Seagram, who had bought the studio from the electronics giant Matsushita in 1995, to be purchased by the Vivendi water conglomerate in June 2000. Success also meant sequels, standard practice in a studio whose biggest 1997–2002 grossers included *The Lost World: Jurassic Park* and *Jurassic Park 3*, as well as *Nutty Professor 2* and *The Mummy Returns*. Almost inevitably, these sequels would repeat the title of their original films. Long characteristic of big-budget blockbusters such as the *Godfather* and *Superman* series, as well as generic horror and science fiction (such as the *Halloween* and *Star Trek* films), title repetition, differentiated by numerals or subtitles, had also become a stock convention of teen comedy. For the sequels of *American Pie*, this effectively redoubled the déjà vu of national designation, since the inclusion of 'America' or 'American' is in any case so frequent a feature of US film titles. Identified with what one recent commentary has described as 'the mother of all brands' (Anholt with Hildreth 2004), *American Pie* pursued its theme of male sexual maturation in two more movies. The Weitz brothers moved upmarket to co-direct *About a Boy* (2002) for Universal in Britain, but acted as executive producers on *American Pie 2* (directed by J. B. Rogers in 2001) and *American Wedding* (directed by Jesse Dylan, 2003). Retaining writer Adam Herz and the original cast (minus Chris Klein and

Mena Suvari for the third film), the sequels set out to repeat the scenes and situations that made the original film a hit.

America Pie 2 opens a year after its predecesssor, as the cast celebrate the end of their first year of college. With no further sexual experience since the post-prom party, Jim apprehensively accepts an amorous invitation from a female classmate in the opening scene. But his dormitory bedroom can offer no more privacy than that of his suburban home, as his father and mother arrive to discover the couple *in flagrante*. The repetition of the first film's parental incursion into their son's intimate life (itself repeated as first Dad then Mom barges into his bedroom) is itself doubled by another repetition, when Jim's shocked mother drops her signature apple pie and it shatters on the dorm-room floor.

Gripped by its compulsion to repeat every schtick of the first film, *American Pie 2* then reprises Stifler's party and the body-fluid jokes of its predecessor, as well as its characters' circumstances. Meeting afterwards at their old diner, the four protagonists could still be in high school. As each admits (usefully establishing the back story) nothing has changed: Kevin still longs for Vicky, Oz is still involved with Heather, Finch is still obsessed with Stifler's mom and Jim is still traumatized by his failure with Nadia. But if this film must enact the repetition compulsion manifested by film sequels generally, as well as the stifling reflexivity of the nostalgia film, it makes a virtue of this necessity by writing the impasse into its narrative. As one of the boys will later state (in apparent critique of the previous film), 'Times change and things are different. The problem is I don't want them to be.'

Seeking advice (as, again, in the previous film) from Kevin's older brother, the quartet are advised to leave town and spend their vacation at the beach nearby. There, in a palatial summerhouse they rent by taking painting jobs, they again undergo the film's formulaic rites of passage. Cue further reprises of the previous film, ostensibly pursuing its four central pairings but lingering on the relations between the boys. Here the sequel effectively exposes the anxious homoeroticism charging its homosocial quartet when they spy on two women whom they believe to be lesbians. The canny duo quickly turn the tables, offering to perform 'lesbian sex' (in the hilariously exaggerated style of the boys' porn videos) in exchange for similar homosexual performances by them. Desperate to see this sex show, the boys force themselves to enact reciprocal caresses, urged on by the rapacious Stifler. And as it quickly becomes clear, this physical ordeal (like that of the contact sports to which it is directly paralleled in Stifler's willingness to 'take it for the team') offers pleasures difficult to disavow. By the next scene, Kevin's invitation to play a card game called 'asshole' seals the film's self-acknowledged homosexuality – an impression not dispelled when Jim's subsequent reunion with Michelle at band camp is punctuated by his anal penetration with a trumpet mouthpiece.

The third film in this trilogy pursues this theme to Chicago, where Stifler's competitive compulsion leads him into a disco-dancing duel in a gay club and eventual friendship with its denizens, who then attend Jim and Michelle's wedding. The move towards something like contemporaneity marked by this sequence, which 'opens out' the films from their flag-decked suburban setting, is also driven by the sequels' increasing ethnic acknowledgement. Although listed in the first film's cast list as Jim Levenstein, Jim's full name is not spoken until *American Pie 2*. After mistaking superglue for lubricant while masturbating to a lesbian scene in *Pussy Palace*, he is driven from the emergency room back to the beach by his ever-understanding father. When the spectacularly self-circumcised son apologizes for his juvenile behaviour, his affectionate father replies: 'You know, you may be Jimbo or Jumbo or Jimmy Dean to these guys in there, but I want you to know that there are two people who still remember where James Emmanuel Levenstein came from. We're awfully proud of you, son.'

Where James Emmanuel Levenstein came from is revealed in the third film, when Jim's grandmother arrives to attend his wedding to Michelle, and denounces his fiancée as a 'goyim'. At the reception, ethnic misgivings become the source of the comedy, as Michelle's family, now revealed to be respectable Irish Americans, anxiously survey their apparently priapic son-in-law and his chaotic relatives. Here, as in the case of the film's homoerotic teasing, the suppressed ethnic references of the first *American Pie* are emphatically disclosed as the sequels attempt to out-gross their original situations (including in the third film Stifler's ingestion of dog faeces and a hyper-oedipal sex scene with Jim's grandmother that sabotages the trilogy's feminist pretensions).

For actor Jason Biggs, Jim's acquisition of a Jewish persona offered further career opportunities as a sanitized Adam Sandler, and he subsequently took the part of the young Woody Allen surrogate in Allen's 2004 *Anything Else*. Anticipated as far back as *The Graduate* in Dustin Hoffman's performance at another awkward wedding and consolidated by Hoffman thirty-five years later as the father of Ben Stiller's sexually dubious Jewish son-in-law in 2005's *Meet the Fockers* (directed by the now-established Weitz brothers), Jim's ethnicized identity in the third film's comedy of mixed marriage is hardly unique. Moreover, by still avoiding Black and Latino characters, *American Wedding* takes the softest of options. Nevertheless, it does restore some sense of generational history to the timeless adolescence that threatened to imprison its predecessors' juvenile protagonists. But if Jews, and even gays, are finally offered their piece of the national pie, what has 'American' come to mean by the end of this trilogy?

Here a belated return to the pre-title sequence of the first film is in order, from the initial bass line sounded under the Universal logo (the logo that represents the universe with the earth turning to the western hemisphere, its southern continent obscured by the studio's name). The music's pumping rhythm suggests porn, an impression strengthened by female moans and male exclamations as the camera tracks past discarded clothes. But as the shot reveals, the male voice in question is that of Jim, stroking himself through a tube sock while peering at obscured images of a naked couple on his television screen. Thus the film establishes both its similarity to and difference from pornography: rather than a graphic representation of people having sex, it is a graphic representation of people watching simulated representations of people having sex. It is, in other words, a representation of its own spectators.

The opening scene also establishes its teenage protagonists' governing desires, to experiment with sex in private and to observe other people engaging in it. The unity of these compulsions in its randy hero is apotheosized in *American Pie 2*'s rooftop revelation of Jim naked, with one hand glued to his dick and the other to the porn video he's been viewing. (Shannon Elizabeth's apparently aroused contemplation of the sort of magazine she used to pose for and her consequent reframing as webporn for Jim's contemporaries is the earlier film's attempt at a female equivalent of this experience, made banally sexist by the absence of any feminine perspective.) Like the masculine youth and feminine maturity thematized in the first film, the desire for sexual privacy and the desire for sexual spectatorship are both opposed and connected. And these contradictions are what make this trilogy American.

In *Laughing Screaming* (published five years before the release of *American Pie*) William Paul addresses these apparent antitheses in his comments on the national context of gross-out comedy. There he traces the subgenre's origins to the 'sick' comedians of the 1960s – Shelley Berman, Lenny Bruce, Mel Brooks, Dick Gregory and Mort Sahl, whose abrasive sexual humour shifted prevailing distinctions between public and private expression by moving the obscene on stage. Aided by important judicial decisions relaxing censorship for works of 'redeeming social value', this new comedy shared the ambitions of the liberation movements of the period 'to make the private public property, to bring out into the open precisely those things we have been most inclined to repress' (Paul 1994: 45). But, as Paul points out, the American politics of personal expression did not retain the radical commitments of the 1960s. Indeed, many of the gross-out comedies he surveys were popular products of the Reagan 1980s. Musing on this apparent anomaly, Paul suggests:

> The politics of selfhood, the liberation movements that seek to empower individuals previously marginalized in the social order, may actually have something in common with the 1980s politics of greed. At the very least, both rest on an unresolvable conflict between the demands of the individual and those of the social order, with a strong sense that the commonweal cannot find a common good that will support all its individuals.
>
> (Paul 1994: 429)

Concluding his study in the early 1990s, when the comedy of excess had apparently burned out, Paul wonders whether in the face of economic recession the American social order had finally triumphed over individual indulgence. Half a decade later, when the President of the USA had become the hapless protagonist of a national gross-out comedy in the renamed Oral Office, those forces no longer seemed so opposed (Merck 2000: 177–99). And by 2005, despite unimaginable political changes and the dispersal of its original cast and crew, the American Pie enterprise spawned a fourth franchise, *American Pie Presents Band Camp*, with Stifler's little brother attempting to shoot his own porn video by wiring the cabins with hidden cameras – until he himself falls for another camper. At Universal (by that year turning out high-grossing gross-outs like *The 40-Year-Old Virgin* for yet another owner, General Electric), the torch had passed to a new generation, still profiting on the national comedy of repression and representation.

Notes

1   In a gesture of ostensible modernization, *American Pie* retains the formulaic foursome, but eliminates the 'blimp' or fat boy of previous gross-outs.

2   Susan Kohner is the daughter of Paul Kohner, the Czech-born émigré who produced *The Hunchback of Notre Dame* in 1923 for Universal before becoming head of its European division in the 1930s. Later he opened an important talent agency, whose clients included Marlene Dietrich, Greta Garbo, Henry Fonda, Billy Wilder and Ingmar Bergman. As Universal 'legacies', the Weitz brothers' early success at that studio becomes more explicable.

References

Anholt, Simon with Hildreth, Jeremy (2004) *Brand America: The Mother of All Brands*, London: Cyan Books.

Berlant, Lauren (1993) 'National Brands/National Body: Imitation of Life', in Bruce Robbins (ed.) *The Phantom Public Sphere*, Minneapolis, Minn.: University of Minnesota Press, pp. 173–208.

Bernstein, Jonathan (1997) *Pretty in Pink: The Golden Age of Teenage Movies*, New York: St. Martin's Press.

Charity, Tom (1999) 'American Pie', *Time Out* (London), 6–13 October.

Crook, Simon (2000) 'The 50 Greatest Comedies Ever!', *Total Film*, November.

Deck, Alice A. (2000) '"Now Then – Who Said Biscuits?" The Black Woman Cook as Fetish in American Advertising, 1905–1953', in Sherrie Inness (ed.) *Kitchen Culture in American Representatives of Gender and Race*, Philadelphia, Pa.: University of Philadelphia Press, pp. 69–93.

Finler, Joel W. (2003) *The Hollywood Story*, London: Wallflower.

French, Philip (1999) 'American Pie', *Observer* Review (London), 10 October.

Greven, David (2002) 'Contemporary Teen Comedies and New Forms of American Masculinity', *Cineaste*, 27 (3): 14–21.

Hurst, Fannie (2004) *Imitation of Life,* ed. and introd. by Daniel Itzkovitz, Durham, NC: Duke University Press.

Itzkovitz, Daniel (2004) 'Introduction', in Fannie Hurst, *Imitation of Life*, edited and intro. by Daniel Itzkovitz, Durham, NC: Duke University Press, pp. xii–xiv.

Jameson, Fredric (1991) *Postmodernism or, The Cultural Logic of Late Capitalism*, Durham, NC: Duke University Press.

—— (2002) *A Singular Modernity*, London: Verso.

Kadir, Djelal (1986) *Questing Fictions: Latin America's Family Romance*, Minneapolis, Minn.: University of Minnesota Press.

—— (2003) 'Introduction: America and Its Studies', *PMLA*, 118 (1): pp. 9–24.

Kaveney, Roz (2006) *Teen Dreams*, London: I. B. Tauris.

Laplanche, J. and Pontalis, J.-B. (1980) *The Language of Psycho-Analysis*, London: Hogarth Press.

Leigh, Danny (1999) 'The Pie Who Loved Me', *Guardian*, 1 October.

Macaulay, Sean (1999) 'No Escape from the Zitgeist', *Times*, 13 July.

Maher, Kevin (1999) 'American Pie', *Sight and Sound*, 9, pp. 37–38.

Merck, Mandy (1993) *Perversions: Deviant Readings*, New York: Routledge.

—— (2000) *In Your Face: Nine Sexual Studies*, New York: New York University Press.

Mulvey, Laura (1996) *Fetishism and Curiosity*, London: British Film Institute.

Osborne, Peter (1996) 'Times (Modern), Modernity (Conservative)', *New Formations* 28: pp. 132–41.

Paul, William (1994) *Laughing Screaming: Modern Hollywood Horror and Comedy*, New York: Columbia University Press.

Rogin, Michael (1996) *Blackface, White Noise: Jewish Immigrants in the Hollywood Melting Pot*, Berkeley, Calif.: University of California Press.

Roth, Philip (1969) *Portnoy's Complaint*, London: Cape.

Shary, Timothy (2002) *Generation Multiplex*, Austin, Tex.: University of Texas Press.

Solotaroff, Theodore (1982) 'Philip Roth: A Personal View', in Sanford Pinsker (ed.) *Critical Essays on Philip Roth*, Boston, Mass.: G. K. Hall.

Williams, Alan (2002) 'Introduction', in Alan Williams (ed.) *Film and Nationalism*, New Brunswick, NJ: Rutgers University Press, 1–22.

Wood, Robin (2002) 'Party Time or Can't Hardly Wait for That American Pie', *Cine-Action*, 58: pp. 2–10.

Wylie, Philip (1955) *A Generation of Vipers*, New York: Pocket Books.

Chapter 14

American Splendor
(2003)

Esther Leslie

Comics, mass-reproduced, serial in form and based upon a character, are about 120 years old. A few black-and-white panels illustrating a modest gag developed by the turn of the century into full-colour Sunday supplements, four to eight pages long, syndicated nationwide. Part of the polyglot urban proletarian culture which absorbed and refracted the energies of the dynamic capitalism that spawned it, these comics fizz with possibility. Some of the most famous, such as *The Yellow Kid*, *The Katzenjammer Kids* and *Little Nemo in Slumberland*, however absurd or fantastical their storylines, are urban-industrial in setting, or more specifically in New York City or a similar skyscrapered place. It is not just a location. The city, the buildings, streets, docks, rivers and alleyways become active participants in the storylines, wielding a monstrous power to crush, oppress, damage. Or, humans running amok, in turn, damage them.

Little Nemo's adventures incorporate the fear of being pursued by tall buildings, or knocking them down, because the proportions between humans and buildings have been suddenly and inexplicably reversed (Marschall 1997). Little Nemo's city is a place of constant disasters. Played out in the elegant rectangles of the strip is a tangible anxiety about the relationship between city inhabitants and the environment in which they find themselves. Winsor McCay was one of the first US animators. Where his drawn comic strips gestured at a city in motion, their long panels stretching themselves precisely to accommodate the new dimensions of city life, vertical not horizontal, the geometrics of buildings not humans, his animations used the rhythms of modernity concretely. His first one from 1911 transferred Little Nemo to the screen. Inside the boxes of New York offices, men conspire to give flat shapes life and colour. There is no story to this animation –

it is simply unmotivated, illogical squashing and stretching, the very principle of cartooning.

Modern cities have long been understood as crucibles of alienation. The diminution of the city dweller adrift amongst towering buildings is expressed in Brecht's 1930 poem, 'Late Lamented Fame of the Giant City of New York' (Brecht 1979: 167–(74), which presents a bleak picture of the once hopeful melting pot that 'received everything that fell into it and converted it within twice two weeks into something identifiable'. The immigrants melted optimistically into the new great city, but their reward was to expose themselves to exploitation, for the men, 'broad-chested', 'raised up their gigantic buildings with incomparable waste of the best human material'. Brecht writes in the Depression, describing how machinery lies rusting in giant heaps. Unlike McCay's drawings of overlively buildings, his poem laments the actual deadliness of a world from which all human purpose has been withdrawn. Here columns of people 'hurry day and night through the empty canyons of lifeless stonepiles', 'empty skyscrapers' from which failed managers plummet, and those who remain hope beyond hope that tomorrow the rain will fall upwards. Even if the buildings remain 'safe as houses', the people are now barred from entering them. Brecht's words speak into a bleak age. The hopes of labouring people have been quashed. The towers which were products of their bodily power now block their paths or crumble from disuse.

It is into such a world that the superheroes are summoned in the 1930s, to avert disaster by resurrecting masculine power. The ludicrous humour or surrealist reverie of early comics cedes ground in this period. Life from the perspective of the street, with micro-narratives of anxious efforts to fit into a New World, gives way to a view from above. This is when the man endowed with special powers arrives, the fetishized human being, a godlike creature. Comic-book supermen first appeared in the form of the action strip, such as *Tarzan* and *Buck Rogers* in 1929, then *Dick Tracy* (1931) and *Flash Gordon* (1934). In the late 1930s, *Superman* arrived on a mission 'to fight for truth, justice and the American Way', heralding proper the age of the superhero. A raft of comics appeared featuring superheroes with extraordinary powers. Like the newspaper funnies before them, these comics were frequently set in an urban present or future. They incorporated disaster into scenarios, for how else could a superhero prove his worth? These were disasters, though, that even if elaborated to the ultimate degree, were erased from memory by the next story. The damage was not lasting. The city recovered. The supermen prevailed.

Recently, the supermen of comics have been challenged, shown to be impotent in New York or Chicago, Cleveland or outer space. This is a theme in comic books and films alike. A contradiction ensues: while superheroes are still called upon by the hegemons in a post-1960s world of black and white, good and evil, over the past two decades Superman has become a cipher of failure and betrayal. That the superheroes are under attack can be mapped initially through an analysis of a celebrated 1990s comic, *Jimmy Corrigan, The Smartest Kid on Earth* (Ware 2001). The title of Chris Ware's comic sounds as if it upholds the tradition of supermen. But one glance at the slope-shouldered protagonist on the cover gives the lie to the epithet, for the Jimmy Corrigans here, all three generations of them, are far from 'smart', each being emotionally 'dumber' than his father before him. The grandfather, Jimmy Reed Corrigan, is beaten and neglected as a child in Chicago in the 1890s and lives a century without expressing feelings for his son. The father, James William Corrigan, a misogynistic bartender in Michigan, loses touch with his son, Jimmy Corrigan, an agonizingly shy Chicago office worker in his mid-thirties, who looks sixty and acts like a now bashful, now vicious six-year-old. Jimmy has never kissed a girl and phones his mom every day, in typical geekish fashion, until the day he receives a letter from his pop, after thirty years of silence.

The aching stories of three generations of men twist together into this examination of American history and home life, fantasy and disappointment. Here the avenging force of the superhero is commuted into the unwarranted power of the patriarch, but its violence stems not from a warranted superiority but rather from ignorance and weakness. The youngest Jimmy, who reads superhero comics while eating his cereal every morning, has to learn *over and over* that Superman and all the other American superheroes on the comic page are, in real life, only dressed-up pretenders, like the caped imposter who has a sordid one-night stand with Jimmy's mother after a 'Meet the Superman' show, or the suicide in a Superman costume who jumps to his death from a skyscraper opposite Jimmy's office, or the lying dads who wear T-shirts with the logo 'Number One Dad'. These scenes illustrate the crushing realization that superheroes are mythic, as mythic as the benevolence of patriarchal family structures. Chris Ware's novel is not just about the failure of a family but the failure of fantasy. Repeated failure, the lessons that are taught but never learned, the relay of emotional mutilation from generation to generation, the recurrence of racial hatreds, these are the themes that bind this book and bound the weekly newspaper strip in which it found its first form, from 1993–9, in the Chicago newspaper *New City* and intermittently serialized in Ware's own periodical, the *Acme Novelty Library*.

Comic strips and cartoons are frequently based on repetition. Over and over a character undergoes the same humiliations at the hands of the same antagonist – Tweety Pie versus Sylvester, Tom versus Jerry, Bugs Bunny versus Elmer Fudd, Road Runner versus Wile E. Coyote. Repetition is necessary for the scenario to default to zero, enabling the next near-identical instalment. Unlike Tom and Jerry and their flat mates, the Corrigans move in historical time, but, just as in regular cartoons, the set-up is predictable, the violence repetitive, handed down through the generations like a sturdy winter coat. The sons suffer, mete out emotional violence and fall prey to accidents. Men hurt themselves throughout this story, and the son Jimmy hobbles around on a crutch, the one thing he dares lean on. Each Jimmy Corrigan is harmed both by the proximity of his father and by his distance. Historically, of course, comic-book superheroes should be orphans – orphaned Billy Batson turns into 'world's mightiest mortal' Captain Marvel, while orphaned Bruce Wayne avenges his parents' death as Batman, and Superman's mother and father save him by sending him to Earth. Abandonment confers a motive and, with that, secret powers. But the Jimmys have none. Doomed to be victims, they have nothing up their sleeves. Repetition inhabits the very panels here. Rather than comic-strip tableaux that blast action-packed moments into focus, a banal image gets repeated, identically or with the smallest shifts, in order to express muteness, stuntedness and embarrassment. These dumb durations yield echoes of the metro-loneliness of Edward Hopper paintings. Inactions do not need the dynamic stellar climaxes of 'WHAM!', 'POW!', 'ZAP!'. This is a comic that not only avoids superheroism. It deconstructs it.

From September 2001, cartoonist Art Spiegelman drew a series of tabloid-size strips, gathered together in 2004 under the title *In the Shadow of No Towers* (Spiegelman 2004). The subject was the aerial attack on the World Trade Center and its subsequent aftermath, including the war in Afghanistan and the US election of 2004. These historical events were addressed in relation to mental trauma, an intertwining familiar from Spiegelman's previous two-volume Holocaust comic *Maus*. The cartoonist witnessed the attacks with considerable anxiety, as his daughter was in the vicinity of the World Trade Center. Like Ware, he incorporates, alongside a reflection on US history and the politics of the family, a self-conscious relationship to the history of comic strips. There are frequent references, in the drawings as well as in Spiegelman's accompanying essay, to previous comic characters and to a raucous optimism embodied in the turn-of-the-century commercial comic culture. It is as if this turn to the comic past reveals something about the essence of New York, something more authentic than the redneck Bush agenda thrust on the city in the wake of the attack.

As in *Jimmy Corrigan*, where suicide is committed in a Superman suit, the failure of superheroism is signalled in the falling body. Spiegelman is haunted by the bodies falling from the World Trade Center. He transmutes them into the characters from the old comics, embodiments of an anarchic and potential-laden New York. The city's mythology has failed. In Spiegelman's response to the events of 11 September 2001 and after, the towers become like wretched bodies for a moment before collapsing. In this collapse, the streets of New York are rattled, and it is this shock, this urban shudder, that releases the ghosts of the past, the Yellow Kids, the Katzenjammer Kids, Little Nemo, the runts of Hogan's Alley, the Upside Downs, the Kinder Kids, all of the comic-book anti-heroes who were swept away by the superheroes.

The strip has at its centre two buildings and their fate. As in Winsor McCay's elongated strips, here too the buildings are made analogous to the form of the comic – only a large sheet could encompass their dimensions. But it seems clear that it is only in their demise that these buildings become beautiful, a part of experience, of memory and the city. Spiegelman is haunted by an image of a building's glowing skeleton. In 'The Sky is Falling', the introduction to *In The Shadow of No Towers* (Spiegelman 2004: n. p.), he notes: 'The pivotal image from my 9/11 morning – one that didn't get photographed or videotaped into public memory but still remains burned on the inside of my eyelids several years later – was the image of the looming north tower's glowing bones just before it vaporized.' It is only when their substructure is exposed that the towers, previously unnoticed, become affecting. The transience and fragility of buildings in *Little Nemo* and other urban strips is reinvoked not as a moment of fantastic reverie (a translation of commodity fetishism into built form) but as an actuality. Given the chain of events that follow the attack, it seems as if the concrete blocks of reality crumble in a firestorm to reveal the motive forces of US imperialism. Political revelation ensues.

The motif of the glowing building suggests a turning point: the building as vulnerable, the processes of historical change, built by humans, destroyed by humans. The glowing tower signals a charged moment, pointing to past and present and future. But it was the moment unseen by any camera. Perhaps it was only a fantasy, a false memory. Nevertheless, like Nemo's dreams, it exerts a power, a gesture towards potential. Better for Spiegelman that he did not literally witness this and suffer an occlusion of memory, a freezing of historical possibility. Through not seeing, Spiegelman is able to transform the falling bodies and buildings into a better past that floods back into the imagination at a moment when the future is not yet guaranteed. This is a moment before the entry of the supermen who ostensibly came to save the city but really brought violence and order to its heart. The comic strip's fantastical possibilities – that is, its independence from documentary reality – are yoked for utopia.

While Spiegelman was still reeling from the shock of 9/11, Spider-Man was back out on the streets of New York. *Amazing Spider-Man*, Volume 2, No. 36, published by Marvel Comics, written by J. Michael Straczynski and drawn and inked by John Romita Jr. and Scott Hanna, appeared in the weeks after the attack. The cover was black, indicating an initial failure to make images or imagine what had occurred. But inside the pages of *Amazing Spider-Man*, all the resources of imaginative projection were reassembled to produce an episode that, unlike so many others, was about failure and incomprehension. On that fateful day, Spider-Man arrives too late, failing to prevent the worst. He surveys the ruins, which adopt a cathedral-like aura, while the people of New York are elected to suffer a moment chosen out of all history. We are told that what has occurred is beyond words, beyond comprehension and, in addition, beyond forgiveness. The comic form has failed.

Spider-Man could not prevent and cannot repair the damage. Captain America appears too, helpless. Even at the heart of mainstream comic culture, the superman has proven impotent.

More than that though, the comic form betrays its own tenets. Gathered before the fallen skyscrapers are a number of arch-villains: Doctor Doom, Doctor Octopus, the Juggernaut, the Kingpin and Magneto. Even these agents of doom and destruction, absolute dictators, hostage-takers, mad scientists and nuclear terrorists are distressed by what they see. One weeps. Aware of this contradiction, the captions declare: 'Because even the worst of us, however scarred, are still human. Still feel. Still mourn the random deaths of innocents.' The comic-book superheroes have to give way, of course, to the real heroes of the event and, for once, the labouring and servicing people of Manhattan are acknowledged. The capital of capital is transformed through disaster into the site of a human collective on the streets, where all the past returns to witness what might possibly happen now normality is suspended. But any utopian gesture is counter-acted in the assertion of a new strength, the bodies of each New Yorker turned building, turned armature. Rattled the superheroes might be, but obdurately unyielding, redoubled in their refusal to be transformed by experience. A caption exhorts New Yorkers: 'They knocked down two tall towers. Graft now their echo onto your spine. Become girders and glass, stone and steel, so that when the world sees you, it sees them and stands tall.' The body is a building. It takes over the building's role. Rather, the building has usurped the body. To be human is to be the building. Fetishism is reasserted. The city's victory over its people is made graphic. Each person must become as hard and invincible as fantasy buildings and fantasy men. Where the superheroes have failed, an entire population must succeed.

Hollywood cameras and news-gatherers colluded in the world's memories of the events. The images of the towers' collapse beamed from satellite to satellite across global media led to a new round of speculation on postmodern themes concerning the event, the image and mediation (see, for example, Baudrillard 2002, Virilio 2002 and Žižek 2002). Was history still at an end in these hypermedia times or had it been jumpstarted by the catastrophe? Was its halt since the fall of the Berlin Wall, another seemingly architectural rather than human event, now over? But fiction film had a particular role in this tale. Cameras had caught the towers when they still existed, inscribed – intentionally or otherwise – in film footage. Editing eradicated them afterwards. In the marketing campaign for the film of *Spider-Man* made in 2001, the World Trade Center featured prominently. In the trailer for the film, Spider-Man spun his web between the two towers and used it to snare villains. This had to be erased when the film was released the following year. Film's techniques, the special effects and new digital processes, which make it so adaptable for superheroics, were used to efface historical reality. A rattled America had the tools to revise and reshape its image in the face of a crisis of legitimacy.

From Spiegelman's efforts to find a chink of hope in 9/11 by asserting a myth of old New York to an unnerved Spider-Man witnessing the temporary transfer of powers to a city's working class, the panorama of the American landscape of possibility is scaled down in the contemporary moment. Comics absorbed the energies of capitalism at the start of the century, and they stretched panels and invented narrative devices to explore the dynamics of land and property. Superheroes turned their bodies into armour, concentrations of physical power to console the Depression's economic woes and consolidate the fortunes of a post-war superpower. Underground comics junked the superhero system at a time when historical futures appeared open. But the future closed again, and the superheroes did not go away, despite their faltering. After the great assault on the model metropolis, they have been called on again, and their powers are transferred to the wider population, rallied at a time of crisis. In such a time, any residual 'underground' values seem merely 'alternative', a personal choice, not a social vision. It is this context that accounts for the ambivalences of the film *American Splendor* (Shari Springer Berman and Robert Pulcini, 2003) as it addresses fame, fortune and family and normalizes the comic inheritance.

The opening scene of the film *American Splendor* depicts the comic-book writer Harvey Pekar as a little boy. The crotchety child protests to the camera that 'he ain't no superman'. The scene cuts to the titles and the adult Pekar wandering Cleveland's unremarkable streets lined with telephone wires and factories pumping chemicals into the grey air. The titles are framed in comic-book style, photographic echoes of Robert Crumb's hand-drawn comic panels, carefully retracing industry and street clutter, the overlooked early 1960s furniture of everyday environments. Crumb even drew Cleveland's streets in the early 1960s (Crumb 1997: 47). This is not Superman's America of skyscrapers and swish offices in burgeoning deco. This is 'average' America where 'the average is dumb', a line Pekar overhears and includes in one of his early comics.

The word 'American' in the title is significant, as might be discerned from the fact that Chris Smith was originally considered as director, which would have made this the third film in his 'American Trilogy', after *American Job* (1995) and *American Movie* (1999). *American Job* is a study of US low-wage culture, pain and boredom, while *American Movie* is a docuportrait of a frustrated no-budget film-maker pursuing in his idiosyncratic fashion 'the American Dream', as Sundance Film Festival founder Robert Redford puts it. *American Splendor* likewise depicts a frustrated protagonist in a low-wage milieu, yet the 'splendor' of the title sets up a certain expectation of glamour and glory. But what could be splendid about the film's American setting, Cleveland? Co-director Robert Pulcini comments on Pekar's comic strip: 'He wanted to do authentic portraits of the things he saw in his life. And, I think there is irony in the title, "American Splendor," but it is also not ironic, you know? I think there is some really genuinely heartfelt moments in his comics that make you want to cry' (Berman and Pulcini 2005). American splendour inheres in authentically experienced everyday life. It may be found in the most ordinary places and experiences: from old blues records to telephone poles, diners and work camaraderie.

The interest of the film, like its comic-strip precedent, lies less with its narrative and more in the micro-details of observed situations. However, the bare bones of the plot are as follows: Harvey Pekar, a temperamentally grouchy file clerk in a Cleveland hospital, meets comic-strip artist Robert Crumb in 1962 at a garage sale. Pekar is a comics fan. He decides to produce his own comic strip. Rather than copying Crumb and focusing on 'freak' and hippie culture, Pekar's comic strip is about his own life, which consists of little that could be called dramatic. The strip presents situations from his menial job and his uneventful personal life. Crumb agrees to draw images for Pekar's words, and the comic *American Splendor* takes off, enjoying moderate success. Among its fans is Joyce Brabner. She contacts Pekar one day, having failed to obtain a particular issue. They arrange to meet and are soon in a relationship. Pekar's fortunes as a cartoonist grow, and a play is made based on scenes from his comic. He is invited to be a regular guest on *Late Night with David Letterman*, where he appears eccentric and irascible. The invitations cease after he criticizes the television network live on air. Illness strikes. Pekar is diagnosed with lymphoma but recovers. He and Joyce become guardians of a child called Danielle. Ultimately he swaps his hospital colleagues with their 'various personality tics' for the 'unlikeliest of nuclear families' (HBO 2005).

The America of *American Splendor* echoes the stasis of Chris Ware's drawn world. It details cramped living in Cleveland, boring administrative work, compromised love, a non-heroic struggle against illness and a story in which increasing success is really a type of failure, either because it is a 'sell-out' or because it is never successful enough. In many ways, Pekar's themes are those of Ware: in short, the banality of existence, despite all railing against it. Both Ware and Pekar doubt the reality of Superman as benevolent patriarch. Both also refer knowledgeably to the history and conventions of cartooning, self-reflexively working their chosen medium. Ware references the extraordinary characters of superhero comics in his epithet 'the Smartest Kid on Earth', while Pekar reveals in an interview with HBO that the 'American' in *American Splendor* came from the old D. C. comics, with their titles such as 'Star Spangled Comics' or 'All American Comics' (Pekar 2005b). Both Ware and Pekar are conscious of place. A once-glorious Chicago with its dream architecture has declined into a world of synthetic sounds and boring offices and hospitals. Pekar's formerly proud Cleveland is now located in the decaying post-industrial rustbelt, and Pekar works specifically at a Veterans' Administration Medical Center, ministering to incapacitated soldiers, another sign of disability and damage. In the underground and alternative comic-book tradition, all these themes are articulated as part of a progressive voice that separates itself consciously from contemporary mores, delving into the past and sharpening the critique of contemporary life, even if, as in Ware's case, this takes on the most hopeless and melancholic of forms. Both protagonists are traumatized. But in the film *American Splendor* there is the pressure on Pekar to normalize. A grouchy Harvey Pekar mutates underground comic-book values into a contemporary idiom of domesticity and security.

Harvey Pekar's America, as represented in the film and the comic strip on which it is based, is a world without glamour and aspiration. It is mundane, trashy and unhappy. Pekar's home life is full of disappointments. In his day job as file clerk in a Cleveland hospital, Pekar keeps a dull landscape in order. Office life is examined in all its banality, with its petty squabbles, corridor gossip and dull routine. Pekar works with a team of people who are similar to him. They too suffer their boring jobs. In addition, these very ordinary, low-skilled workers are also social misfits – loners and nerds. This is the 'dumb average' – ordinary and strange, at one and the same time. The scenario is ordinary because such types, with all their peculiarities, might be found in any workplace across the USA. It is extraordinary because this world and these idiosyncratic types rarely get represented. Pekar is one of the ordinary guys, but he is also estranged from them, because he draws a comic strip which reflects on their lives and which leads eventually to a degree of success, despite protests that it brings him hassles for little money. Pekar is a misfit even within the world of misfits at the hospital. The film-makers use these characters to assert another vision of America, one in which the guy on the street, with all his foibles, is acknowledged as something wonderful. Perfection is boring and drama is fatuous. Instead, defects and doldrums are celebrated. From this vantage point, Hollywood's scenarios seem tediously fantastic: they serve up 'idealized bullshit', Pekar's term for the type of popular culture he despises, and they exclude the working day and working class from representation. Pekar is an extraordinary character in film because he is a regular working man, with all the usual weaknesses, frustrations and neuroses. The world he inhabits is unusual because it is so normal.

American Splendor's promotional tagline proclaims 'ordinary life is pretty complex stuff'. However, the ordinary life of Harvey Pekar is not especially complex, though it is traumatic. Indeed, things happen more predictably than is usual in the movies. Work is routine, life is dull and even the crises are fairly straightforward: Pekar's first wife leaves him, as does his voice – literalizing the sense in which 'the average is – dumb'. Pekar's voice – that of the real Harvey Pekar whom we glimpse at points in the film, just as much as that of the acted Pekar, played by Paul Giamatti – is wobbly. (Pekar has had a vasectomy, which reinforces this sense of emasculation.) His workmate Toby Radloff speaks in an over-emphatic and stilted way. Pekar's friend Robert Crumb sounds odd too. Their distorted voices set them apart from other Americans in films. Their syndrome is a well-acknowledged one in US stereotypes: nerdishness. The nerd is an idiot-savant, who at the same time knows too much (about what matters to him) and too little (about social interaction and the business of life). One of the nerd's guises is the comic-book reader, lost in a world of drawings, fantasies, infantilized reverie. Crumb and Pekar are nerdishness redoubled. They are the clichéd 'geeks' – another term for a social misfit, often applied to comic-book readers – who consume as well as make comic culture, and they are also the geeks represented in the same comics, for they represent themselves. But their comic culture is different from the traditional geek culture of wish-fulfilling superheroes, where nerds such as Clark Kent and Peter Parker turn into champions. Their comic culture is all nerds with no superheroes.

The (stereo-)typically male reader of comics is usually disdained for his obsessive absorption in a trashy, irrelevant cultural form. Pekar and Crumb, meeting in 1962 as they trawl through old 78s at a garage sale, address this truism. At the heart of *American Splendor* is the question of value. Comics, like old records, generally have low economic and cultural value. Pekar revels in both, transforming junk into something that is culturally valuable *for him*. He has his own hierarchy of value within popular culture, and through it he pursues 'real life', or rather ordinary, unembellished life; his literary preference is for naturalism. Pekar's is an anti-comic, as much as the film *American Splendor* is an anti-film. Its directors come from a documentary background and this was their dramatic debut: however, they reinvent the form. Its genre-defying intermeshing of documentary, drama, comic strip and animation has little narrative drive, and its hero is unsympathetic. The inversion of the mainstream comic world is suggested in the directors' conception of the relationship between Pekar and Toby Radloff: 'Radloff is like Robin to Batman, Harvey's Batman' (Berman and Pulcini 2005). That this can only be meant ironically is indicated in the film's pre-credits scene when the young Pekar objects, while trick or treating with friends dressed as Superman, Batman, Robin and the Green Lantern, 'I ain't no superman – I'm just a kid from the neighbourhood'. Pekar is no superhero but rather an 'Everyman in Everyman situations' (Giamatti 2005).

Banality and freakdom (in a variety of senses) are the coordinates of the American splendour here on show. The film rescues for representation social misfits and the extraordinary that is, in fact, ordinary. As Pekar sees it, that which seems idiosyncratic or extraordinary to the individual is, in fact, a common experience, and *American Splendor* can bring consolation in providing a figure for identification:

> A lot of people get worried. They think, Jesus, I'm the only person in the world like this. I'm really fucked. But they don't know that there are a lot of people that are fucked out there. See? [. . .] It makes you feel good to know that there's other people afflicted like you.
>
> (Pekar 2005b)

The film also reflects on the possible negative aspects of the representation of misfits in commercial culture. For example, Pekar's colleague Radloff persuades Pekar and his wife to see the film *Revenge of the Nerds* (Jeff Kanew, 1984). Pekar recognizes something exploitative in these Hollywood nerds, but Radloff feels the film is truly a positive – and therefore atypical – representation of his and Pekar's world. The dilemma is repeated in the take-up of Radloff by the music-video channel MTV. For Radloff, MTV offers a platform for his 'nerd pride', an absurdist variation on sundry civil-rights struggles. He is able to represent himself and be lauded and confirmed in his identity. Pekar, in contrast, recognizes Radloff's media exposure as commercial exploitation. But commercial exploitation is a tactic that he and Joyce also attempt to use in relation to television exposure, with their self-marketing and promotion on the David Letterman show. ('Gourmet' jellybeans form an idiosyncratic analogue to the film's double-coding of value. Radloff praises the authenticity of the flavours, especially piña colada, which he pronounces with his own over-emphatic emphasis on the y-like sound in piña, making an effort at an accurate pronunciation of the Spanish. But the jellybean flavour is a chemical imitation of a gringo's coconut cocktail, and not even authentically alcoholized.)

In its examinations of the media, *American Splendor* reflects on authentic value, in cultural and personal terms, a theme dear to the counterculture with its abhorrence of 'selling out'. Authentic value is cross-indexed to questions of fame and recognition. Value may be confirmed or denied by fame. Economic value is usually increased by fame. Truth to one's principles and milieu is countermanded by fame. Pekar sways ambivalently between frustration and acceptance of not being 'recognized' – a theme visualized in the multiplicity of his identities. If one's self-image is an image of failure, then a contradiction opens once weakness forms the basis of success. The question of authenticity is played out most vividly in the film segment on Pekar's television fame. The highpoint of his celebrity is a number of appearances on the *Late Night with David Letterman* chat show in the late 1980s. Letterman describes Harvey Pekar, semi-ironically, as the 'embodiment of the American dream'. But Pekar assaults the value system of the chat show, asserting. 'I'm no showbiz phony – I'm telling the truth.' Sporting an 'on strike against NBC' T-shirt, Pekar explodes on air, attacking the 'military-industrial' connections of NBC's corporate parent General Electric. He also characterizes himself as a 'sell-out hack' who has been 'co-opted'. *American Splendor* emanates from the culture it attempts to bring to the screen and, in addition, thematizes the ways in which a subculture will be recuperated by the mainstream.

Beginning with Superman and Batman in the 1940s, films of comic books were for a long time largely synonymous with superhero tales, barring the odd underground animation in the late 1960s and 1970s, such as Ralph Bakshi's *Fritz the Cat* (1972). In the 1980s, mainstream film continued to draw on comic-book stories and scenarios, but there emerged an increasingly ironic or even camp take on the comic-book heritage, as seen, for example, in Robert Altman's *Popeye* (1980) or Warren Beatty's *Dick Tracy* (1990), but already present in the television series *Batman* (1966–8) and the Lex Luthor character in the first lavish super-hero blockbuster, *Superman* (Richard Donner, 1978). Superheroes never really disappeared, but they were periodically subjected to questioning and analysis: for example in Stan Lee's Marvel comics in the 1960s, when Spider-Man, the Hulk and the X-men discovered self-consciousness and posed questions about their *raison d'être*.

The 1990s series *Kingdom Come* and *Planetary* extended the line in critical, deconstructed superheroes begun in the 1980s in Alan Moore's and Dave Gibbons's *Watchmen* and Frank Miller's *The Dark Knight Returns* and *Batman: Year One*. Aspects of these revised superheroes found their way into Tim Burton's *Batman* films and Christopher Nolan's *Batman Begins* (2005). Intensifying Marvel's reconsideration of the superhero figure, a filmed comic book is now as likely to be drawn from the world of subcultural or 'alternative' comics. The Dark Horse comics *Hellboy* (2004) and *Frank Miller's Sin City* (2005) brought cult comics successfully to the screen. *Hellboy* presents a twisted superhero, the result of Nazi experiments, who teams up with fellow 'freak' Abe Sapien in a bureau of paranormal research. *Sin City* returns the noirish atmosphere of the comic to its filmic origin in a story centred on avenging men, including a streetfighter and a violent policeman who risks his life in protecting a girl from a deformed paedophile.

But more and more film-makers are turning to comics free of zaps, whams, cartoon violence and action scenes. Over the past ten years, alternative comics, or 'comix', have stimulated films, and there are no superheroes in sight. The adaptation of an 'indie' comic into a movie is now unsurprising. A key year was 2001. It saw the collaboration between comic-strip author Daniel Clowes and director Terry Zwigoff in *Ghost World*, as well as the first adaptation of an Alan Moore graphic novel, *From Hell*, later followed by *The League of Extraordinary Gentlemen* (2003), *Constantine* (2005) and *V For Vendetta* (2006). *From Hell* is a grimy tale of a nineteenth-century London stalked by Jack the Ripper. Moore follows Stephen Knight's theory that the murderer is Sir William Withey Gull, a royal physician, in a conspiracy to conceal the birth of an illegitimate baby fathered by Prince Albert Victor, Duke of Clarence. The world conjured up in the film is dark and hallucinatory. Taking off from the graphic novel, the film is less about detection and crime-solving and more an atmospheric meditation on themes such as tabloid sensationalism and emergent commodification, all set against the anatomizing of a class system and its values. *From Hell* earned more than $11 million in its opening weekend in the USA, and went on to take an estimated $45 million worldwide (Hughes 2003). *Ghost World* was also a dissection of horror, but a banal, suburban modern horror. Its sensibility – summarized in its tagline 'accentuate the negative' – mirrors that of *American Splendor*.

Ghost World is a study of alienation as experienced by Enid Coleslaw (Thora Birch), a freshly graduated high-school student living in a suburb of Anytown, USA. Her habitat is drab. Billboards clutter the landscape. Corporate brandnames are everywhere. Power lines and cables slice the sky. Shabby diners fill up with creeps. Interviewed for *Movie Maker*, Zwigoff outlines a bleak vision of an America that is all surface and where freedom of choice becomes no choice at all: 'Anything that's authentic and genuine, anything that grew out of any sense of tradition, is wiped out. We're left with this bland monoculture that's swept over the whole country' (Zwigoff 2002a). The film-makers chose a Californian suburb for shooting because, as author Daniel Clowes noted, 'it looks like any place in modern America – just one big happy corporate strip mall filled with Gaps and Starbucks and Burger Kings', where Enid is unable 'to find something authentic to connect with' (Hughes 2003: 206). Such a critical and disaffected female lead (whose name is an anagram of the male who created her) deviates from the norm. Enid is an observer of a world she finds repellent. Like Pekar, she also draws it, signalling her place in the comic-book lineage subtly. Her sketches of strangers in diners, such as the 'Satanic couple', echo those of comic-book artists – they are in fact the work of Crumb's daughter Sophie.

Enid's drawings are genuinely expressive, unlike the work produced in her compulsory summer art class, where a pretentious teacher, adept at dishing out postmodern discourse, is unable to distinguish 'real' from 'fake' artistic expression. She grows apart from her schoolfriend Rebecca (Scarlett Johansson), who is increasingly drawn into a more 'normal' social circle. Enid finds another misfit, with whom she eventually has a one-night stand. This figure, a composite of two people from the original comic book but also a fusion of Crumb and Zwigoff, is an older man, Seymour (played by Steve Buscemi), who has had no success with women. Seymour is a collector of blues records and is especially excited by '78s, just like the real-life R. Crumb and director Terry Zwigoff. Seymour's collecting is not simply a positive rejection of commercial culture. It is a symptom of his own self-diagnosed inability to connect with people, 'so you fill your life with stuff'. However, this 'stuff' touches Enid in a way that contemporary teen pop or the 'pseudo-bohemian' sounds of reggae do not. Just as the opening sequence's Bollywood soundtrack offers Enid the possibility of genuine physical abandon, unlike commercial pop, so too the blues presents an emotional authenticity absent in contemporary chart music.

Zwigoff made strenuous efforts to counter external pressures on the film. His first film *Crumb* (1994), a desolate study of the artist and his family, was an independently financed documentary. For *Ghost World*, financial backing from Hollywood was declined, and, instead, a deal guaranteeing Zwigoff editorial control was forged with the European producers Granada Film. United Artists distributed the film in a 'negative distribution' deal, securing them no influence on the final product. Consequently, the closing scene eschews the expected narrative closure, leaving things unresolved: Enid's ride out of town on a bus that should have been decommissioned appears as a journey into a possibly better unknown or as a passage into death. But, despite Zwigoff's maintenance of editorial control, self-censorship kicks in when it comes to film. Clowes and Zwigoff have commented on how they toned down the ending (originally Seymour was to commit suicide) and they intensified the film's colour, visually and thematically, because 'You have to make a colorful film or people just think it's too bleak and cheap-looking' (Zwigoff 2002b).

Adaptations of comic books are now standard fare in Hollywood and very successful financially. To take just a few examples, *Fantastic Four* (2005) opened with $56.1 million at 3,602 theatres; *Spider-Man* (2002) earned over $403 million for Sony and Marvel Comics domestically, and its worldwide receipts totalled over $800 million; $373 million was taken domestically for *Spider-Man 2* (2004); Warner Bros. *Batman Begins* (2005) grossed $191 million domestically (Hughes 2003, Hetherington 2005). The 'indie' films are in a different league to the superhero films economically, though it is still a multi-million-dollar one. Frank Miller's *Sin City* (2005) brought in over $74 million in its domestic market, while *Hellboy* grossed $59 million. The more off-beat *Ghost World* took over $8 million worldwide, the same amount as *American Splendor*, which gained the highest per-screen box-office average on its opening weekend.

Hollywood perceives graphic novels as already existing storyboards. On the surface, it appears simple to translate them into film. This, of course, is an illusion. The space between frames in a graphic novel or comic book is a different space to that between frames – or scenes – in a film. Graphic novel readers have learned modes of reading that bridge the gaps, understanding how absence is suggestive. Linearity is not expected – a reader can rifle backwards and forwards at will. Perspective changes rapidly and without explanation. Readers accommodate themselves to a comic's particularity through immersion in it, possibly over long periods of time. Film audiences, by contrast, generally expect to see all relevant action take place on screen. Too strict an adherence to the comic-book aesthetic can paralyse a film, for comic books are an anti-filmic still medium, comprised entirely of cuts. Terry Zwigoff's direction in *Ghost World* retains this aspect and, in an interview published in *ImageText*, he acknowledged that he went too far in this respect (Zwigoff 2002b). The film's camera is static or tracking, using standard medium shots. The one exception to this is the opening pan which culminates in the only energetic movement in the film: Enid's wild dance to a Bollywood soundtrack. It makes for an inertness that could be read as significant: America is paralysed or, worse, embracing (cultural, technological, critical) paralysis, as indicated by the wheelchair-using coffee-shop customer, with his laptop on his knees, who is reputedly 'faking it'.

If there are difficulties in translating comics to film, there are also facilitating factors. The first comic-book superheroes of the 1930s quickly translated into animated shorts. They also took on the shape of live action figures, in children's television series such as *Batman* and, later, in studio blockbusters. The superhuman exploits of Spider-Man, Superman and the rest can be rendered easily in cel animation, which is the translation into mobile form of the comic books' drawn panels. Nothing is unstageable in the world of animation, which demands no gravity or time–space coherence. The studio film also found ways of emulating the comic-book look for non-animated film: a visual world of props, dramatic lighting and exaggerated camera angles. The special effects available to cinema from the beginning – slow-motion, time-lapse and film reversal and editing – allow super-heroics to be performed before the camera. In certain respects, the contemporary comic-book form anticipates a wider contemporary shift in commercial film production where, given digital technology and storyboarding, much of film has become animation and episodic. Animation, like the digital, allows an endless and absolute manipulation and revision of filmic material. And with DVD technology the episodic nature of contemporary film seems underlined, as films are clearly composed of divisible segments. But many of these new processes are expensive. As Daniel Clowes observes, the popularity of underground comics as film material might be explained economically. They can be more cheaply transferred to the screen, as their non-superheroic stories require no elaborate special effects and there are fewer problems and costs associated with acquiring rights that are owned by large corporations or tied up in long-standing deals (Vazquez 2004).

Some of the 'indie' comic-book films seek ways of translating the comics' episodic and inventive modes of storytelling and particular visual styles into film form. But the commercial pressures of film-making mean that there are often compromises in terms of story and look. For example, the film version of Alan Moore's *From Hell* (Allen and Albert Hughes, 2001) renders its Jack the Ripper story in conventional filmic Gothic horror mode and excises the comic's play with psycho-geography and myth, the 'fractal' nature of truth and the simultaneity of events. Lost are the dense cross-references that dart across the original graphic novel and its critical dialogue with historiography.

Conversely, in its efforts to render the comic-book origins of its source material, *American Splendor* is outstanding. The film is as much about the comic-book format as it is about Harvey Pekar. Its episodic nature emulates the comic-strip format, a series of fairly self-contained scenes with little development across them. As in the comic, chronology is not strictly adhered to, although the overarching narrative is the story of Pekar's life and his comic's fortunes. The absence of chronology allows the starting point to be, self-reflexively, the film's own existence, though in terms of 'the Harvey Pekar story', it, of course, logically comes at the end. The film's origins are also indicated in scenes using drawn panels which appear to be taken directly from the comic. Episodes begin with a title, such as 'Meanwhile in Delaware', turning the opening photographic frame into a comic panel. In one episode, Pekar sits in a diner, and the scene transforms into a drawing with a thought bubble emerging from Pekar's head.

The comic source is also apparent in the segment 'Who is Harvey Pekar?'. Here the screen is completely white, like a blank page. As the actor representing Pekar traverses the screen, a drawn line appears indicating the dimensions of a room. Then other lines and a telephone appear, all unmistakably in Crumb's style. Film and comic are combined. The scene cuts to Pekar on a filmed street. He steps from it through a drawn window back into a drawn room, before the scene fades to white, indicating the unmarked page once more. Animation makes the process of drawing visible, and this is shown to be of a different order to film, whether documentary or dramatic. The theme of the episode is identity. Pekar's identity is shown to straddle the documentary, the dramaticized and the drawn world. The audience is asked to judge which is more real.

The question of identity is also foregrounded in the scene depicting Pekar and Brabner's first meeting. Knowing Pekar only from his comics, Joyce is anxious about what sort of man will greet her at the airport. Meshing real-life action and comic, Pekar lounges on various seats in the airport, drawn in divergent ways by different illustrators. In a broader sense, the relationship between Pekar and his 'fictional' selves is indicated in the film by the use of several modes of representation: Harvey Pekar himself, a film actor and a stage actor playing Pekar, and the drawn Pekar. (Joyce Brabner likewise both plays herself and is represented by Hope Davis). Cutting between the documentary and the fictional, the filmic and the drawn foregrounds issues of representation: we see something of Pekar's sense of his own biography in the documentary portions, and we see how his life is represented by the film-makers (and, briefly, by a playwright). Such a strategy matches a prevalent scepticism about representation and a self-consciousness about film-makers' intentions often played out in non-mainstream film-making. For example, Andrew Jarecki's *Capturing the Friedmans* (2003), a portrait of a family torn apart by accusations of paedophilia, has the tagline 'Who do you believe?', a reference to the discrepant testimonies in the film as well as to the various filmic documents, including those produced by the Friedmans, who 'captured' themselves extensively on 8-millimetre film and video.

American Splendor and other alternative comics provide material for film adaptation. But it is not so much the comic-book look that is attractive or the fact that Hollywood's special effects are particularly well adapted to render the drawn universe filmically. The comic books' cult status and existing fan base make it a good commercial gamble. In addition, they communicate an attitude and set of values, or anti-values, which appeal to the ageing hipsters of the 'boomer' generation as much as to 'Generation X'. They also appeal to film critics. These films are cinephiles' films, garnering extensive publicity in broadsheets, magazines, on web sites, radio and television. Their self-reflexivity and their hip attitude flatter film-savvy audiences. Many of them have been enthusiastically taken up on the alternative circuit and showered, like *Ghost World*, with awards. The web site for *American Splendor* lists twenty-four awards from fourteen awarding bodies, largely film critics' associations. It was nominated for a Best Adapted Screenplay Academy Award in 2002. A week after nomination, it appeared on DVD, generating more income, alongside the enhanced sales of the comic book and its spin-offs. These films stand out – offering 'something different'.

This could also be said of the original comic, since *American Splendor* emerged from the counter-culture of the 1960s and 1970s, when 'underground' comics for adults first appeared, most enduringly drawn by Crumb. But Pekar's effort – first published in 1976 – is a faint echo of its predecessors, translated as it was into the post-hippie America of work, routine, disappointment and a solitude which could be relabelled positively as individualism or negatively as manic egoism. By the time *American Splendor* appeared, the splendour of comics – inaugurated in the mainstream, in the superhero comics, but raised to a higher (intellectual) level in the counter-culture – was over. Also consigned to the past was the golden age of protest that fuelled the underground comic scene of the 1960s and 1970s, refused superheroics and developed ever more self-referential and sophisticated forms. By the end of the century, the market for adult comics had shrunk. Successive Republican administrations and Clintonian centrism had subjected the underground values of the 1960s to concerted ideological onslaughts. *American Splendor* is a reinvention of the 'alternative' comic book amidst enervated social and collective visions. Pekar's insistence on the ordinary signals the 'return to normality' after a period of social and political experimentation.

Moreover, Pekar's forceful political convictions are further muted in the film. When he has his outburst against Letterman, the motivation seems to be not political critique but loneliness and the cancer lump. Crumb's presence as illustrator retains a link to the freak scene of the 1960s and 1970s, but the social context of the comics has changed. In 2003, the film of the comic arrives in another, different America, with memories of Vietnam and social protest obscured by new wars, including the infinite War on Terror. In addition, transposed into a new finance-gobbling medium, even the residues of a countercultural moment are erased. In comic-book subculture, the distinction between mainstream and underground/alternative traditions can be maintained, but the vast capital investment required for film and, consequently, the need for large audiences, means that very little is able to hold out against subsumption by mainstream conventional values.

It is for this reason that *American Splendor* plays as a love story, if an unconventional one. Deviating from the comic-book story which provided the initial filmic idea, *Ghost World* is likewise organized around a love story – although it falls apart as soon as it is consummated. Despite its apparent countercultural values, the film *American Splendor* seems compelled to translate everything into a spectacle of normativity: fame and fortune, family and future. At the close of the film, the family is ushered in to provide an ending which is relatively conventional – the tinge of weirdness manifesting itself only because this is not natural parenthood but guardianship (or rescue) of a fictional illustrator's uncared-for daughter. The future is held open by Harvey Pekar's recovery from cancer, the stabilization of his family unit (notwithstanding the reassuringly usual attendant chaos) and the promise of fame as a consequence of the film itself. Pekar's intriguing mesh of the extraordinary and the ordinary is separated out into a more conventional ordinariness (family life) and extraordinariness (celebrity). The promotional blurb on the DVD box expresses the full normalization of the story, albeit in a way that denies the film's more nuanced texture: 'he achieves critical acclaim, celebrity status and, most unlikely of all, finds true love'. Furthermore, Pekar's disastrous performance on television, which cuts him off from media exposure, is comfortingly recuperated by the very fact of the present film and its attendant spin-offs, in re-released *American Splendor* comic anthologies (Pekar 2003, 2005a) and the all new *Our Movie Year* (Pekar 2004).

The paradox of success is not only thematized in the film. It is played out in the film's fate. The documentary aspect of the film points to the world outside the film, and it is the further success of the film (and therefore of Pekar) that comes to be of interest. The predominant form of self-reflexivity in *American Splendor* is the fact of the film's filming. This acknowledgement of the film as artefact is revealing, producing a disruption in the storytelling and foregrounding questions of representation. However, it also distorts the original subject matter, as the themes of success and celebrity come to dominate, taking over from the comic's initial impulse: to document the ordinary. Putatively offered as a corrective to the dominant images in commercial film, the film cannot fully escape the values of mainstream cinema. *American Splendor* can be seen as a renormalization, after the counterculture's demise, but echoing enough of its critical affect to appear 'alternative'. Artefacts such as *American Splendor* are the alternative forms in an epoch of no alternative.

References

Baudrillard, J. (2002) *The Spirit of Terrorism and Requiem for the Twin Towers*, London: Verso.

Berman, S. S. and Pulcini, R. (2005) 'Interview', available on-line at <http://www.hbo.com/films/americansplendor/interviews/directors.html> (accessed 7 August 2005).

Brecht, B. (1979) *Poems 1913–1956*, London: Methuen.

Crumb, R. (1997) *The R. Crumb Coffee Table Art Book*, Boston, Mass.: Kitchen Sink Press Book, Little, Brown & Company.

Giamatti, P. (2005) 'Interview', available on-line at <http://www.hbo.com/films/americansplendor/interviews/paul_giamatti.html> (accessed 7 August 2005).

HBO (2005) 'Synopsis', available on-line at <http://www.hbo.com/films/americansplendor/synopsis> (accessed 7 August 2005).

Hetherington, J. (2005) 'Graphic Novels Go Hollywood', *Animation World Magazine*, 29 July 2005, available on-line at <http://mag.awn.com/index.php?ltype=pageone&article_no=2578> (accessed 1 April 2006).

Hughes, D. (2003) *Comic Book Movies*, London: Virgin.

Marschall, R. (ed.) (1997) *The Best of Little Nemo in Slumberland*, New York: Stewart, Chabori and Chang.

Pekar, H. (2003) *American Splendor: The Life and Times of Harvey Pekar*, New York: Ballantine Books.

—— (2004) *Our Movie Year*, London: Titan Books.

—— (2005a) *Best of American Splendor*, New York: Ballantine Books.

—— (2005b) 'Interview', available on-line at <http://www.hbo.com/films/americansplendor/interviews> (accessed 7 August 2005).

Spiegelman, A. (2004) *In The Shadow of No Towers*, London: Penguin/Viking.

Straczynski, J.M. and Romita Jr, J. (2002) *The Amazing Spider-Man:Coming Home* (Reprint of Marvel Comics, Amazing Spider-Man, Vol. 2, issues 30–36), Tunbridge Wells: Panini.

Vazquez, V. (2004) 'Alternative Comics', available on-line at <http://www.youthradio.org/ae/npr2002_ape.shtml> (accessed 7 August 2005).

Virilio, P. (2002) *Ground Zero*, London: Verso.

Ware, C. (2001) *Jimmy Corrigan, The Smartest Kid on Earth*, London: Random House/Jonathan Cape.

Žižek, S. (2002) *Welcome to the Desert of the Real! Five Essays on September 11 and Similar Dates*, London: Verso.

Zwigoff, T. (2002a) 'Interview', available on-line at <http://www.moviemaker.com/hop/06/screenwriting.html> (accessed 1 April 2006).

—— (2002b) 'Interview', available on-line at <http://www.english.ufl.edu/imagetext/archives/volume1/issue1/after> (accessed 21 April 2006).

Index

Related titles from Routledge

American Civilization

An Introduction
Fourth Edition

David Mauk and John Oakland

Thoroughly revised, this fourth edition of a hugely successful text provides students of American studies with the perfect background and introductory information on contemporary American life.

Brought up to date with new illustrations and case studies, the book examines the second Gulf War, the War on Terror and the 2004 presidential election.

Like its three excellent predecessors, this new edition covers all the central dimensions of American society from geography and the environment, government and politics to religion, education, media and the arts.

American Civilization:

- covers all core American studies topics at introductory level
- contains essential historical background for American studies students at the start of the twenty-first century
- analyzes gender, class and race, and America's cosmopolitan population
- includes photos, case studies, questions and terms for discussion, and suggests websites for further research.

This text enables all students of American studies to lay solid and sound foundations in their degree course studies.

ISBN13: 978–0–415–35830–9 (hbk)
ISBN13: 978–0–415–35831–6 (pbk)

Available at all good bookshops
For ordering and further information please visit:
www.routledge.com

Related titles from Routledge

Contemporary Hollywood Cinema

Steve Neale and Murray Smith

Contemporary Hollywood Cinema is a comprehensive overview of Hollywood today. The book brings together leading international scholars to provide an indispensable guide to:

- The principal and defining characteristics of contemporary Hollywood cinema
- The structure, technology, aesthetics and ideology of recent Hollywood cinema
- Key movies of contemporary Hollywood, including *Batman, Bram Stoker's Dracula, Blue Steel, The Player, Pulp Fiction* and *Fargo.*

The contributors consider the idea of New or Post-Classical Hollywood and ask how New Hollywood differs from the Old. They explore key features of the contemporary movie industry, including:

- The growth of independent and package production
- The significance of 'major independents' such as New Line and Miramax
- The impact of television
- The globalization of Hollywood's markets.

ISBN13: 9–78–0–415–17009–3 (hbk)
ISBN13: 9–78–0–415–17010–9 (pbk)

Available at all good bookshops
For ordering and further information please visit:
www.routledge.com

Introduction to Film Studies

Fourth Edition

Edited by Jill Nelmes

Introduction to Film Studies is a comprehensive leading textbook for students of cinema. This completely revised and updated fourth edition guides students through the key issues and concepts in film studies, traces the historical development of film and introduces some of the worlds key national cinemas. A range of theories and theorists are presented from Formalism to Feminism, from Eisenstein to Deleuze. Each chapter is written by a subject specialist, including three new authors, and a wide range of films are analysed and discussed. It is lavishly illustrated with over 123 film stills and production shots, many of them in colour. Reviewed widely by teachers in the field and with a foreword by Bill Nichols, it will be essential reading for any introductory student of film, media studies or the visual arts worldwide.

Key features of the fourth edition are:

- full coverage of important topics for introductory level
- updated coverage of a wide range of concepts, theories and issues in film studies
- in-depth discussion of the contemporary film industry
- new chapters on Rediscovering Film; Ethnicity, Race and Cinema; Documentary; Film, Form and Narrative; British Cinema; Approaches to Cinematic Authorship
- new case studies on films such as *Bamboozled, Wild Strawberries, Run Lola Run, Grey Gardens, Grizzly Man, Boy's Don't Cry, Love Actually*, and many others
- marginal key terms, notes, cross-referencing
- suggestions for further reading, further viewing and a comprehensive glossary and bibliography
- website resources including updated popular case studies from previous editions, a chapter on German Cinema and links to supporting sites.

ISBN13: 9–78–0–415–40929–2 (hbk)
ISBN13: 9–78–0–415–40928–5 (pbk)